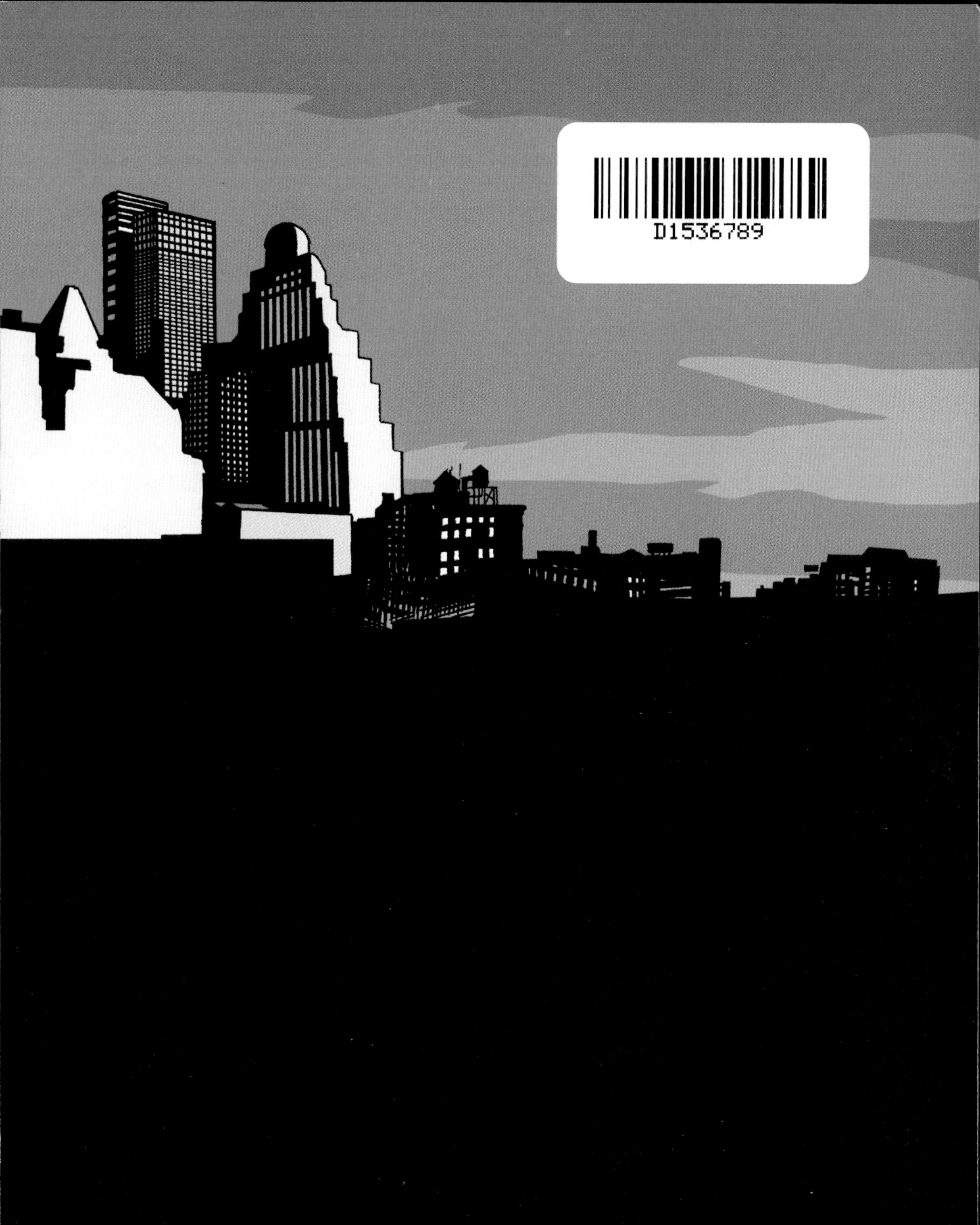

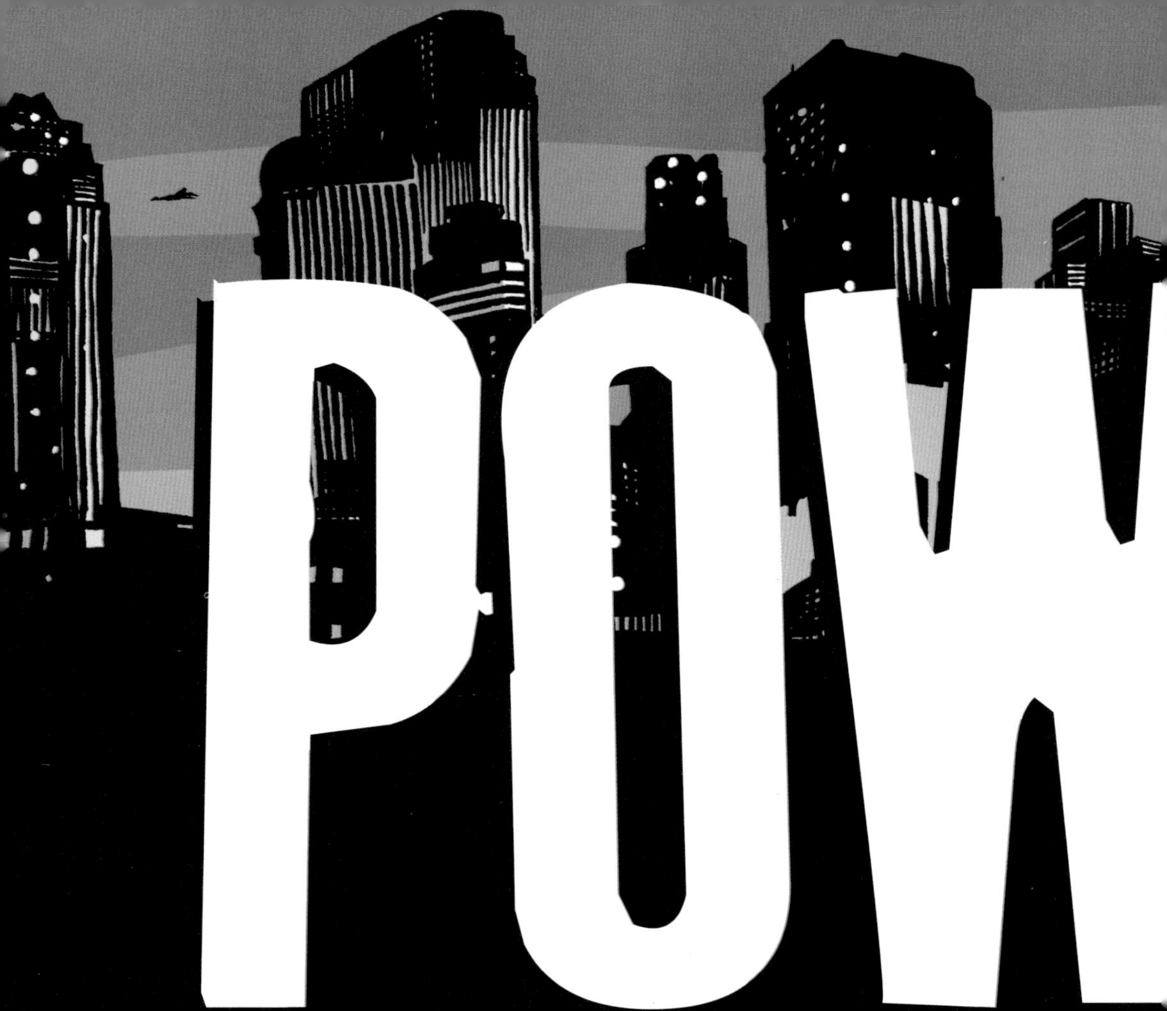

POW

CREATED AND PRODUCED
BY
BRIAN MICHAEL BENDIS
AND
MIKE AVON OEMING

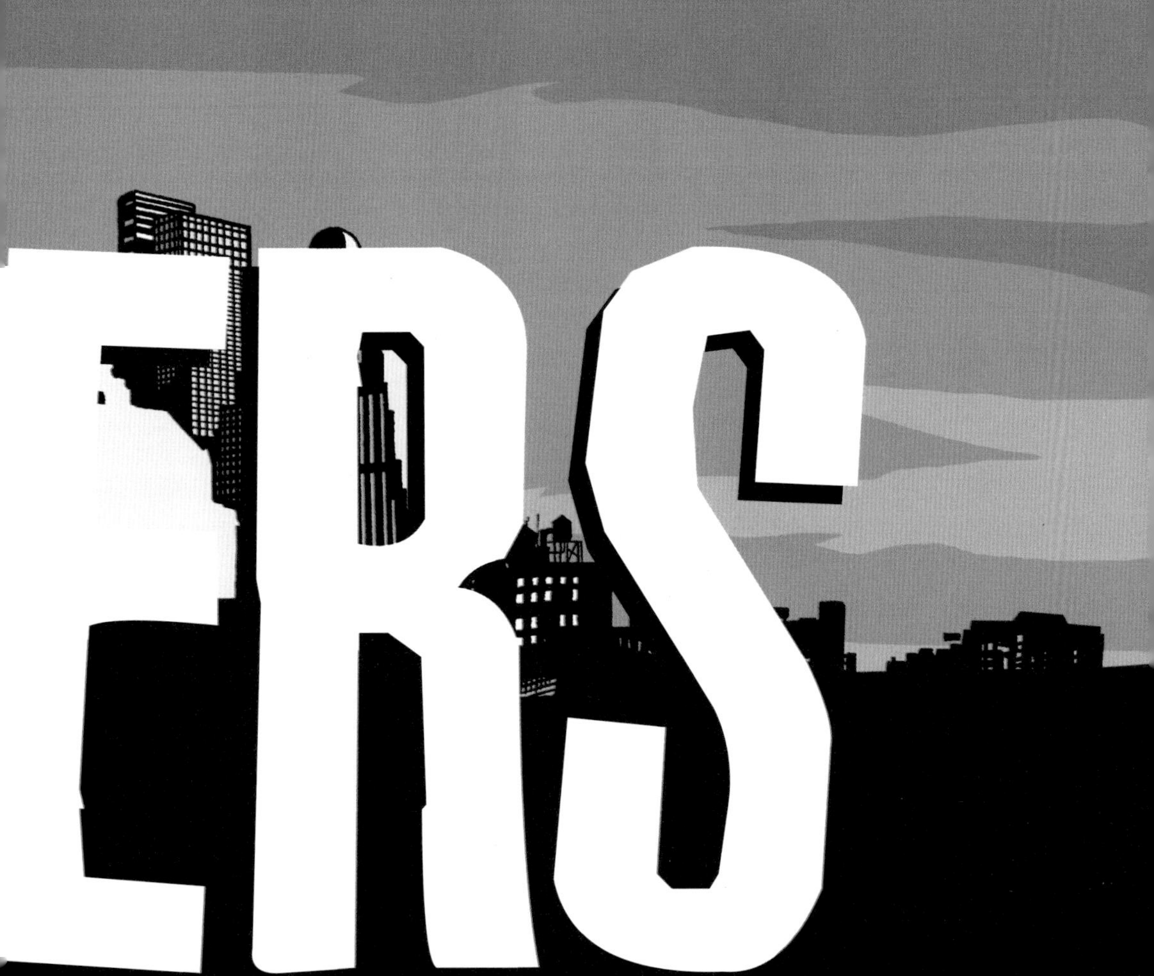
ERS

COLORING
NICK FILARDI

LETTERING AND PRODUCTION
CHRIS ELIOPOULOS

PROOFREADER
K.C. McCRORY

EDITING
C.B. CEBULSKI

BUSINESS AFFAIRS
ALISA BENDIS

COLLECTION EDITOR
JEN GRÜNWALD

COLLECTION DESIGNER
PATRICK McGRATH

Previously in Powers:

Homicide Detectives Christian Walker and Deena Pilgrim investigate murders specific to superhero cases...

The Millennium Guard, a secret grouping of intergalactic guardians, offer Walker the choice to be this world's latest secret guardian against the growing threats of alien invasion. Walker, an ex-superhero, accepts the responsibility and the powers that come with it.

Pilgrim is hiding a dark secret. She contracted a powers virus from a fight with an underworld thug and it is eating her alive inside. She accidentally murdered her ex-boyfriend in an act of self-defense and hid the evidence. Deena is now under investigation by Internal Affairs.

After discovering Walker's secret, she disappeared. That was months ago...

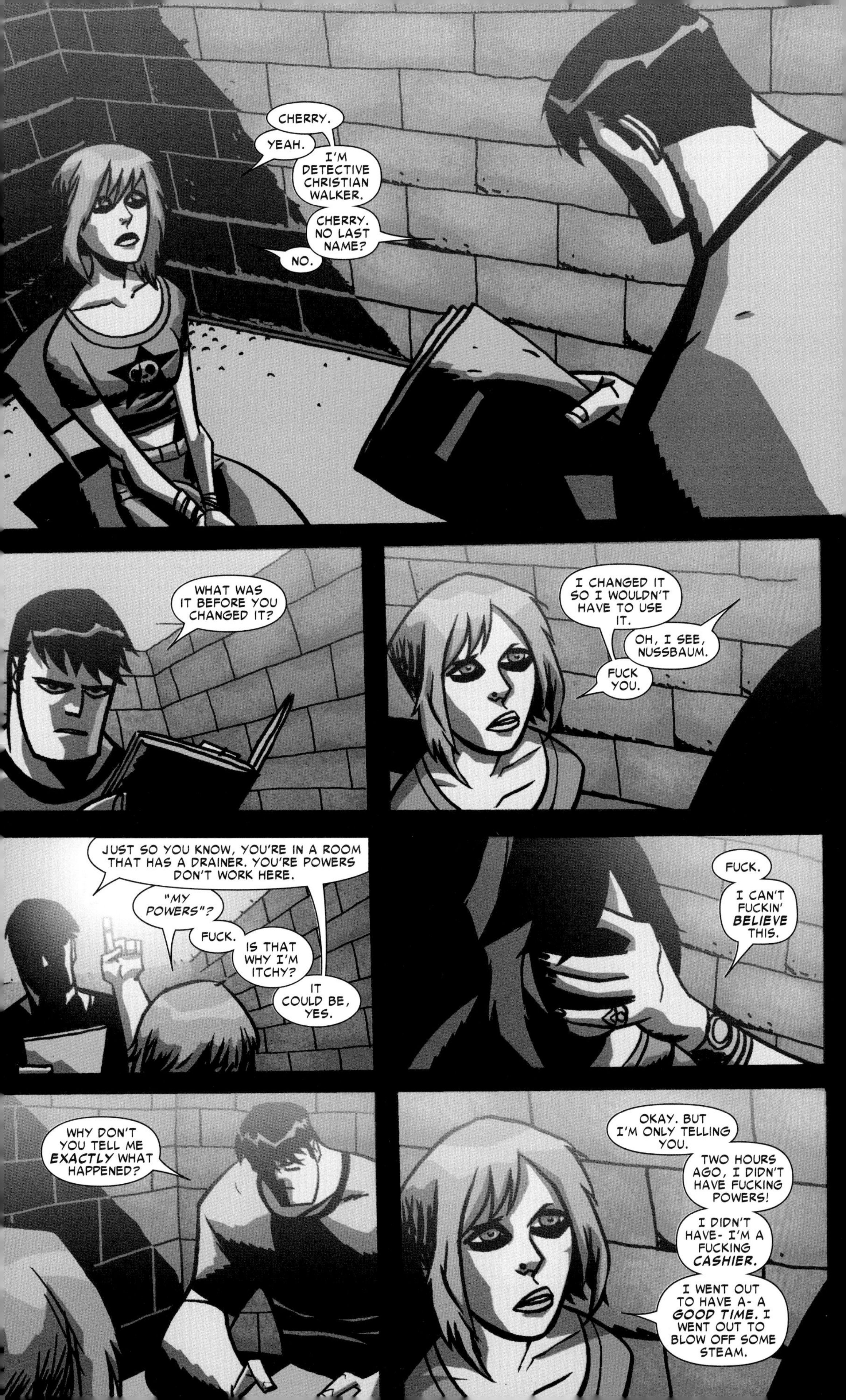
CHERRY.
YEAH.
I'M DETECTIVE CHRISTIAN WALKER.
CHERRY. NO LAST NAME?
NO.
WHAT WAS IT BEFORE YOU CHANGED IT?
I CHANGED IT SO I WOULDN'T HAVE TO USE IT.
OH, I SEE, NUSSBAUM.
FUCK YOU.
JUST SO YOU KNOW, YOU'RE IN A ROOM THAT HAS A DRAINER. YOU'RE POWERS DON'T WORK HERE.
"MY POWERS"?
FUCK.
IS THAT WHY I'M ITCHY?
IT COULD BE, YES.
FUCK.
I CAN'T FUCKIN' BELIEVE THIS.
WHY DON'T YOU TELL ME EXACTLY WHAT HAPPENED?
OKAY. BUT I'M ONLY TELLING YOU.
TWO HOURS AGO, I DIDN'T HAVE FUCKING POWERS!
I DIDN'T HAVE- I'M A FUCKING CASHIER.
I WENT OUT TO HAVE A- A GOOD TIME. I WENT OUT TO BLOW OFF SOME STEAM.

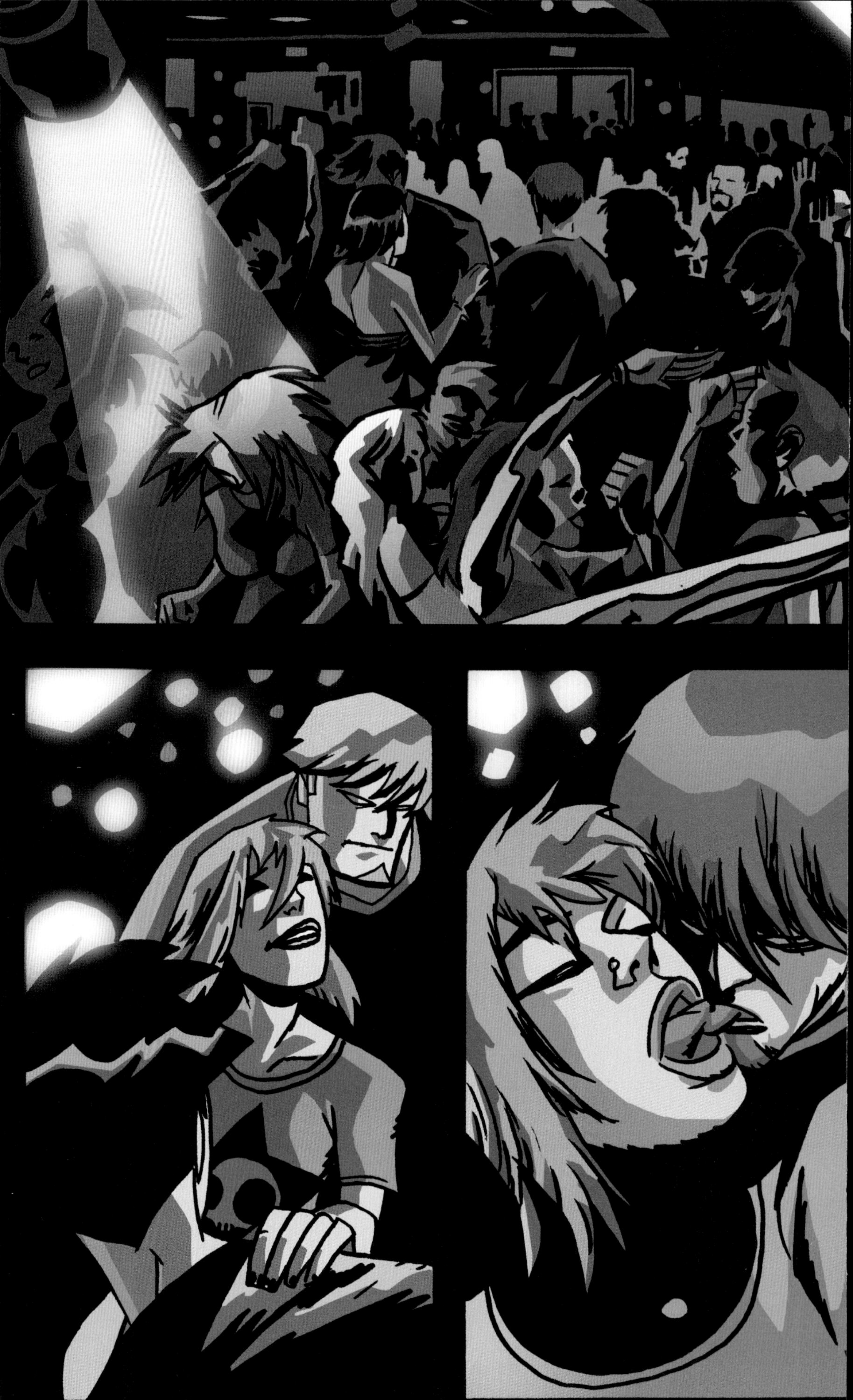

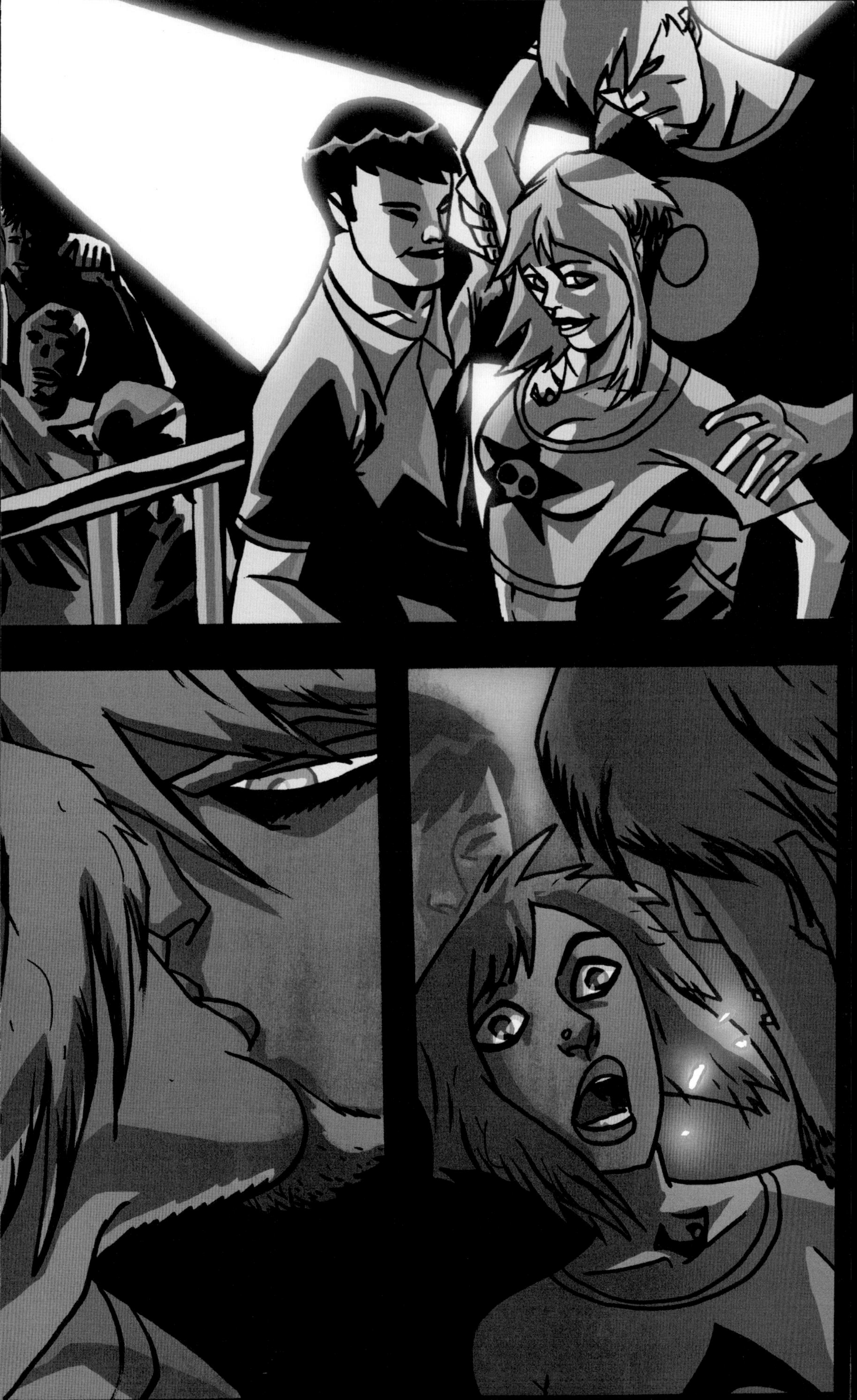

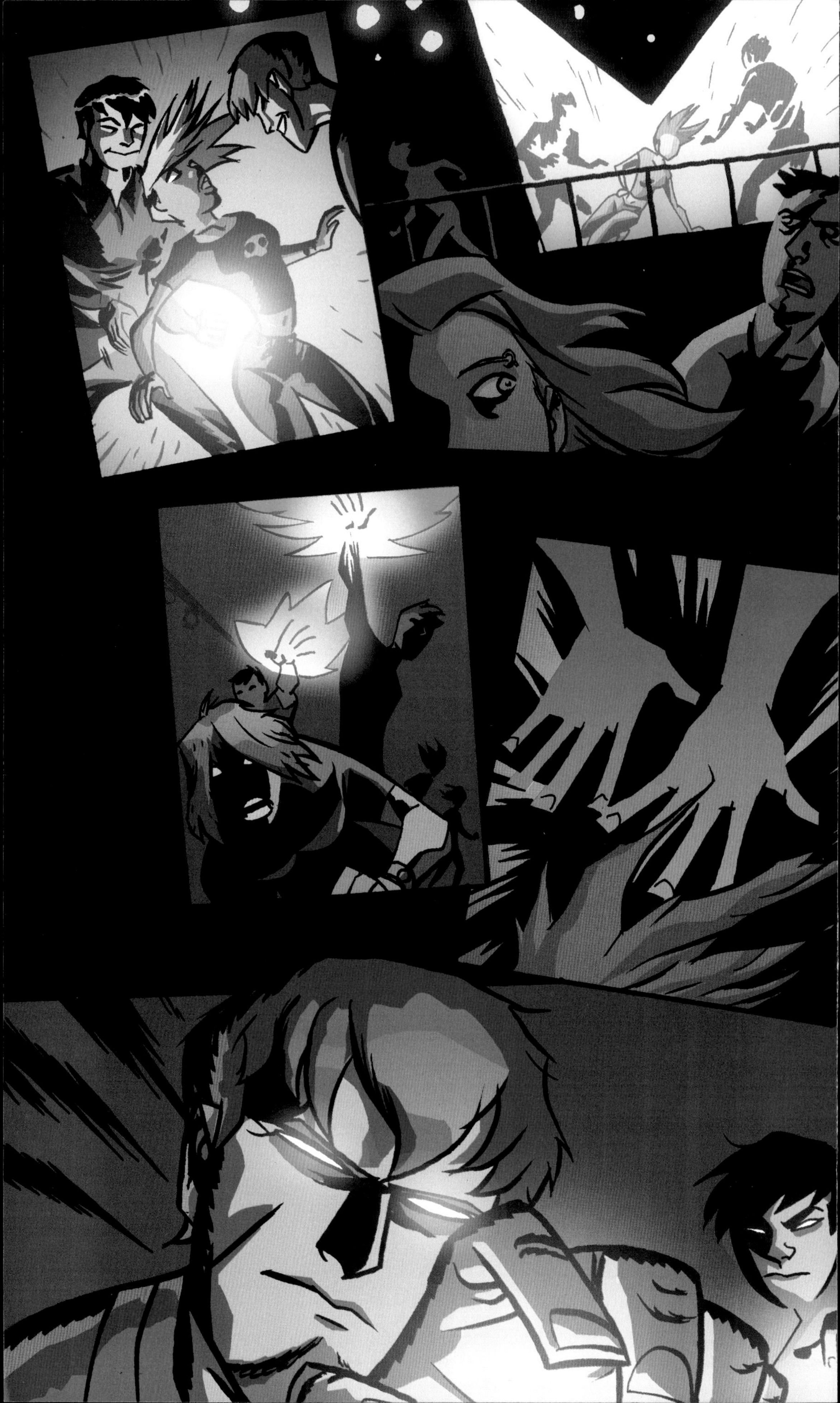

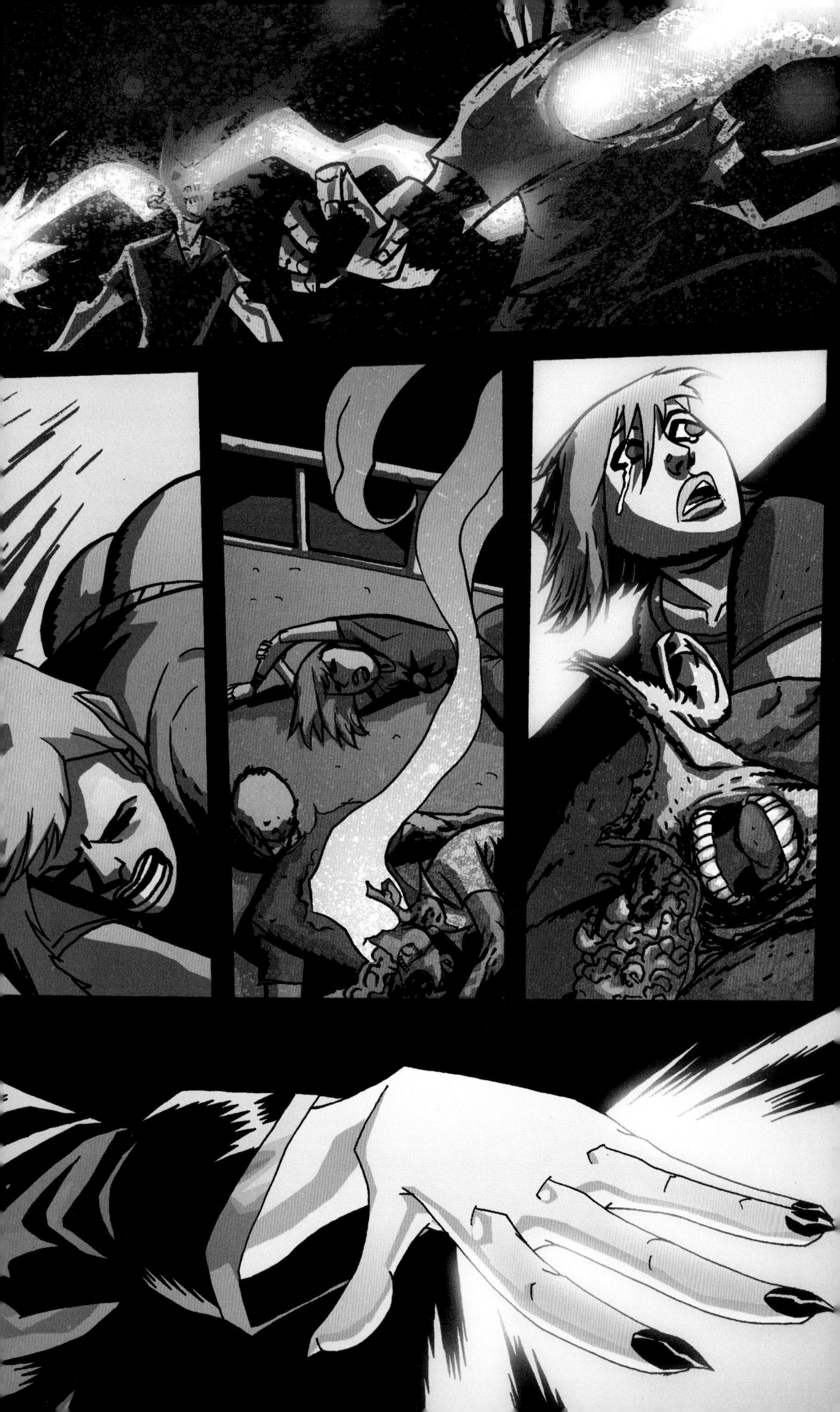

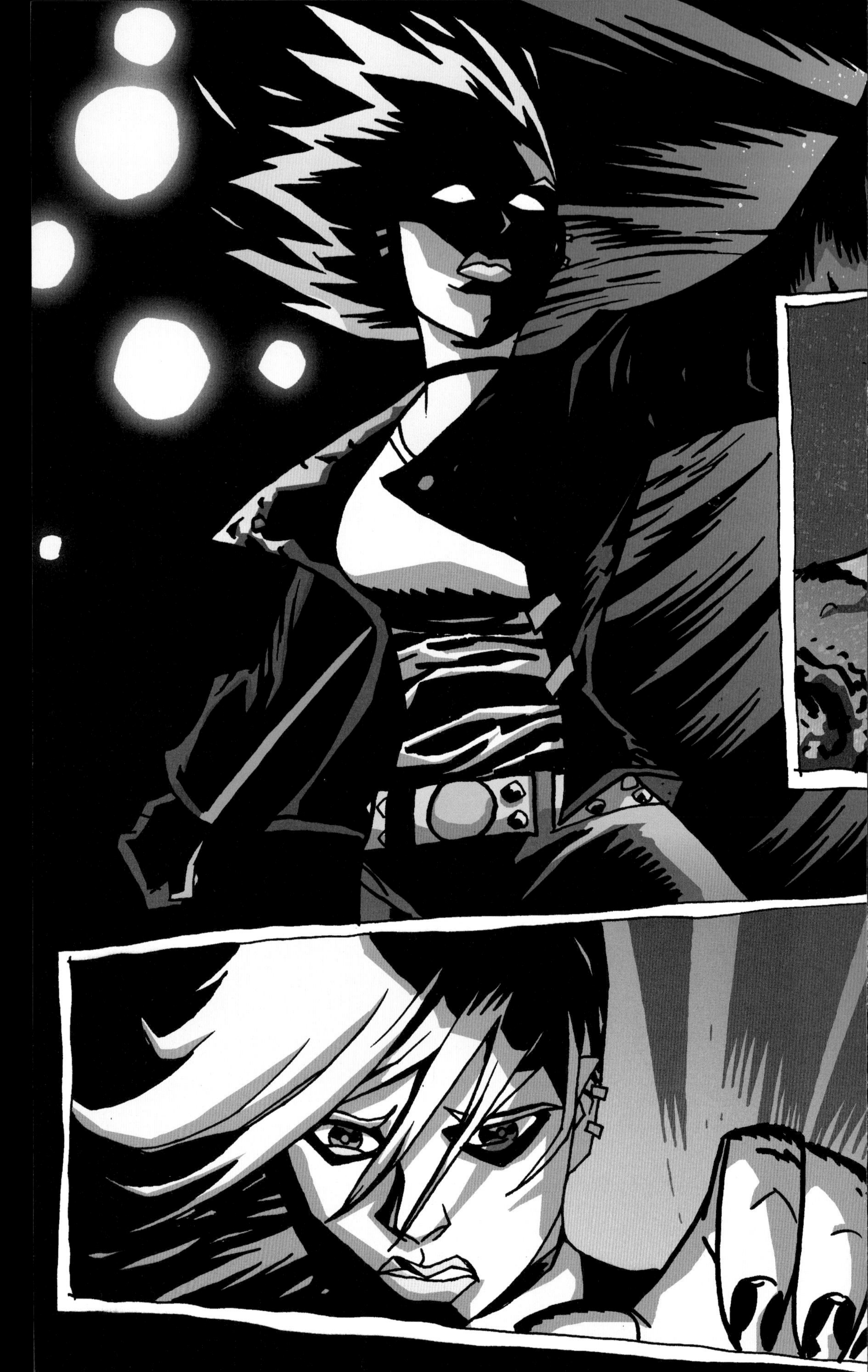

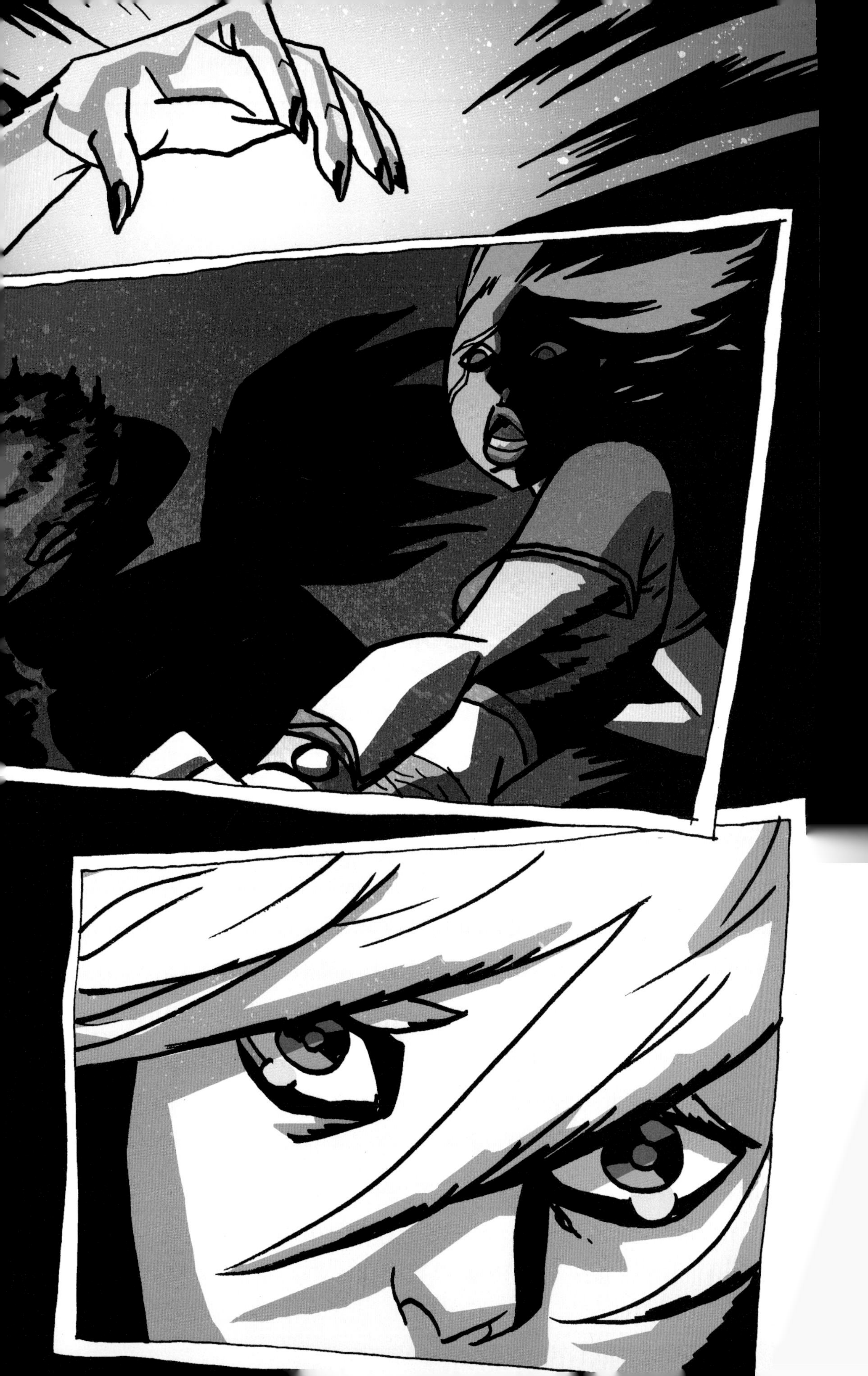

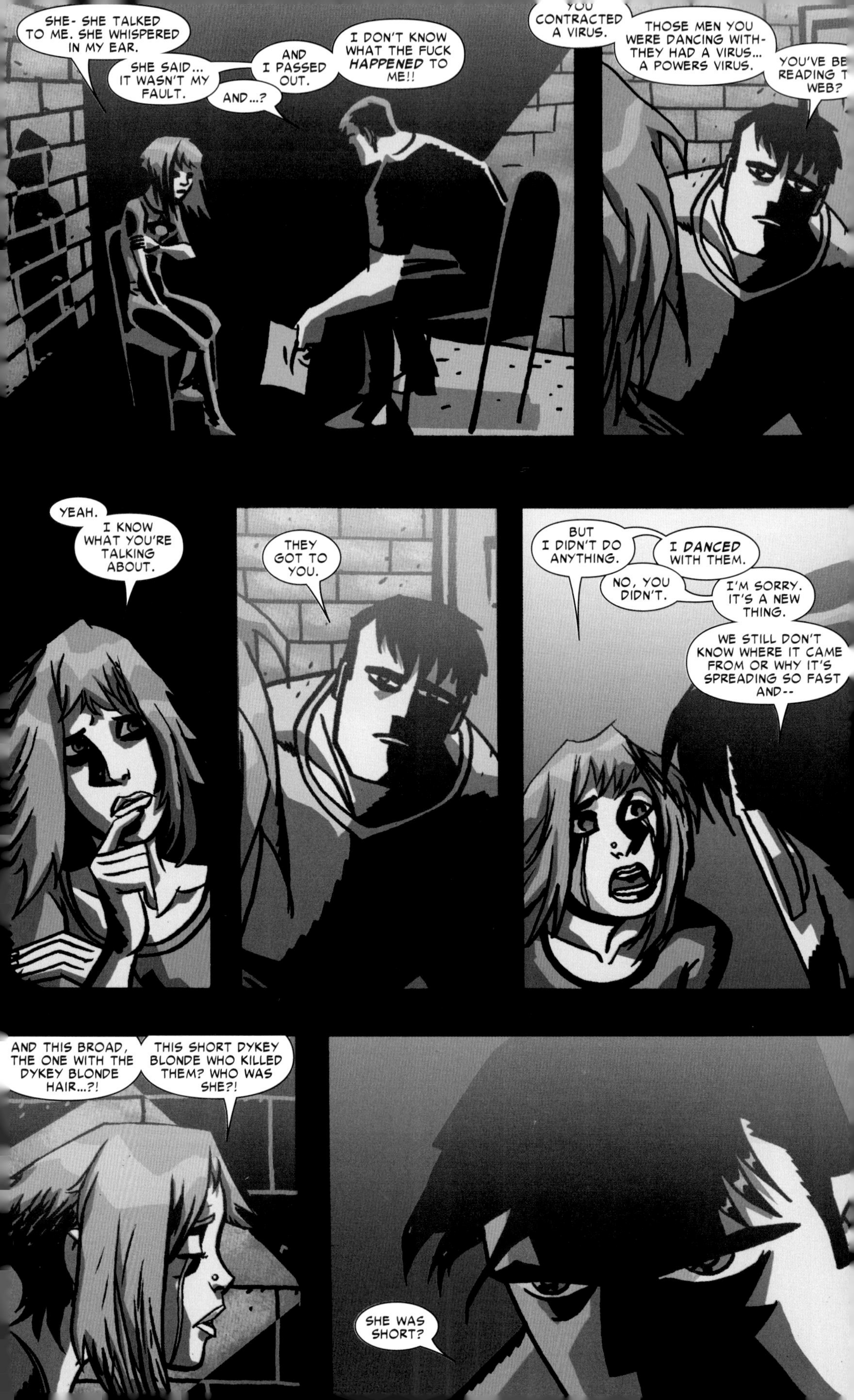
SHE- SHE TALKED TO ME. SHE WHISPERED IN MY EAR.
SHE SAID... IT WASN'T MY FAULT.
AND...?
AND I PASSED OUT.
I DON'T KNOW WHAT THE FUCK HAPPENED TO ME!!
YOU CONTRACTED A VIRUS.
THOSE MEN YOU WERE DANCING WITH- THEY HAD A VIRUS... A POWERS VIRUS.
YEAH. I KNOW WHAT YOU'RE TALKING ABOUT.
THEY GOT TO YOU.
BUT I DIDN'T DO ANYTHING.
I DANCED WITH THEM.
NO, YOU DIDN'T.
I'M SORRY. IT'S A NEW THING.
WE STILL DON'T KNOW WHERE IT CAME FROM OR WHY IT'S SPREADING SO FAST AND--
AND THIS BROAD, THE ONE WITH THE DYKEY BLONDE HAIR...?!
THIS SHORT DYKEY BLONDE WHO KILLED THEM? WHO WAS SHE?!
SHE WAS SHORT?

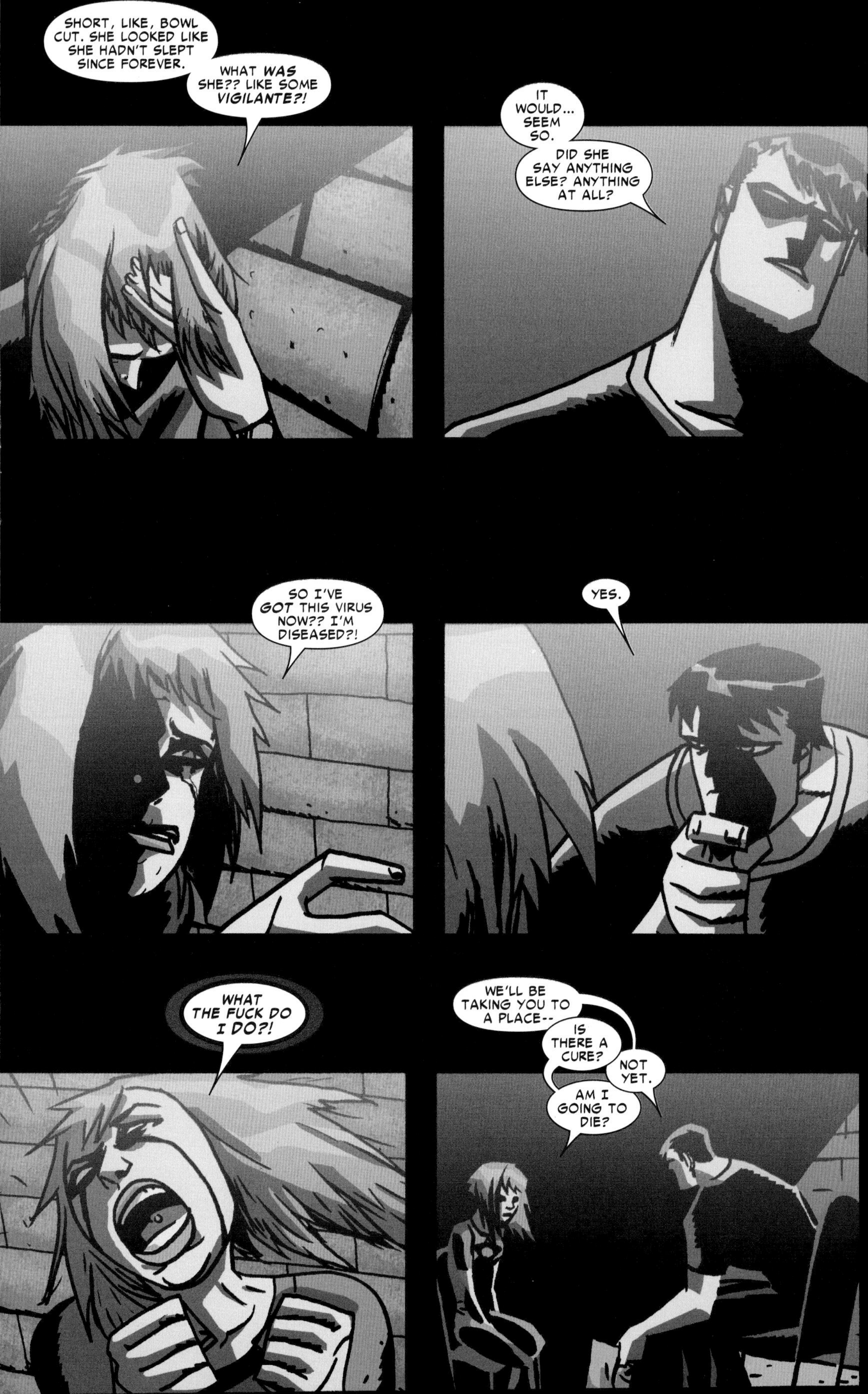
SHORT, LIKE, BOWL CUT. SHE LOOKED LIKE SHE HADN'T SLEPT SINCE FOREVER.
WHAT *WAS* SHE?? LIKE SOME *VIGILANTE?!*
IT WOULD... SEEM SO.
DID SHE SAY ANYTHING ELSE? ANYTHING AT ALL?
SO I'VE *GOT* THIS VIRUS NOW?? I'M DISEASED?!
YES.
WHAT THE FUCK DO *I DO?!*
WE'LL BE TAKING YOU TO A PLACE--
IS THERE A CURE?
NOT YET.
AM I GOING TO DIE?

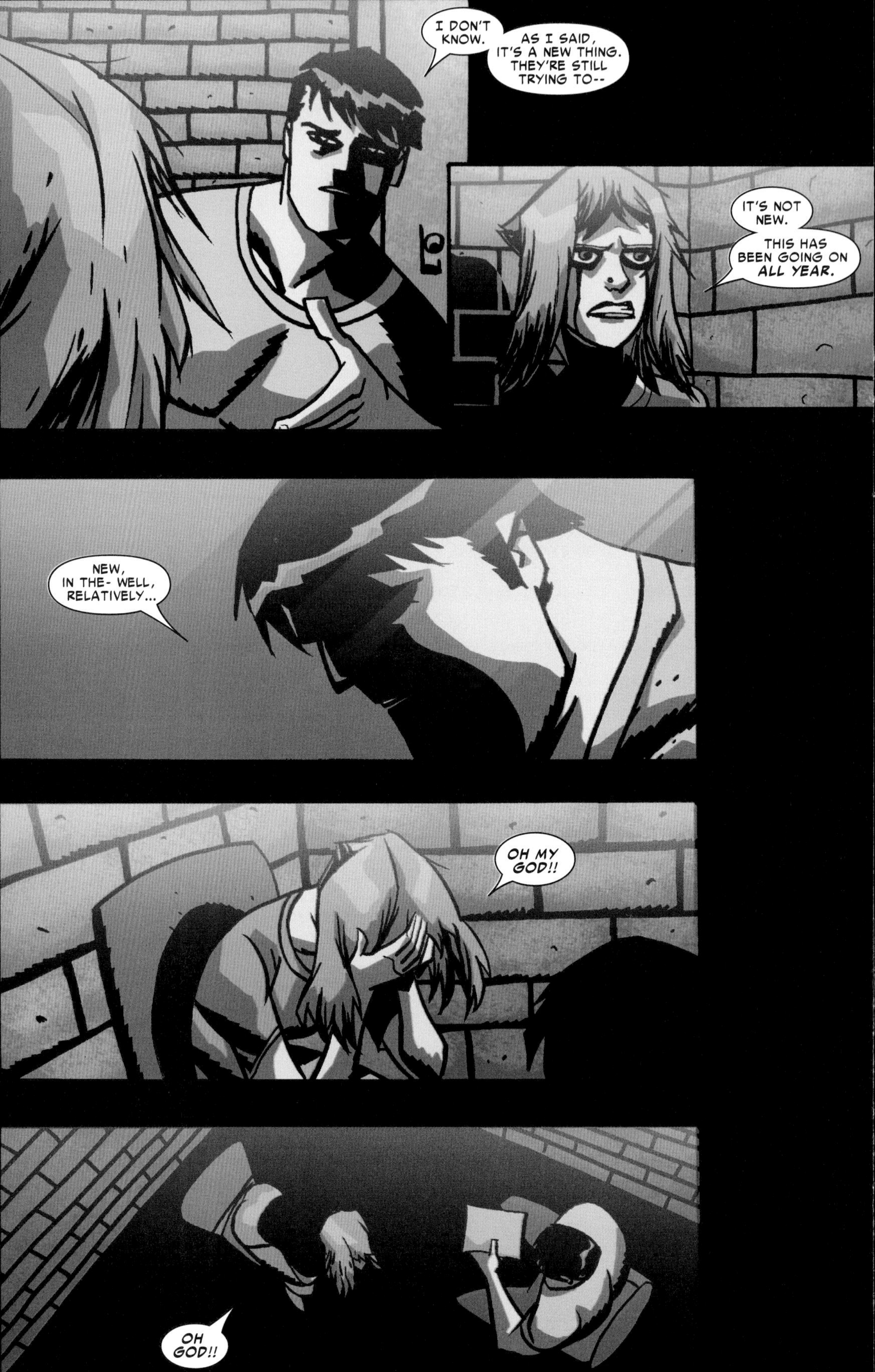
I DON'T KNOW.
AS I SAID, IT'S A NEW THING. THEY'RE STILL TRYING TO--
IT'S NOT NEW.
THIS HAS BEEN GOING ON ALL YEAR.
NEW, IN THE- WELL, RELATIVELY...
OH MY GOD!!
OH GOD!!

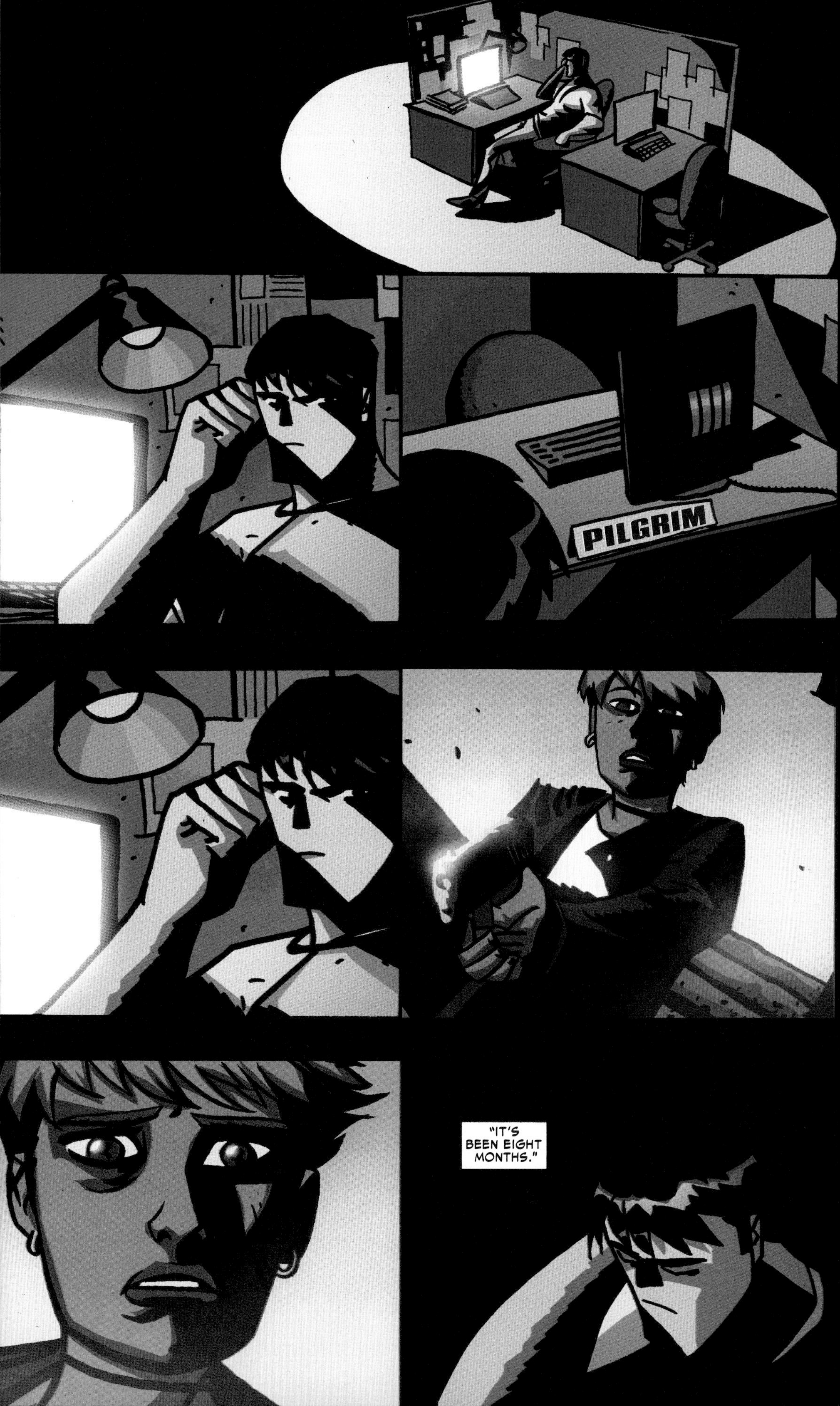
PILGRIM
"IT'S
BEEN EIGHT
MONTHS."

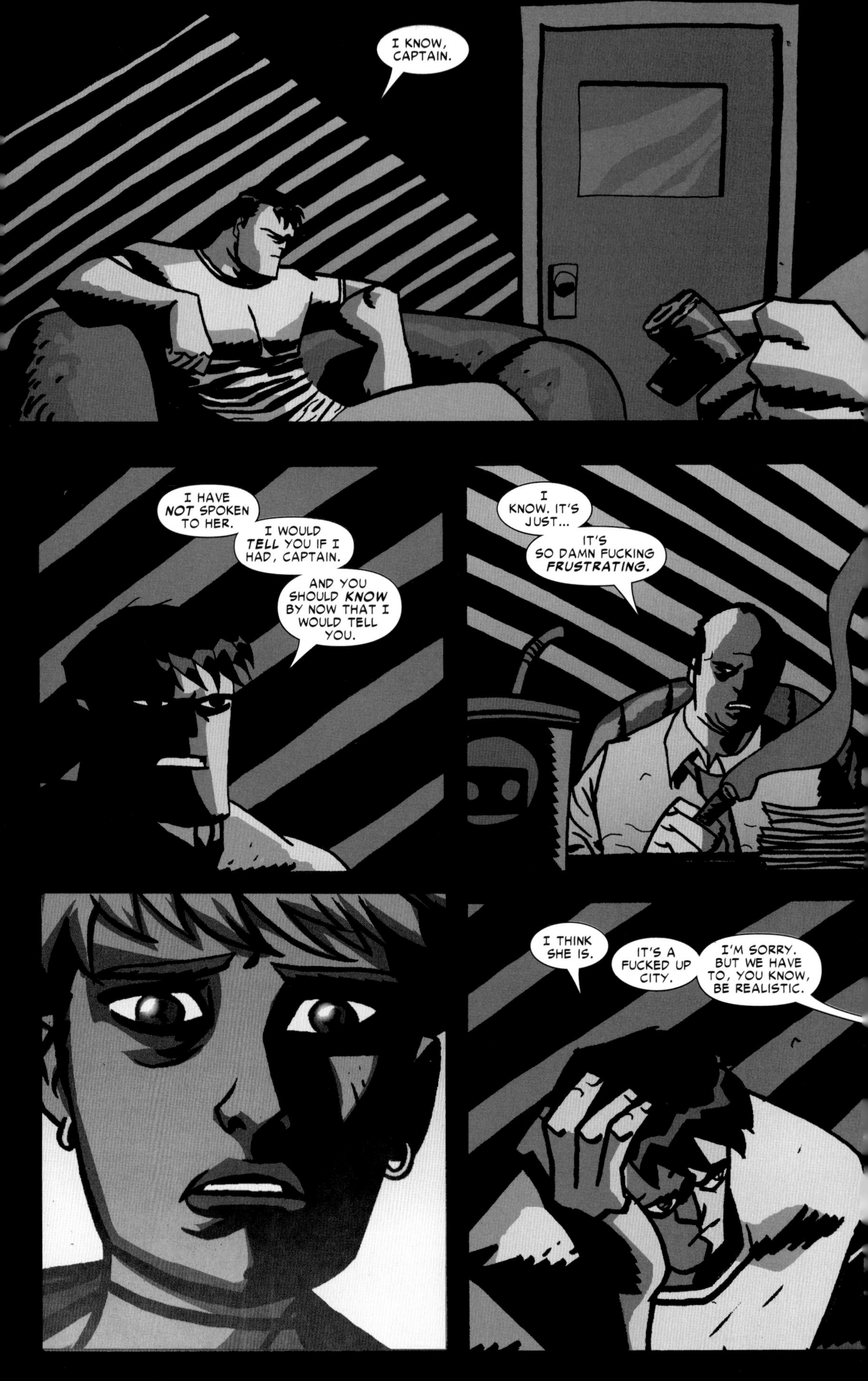
I KNOW, CAPTAIN.
I HAVE NOT SPOKEN TO HER.
I WOULD TELL YOU IF I HAD, CAPTAIN.
AND YOU SHOULD KNOW BY NOW THAT I WOULD TELL YOU.
I KNOW. IT'S JUST...
IT'S SO DAMN FUCKING FRUSTRATING.
I THINK SHE IS.
IT'S A FUCKED UP CITY.
I'M SORRY. BUT WE HAVE TO, YOU KNOW, BE REALISTIC.

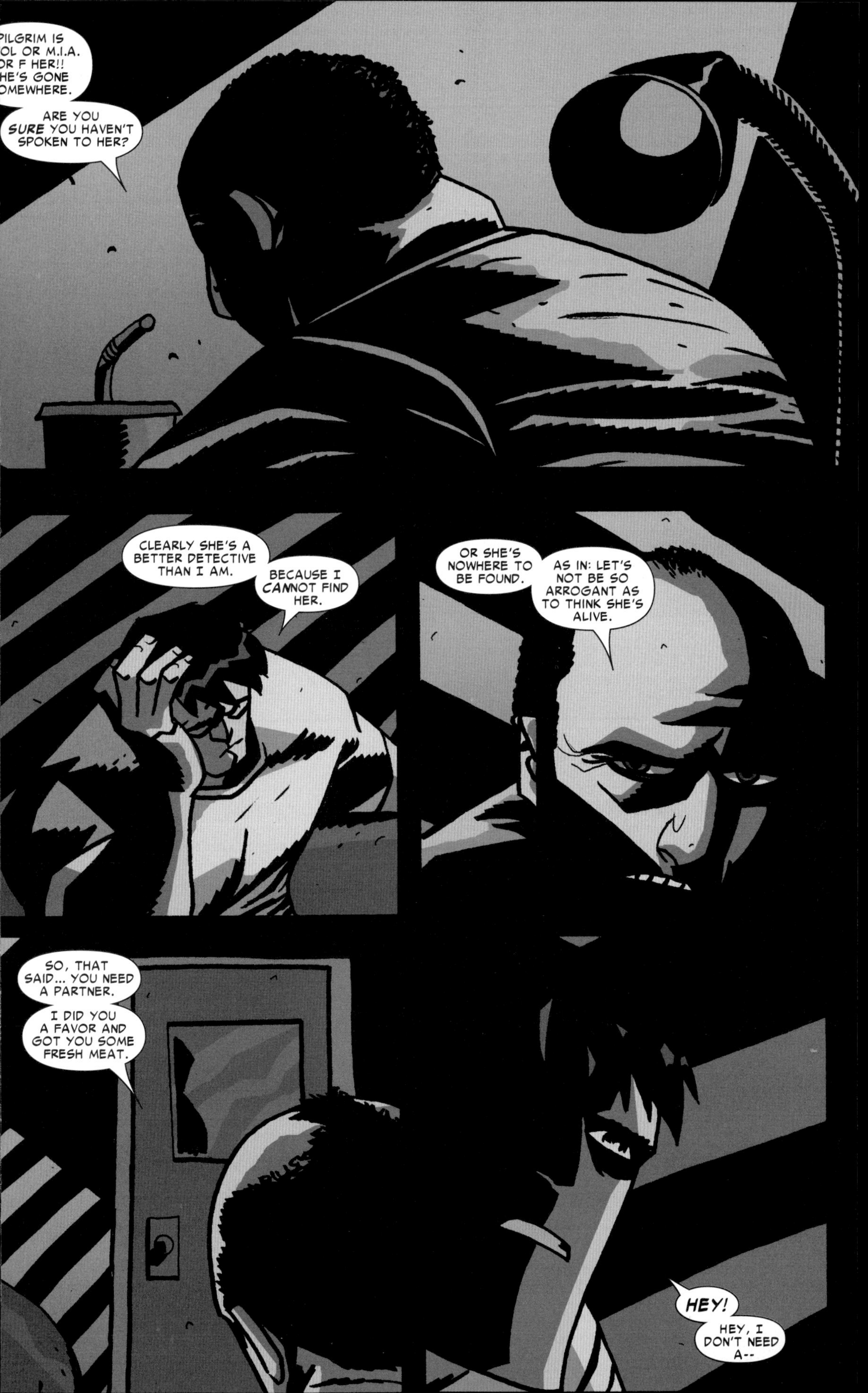

PILGRIM IS OL OR M.I.A. OR F HER!! HE'S GONE OMEWHERE.
ARE YOU *SURE* YOU HAVEN'T SPOKEN TO HER?
CLEARLY SHE'S A BETTER DETECTIVE THAN I AM.
BECAUSE I *CAN*NOT FIND HER.
OR SHE'S NOWHERE TO BE FOUND.
AS IN: LET'S NOT BE SO ARROGANT AS TO THINK SHE'S ALIVE.
SO, THAT SAID... YOU NEED A PARTNER.
I DID YOU A FAVOR AND GOT YOU SOME FRESH MEAT.
HEY!
HEY, I DON'T NEED A--

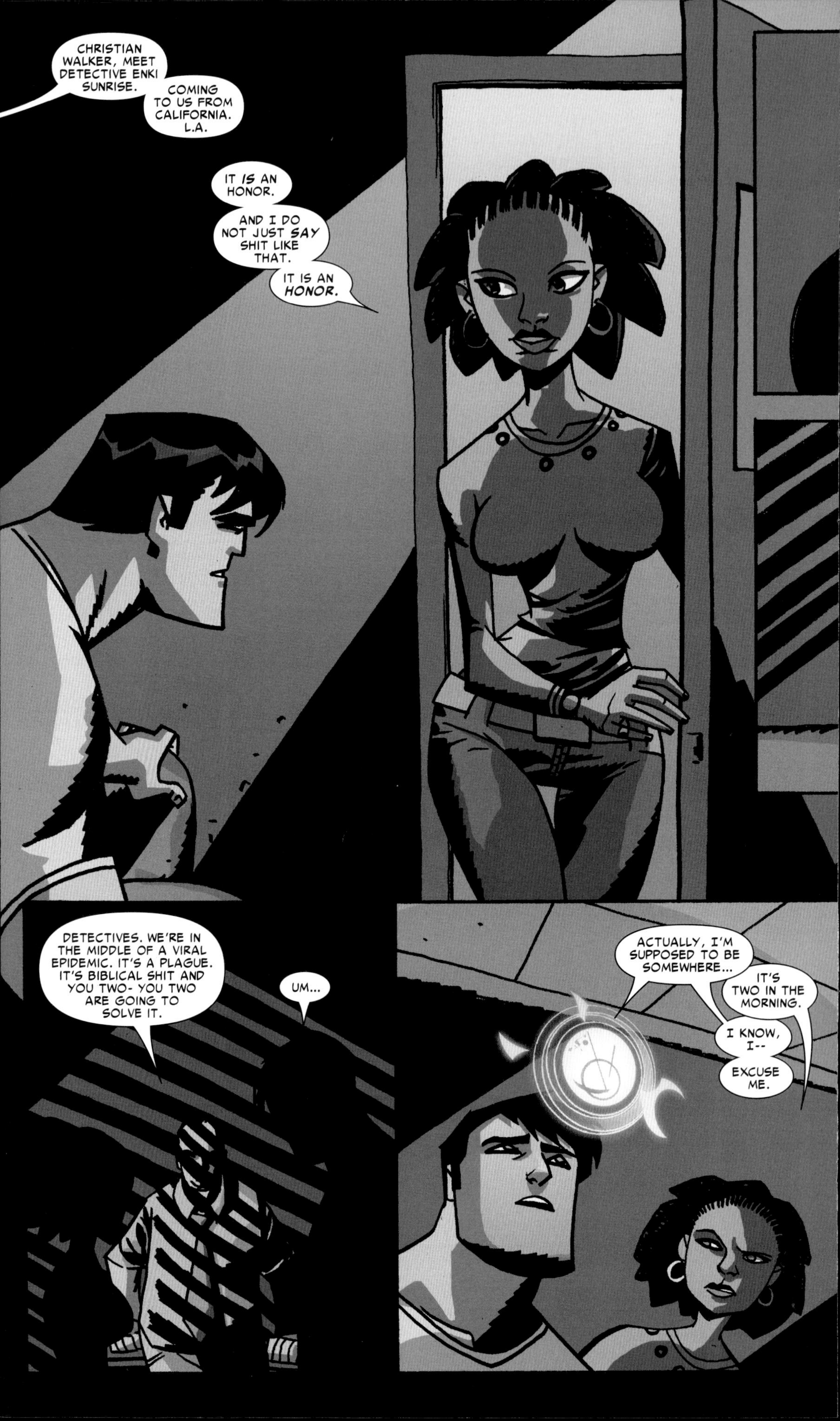
CHRISTIAN WALKER, MEET DETECTIVE ENKI SUNRISE.
COMING TO US FROM CALIFORNIA. L.A.
IT *IS* AN HONOR.
AND I DO NOT JUST *SAY* SHIT LIKE THAT.
IT IS AN *HONOR.*
DETECTIVES. WE'RE IN THE MIDDLE OF A VIRAL EPIDEMIC. IT'S A PLAGUE. IT'S BIBLICAL SHIT AND YOU TWO- YOU TWO ARE GOING TO SOLVE IT.
UM...
ACTUALLY, I'M SUPPOSED TO BE SOMEWHERE...
IT'S TWO IN THE MORNING.
I KNOW, I--
EXCUSE ME.

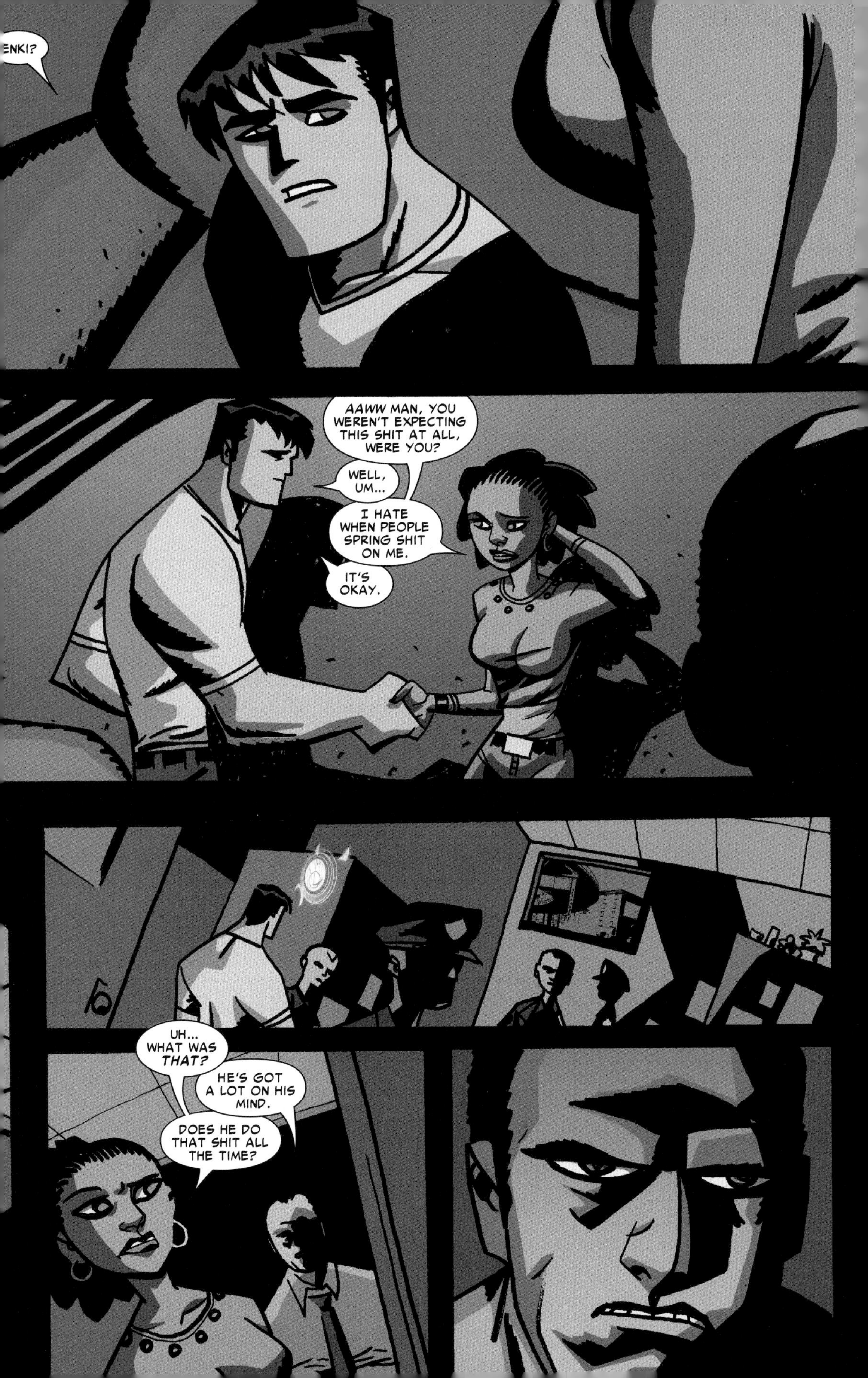
ENKI?
AAWW MAN, YOU WEREN'T EXPECTING THIS SHIT AT ALL, WERE YOU?
WELL, UM...
I HATE WHEN PEOPLE SPRING SHIT ON ME.
IT'S OKAY.
UH... WHAT WAS *THAT?*
HE'S GOT A LOT ON HIS MIND.
DOES HE DO THAT SHIT ALL THE TIME?

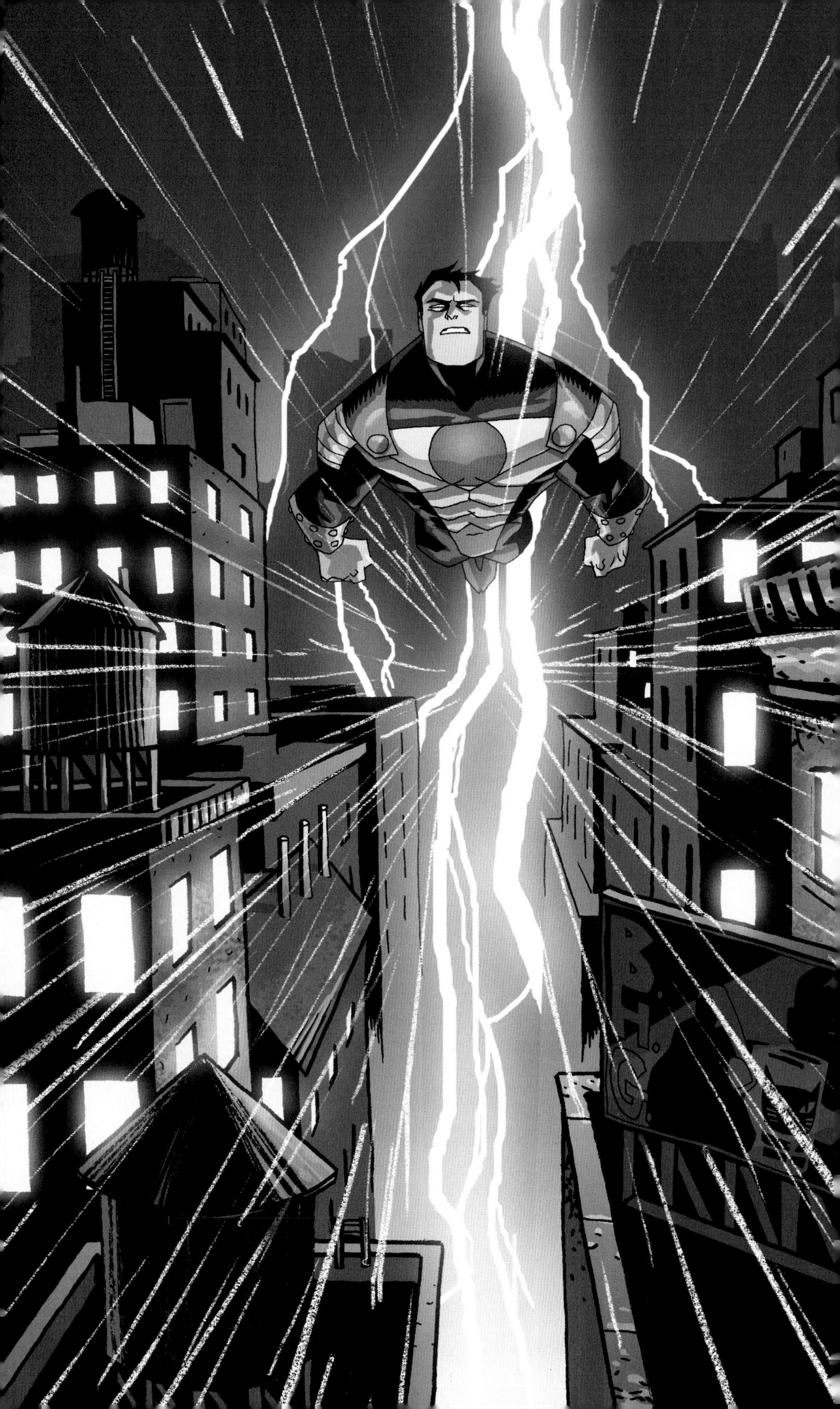

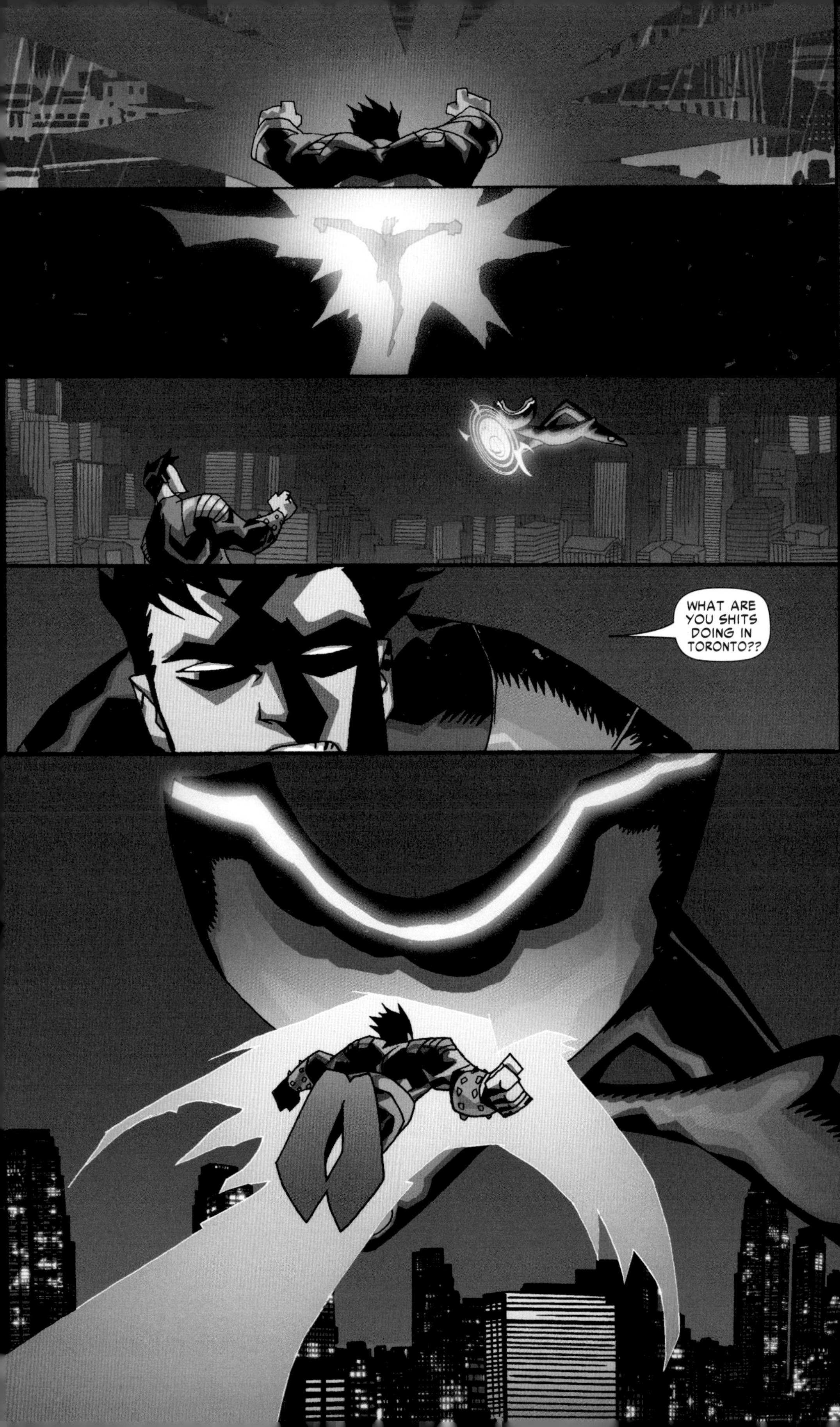
WHAT ARE YOU SHITS DOING IN TORONTO??

HEY!! WHAT ARE YOU GUYS DOING IN TORONTO?!

I ASKED YOU A QUESTION?? WHAT ARE YOU-- **ARGHGH!!**

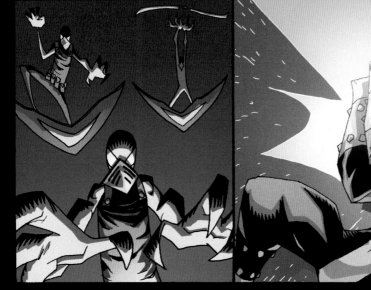

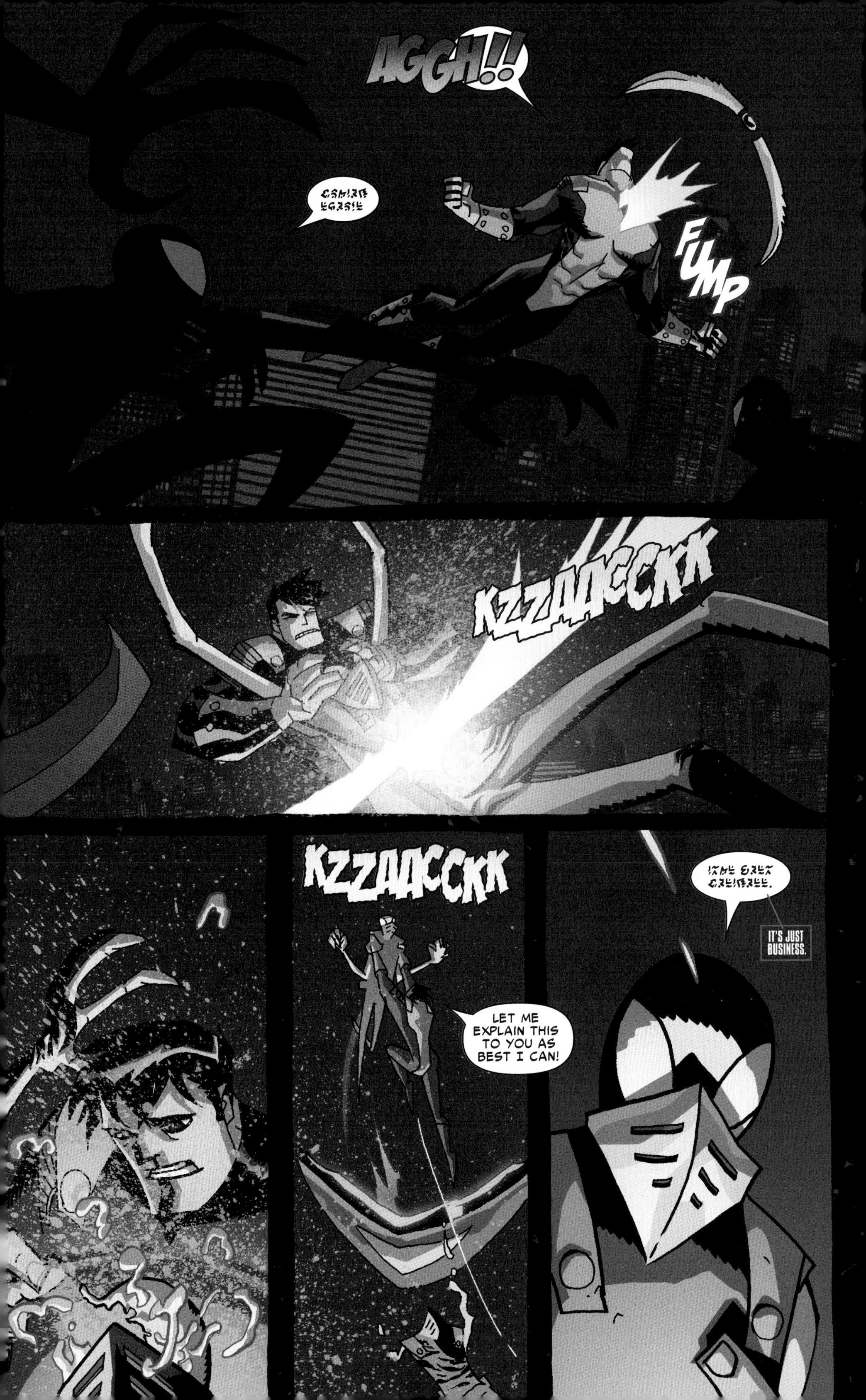
AGGH!!
FUMP
KZZAACCKK
KZZAACCKK
LET ME EXPLAIN THIS TO YOU AS BEST I CAN!
IT'S JUST BUSINESS.

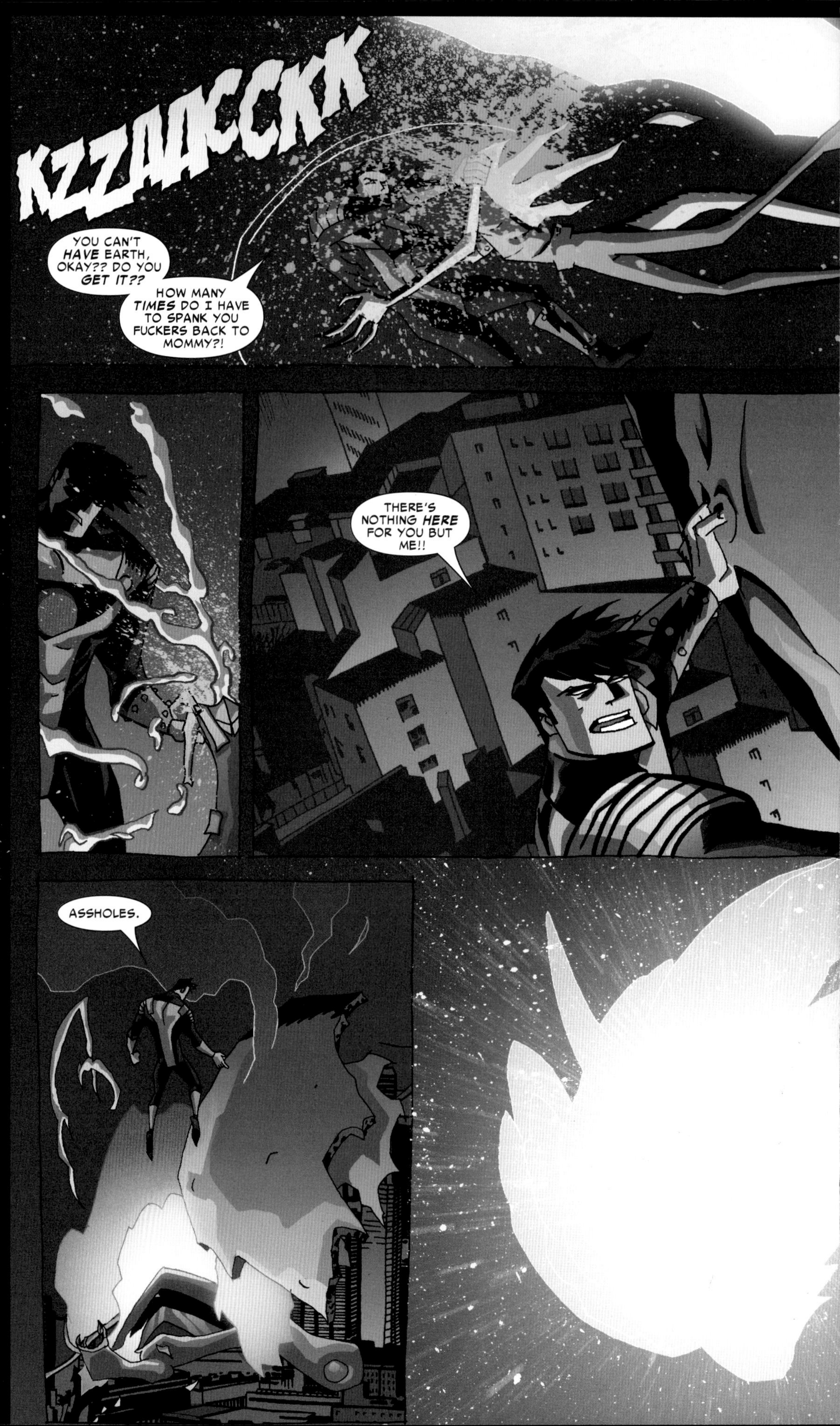
KZZAACCKK
YOU CAN'T HAVE EARTH, OKAY?? DO YOU GET IT??
HOW MANY TIMES DO I HAVE TO SPANK YOU FUCKERS BACK TO MOMMY?!
THERE'S NOTHING HERE FOR YOU BUT ME!!
ASSHOLES.

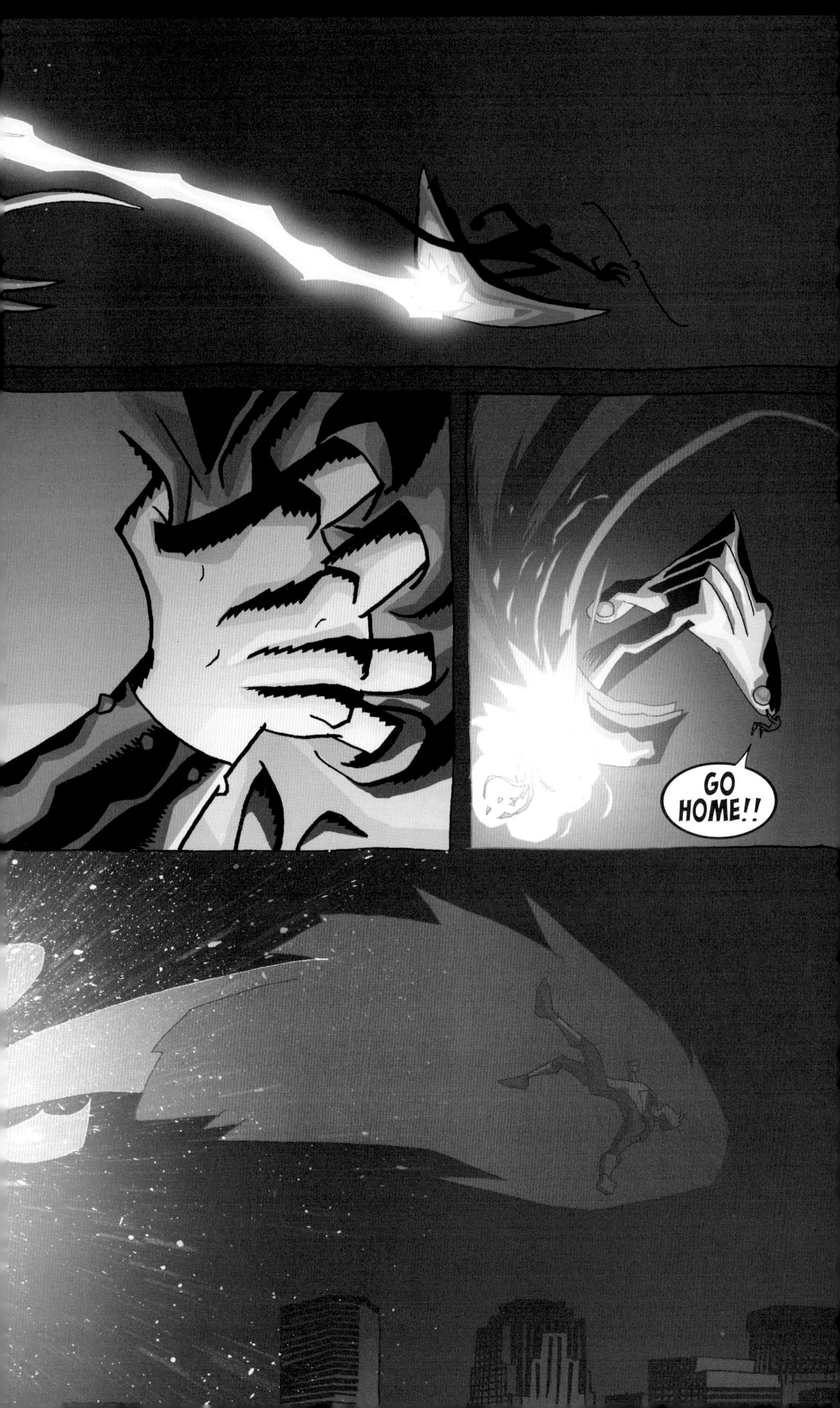
GO HOME!!

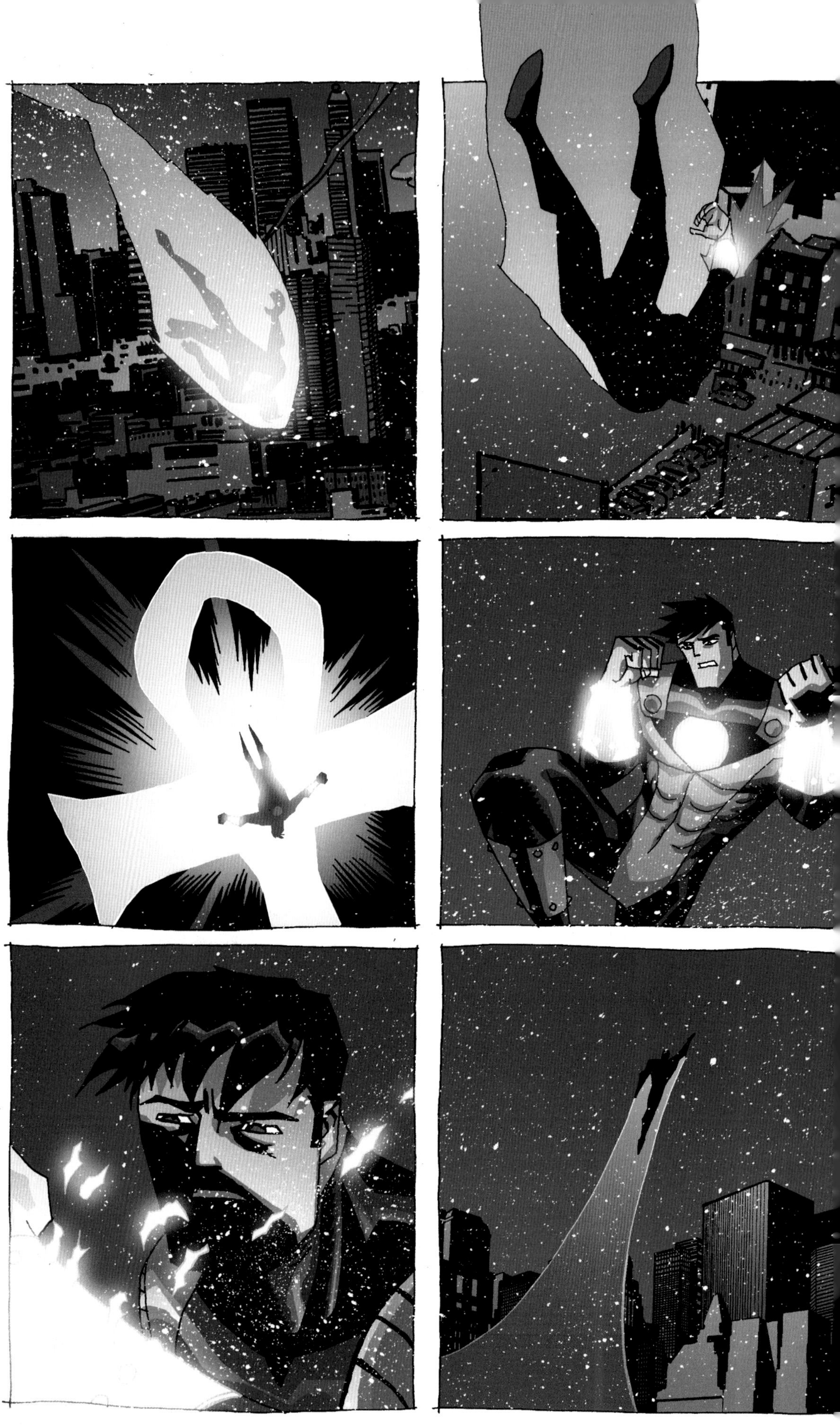

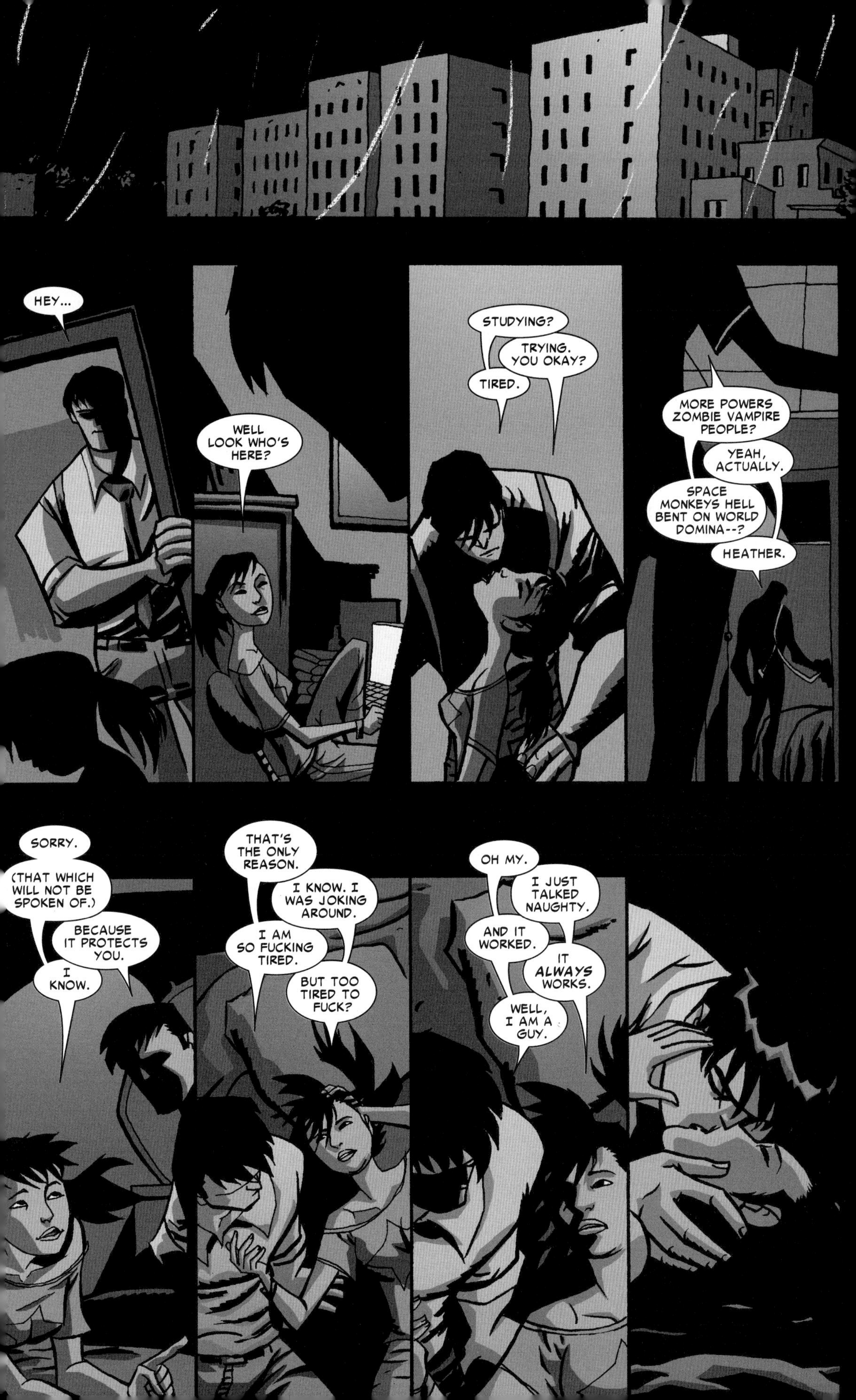
HEY...
WELL LOOK WHO'S HERE?
STUDYING?
TRYING. YOU OKAY?
TIRED.
MORE POWERS ZOMBIE VAMPIRE PEOPLE?
YEAH, ACTUALLY.
SPACE MONKEYS HELL BENT ON WORLD DOMINA--?
HEATHER.
SORRY.
(THAT WHICH WILL NOT BE SPOKEN OF.)
BECAUSE IT PROTECTS YOU.
I KNOW.
THAT'S THE ONLY REASON.
I KNOW. I WAS JOKING AROUND.
I AM SO FUCKING TIRED.
BUT TOO TIRED TO FUCK?
OH MY.
I JUST TALKED NAUGHTY.
AND IT WORKED.
IT ALWAYS WORKS.
WELL, I AM A GUY.

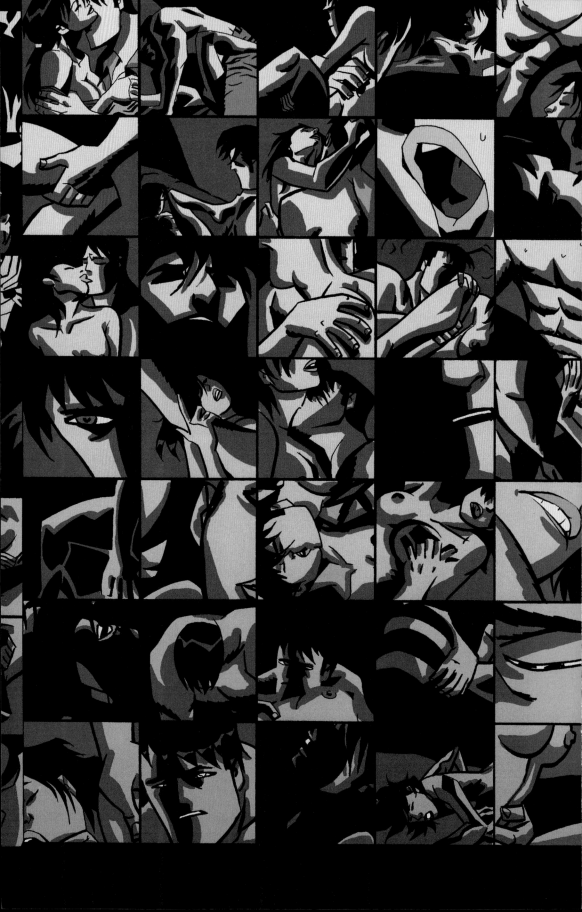

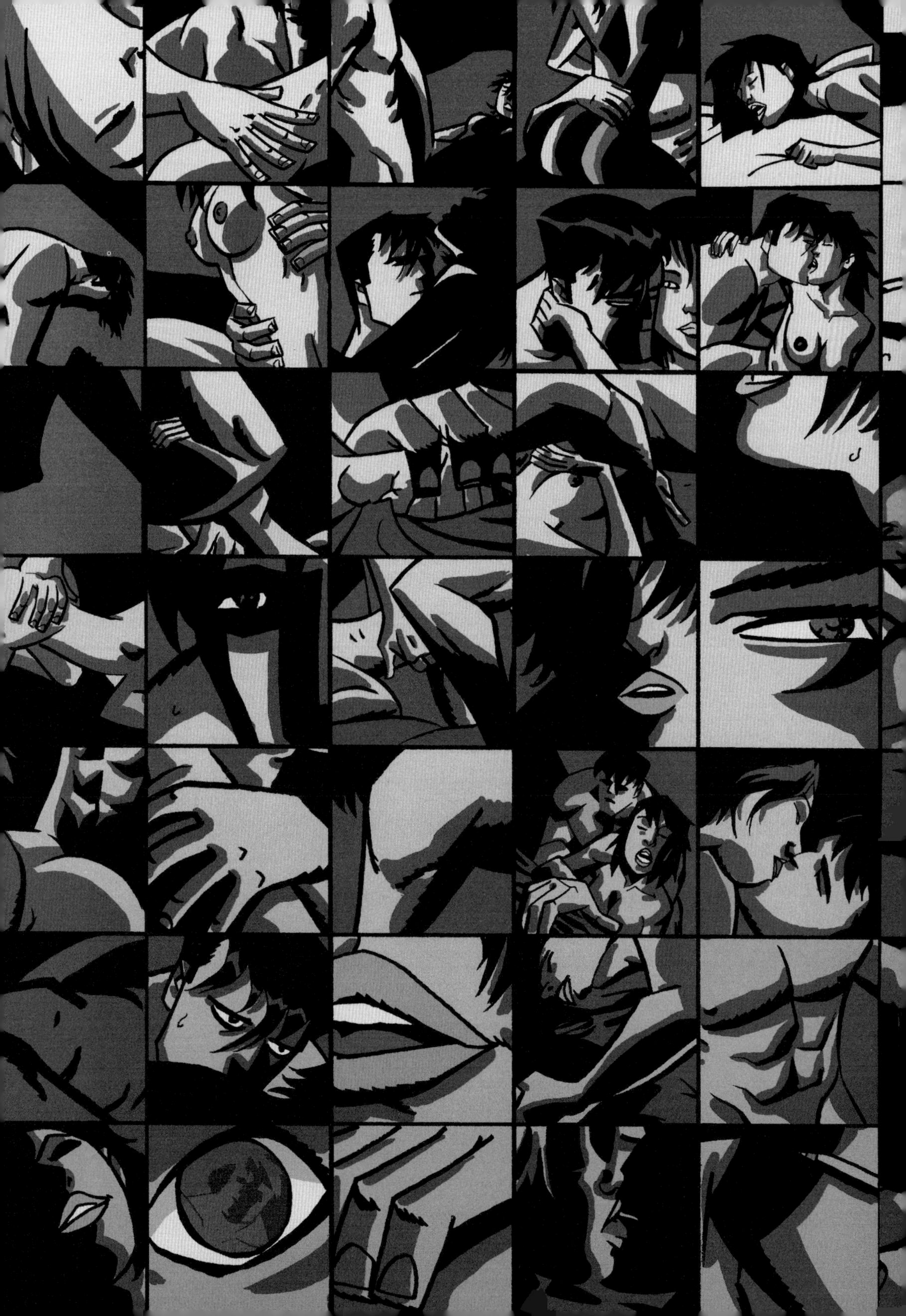

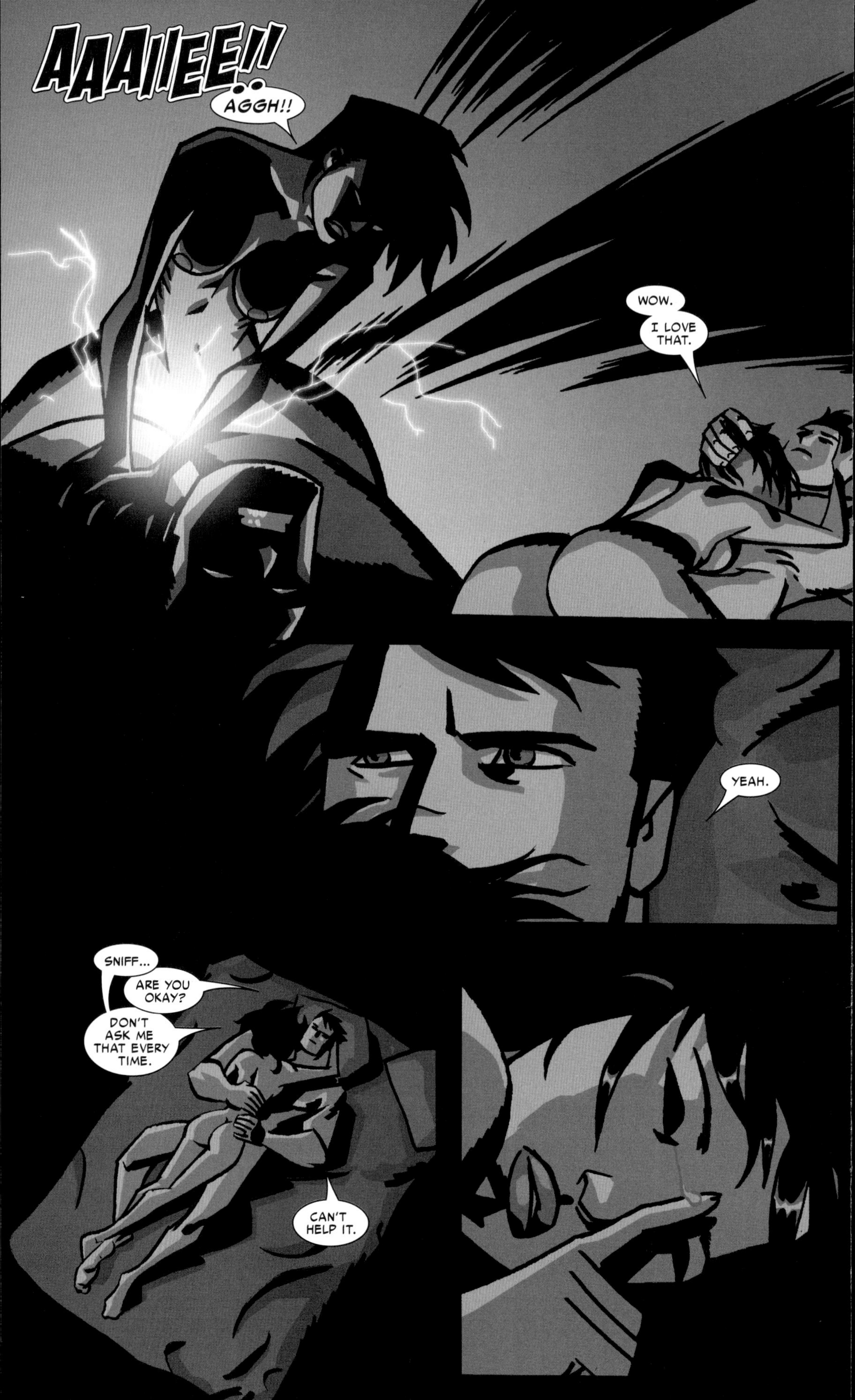
AAAIIEE!!
AGGH!!
WOW.
I LOVE THAT.
YEAH.
SNIFF...
ARE YOU OKAY?
DON'T ASK ME THAT EVERY TIME.
CAN'T HELP IT.

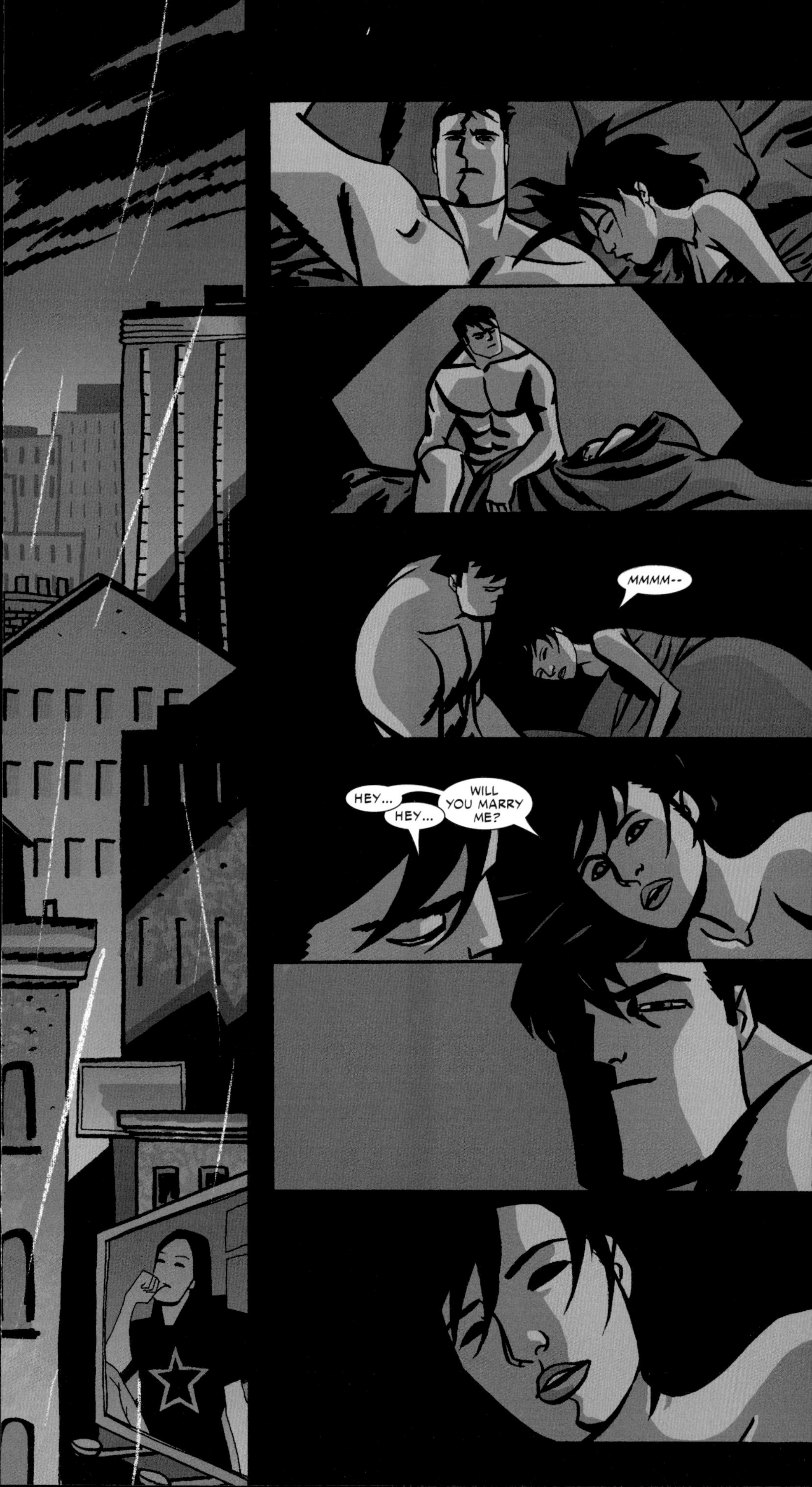
MMMM--
HEY...
HEY...
WILL YOU MARRY ME?

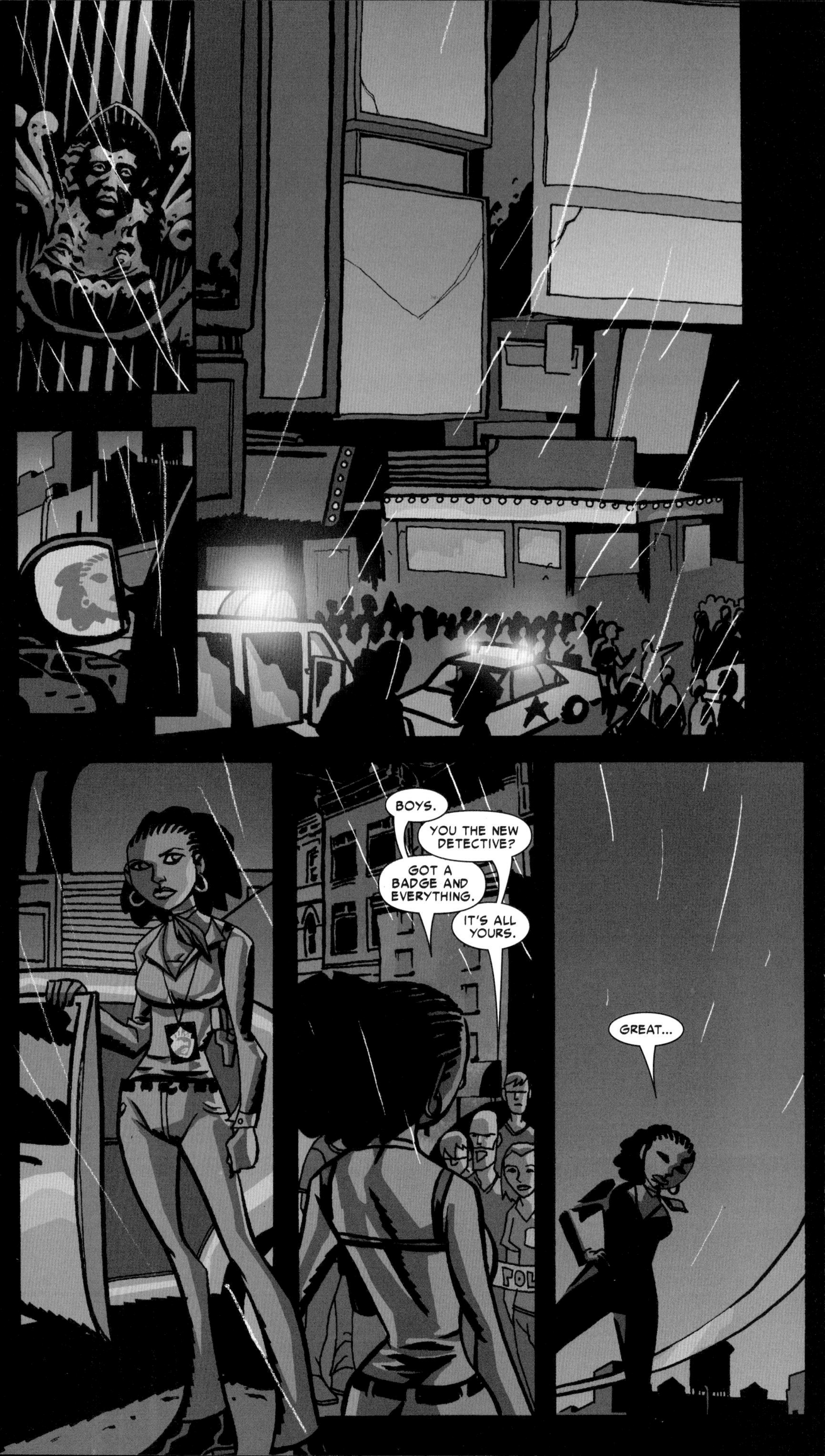
BOYS.
YOU THE NEW DETECTIVE?
GOT A BADGE AND EVERYTHING.
IT'S ALL YOURS.
GREAT...

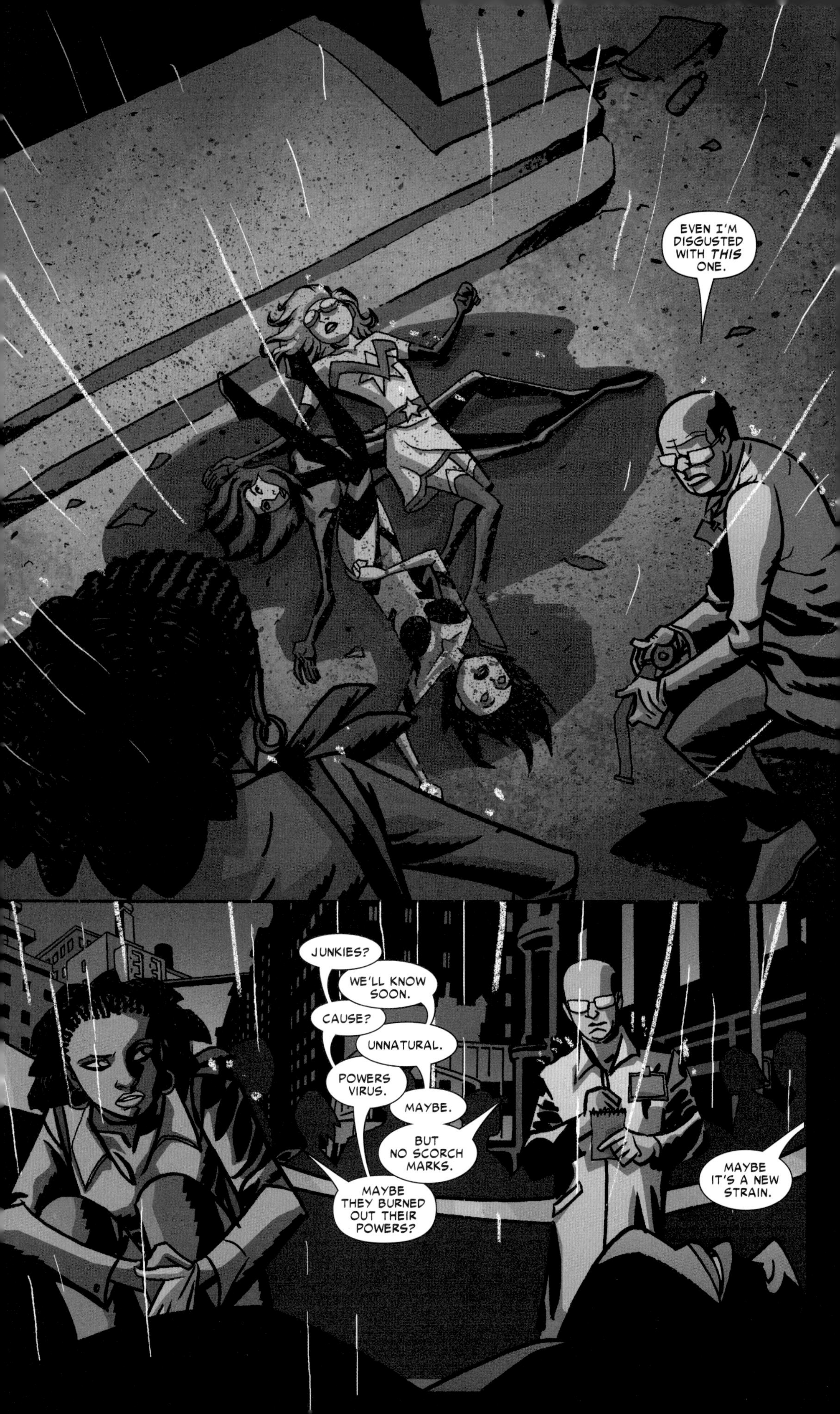
EVEN I'M DISGUSTED WITH *THIS* ONE.
JUNKIES?
WE'LL KNOW SOON.
CAUSE?
UNNATURAL.
POWERS VIRUS.
MAYBE.
BUT NO SCORCH MARKS.
MAYBE THEY BURNED OUT THEIR POWERS?
MAYBE IT'S A NEW STRAIN.

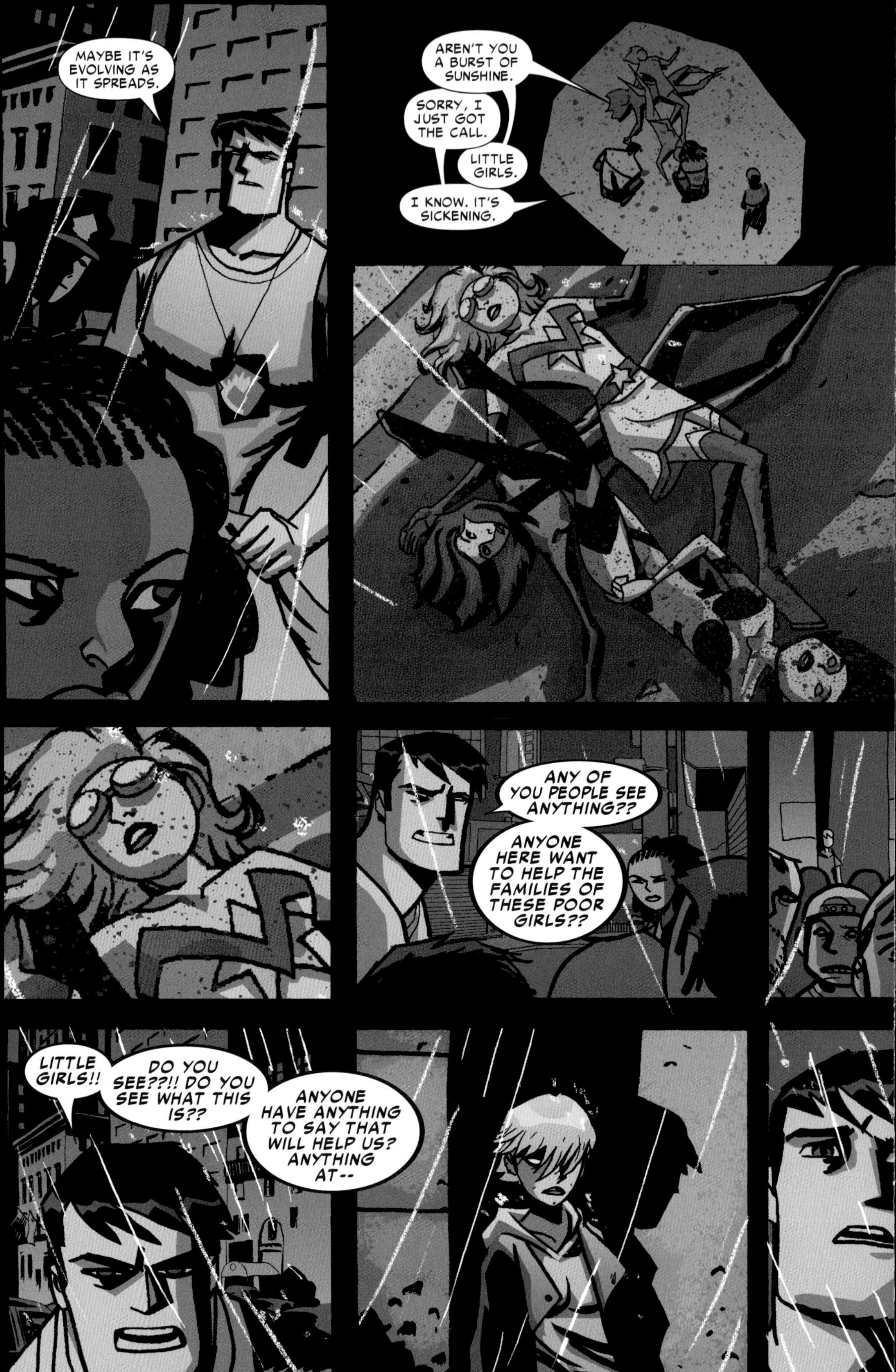
MAYBE IT'S EVOLVING AS IT SPREADS.
AREN'T YOU A BURST OF SUNSHINE.
SORRY, I JUST GOT THE CALL.
LITTLE GIRLS.
I KNOW. IT'S SICKENING.
ANY OF YOU PEOPLE SEE ANYTHING??
ANYONE HERE WANT TO HELP THE FAMILIES OF THESE POOR GIRLS??
LITTLE GIRLS!!
DO YOU SEE??!! DO YOU SEE WHAT THIS IS??
ANYONE HAVE ANYTHING TO SAY THAT WILL HELP US? ANYTHING AT--

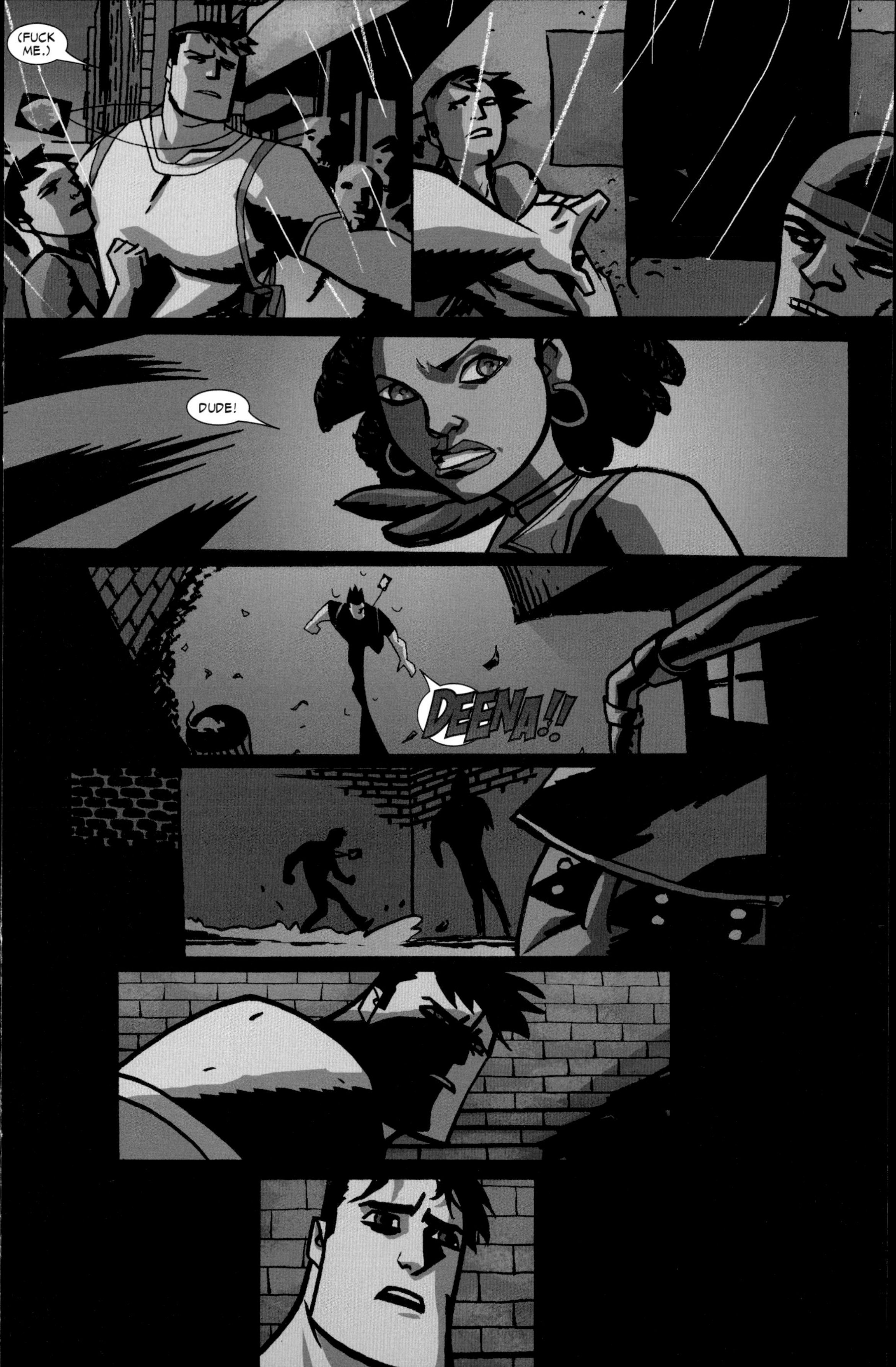
(FUCK ME.)
DUDE!
DEENA!!

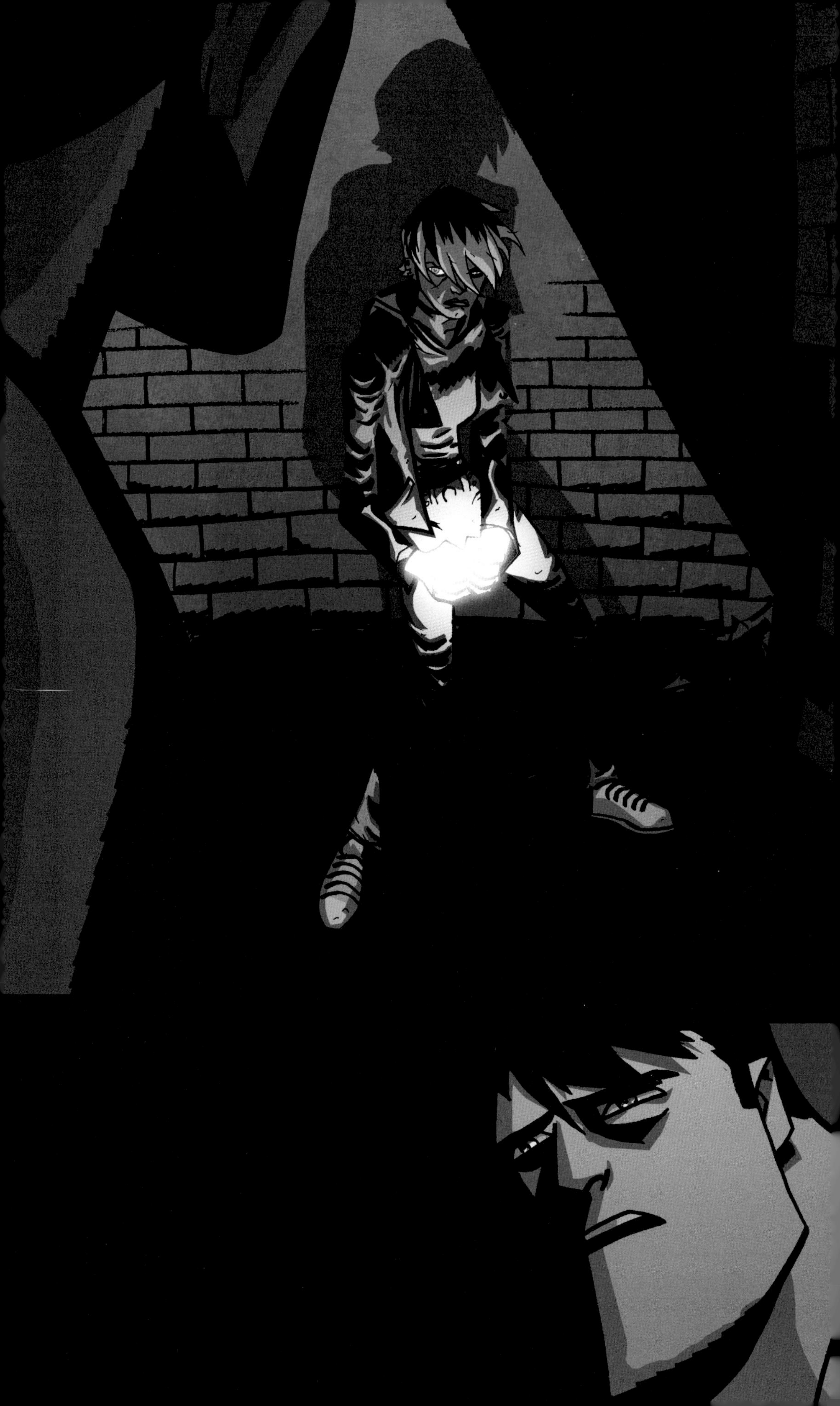

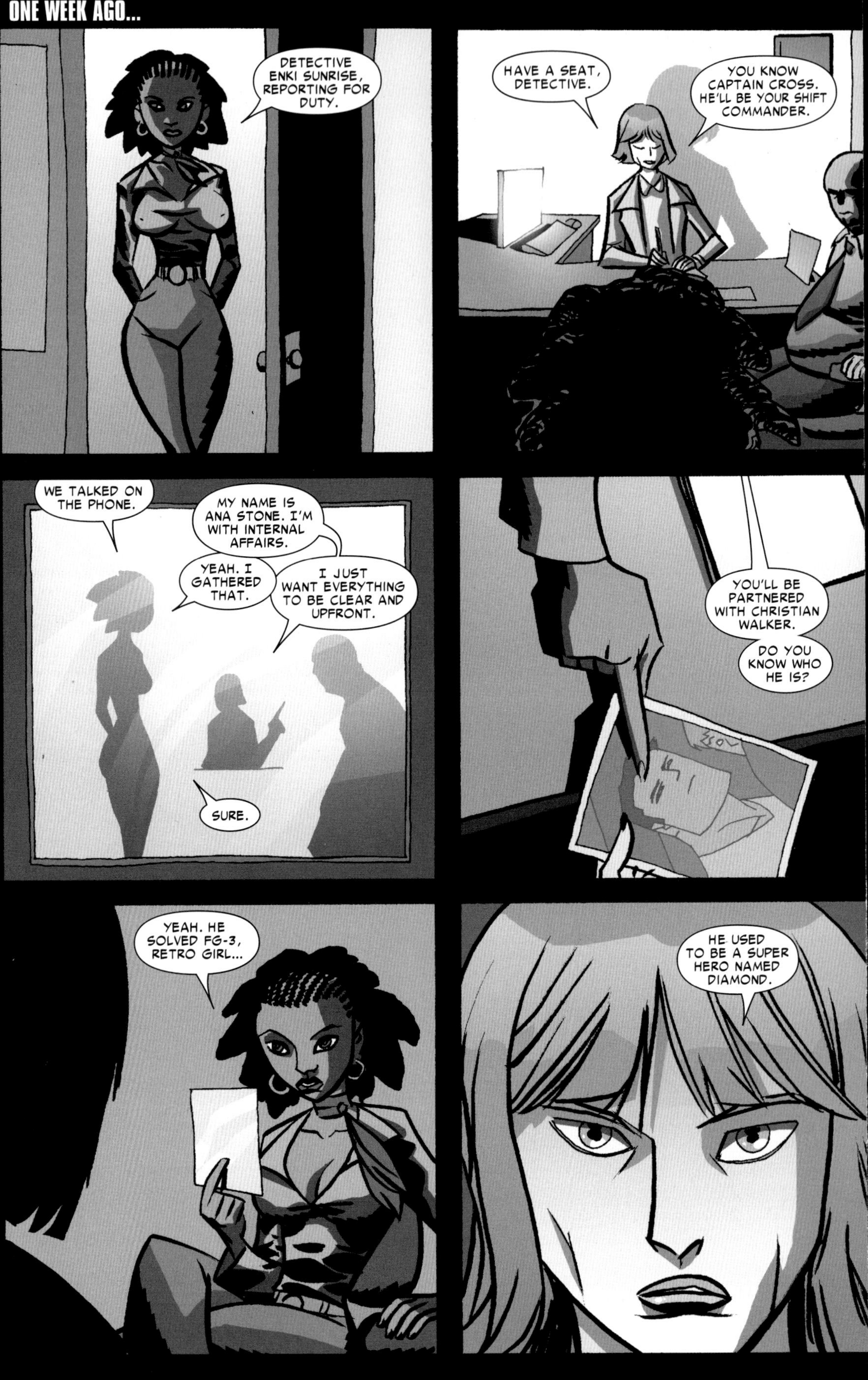

ONE WEEK AGO...
DETECTIVE ENKI SUNRISE, REPORTING FOR DUTY.
HAVE A SEAT, DETECTIVE.
YOU KNOW CAPTAIN CROSS. HE'LL BE YOUR SHIFT COMMANDER.
WE TALKED ON THE PHONE.
MY NAME IS ANA STONE. I'M WITH INTERNAL AFFAIRS.
YEAH. I GATHERED THAT.
I JUST WANT EVERYTHING TO BE CLEAR AND UPFRONT.
SURE.
YOU'LL BE PARTNERED WITH CHRISTIAN WALKER.
DO YOU KNOW WHO HE IS?
YEAH. HE SOLVED FG-3, RETRO GIRL...
HE USED TO BE A SUPER HERO NAMED DIAMOND.

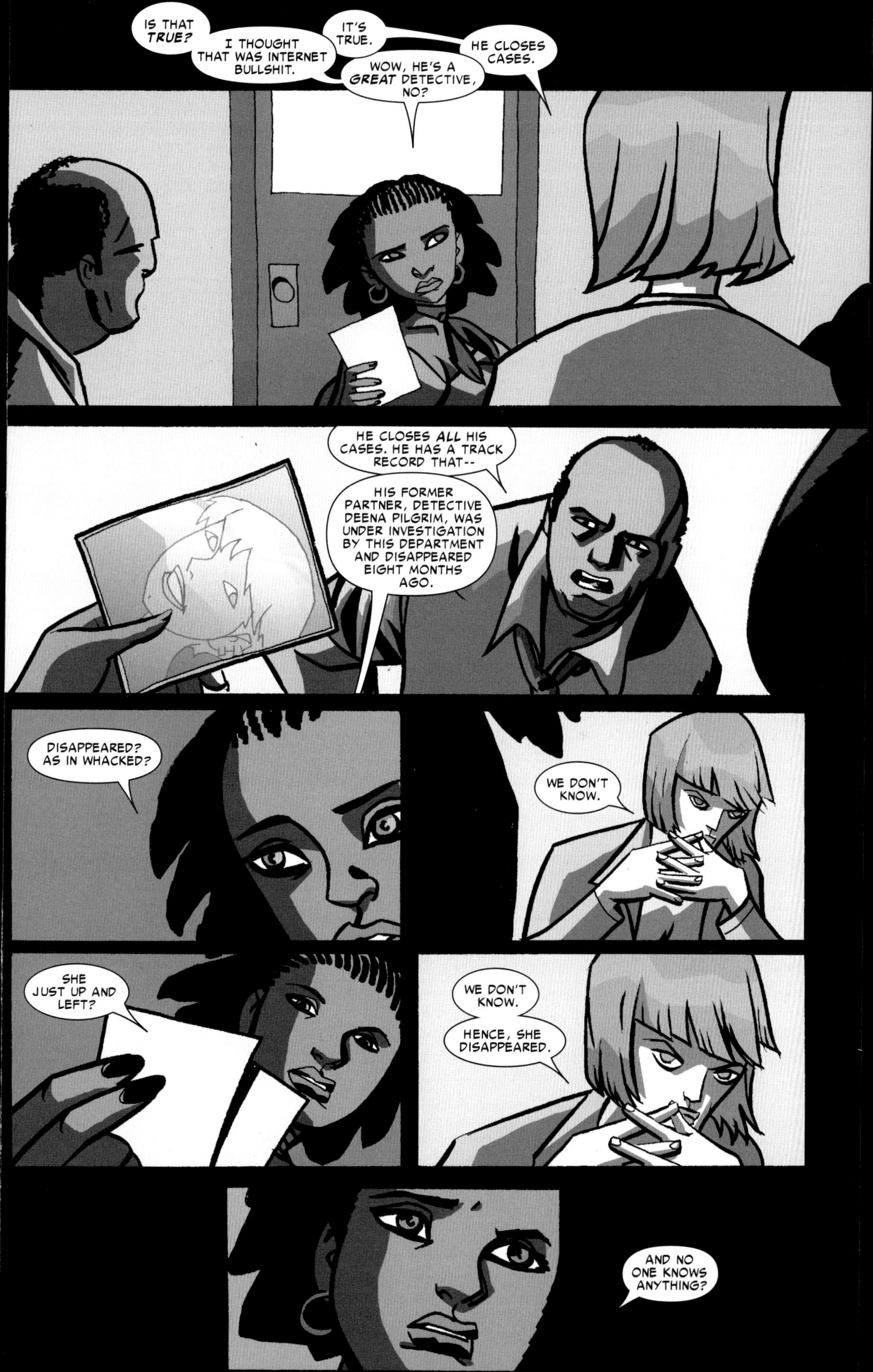
IS THAT TRUE?
I THOUGHT THAT WAS INTERNET BULLSHIT.
IT'S TRUE.
WOW, HE'S A GREAT DETECTIVE, NO?
HE CLOSES CASES.
HE CLOSES ALL HIS CASES. HE HAS A TRACK RECORD THAT--
HIS FORMER PARTNER, DETECTIVE DEENA PILGRIM, WAS UNDER INVESTIGATION BY THIS DEPARTMENT AND DISAPPEARED EIGHT MONTHS AGO.
DISAPPEARED? AS IN WHACKED?
WE DON'T KNOW.
SHE JUST UP AND LEFT?
WE DON'T KNOW.
HENCE, SHE DISAPPEARED.
AND NO ONE KNOWS ANYTHING?

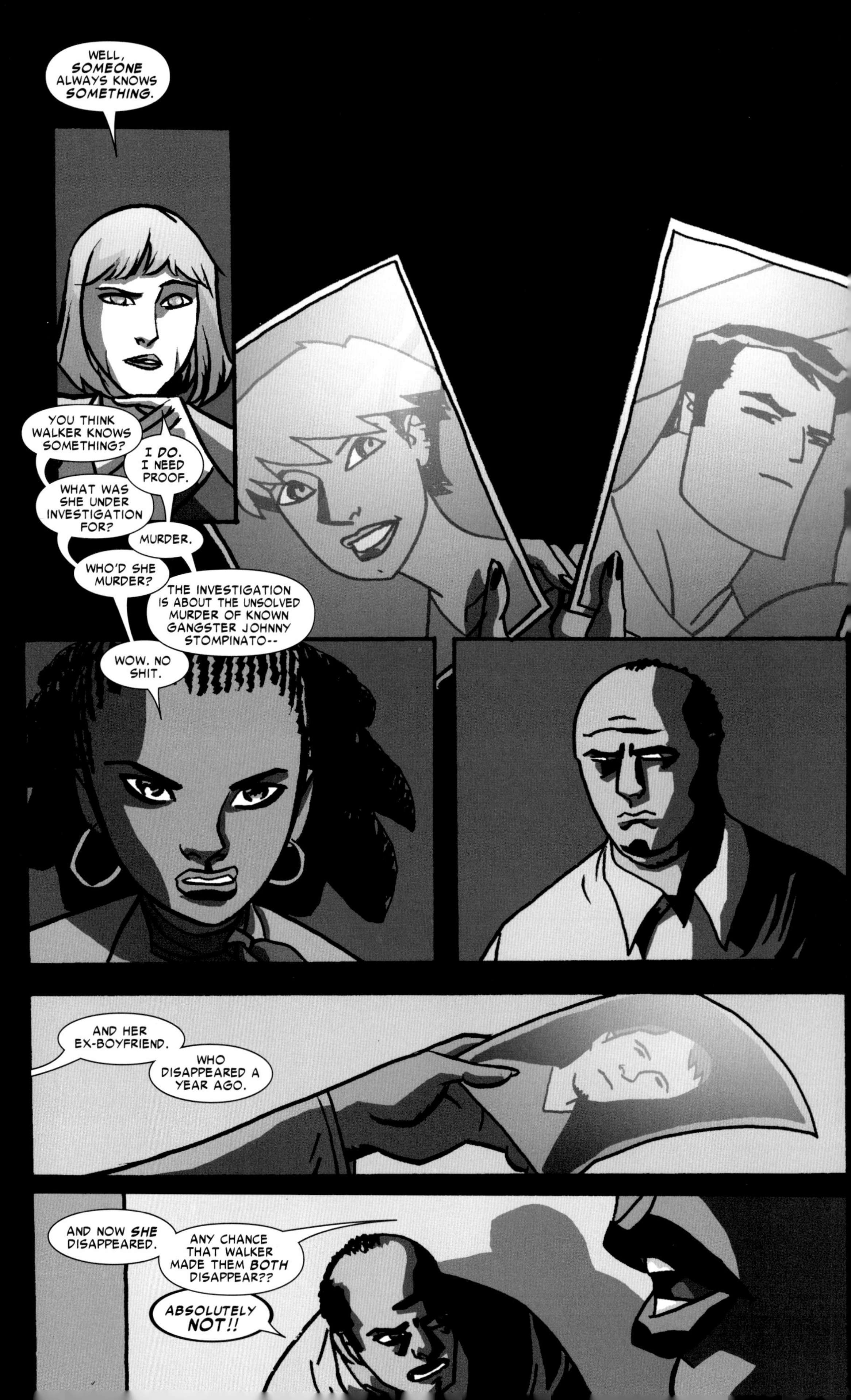

WELL, SOMEONE ALWAYS KNOWS SOMETHING.
YOU THINK WALKER KNOWS SOMETHING?
I DO. I NEED PROOF.
WHAT WAS SHE UNDER INVESTIGATION FOR?
MURDER.
WHO'D SHE MURDER?
THE INVESTIGATION IS ABOUT THE UNSOLVED MURDER OF KNOWN GANGSTER JOHNNY STOMPINATO--
WOW. NO SHIT.
AND HER EX-BOYFRIEND.
WHO DISAPPEARED A YEAR AGO.
AND NOW SHE DISAPPEARED.
ANY CHANCE THAT WALKER MADE THEM BOTH DISAPPEAR??
ABSOLUTELY NOT!!

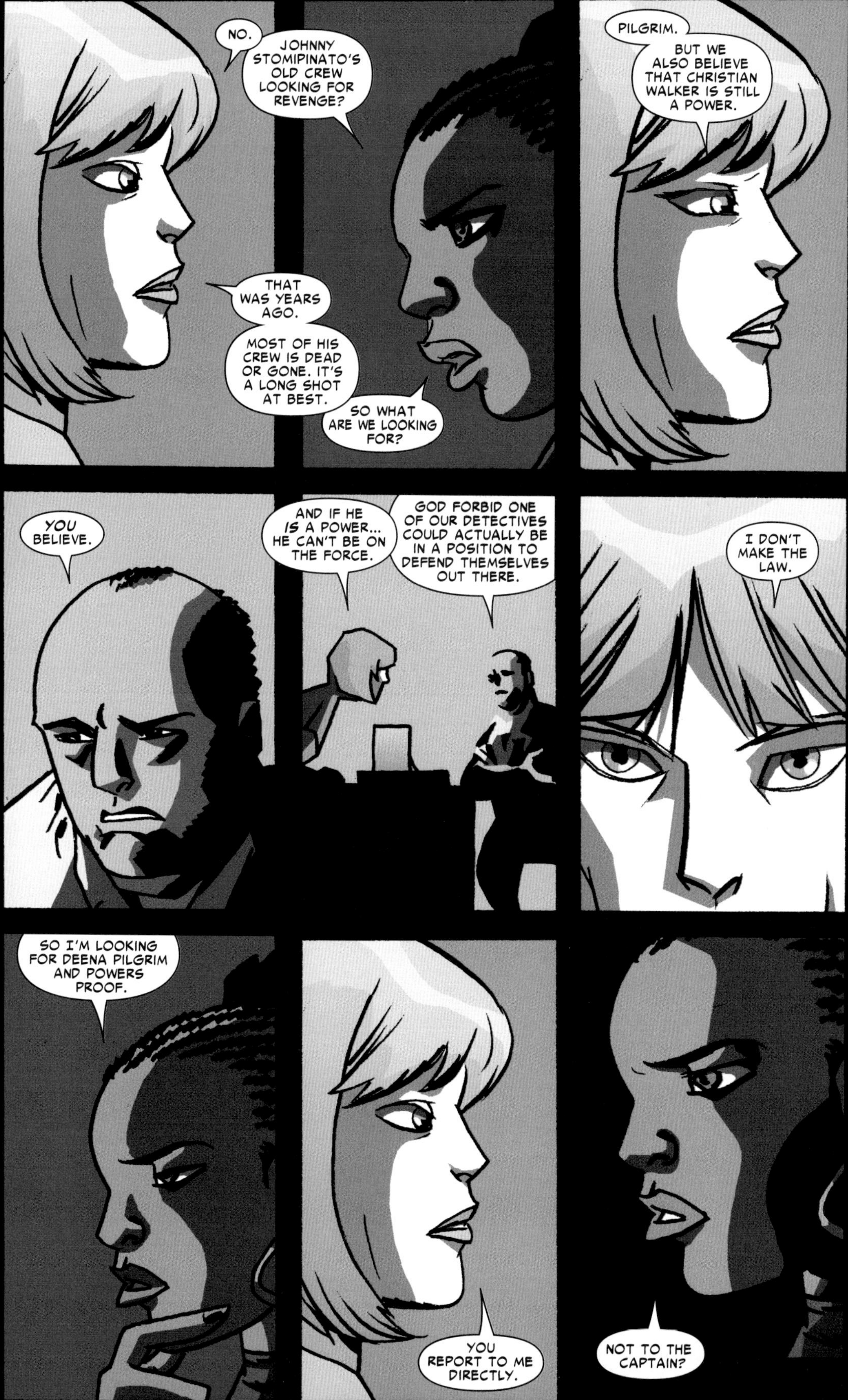
NO.
JOHNNY STOMIPINATO'S OLD CREW LOOKING FOR REVENGE?
THAT WAS YEARS AGO.
MOST OF HIS CREW IS DEAD OR GONE. IT'S A LONG SHOT AT BEST.
SO WHAT ARE WE LOOKING FOR?
PILGRIM.
BUT WE ALSO BELIEVE THAT CHRISTIAN WALKER IS STILL A POWER.
YOU BELIEVE.
AND IF HE *IS* A POWER... HE CAN'T BE ON THE FORCE.
GOD FORBID ONE OF OUR DETECTIVES COULD ACTUALLY BE IN A POSITION TO DEFEND THEMSELVES OUT THERE.
I DON'T MAKE THE LAW.
SO I'M LOOKING FOR DEENA PILGRIM AND POWERS PROOF.
YOU REPORT TO ME DIRECTLY.
NOT TO THE CAPTAIN?

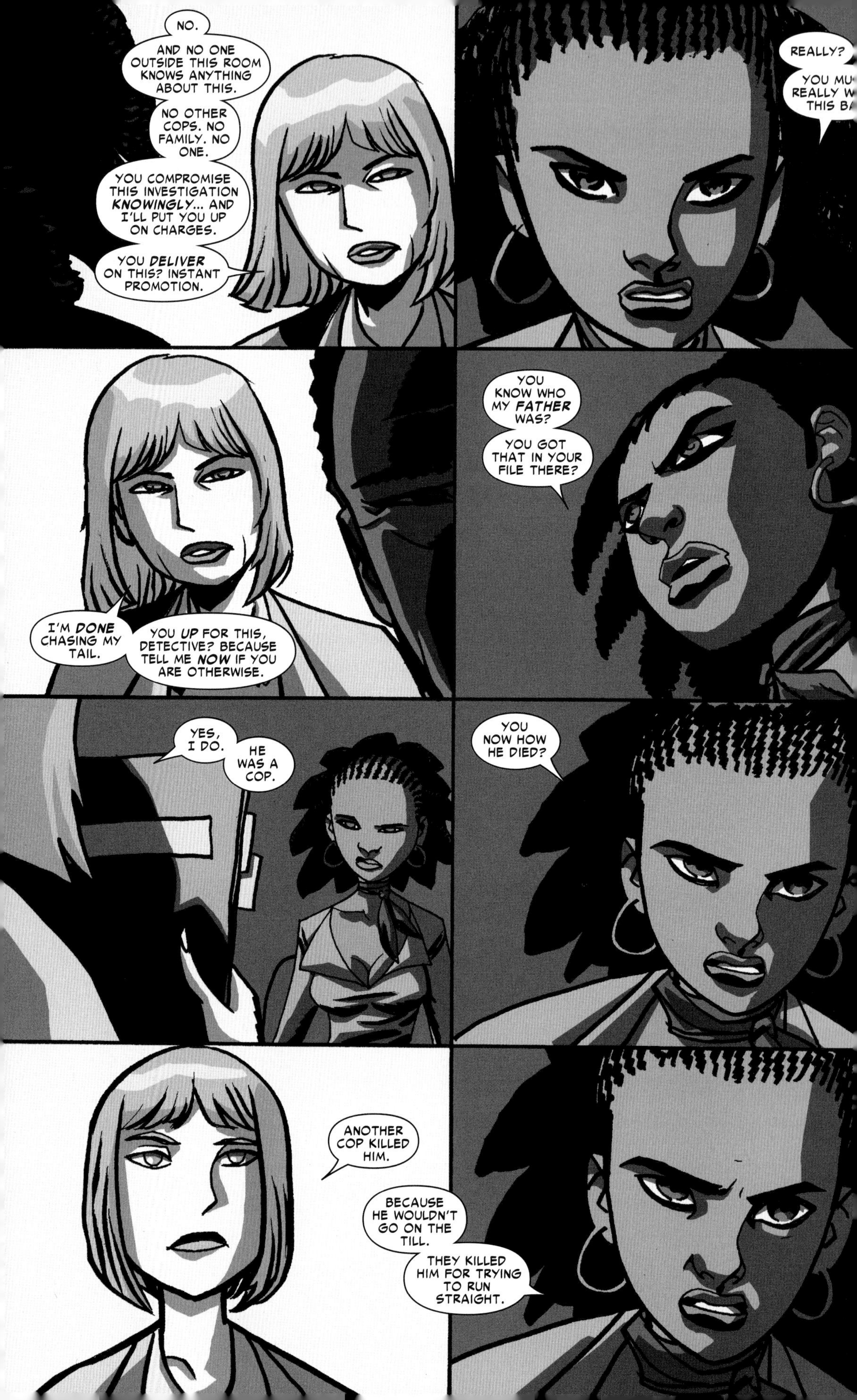
NO.
AND NO ONE OUTSIDE THIS ROOM KNOWS ANYTHING ABOUT THIS.
NO OTHER COPS. NO FAMILY. NO ONE.
YOU COMPROMISE THIS INVESTIGATION KNOWINGLY... AND I'LL PUT YOU UP ON CHARGES.
YOU DELIVER ON THIS? INSTANT PROMOTION.
REALLY?
YOU KNOW WHO MY FATHER WAS?
YOU GOT THAT IN YOUR FILE THERE?
I'M DONE CHASING MY TAIL.
YOU UP FOR THIS, DETECTIVE? BECAUSE TELL ME NOW IF YOU ARE OTHERWISE.
YES, I DO.
HE WAS A COP.
YOU NOW HOW HE DIED?
ANOTHER COP KILLED HIM.
BECAUSE HE WOULDN'T GO ON THE TILL.
THEY KILLED HIM FOR TRYING TO RUN STRAIGHT.

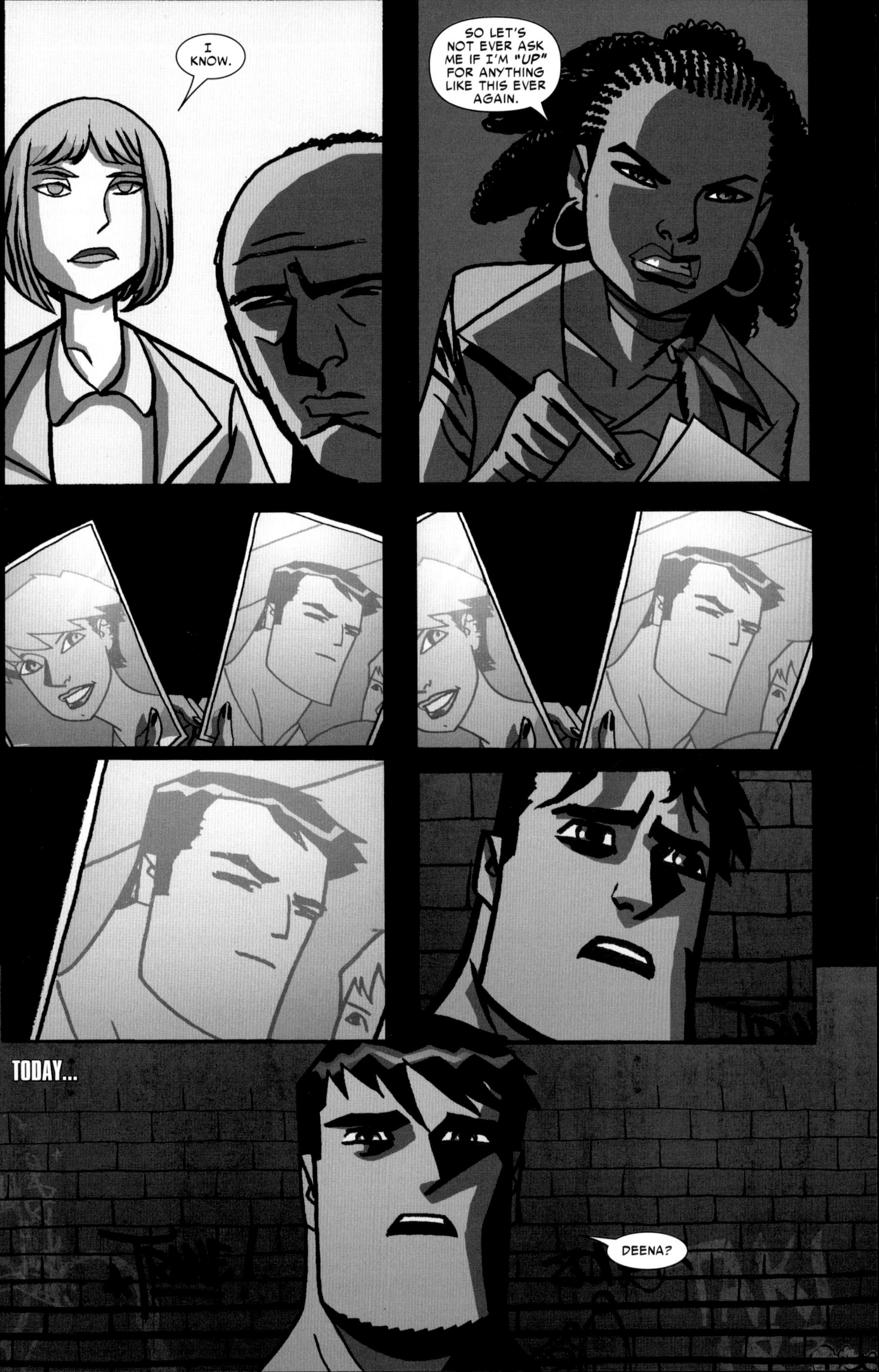
I KNOW.
SO LET'S NOT EVER ASK ME IF I'M "UP" FOR ANYTHING LIKE THIS EVER AGAIN.
TODAY...
DEENA?

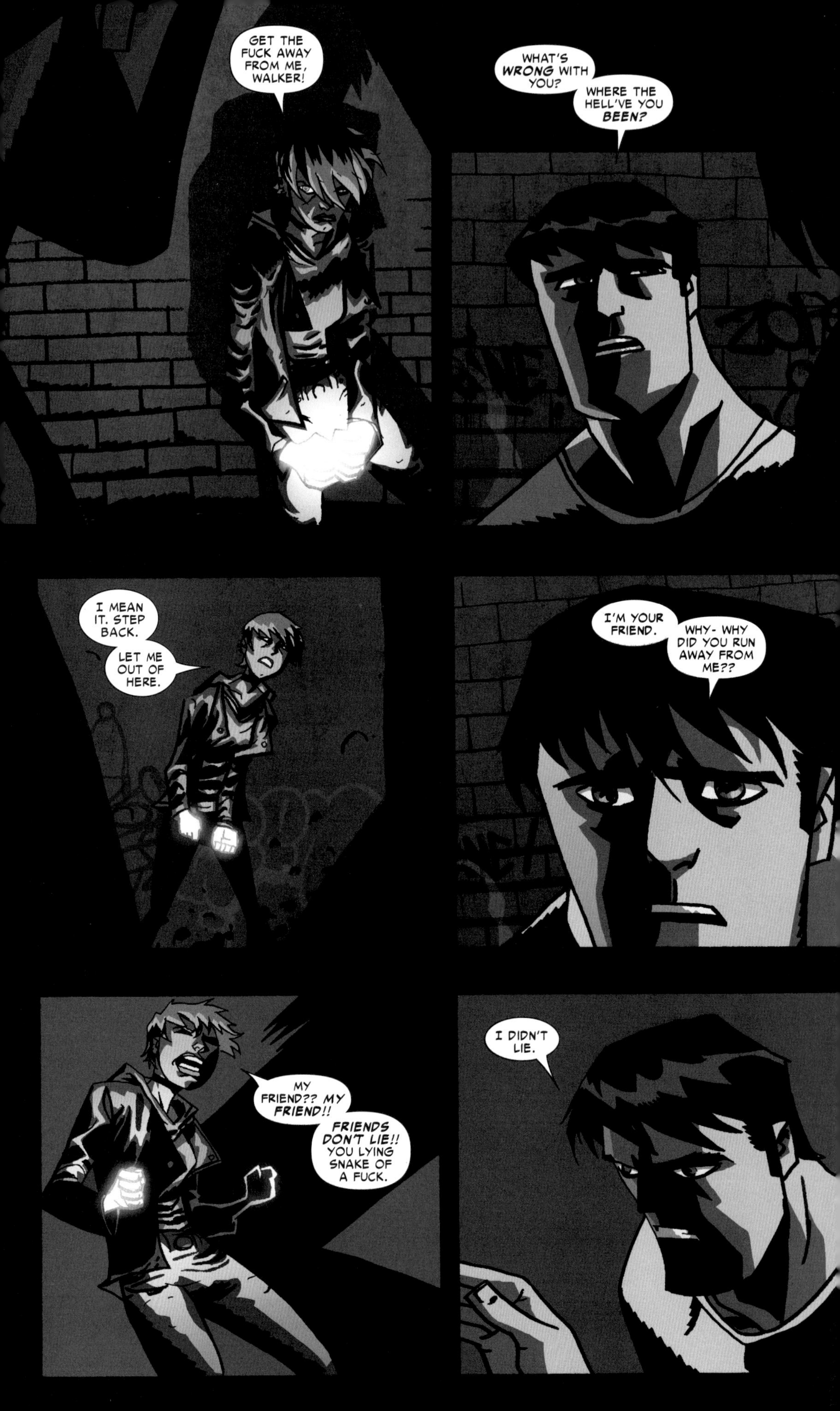
GET THE FUCK AWAY FROM ME, WALKER!
WHAT'S **WRONG** WITH YOU?
WHERE THE HELL'VE YOU **BEEN?**
I MEAN IT. STEP BACK.
LET ME OUT OF HERE.
I'M YOUR FRIEND.
WHY- WHY DID YOU RUN AWAY FROM ME??
MY FRIEND?? MY **FRIEND!!**
FRIENDS DON'T LIE!! YOU LYING SNAKE OF A FUCK.
I DIDN'T LIE.

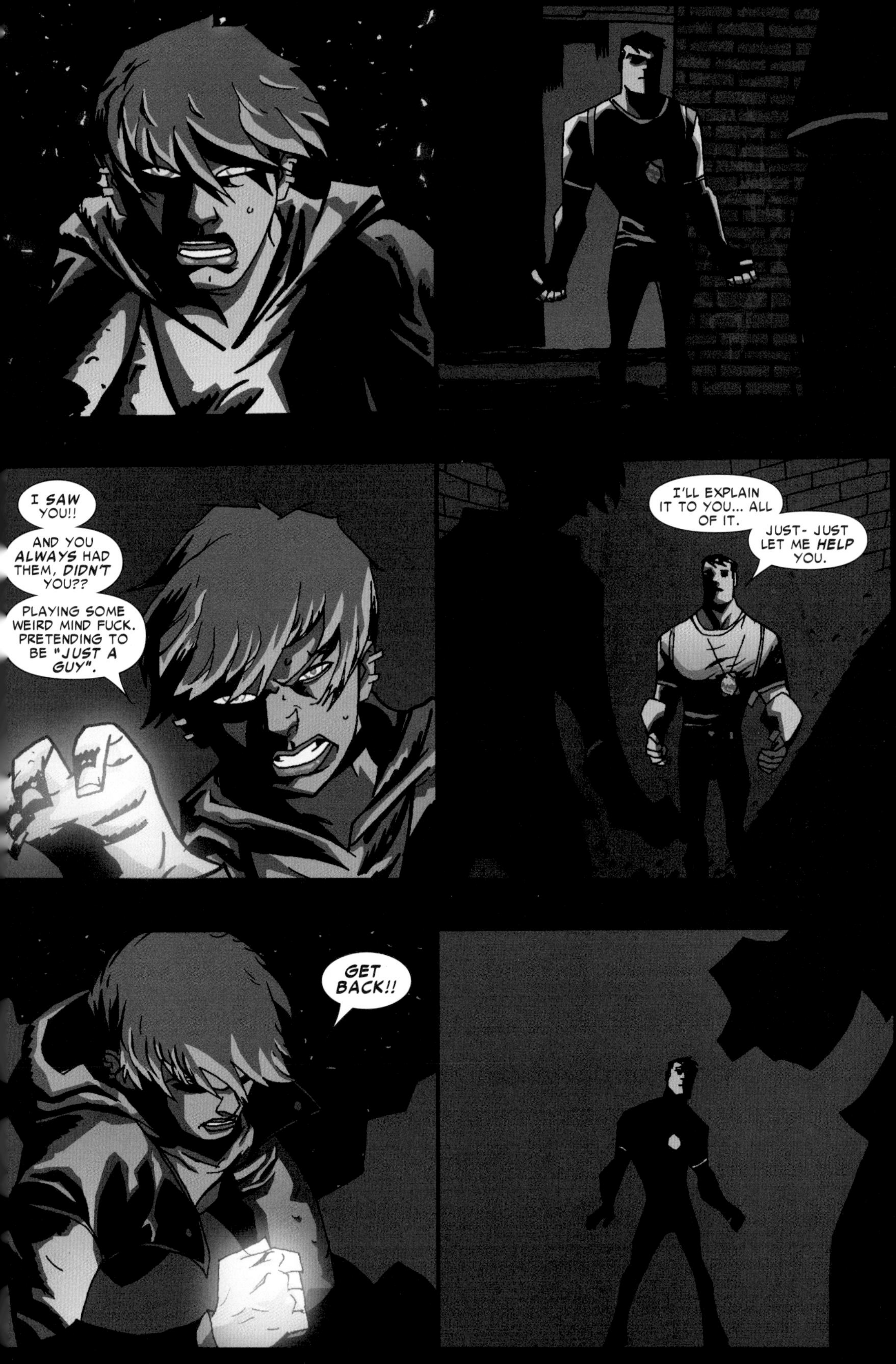
YOU HAVE POWERS!! YOU LYING FUCK!!!
I NEVER LIED TO YOU.
I SAW YOU!!
AND YOU ALWAYS HAD THEM, DIDN'T YOU??
PLAYING SOME WEIRD MIND FUCK. PRETENDING TO BE "JUST A GUY".
I'LL EXPLAIN IT TO YOU... ALL OF IT.
JUST- JUST LET ME HELP YOU.
GET BACK!!

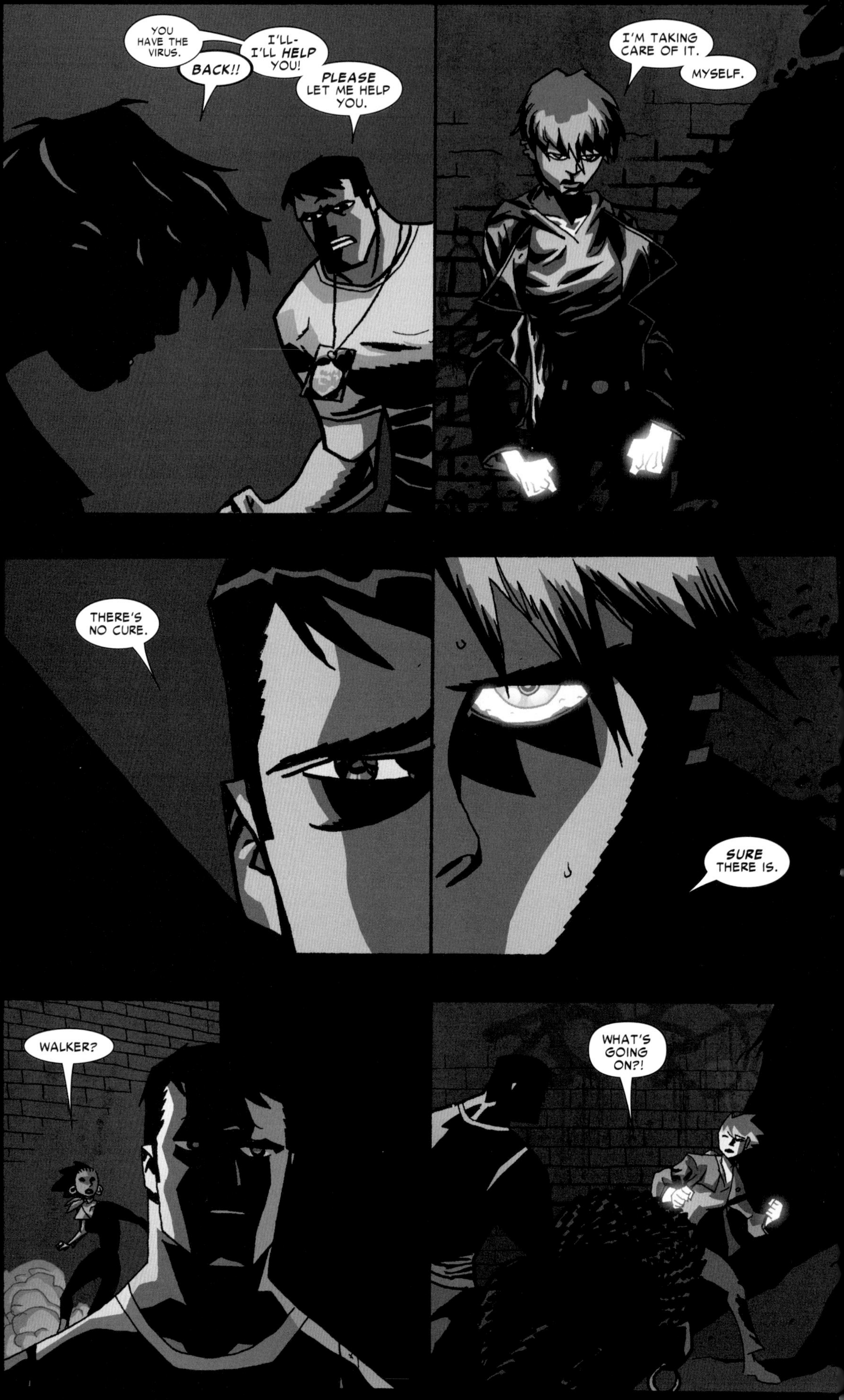
YOU HAVE THE VIRUS.
BACK!!
I'LL- I'LL HELP YOU!
PLEASE LET ME HELP YOU.
I'M TAKING CARE OF IT.
MYSELF.
THERE'S NO CURE.
SURE THERE IS.
WALKER?
WHAT'S GOING ON?!

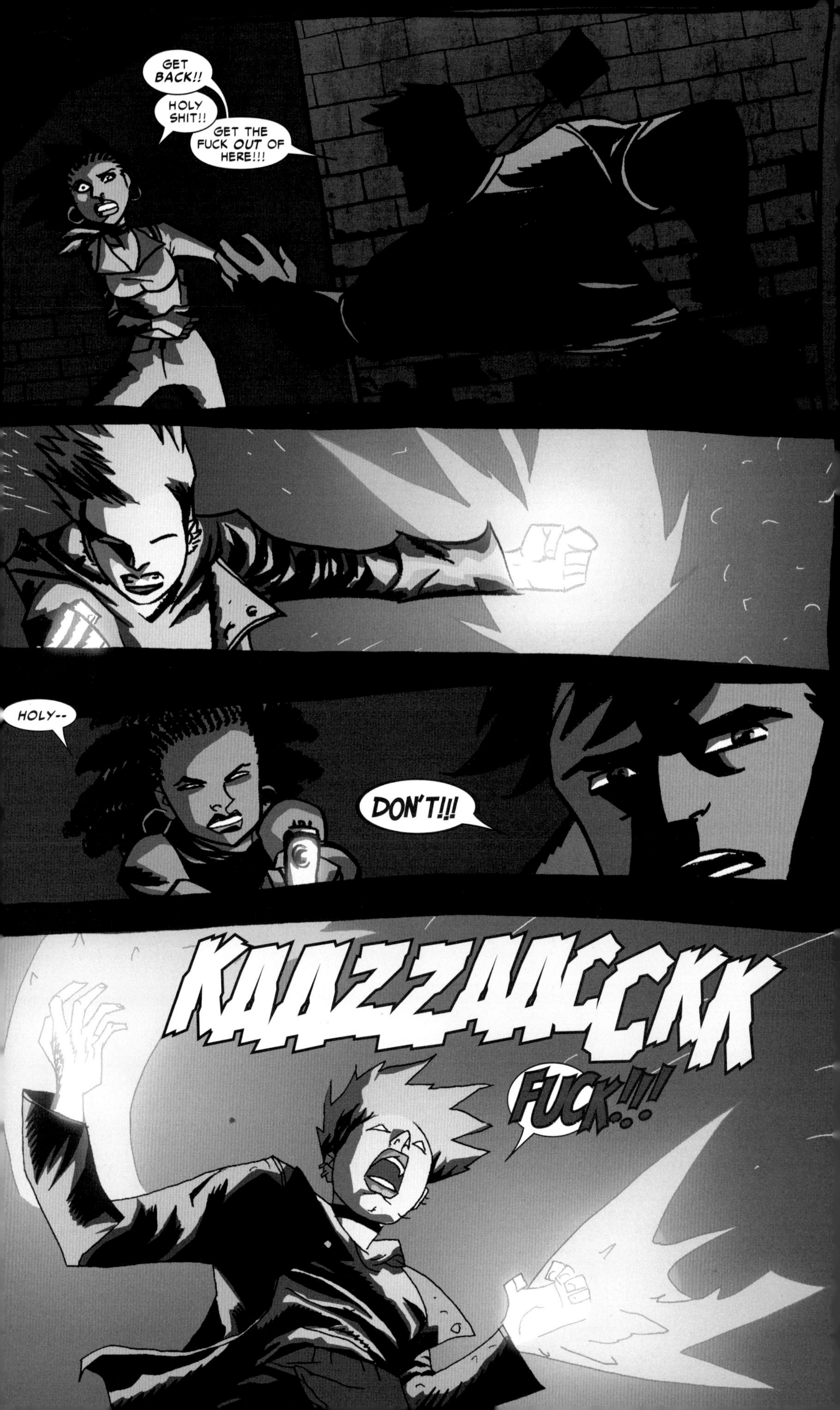
GET BACK!!
HOLY SHIT!!
GET THE FUCK OUT OF HERE!!!
HOLY--
DON'T!!!
KAAAZZAAACCKK
FUCK!!!

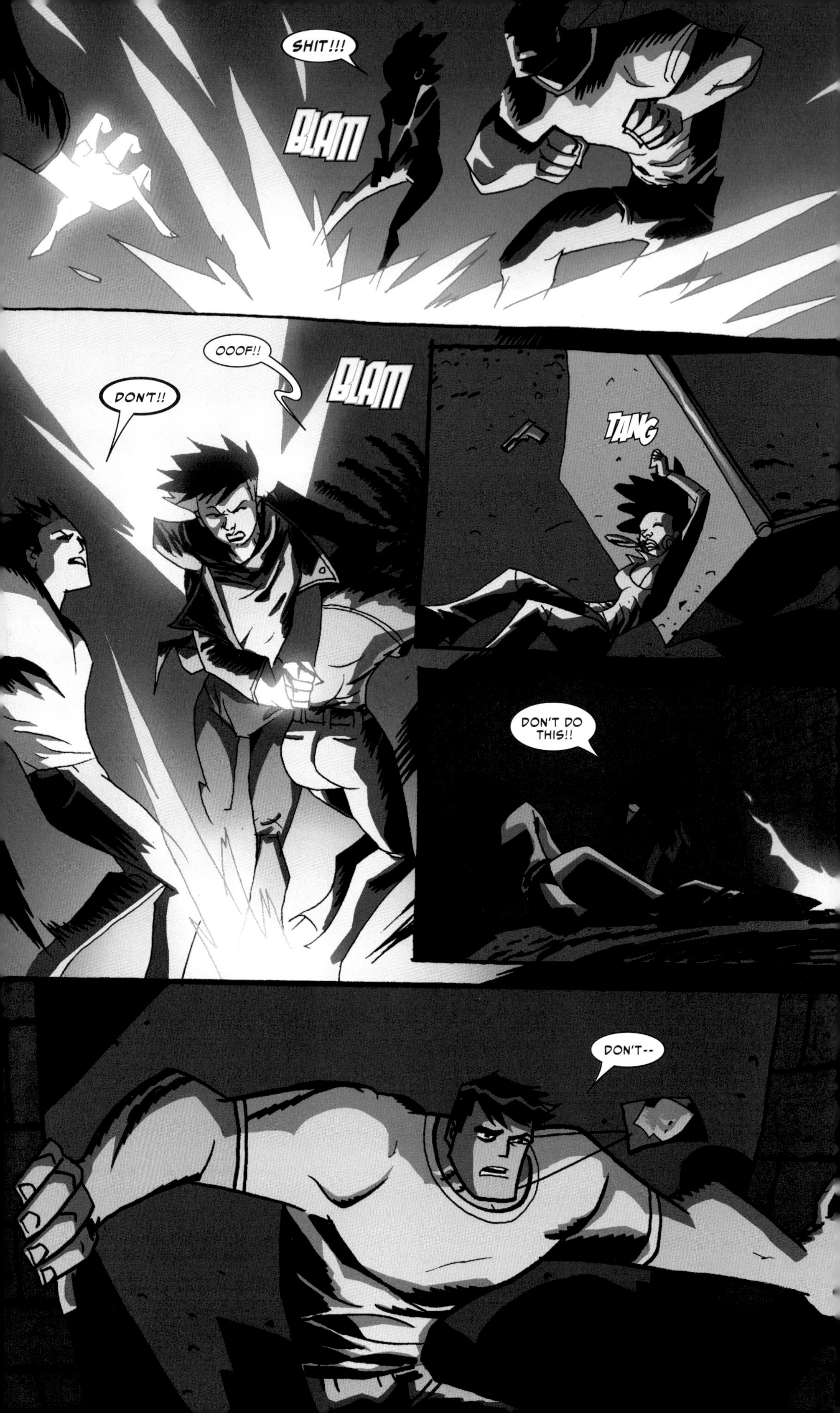
SHIT!!!
BLAM
DON'T!!
OOOF!!
BLAM
TANG
DON'T DO THIS!!
DON'T--

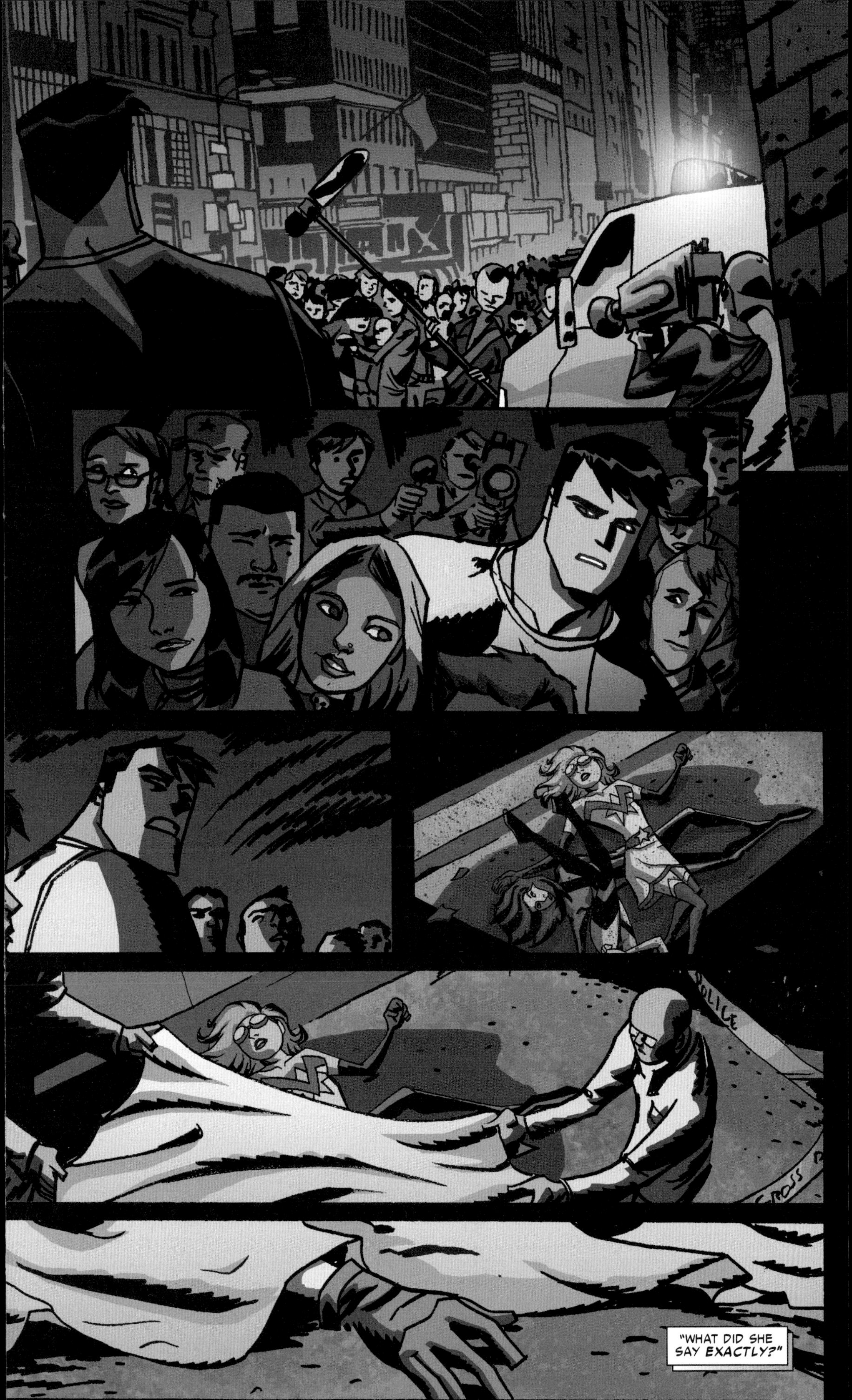
"WHAT DID SHE SAY EXACTLY?"

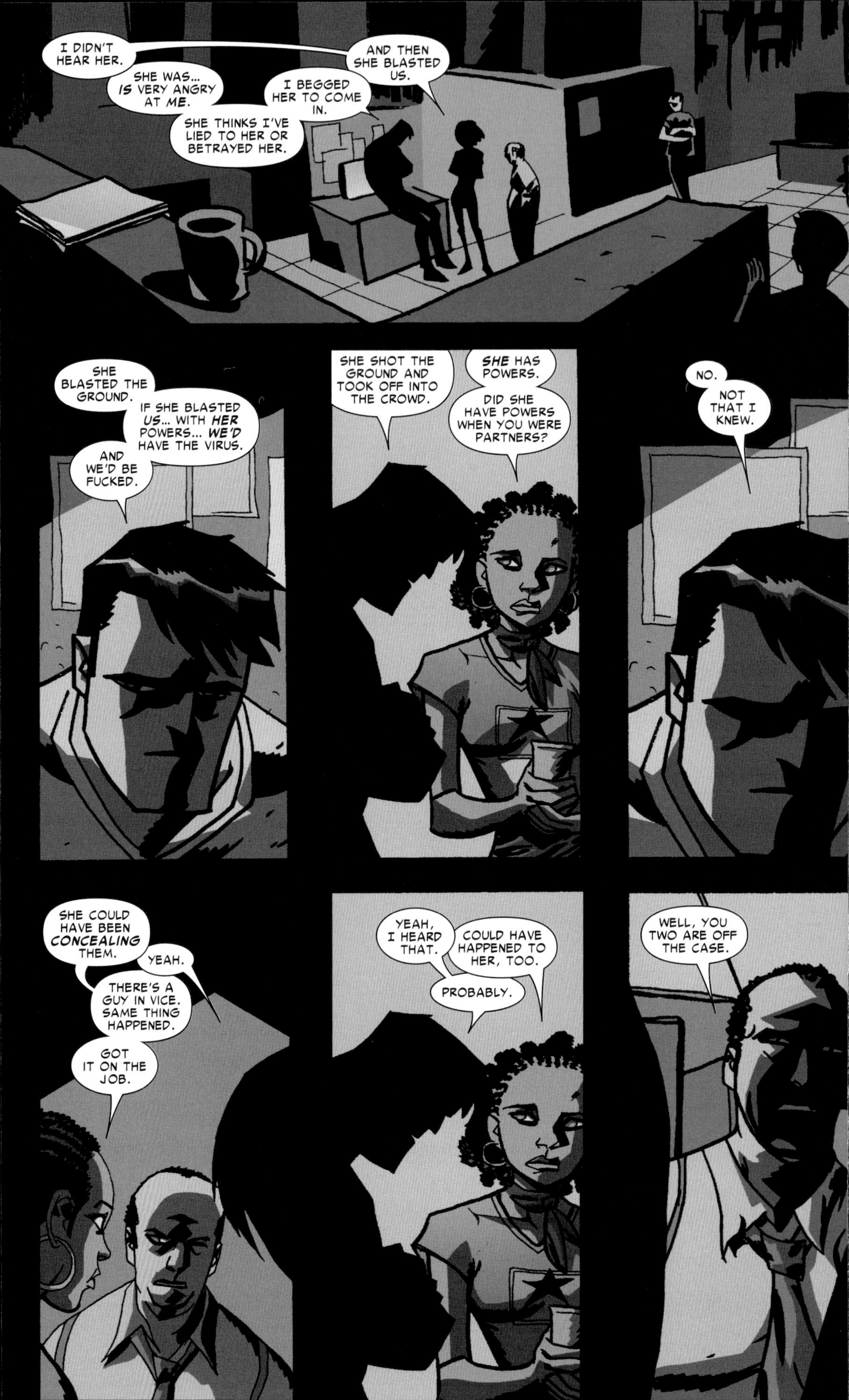
I DIDN'T HEAR HER.
SHE WAS... *IS* VERY ANGRY AT *ME*.
SHE THINKS I'VE LIED TO HER OR BETRAYED HER.
I BEGGED HER TO COME IN.
AND THEN SHE BLASTED US.
SHE BLASTED THE GROUND.
IF SHE BLASTED *US*... WITH *HER* POWERS... *WE'D* HAVE THE VIRUS.
AND WE'D BE FUCKED.
SHE SHOT THE GROUND AND TOOK OFF INTO THE CROWD.
SHE HAS POWERS.
DID SHE HAVE POWERS WHEN YOU WERE PARTNERS?
NO.
NOT THAT I KNEW.
SHE COULD HAVE BEEN *CONCEALING* THEM.
YEAH.
THERE'S A GUY IN VICE. SAME THING HAPPENED.
GOT IT ON THE JOB.
YEAH, I HEARD THAT.
COULD HAVE HAPPENED TO HER, TOO.
PROBABLY.
WELL, YOU TWO ARE OFF THE CASE.

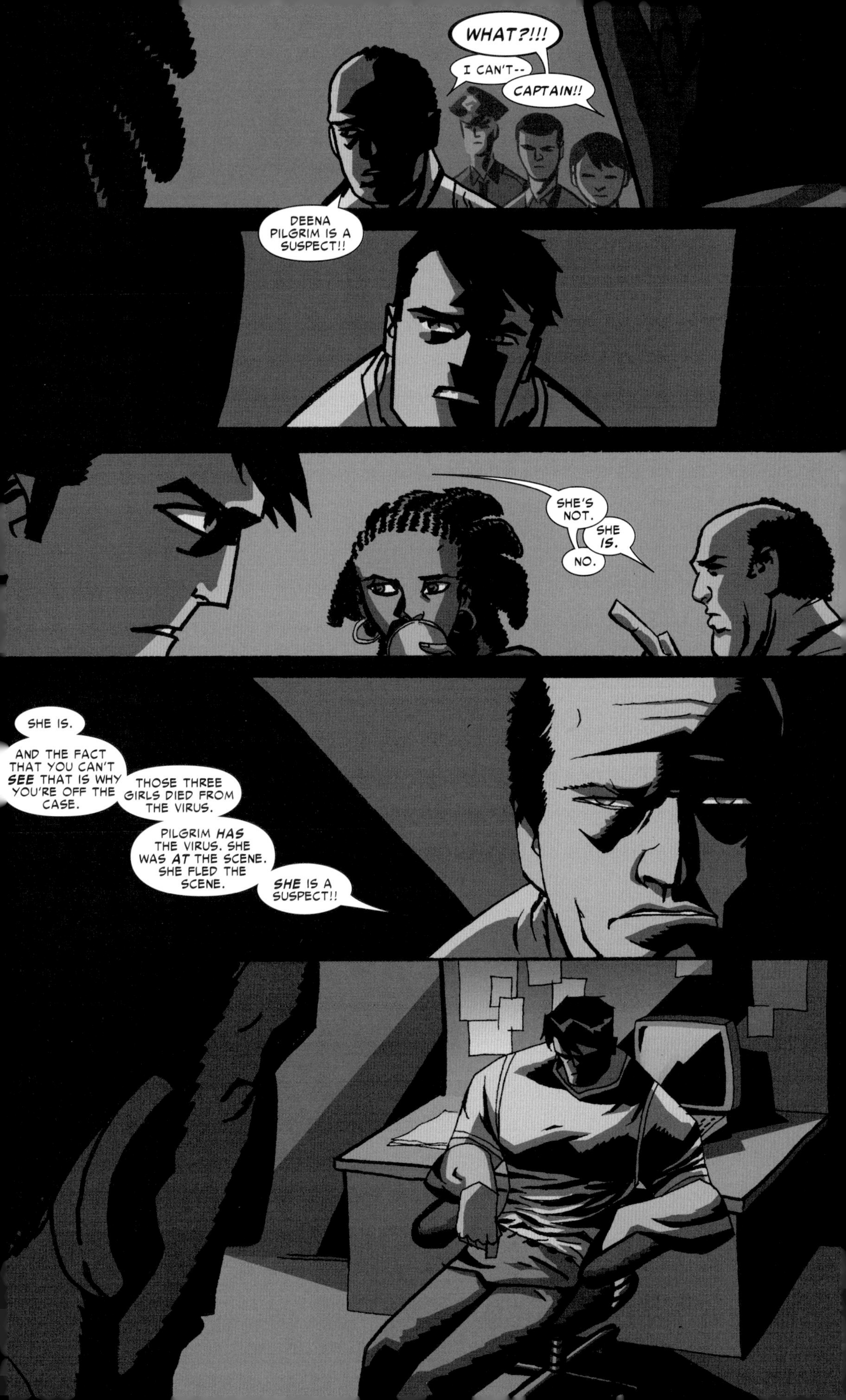
WHAT?!!!
I CAN'T--
CAPTAIN!!
DEENA PILGRIM IS A SUSPECT!!
SHE'S NOT.
NO.
SHE IS.
SHE IS.
AND THE FACT THAT YOU CAN'T SEE THAT IS WHY YOU'RE OFF THE CASE.
THOSE THREE GIRLS DIED FROM THE VIRUS.
PILGRIM HAS THE VIRUS. SHE WAS AT THE SCENE. SHE FLED THE SCENE.
SHE IS A SUSPECT!!

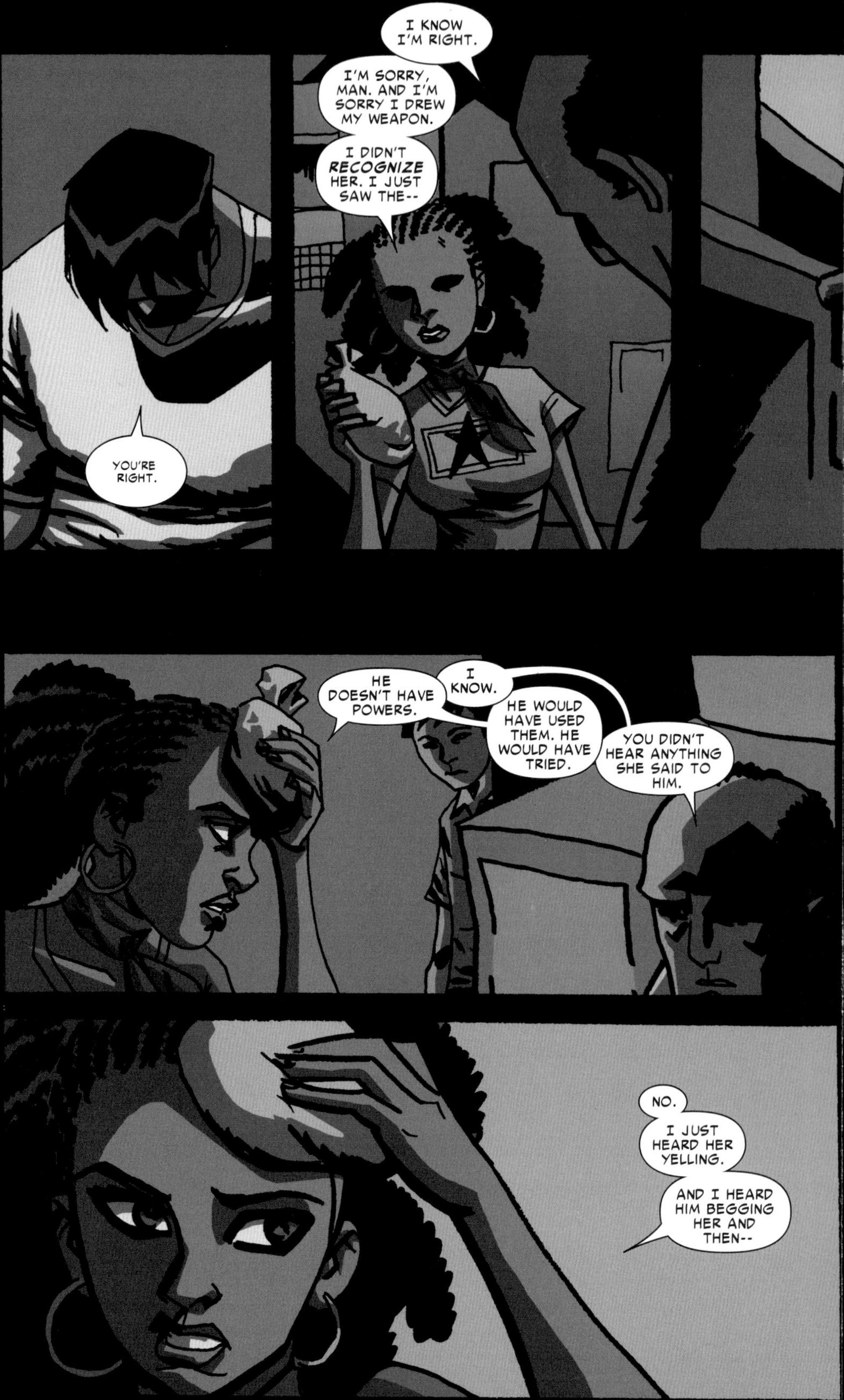
I KNOW I'M RIGHT.
I'M SORRY, MAN. AND I'M SORRY I DREW MY WEAPON.
I DIDN'T RECOGNIZE HER. I JUST SAW THE--
YOU'RE RIGHT.
HE DOESN'T HAVE POWERS.
I KNOW.
HE WOULD HAVE USED THEM. HE WOULD HAVE TRIED.
YOU DIDN'T HEAR ANYTHING SHE SAID TO HIM.
NO.
I JUST HEARD HER YELLING.
AND I HEARD HIM BEGGING HER AND THEN--

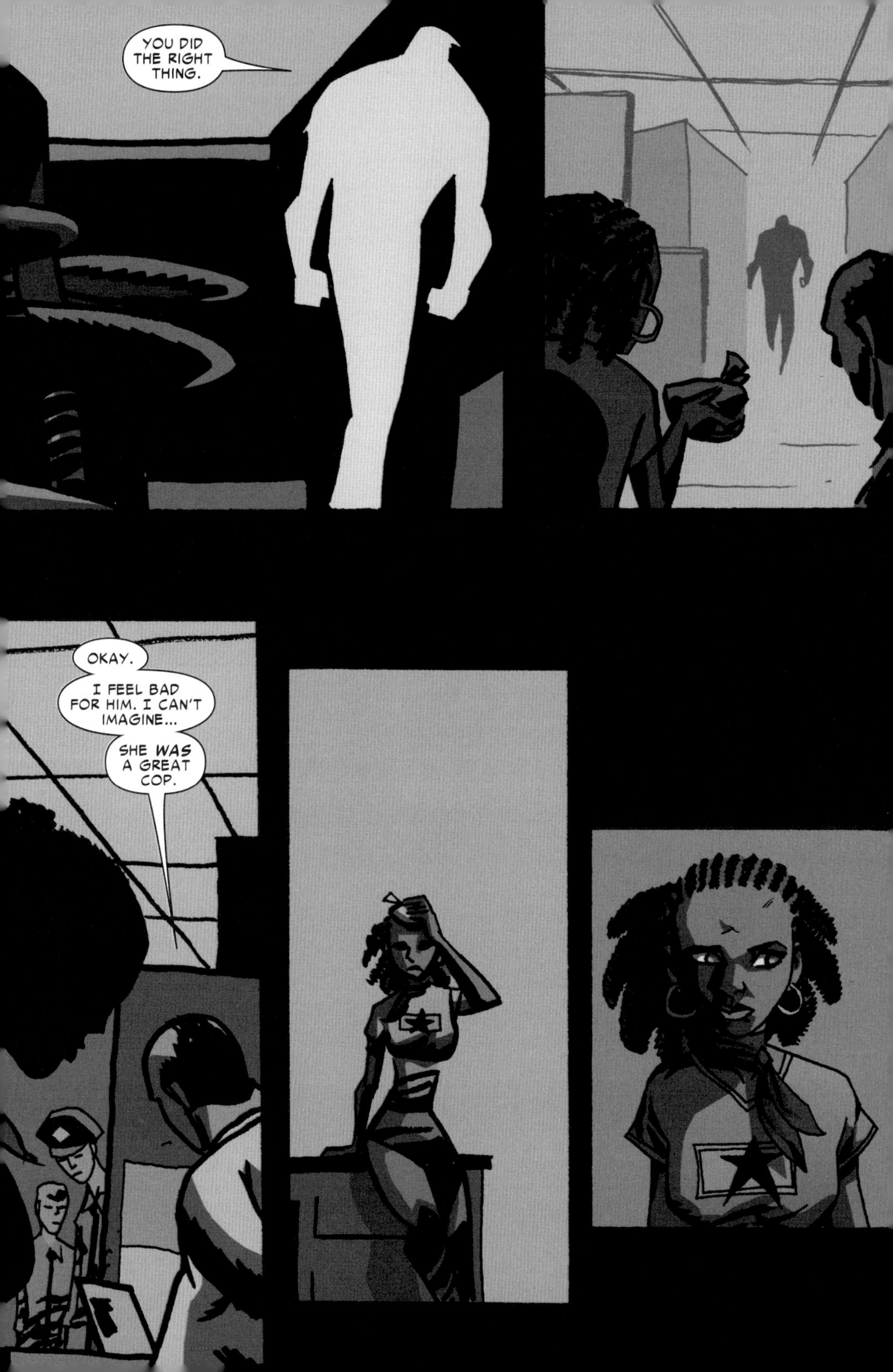
YOU DID THE RIGHT THING.
OKAY.
I FEEL BAD FOR HIM. I CAN'T IMAGINE...
SHE WAS A GREAT COP.

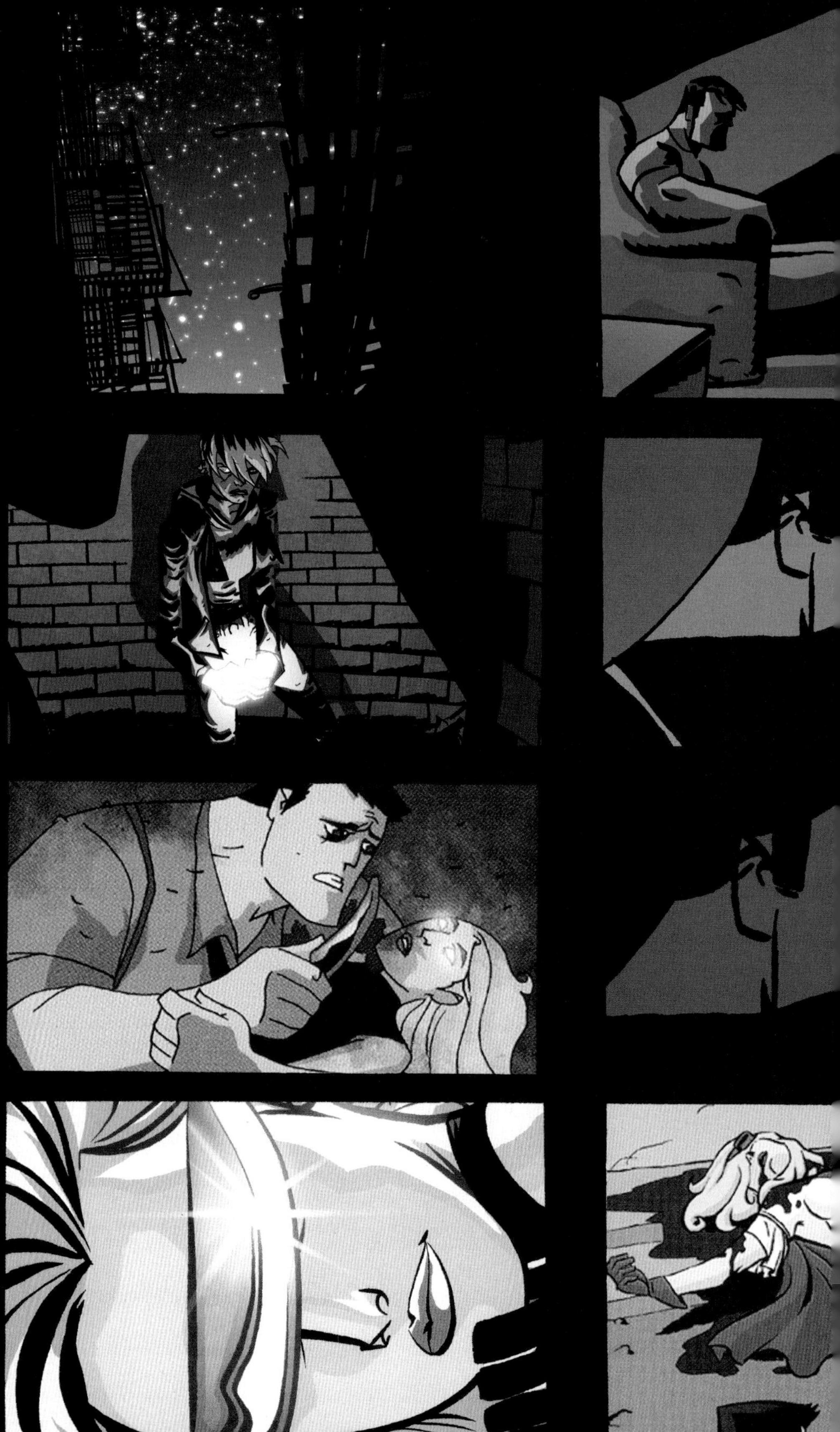

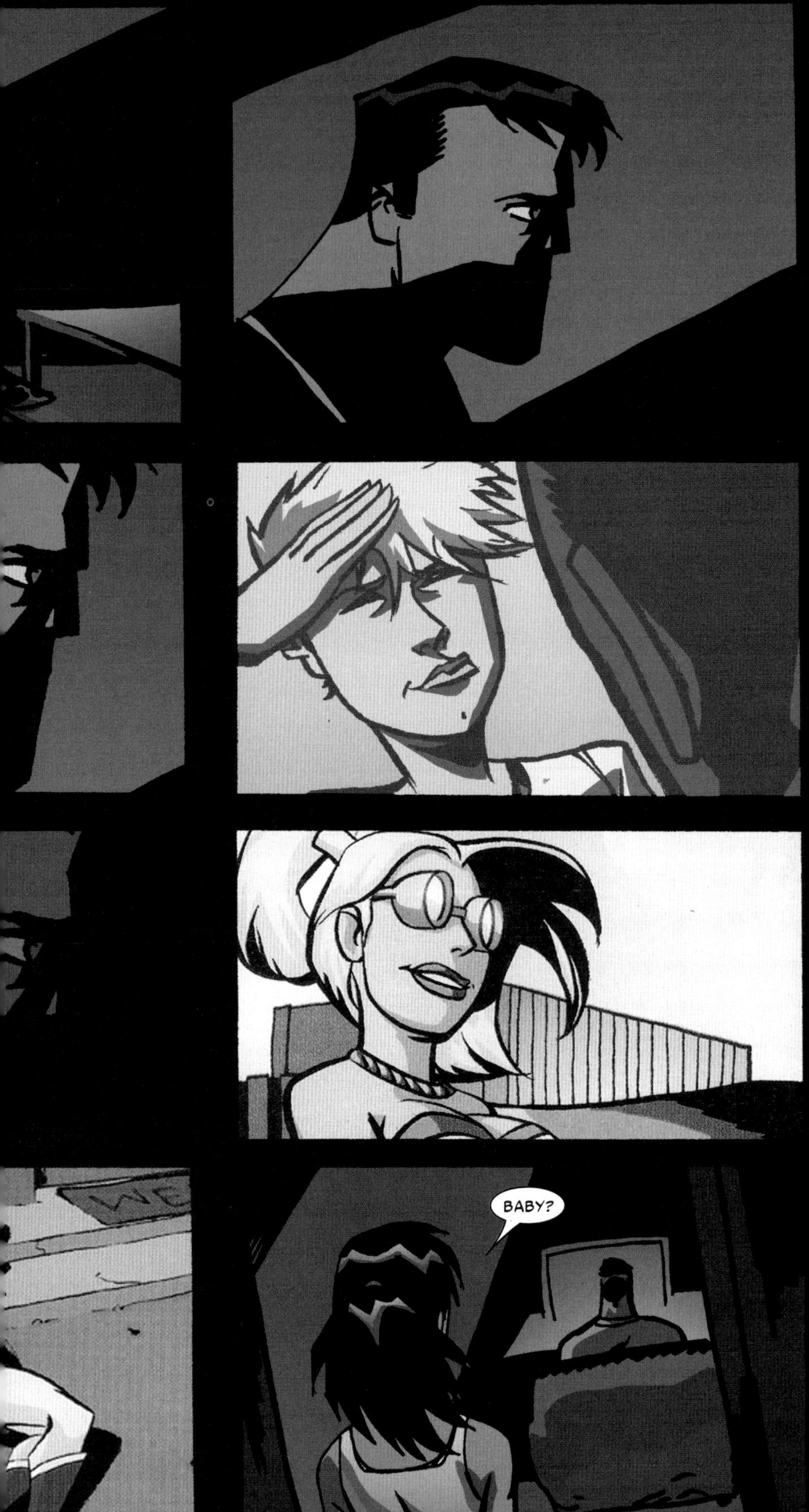
BABY?

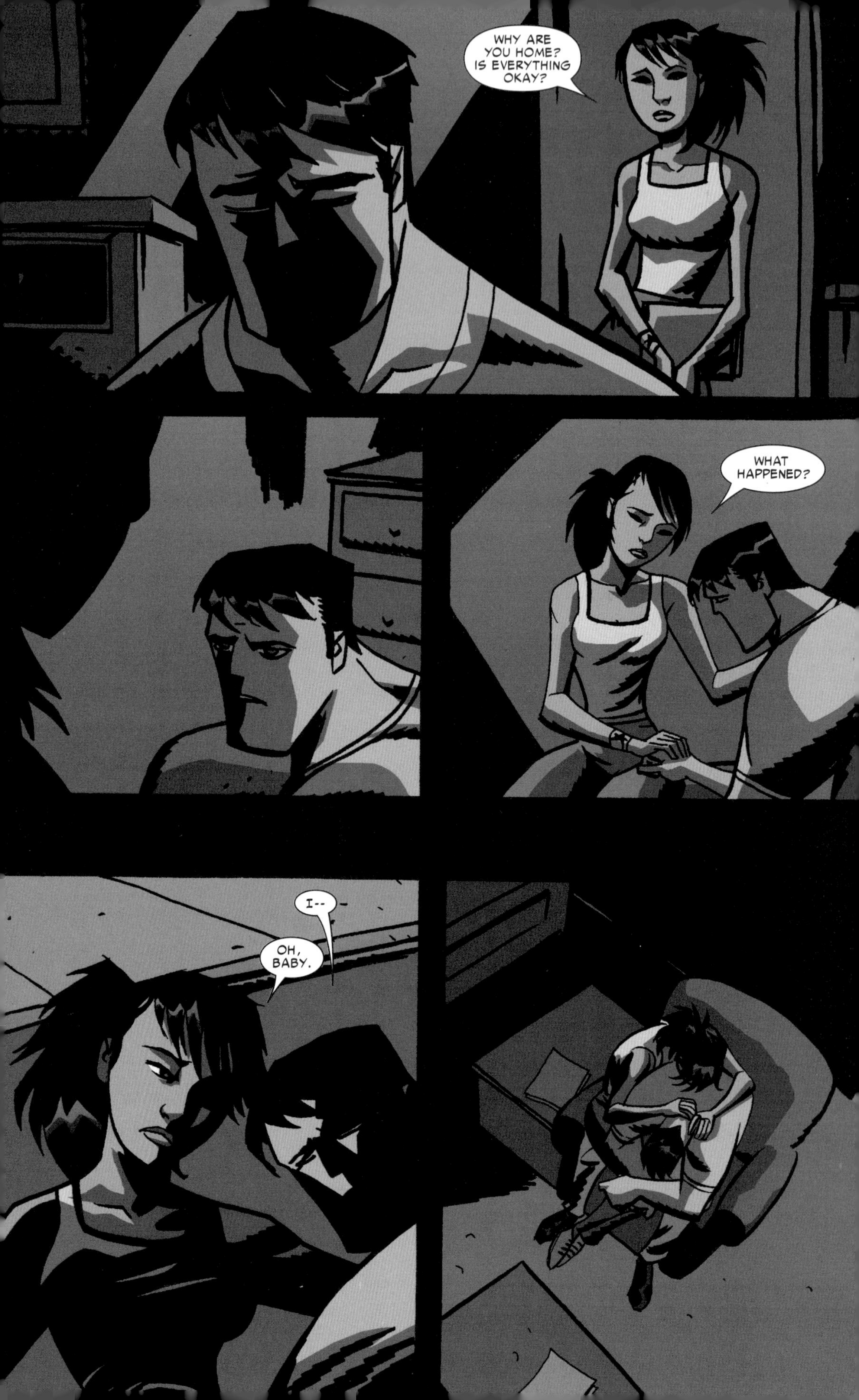
WHY ARE YOU HOME? IS EVERYTHING OKAY?
WHAT HAPPENED?
I--
OH, BABY.

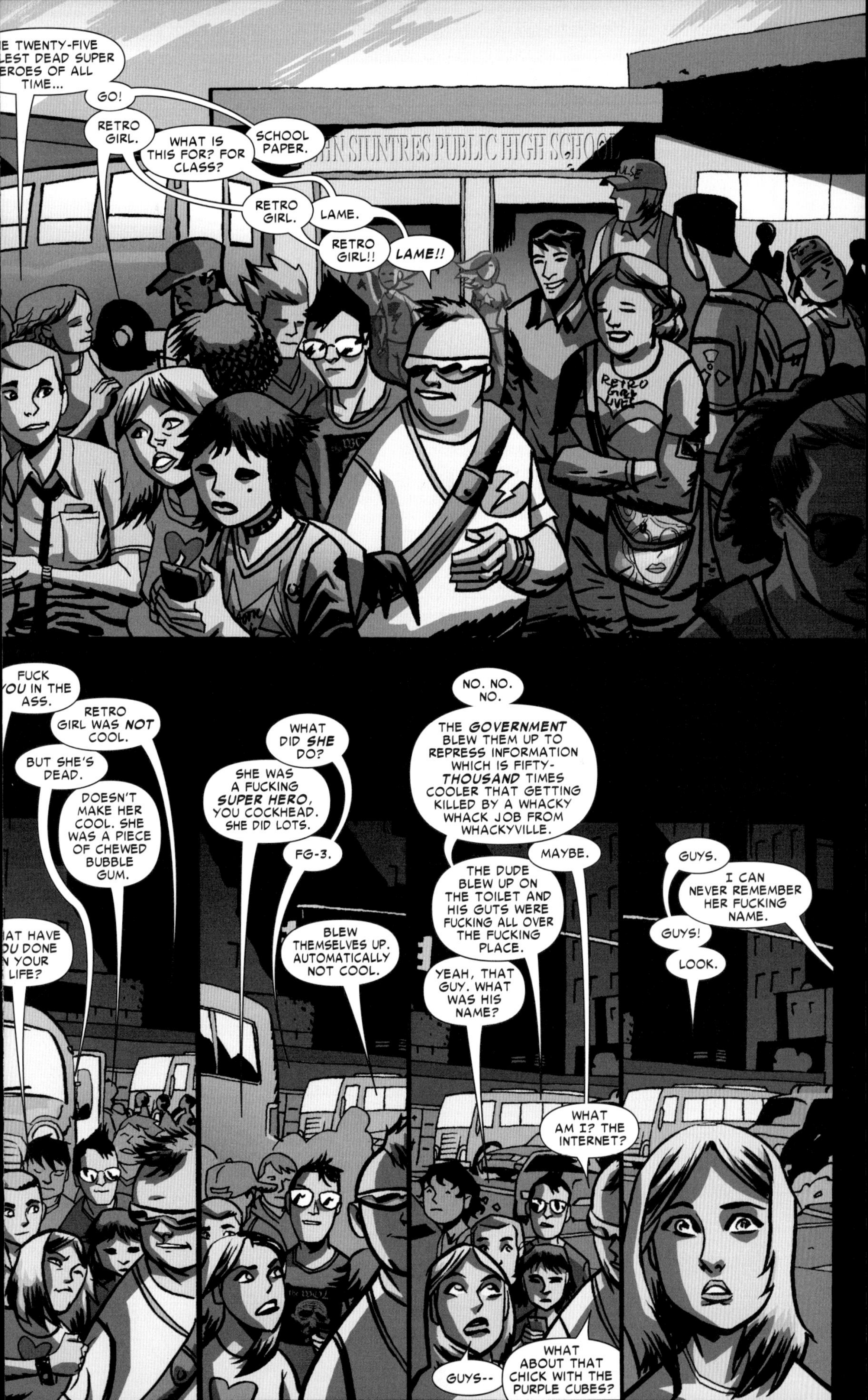
E TWENTY-FIVE LEST DEAD SUPER EROES OF ALL TIME...
GO!
SCHOOL PAPER.
RETRO GIRL.
WHAT IS THIS FOR? FOR CLASS?
RETRO GIRL.
LAME.
RETRO GIRL!!
LAME!!
FUCK YOU IN THE ASS.
RETRO GIRL WAS NOT COOL.
BUT SHE'S DEAD.
DOESN'T MAKE HER COOL. SHE WAS A PIECE OF CHEWED BUBBLE GUM.
AT HAVE OU DONE N YOUR LIFE?
WHAT DID SHE DO?
SHE WAS A FUCKING SUPER HERO, YOU COCKHEAD. SHE DID LOTS.
FG-3.
BLEW THEMSELVES UP. AUTOMATICALLY NOT COOL.
NO. NO. NO.
THE GOVERNMENT BLEW THEM UP TO REPRESS INFORMATION WHICH IS FIFTY-THOUSAND TIMES COOLER THAT GETTING KILLED BY A WHACKY WHACK JOB FROM WHACKYVILLE.
MAYBE.
THE DUDE BLEW UP ON THE TOILET AND HIS GUTS WERE FUCKING ALL OVER THE FUCKING PLACE.
YEAH, THAT GUY. WHAT WAS HIS NAME?
WHAT AM I? THE INTERNET?
GUYS--
WHAT ABOUT THAT CHICK WITH THE PURPLE CUBES?
GUYS.
I CAN NEVER REMEMBER HER FUCKING NAME.
GUYS!
LOOK.

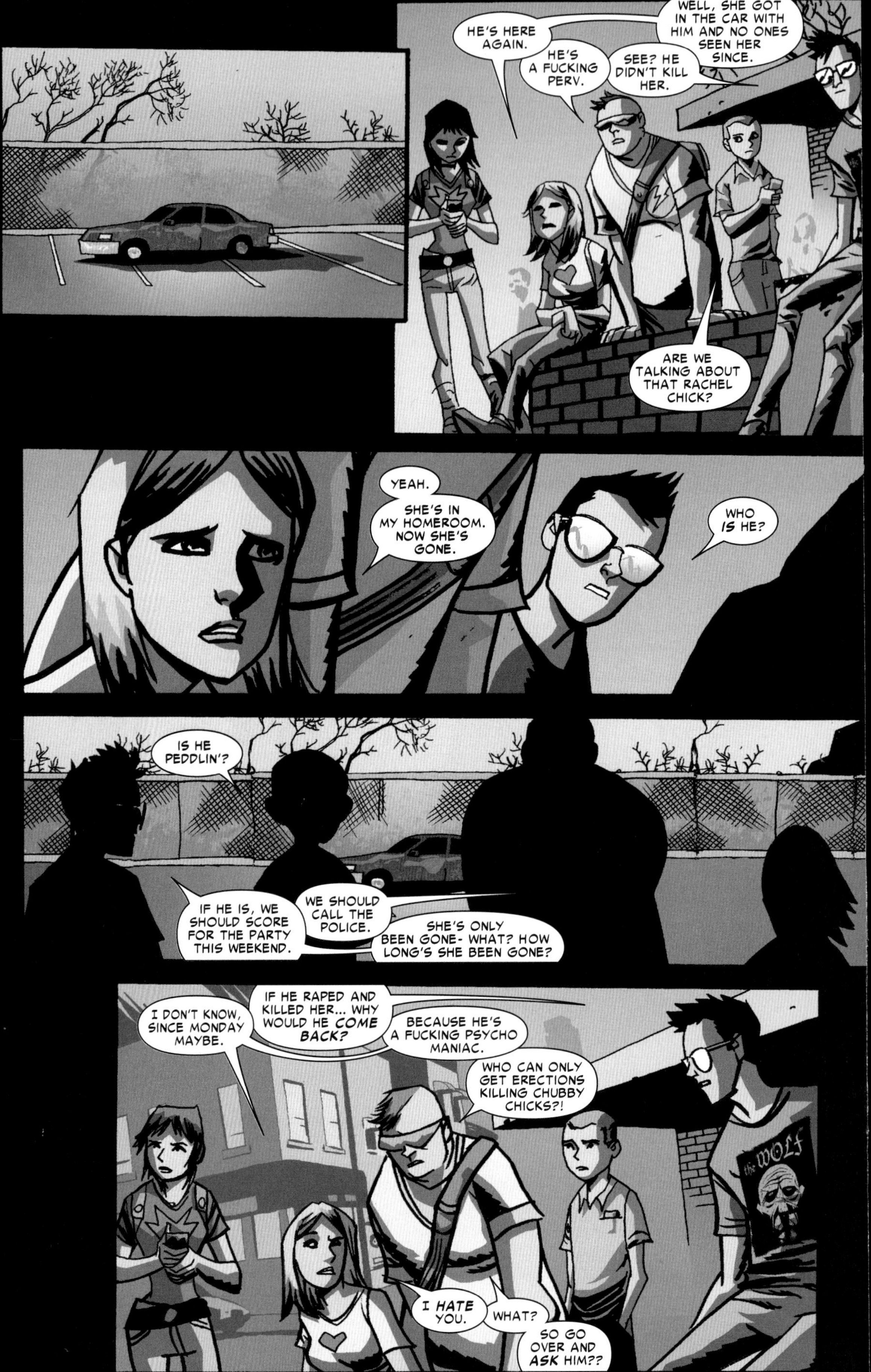
HE'S HERE AGAIN.
HE'S A FUCKING PERV.
WELL, SHE GOT IN THE CAR WITH HIM AND NO ONES SEEN HER SINCE.
SEE? HE DIDN'T KILL HER.
ARE WE TALKING ABOUT THAT RACHEL CHICK?
YEAH.
SHE'S IN MY HOMEROOM. NOW SHE'S GONE.
WHO *IS* HE?
IS HE PEDDLIN'?
IF HE IS, WE SHOULD SCORE FOR THE PARTY THIS WEEKEND.
WE SHOULD CALL THE POLICE.
SHE'S ONLY BEEN GONE- WHAT? HOW LONG'S SHE BEEN GONE?
I DON'T KNOW, SINCE MONDAY MAYBE.
IF HE RAPED AND KILLED HER... WHY WOULD HE *COME BACK?*
BECAUSE HE'S A FUCKING PSYCHO MANIAC.
WHO CAN ONLY GET ERECTIONS KILLING CHUBBY CHICKS?!
THE WOLF
I *HATE* YOU.
WHAT?
SO GO OVER AND *ASK* HIM??

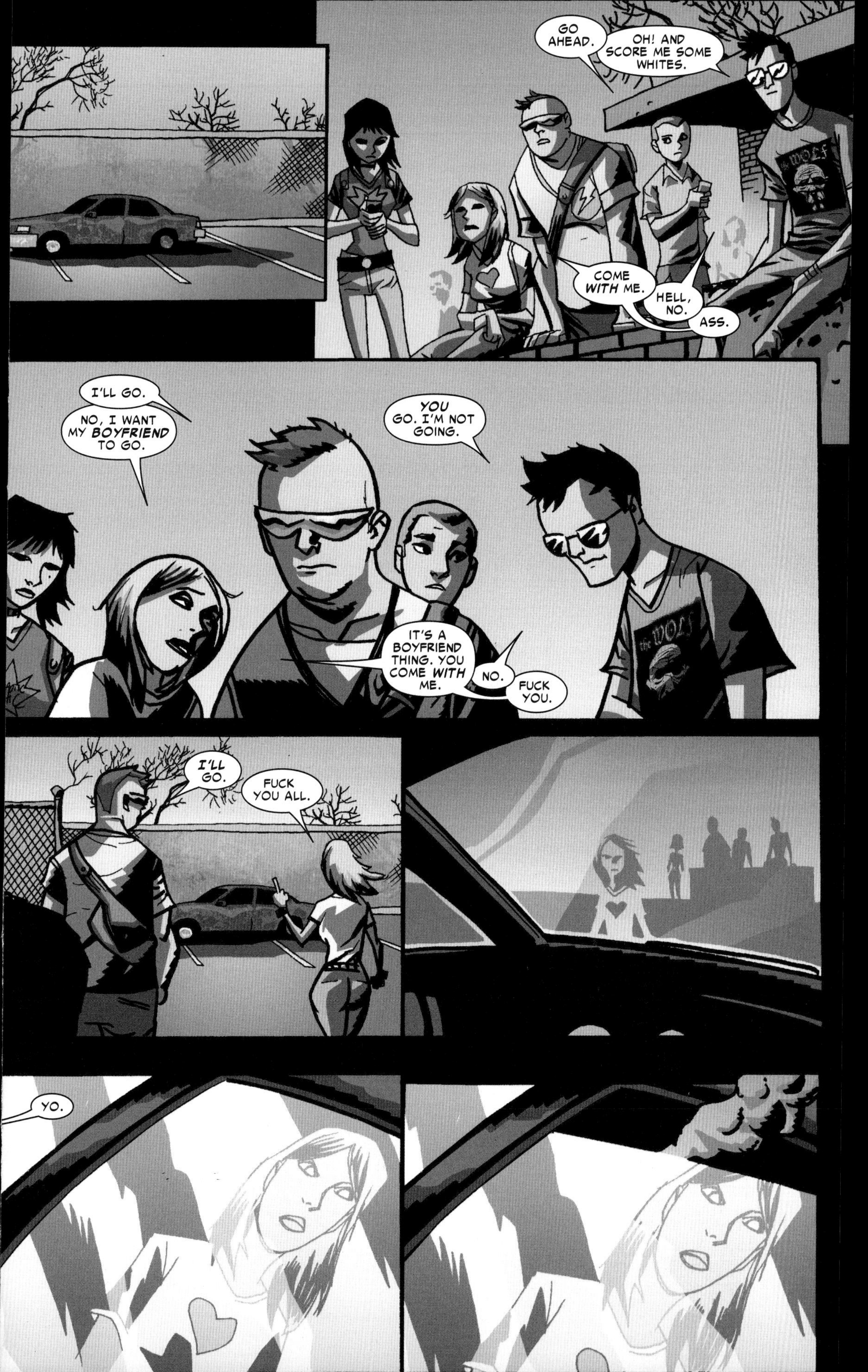
GO AHEAD.
OH! AND SCORE ME SOME WHITES.
COME WITH ME.
HELL, NO.
ASS.
I'LL GO.
NO, I WANT MY BOYFRIEND TO GO.
YOU GO. I'M NOT GOING.
IT'S A BOYFRIEND THING. YOU COME WITH ME.
NO.
FUCK YOU.
I'LL GO.
FUCK YOU ALL.
YO.

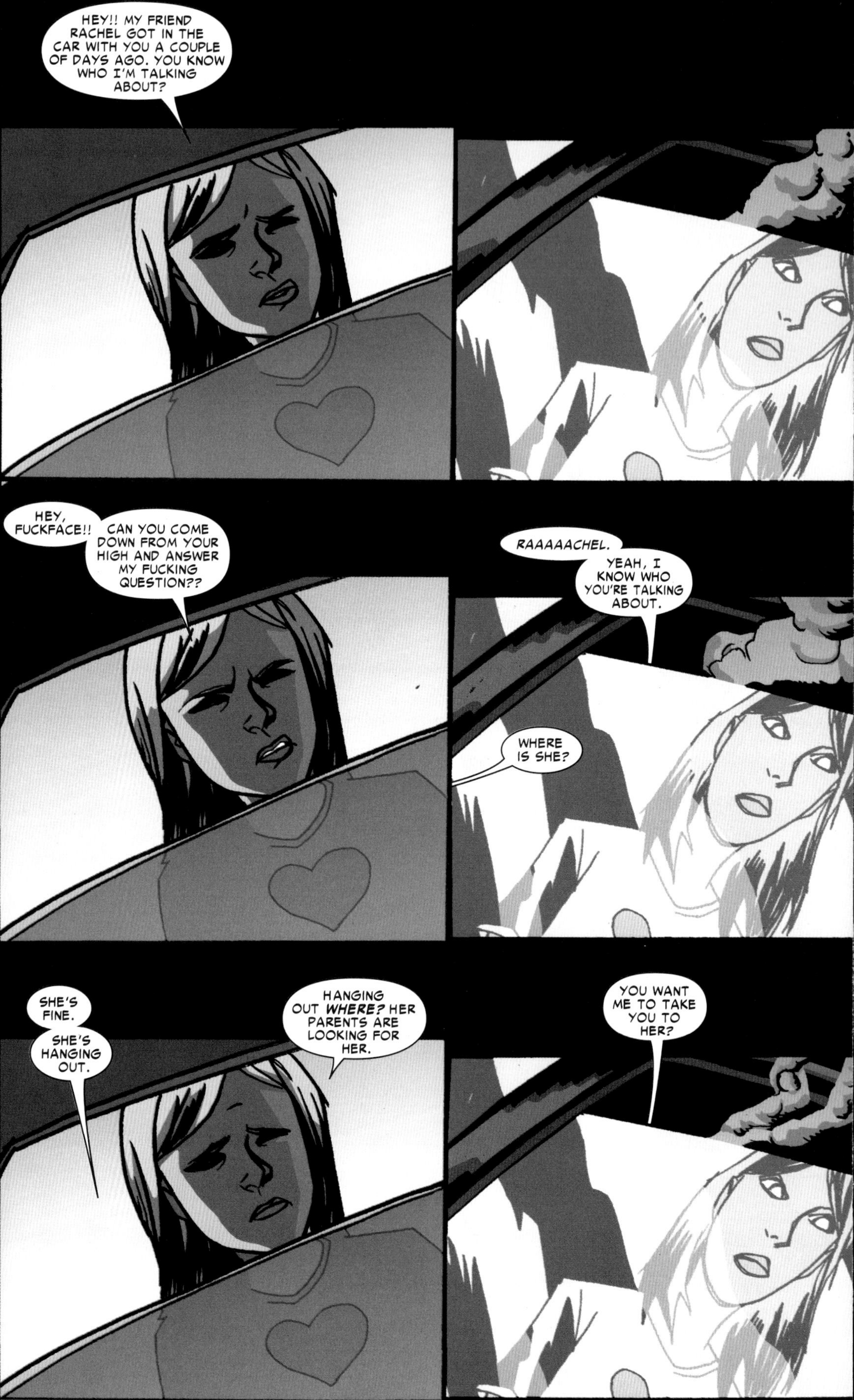
HEY!! MY FRIEND RACHEL GOT IN THE CAR WITH YOU A COUPLE OF DAYS AGO. YOU KNOW WHO I'M TALKING ABOUT?
HEY, FUCKFACE!!
CAN YOU COME DOWN FROM YOUR HIGH AND ANSWER MY FUCKING QUESTION??
RAAAAACHEL.
YEAH, I KNOW WHO YOU'RE TALKING ABOUT.
WHERE IS SHE?
SHE'S FINE.
SHE'S HANGING OUT.
HANGING OUT *WHERE?* HER PARENTS ARE LOOKING FOR HER.
YOU WANT ME TO TAKE YOU TO HER?

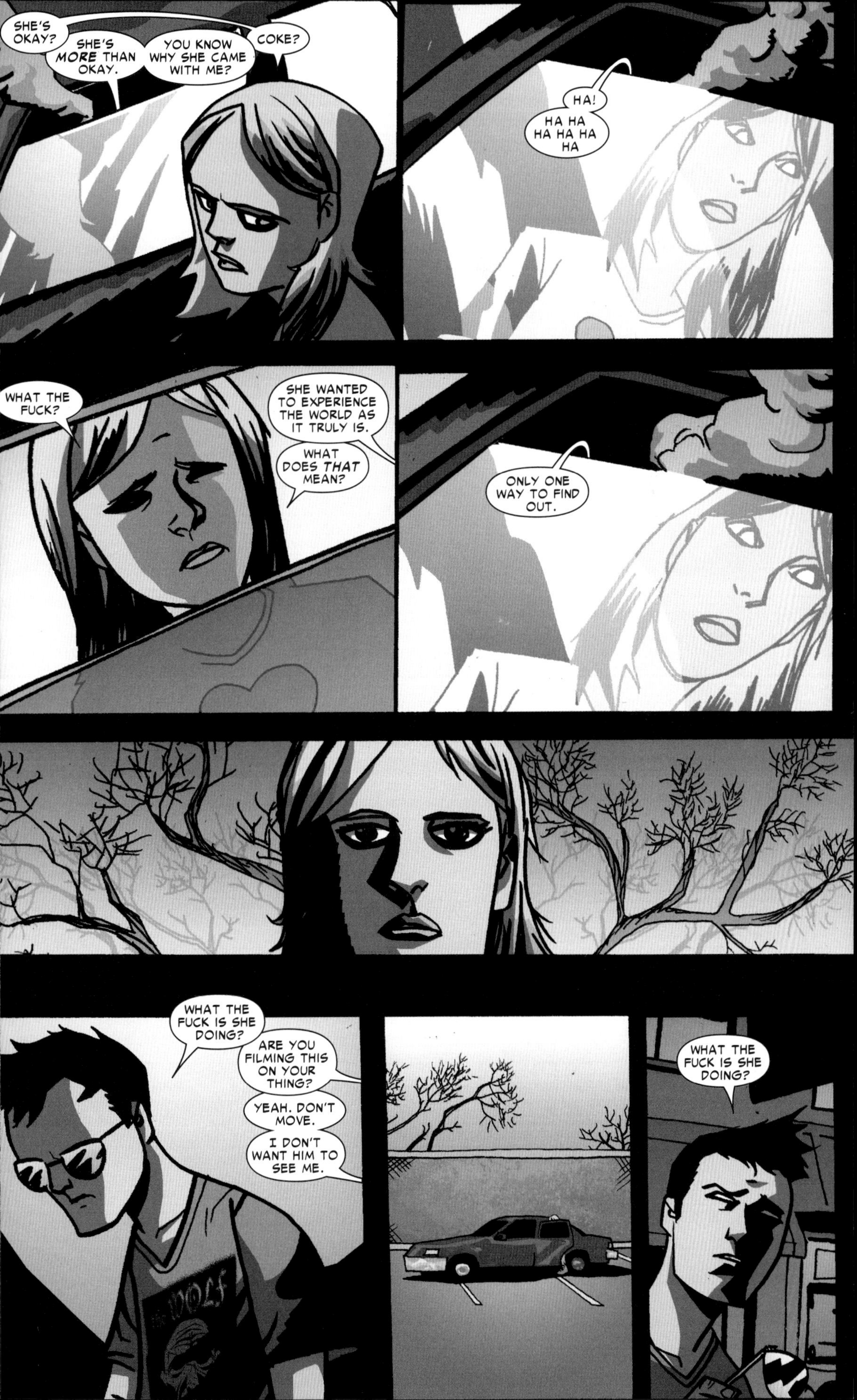
SHE'S OKAY?
SHE'S MORE THAN OKAY.
YOU KNOW WHY SHE CAME WITH ME?
COKE?
HA! HA HA HA HA HA HA
WHAT THE FUCK?
SHE WANTED TO EXPERIENCE THE WORLD AS IT TRULY IS.
WHAT DOES THAT MEAN?
ONLY ONE WAY TO FIND OUT.
WHAT THE FUCK IS SHE DOING?
ARE YOU FILMING THIS ON YOUR THING?
YEAH. DON'T MOVE.
I DON'T WANT HIM TO SEE ME.
WHAT THE FUCK IS SHE DOING?

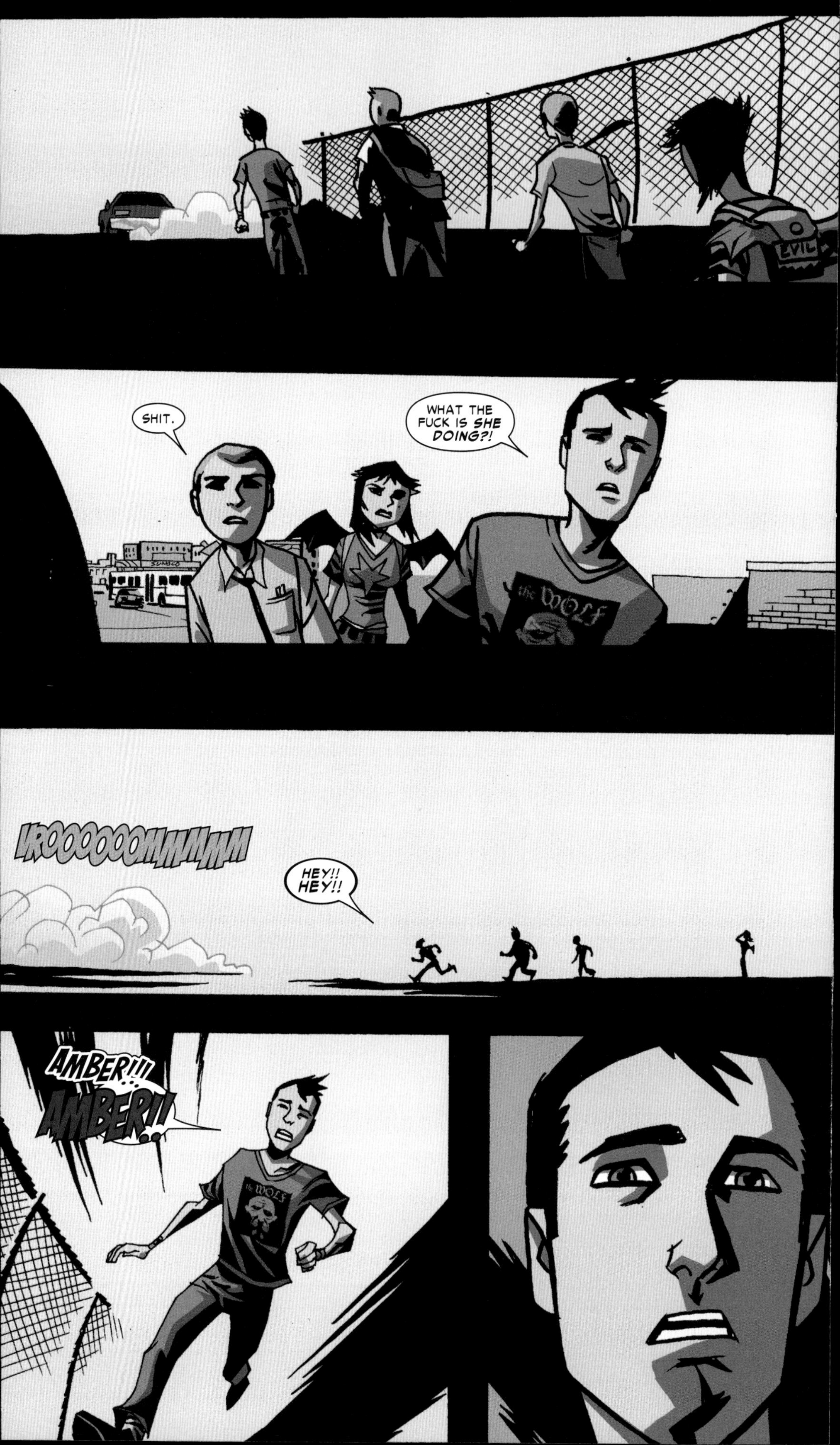
SHIT.
WHAT THE FUCK IS SHE DOING?!
VROOOOOOOMMMMMM
HEY!! HEY!!
AMBER!!!
AMBER!!

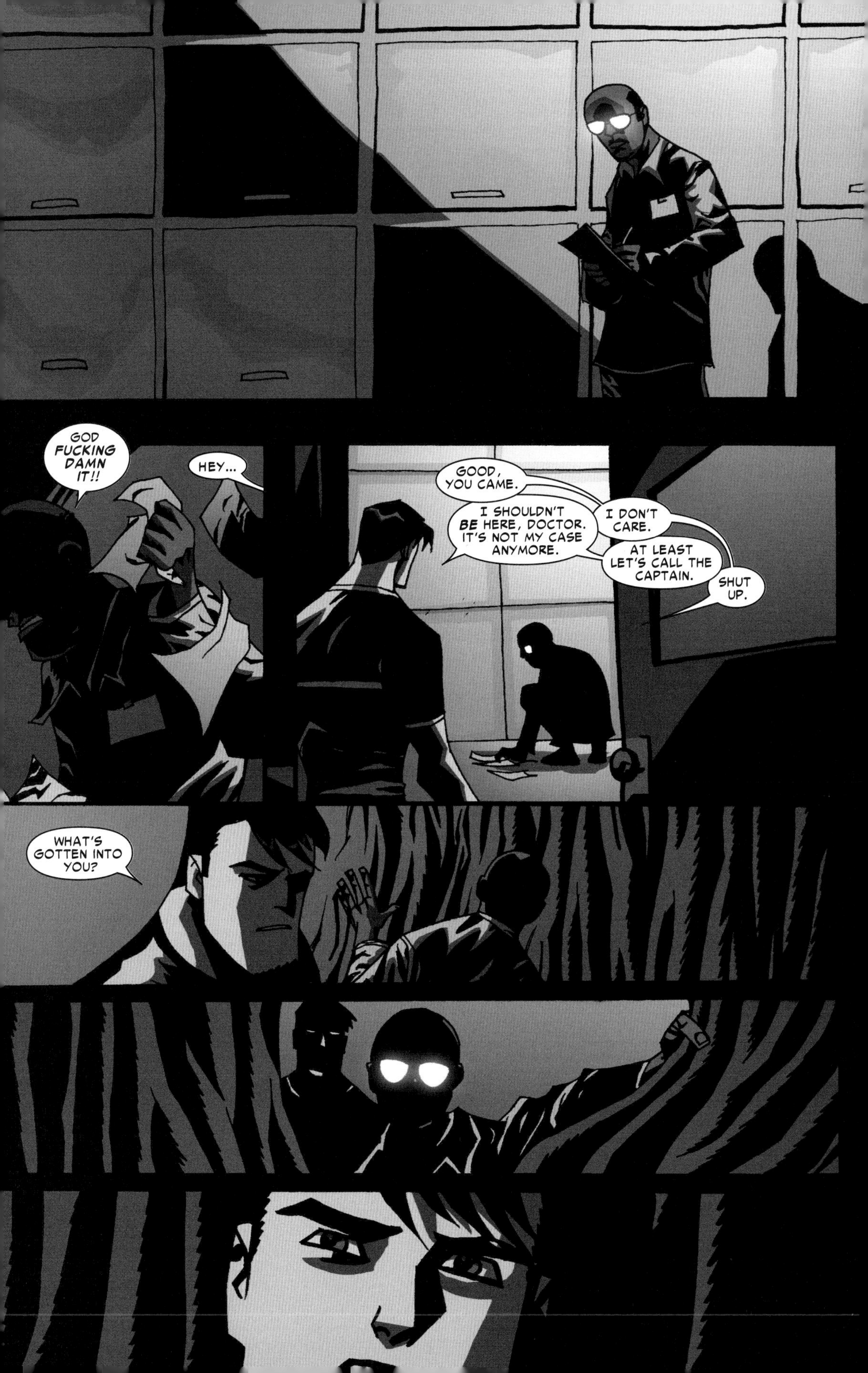
GOD FUCKING DAMN IT!!
HEY...
GOOD, YOU CAME.
I SHOULDN'T BE HERE, DOCTOR. IT'S NOT MY CASE ANYMORE.
I DON'T CARE.
AT LEAST LET'S CALL THE CAPTAIN.
SHUT UP.
WHAT'S GOTTEN INTO YOU?

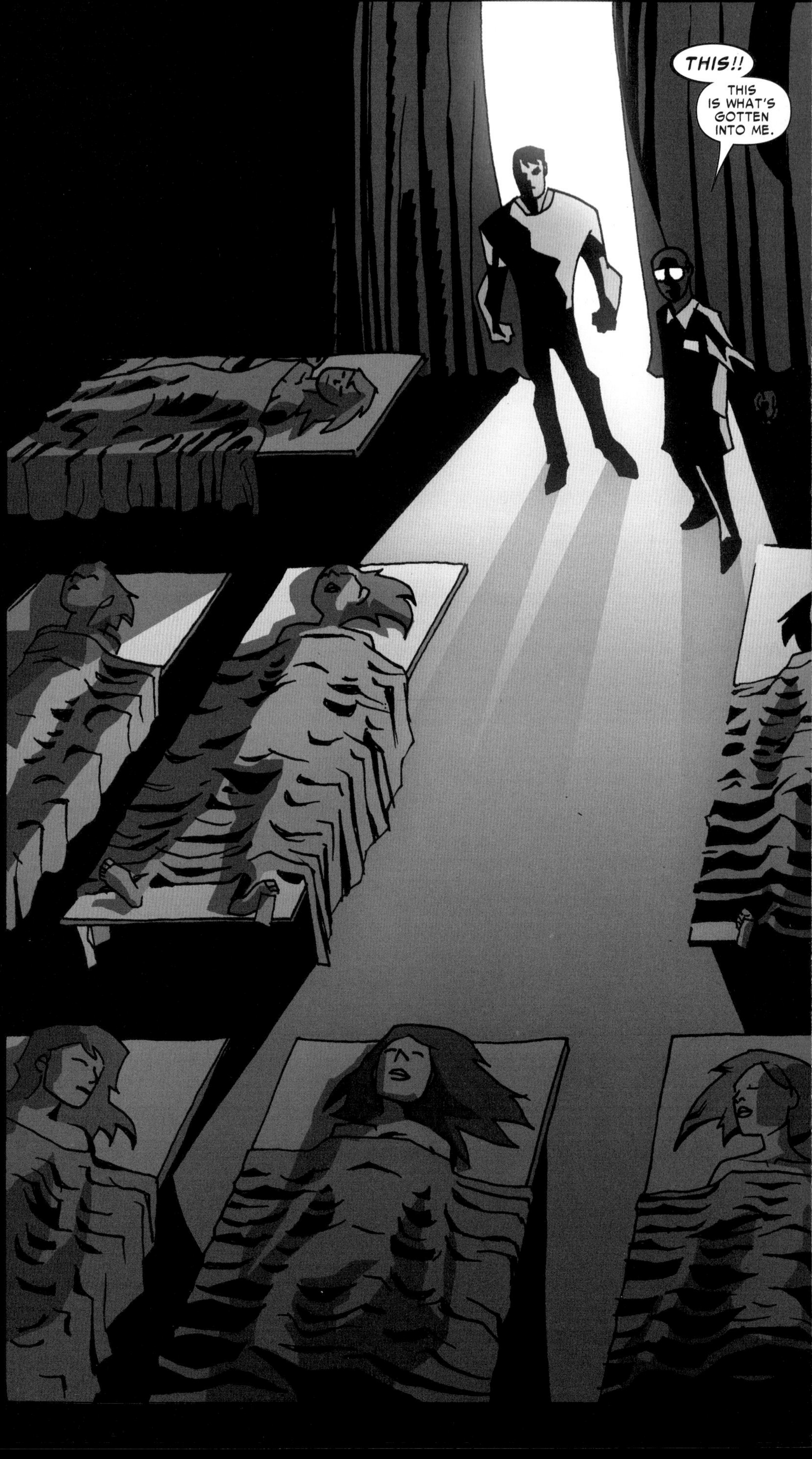
THIS!!
THIS IS WHAT'S GOTTEN INTO ME.

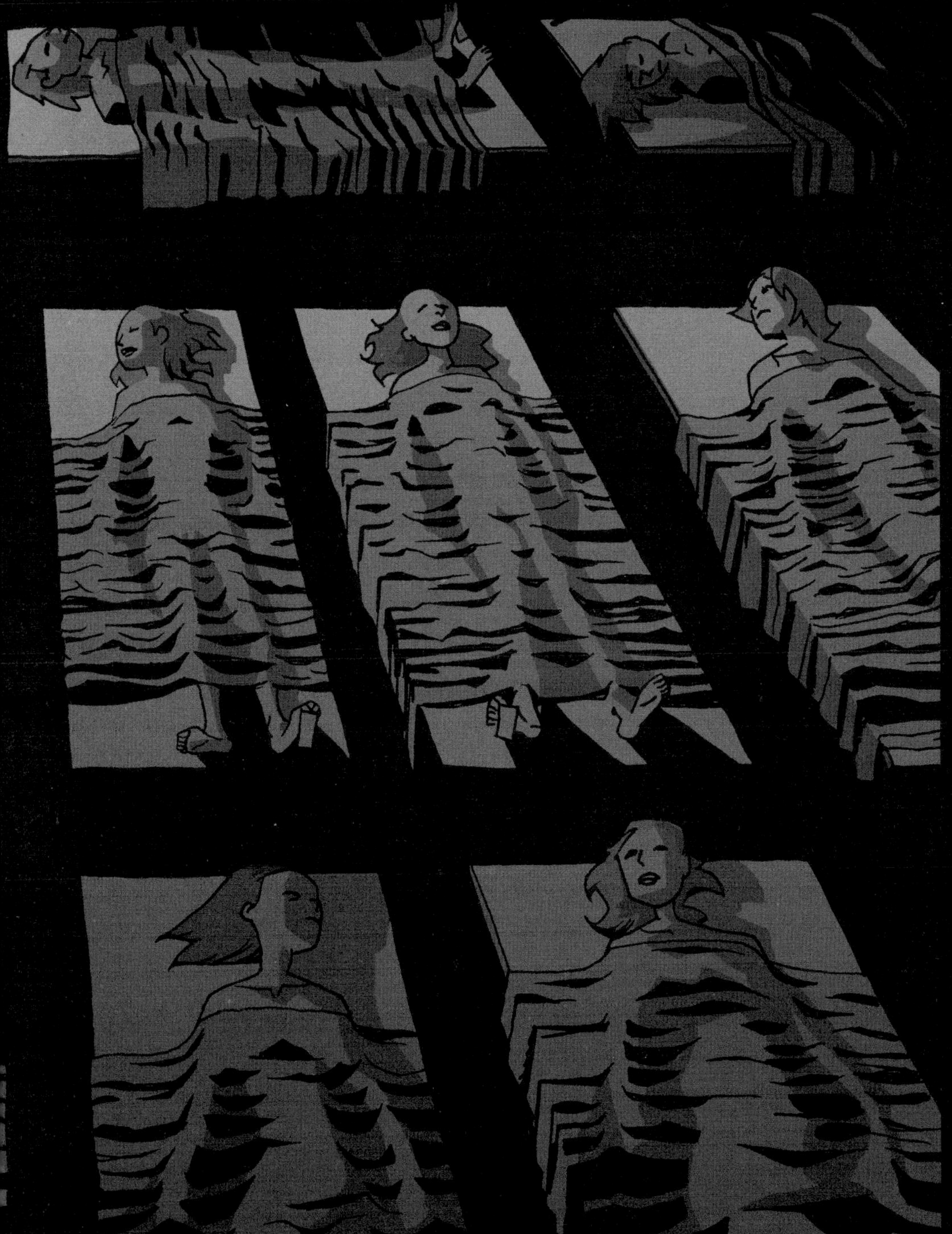

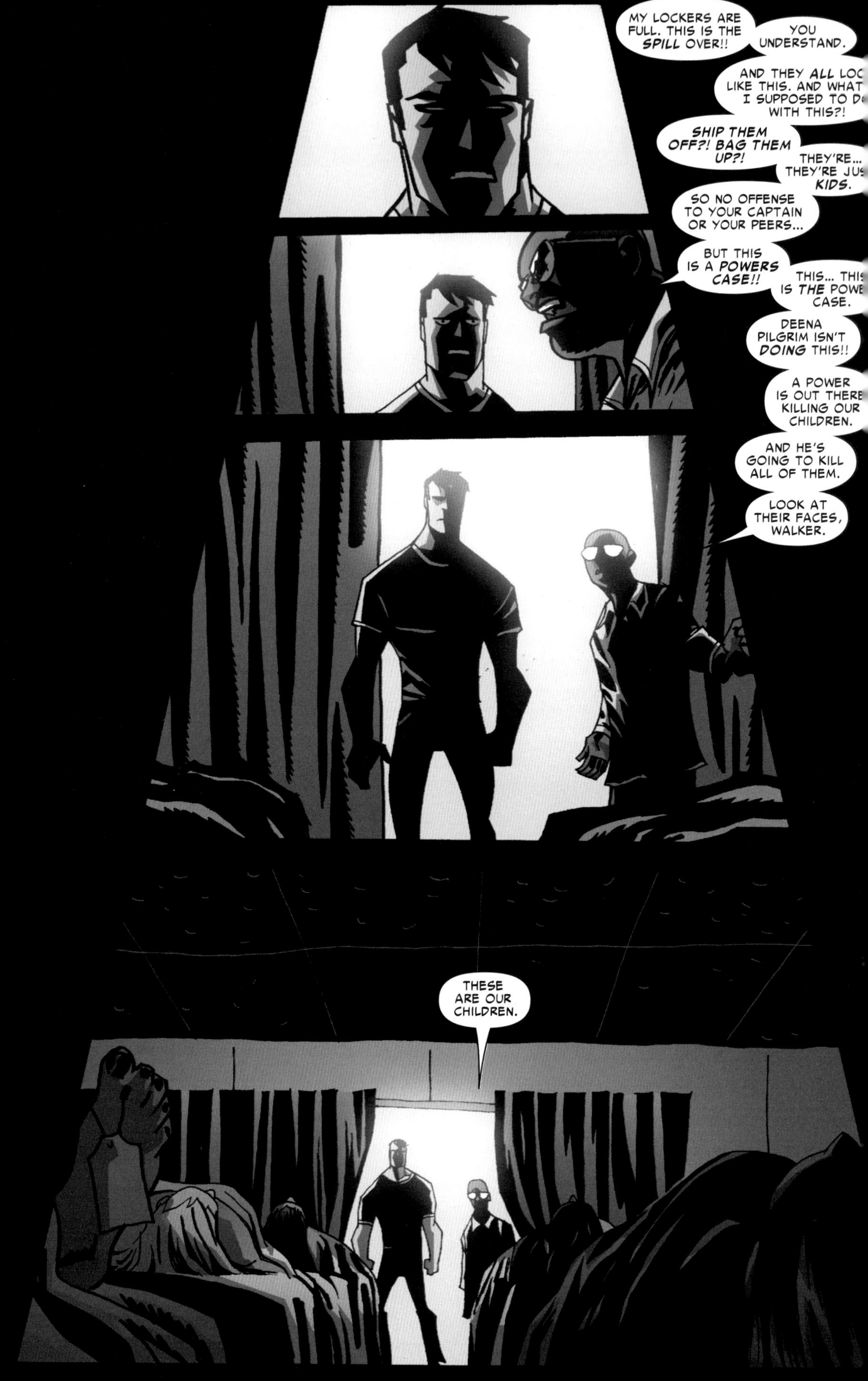
MY LOCKERS ARE FULL. THIS IS THE SPILL OVER!!
YOU UNDERSTAND.
AND THEY ALL LOC LIKE THIS. AND WHAT I SUPPOSED TO D WITH THIS?!
SHIP THEM OFF?! BAG THEM UP?!
THEY'RE... THEY'RE JUS KIDS.
SO NO OFFENSE TO YOUR CAPTAIN OR YOUR PEERS...
BUT THIS IS A POWERS CASE!!
THIS... THIS IS THE POWE CASE.
DEENA PILGRIM ISN'T DOING THIS!!
A POWER IS OUT THERE KILLING OUR CHILDREN.
AND HE'S GOING TO KILL ALL OF THEM.
LOOK AT THEIR FACES, WALKER.
THESE ARE OUR CHILDREN.

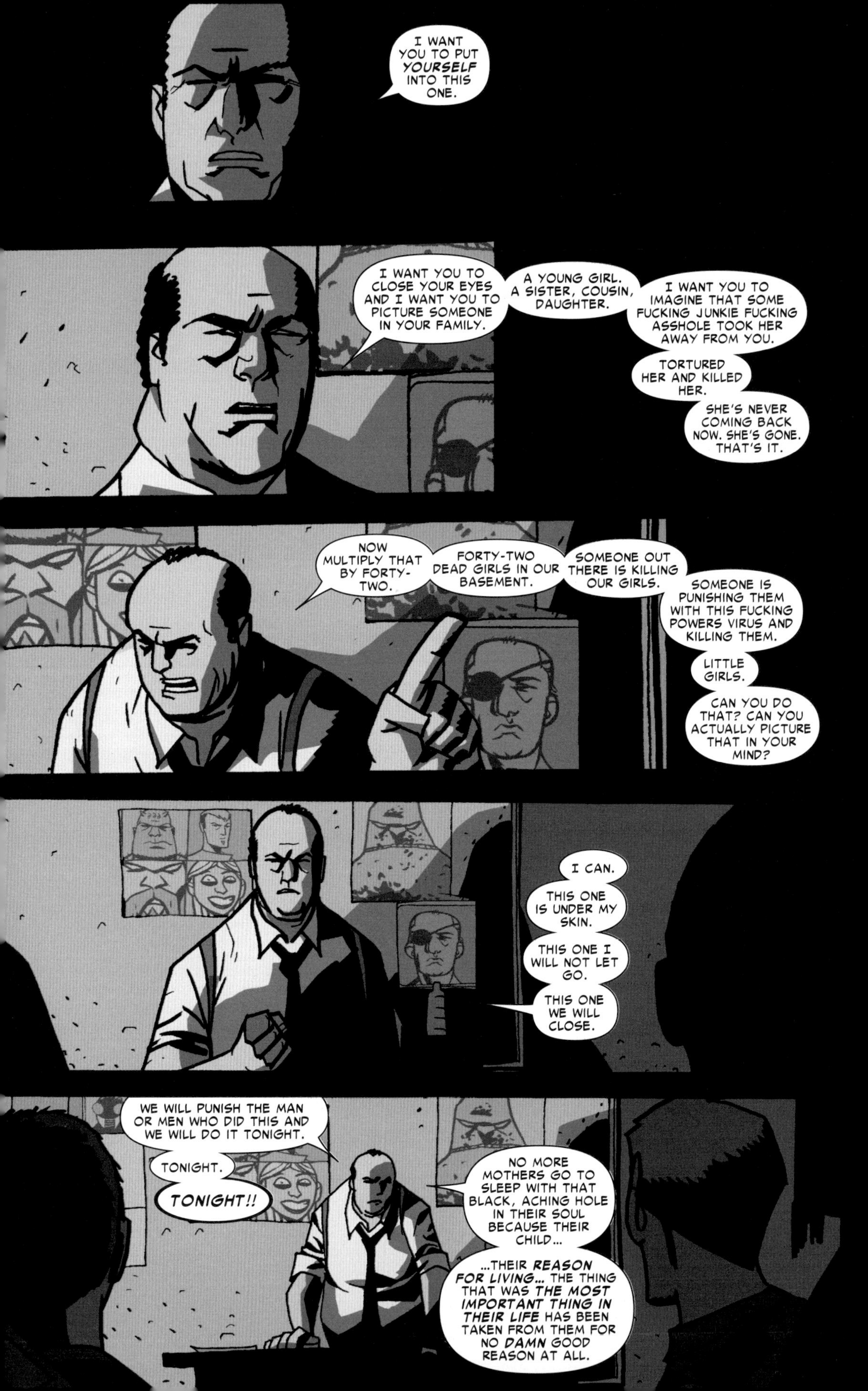
I WANT YOU TO PUT *YOURSELF* INTO THIS ONE.
I WANT YOU TO CLOSE YOUR EYES AND I WANT YOU TO PICTURE SOMEONE IN YOUR FAMILY.
A YOUNG GIRL. A SISTER, COUSIN, DAUGHTER.
I WANT YOU TO IMAGINE THAT SOME FUCKING JUNKIE FUCKING ASSHOLE TOOK HER AWAY FROM YOU.
TORTURED HER AND KILLED HER.
SHE'S NEVER COMING BACK NOW. SHE'S GONE. THAT'S IT.
NOW MULTIPLY THAT BY FORTY-TWO.
FORTY-TWO DEAD GIRLS IN OUR BASEMENT.
SOMEONE OUT THERE IS KILLING OUR GIRLS.
SOMEONE IS PUNISHING THEM WITH THIS FUCKING POWERS VIRUS AND KILLING THEM.
LITTLE GIRLS.
CAN YOU DO THAT? CAN YOU ACTUALLY PICTURE THAT IN YOUR MIND?
I CAN.
THIS ONE IS UNDER MY SKIN.
THIS ONE I WILL NOT LET GO.
THIS ONE WE WILL CLOSE.
WE WILL PUNISH THE MAN OR MEN WHO DID THIS AND WE WILL DO IT TONIGHT.
TONIGHT.
TONIGHT!!
NO MORE MOTHERS GO TO SLEEP WITH THAT BLACK, ACHING HOLE IN THEIR SOUL BECAUSE THEIR CHILD...
...THEIR *REASON FOR LIVING...* THE THING THAT WAS *THE MOST IMPORTANT THING IN THEIR LIFE* HAS BEEN TAKEN FROM THEM FOR NO *DAMN* GOOD REASON AT ALL.

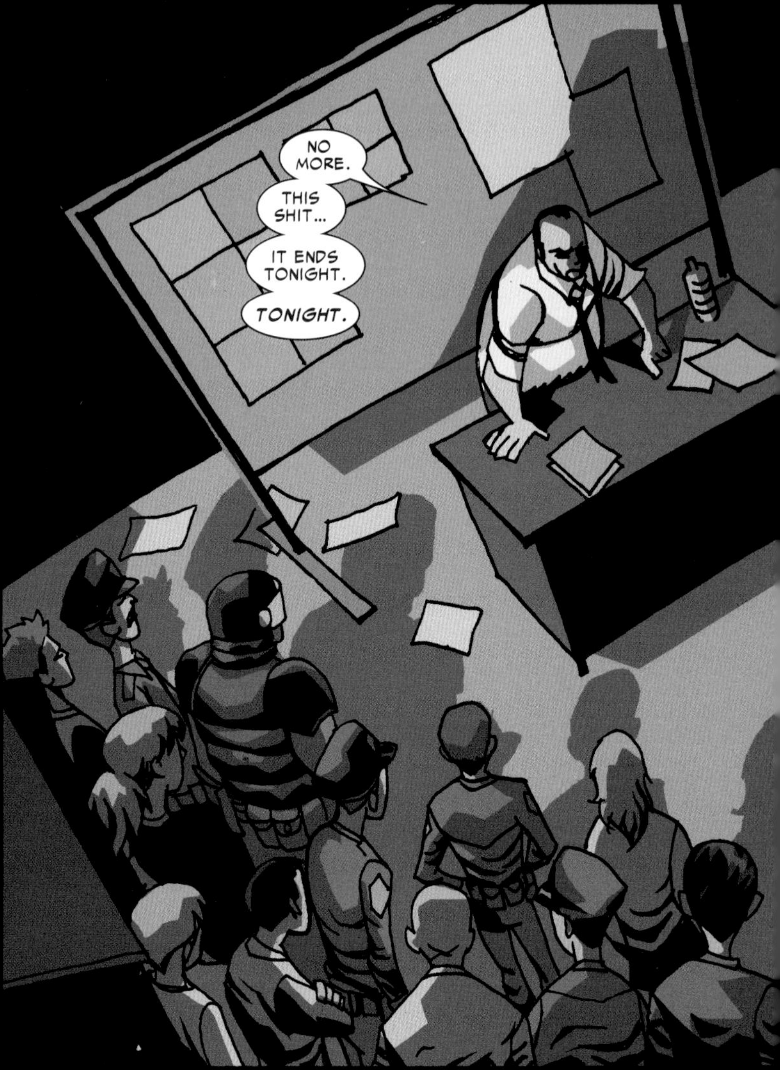
NO MORE.
THIS SHIT...
IT ENDS TONIGHT.
TONIGHT.

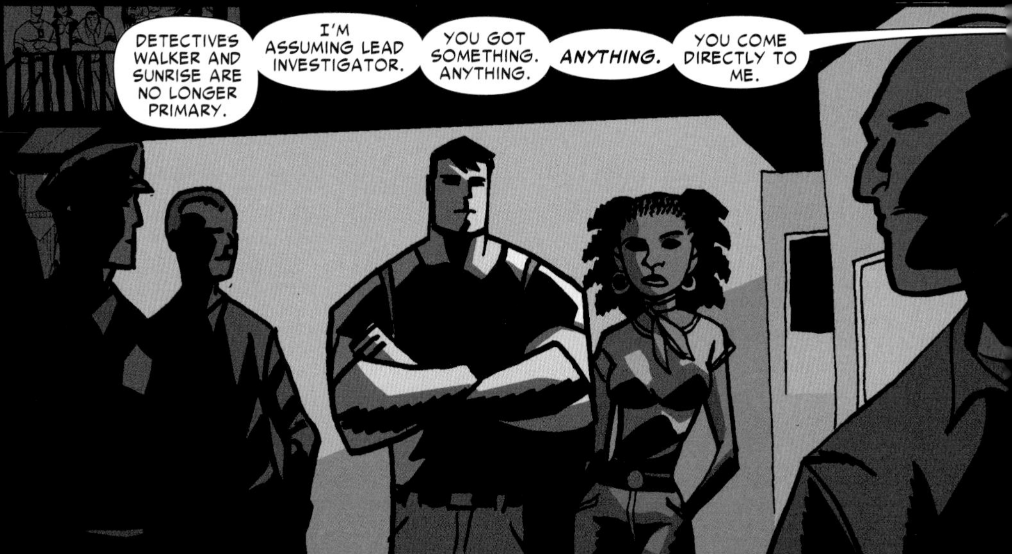
DETECTIVES WALKER AND SUNRISE ARE NO LONGER PRIMARY.
I'M ASSUMING LEAD INVESTIGATOR.
YOU GOT SOMETHING. ANYTHING.
ANYTHING.
YOU COME DIRECTLY TO ME.

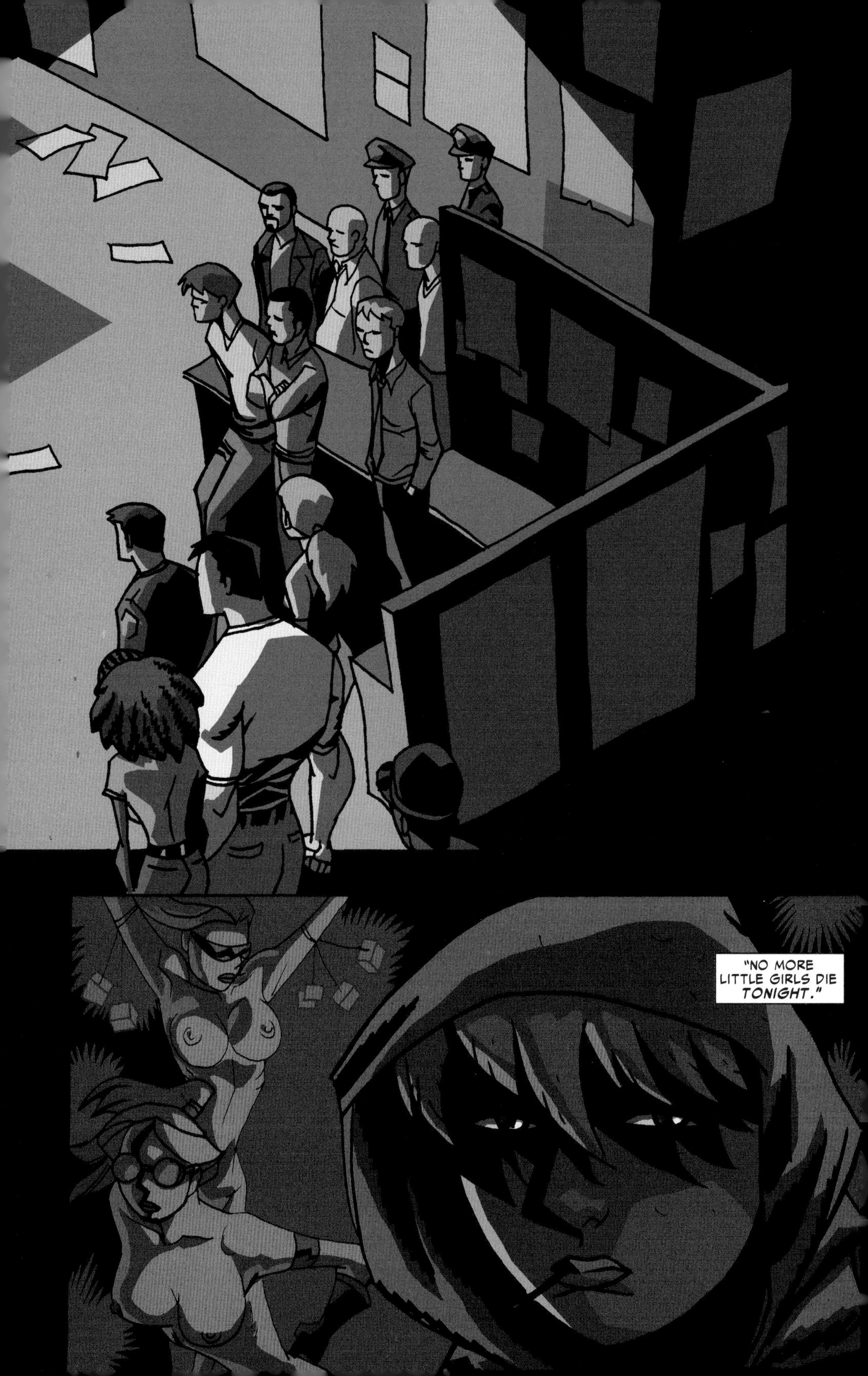
"NO MORE LITTLE GIRLS DIE TONIGHT."

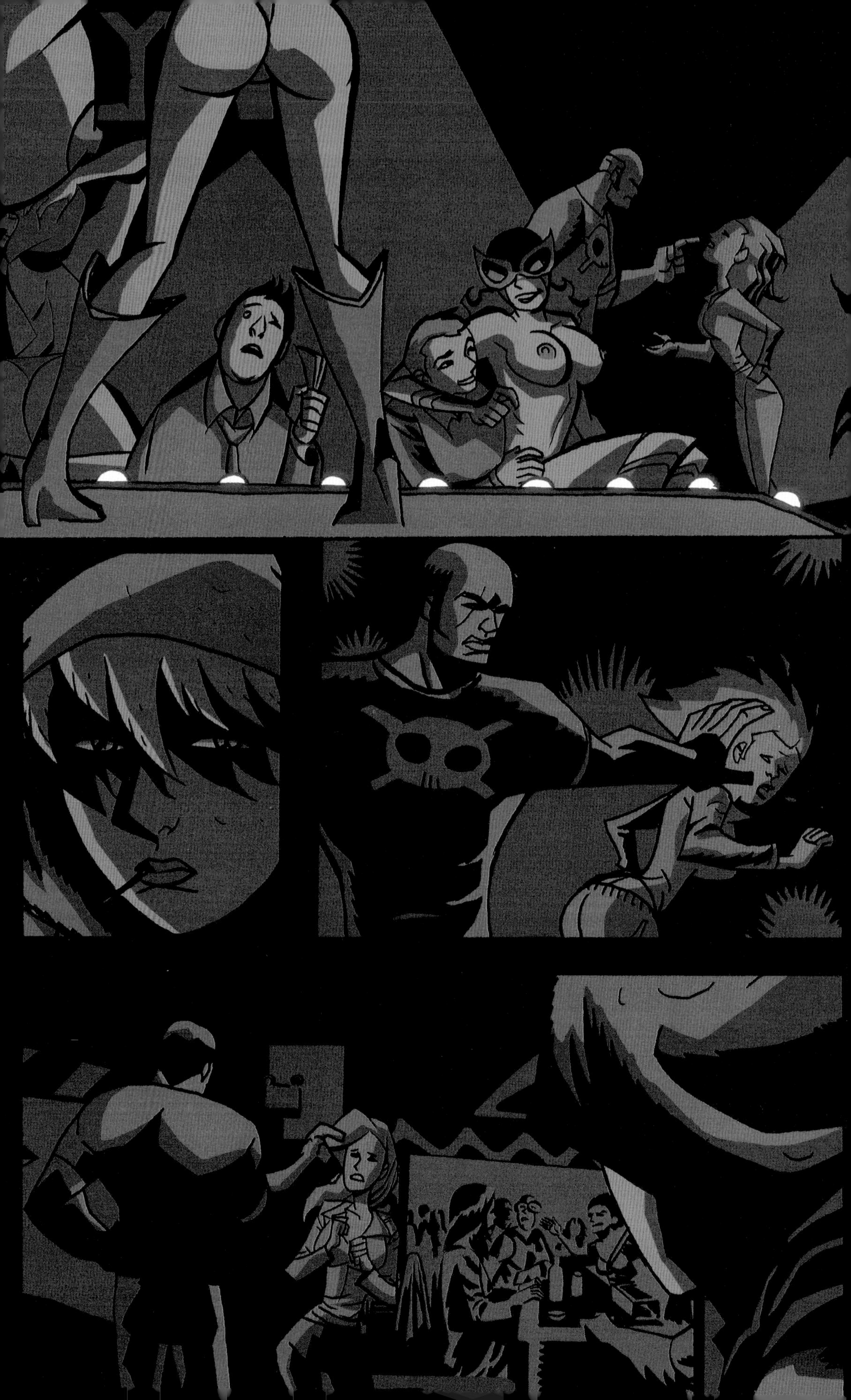

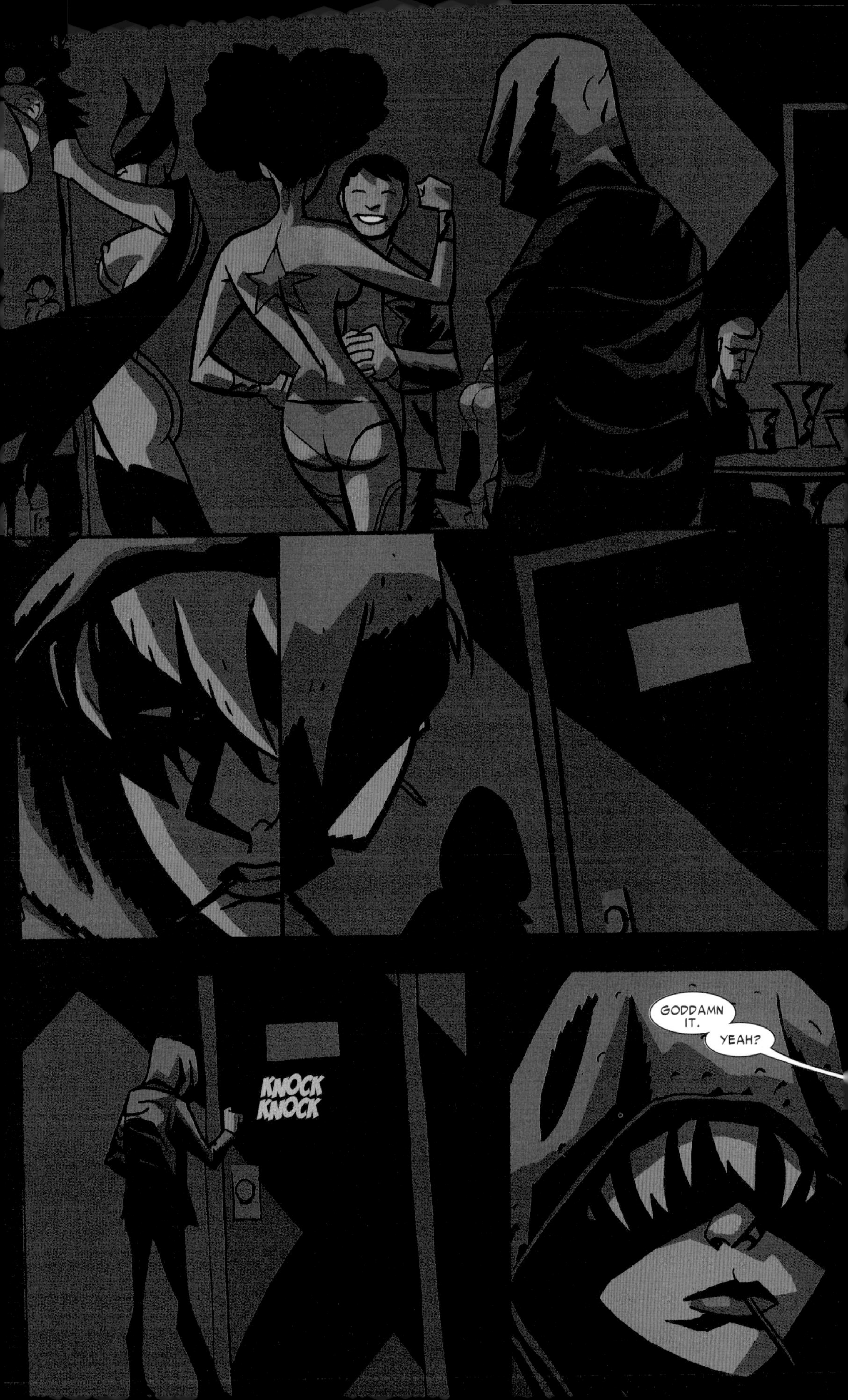
KNOCK KNOCK
GODDAMN IT.
YEAH?

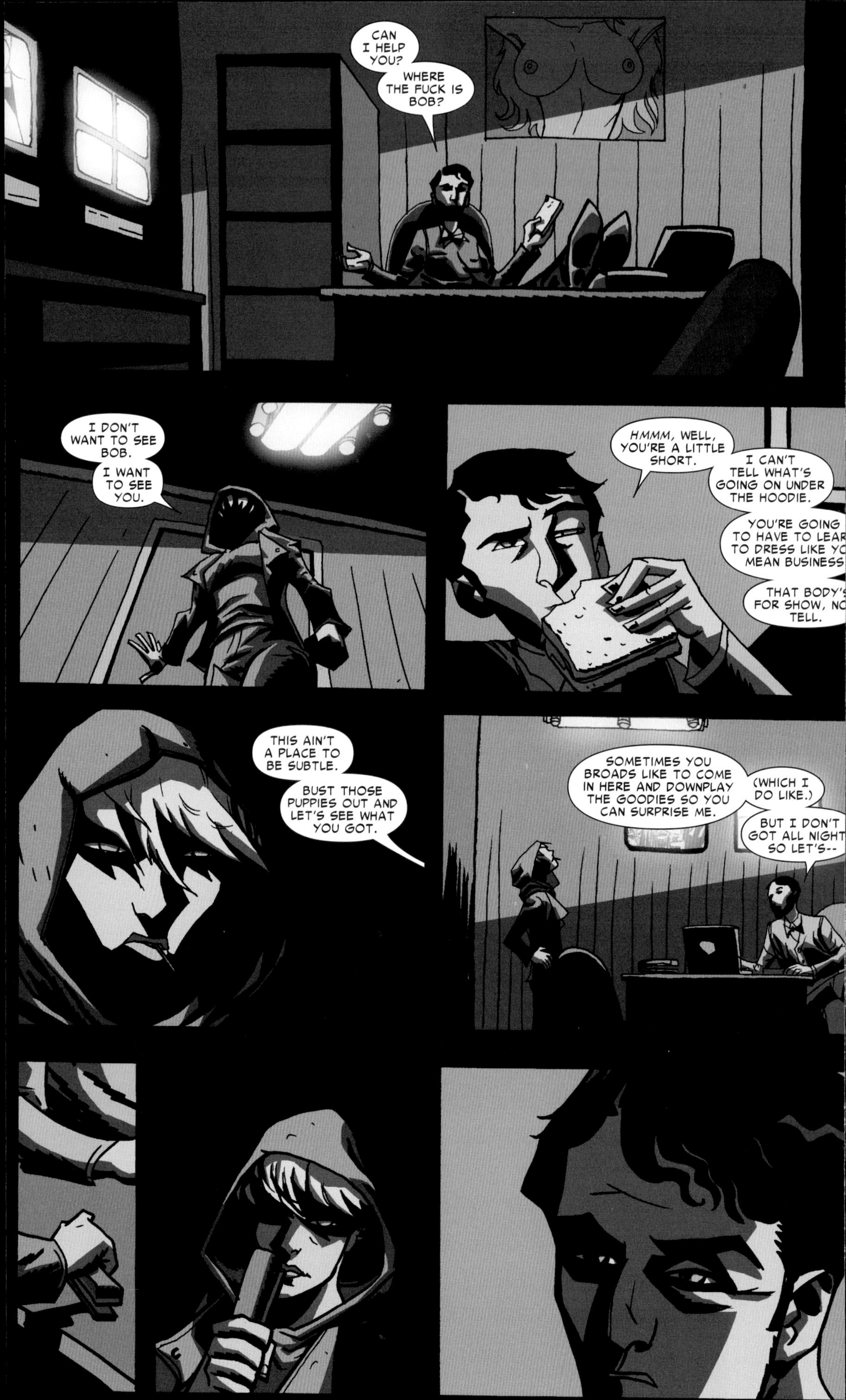
CAN I HELP YOU?
WHERE THE FUCK IS BOB?
I DON'T WANT TO SEE BOB.
I WANT TO SEE YOU.
HMMM, WELL, YOU'RE A LITTLE SHORT.
I CAN'T TELL WHAT'S GOING ON UNDER THE HOODIE.
YOU'RE GOING TO HAVE TO LEAR
TO DRESS LIKE YO
MEAN BUSINESS
THAT BODY'S
FOR SHOW, NO
TELL.
THIS AIN'T A PLACE TO BE SUBTLE.
BUST THOSE PUPPIES OUT AND LET'S SEE WHAT YOU GOT.
SOMETIMES YOU BROADS LIKE TO COME IN HERE AND DOWNPLAY THE GOODIES SO YOU CAN SURPRISE ME.
(WHICH I DO LIKE.)
BUT I DON'T GOT ALL NIGHT SO LET'S--

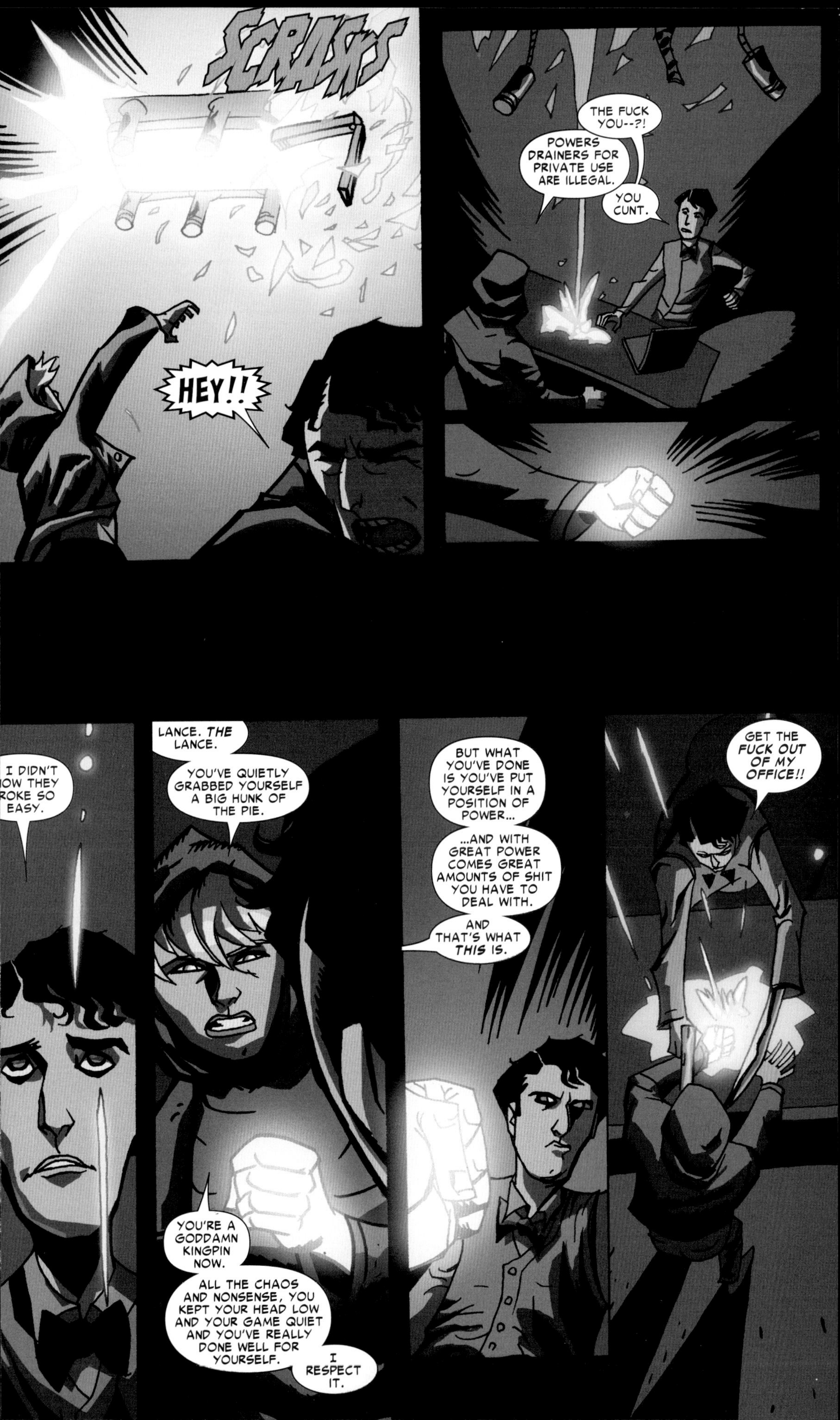
SCRASH
HEY!!
THE FUCK YOU--?!
POWERS DRAINERS FOR PRIVATE USE ARE ILLEGAL.
YOU CUNT.
I DIDN'T
OW THEY
ROKE SO
EASY.
LANCE. THE LANCE.
YOU'VE QUIETLY GRABBED YOURSELF A BIG HUNK OF THE PIE.
YOU'RE A GODDAMN KINGPIN NOW.
ALL THE CHAOS AND NONSENSE, YOU KEPT YOUR HEAD LOW AND YOUR GAME QUIET AND YOU'VE REALLY DONE WELL FOR YOURSELF.
I RESPECT IT.
BUT WHAT YOU'VE DONE IS YOU'VE PUT YOURSELF IN A POSITION OF POWER...
...AND WITH GREAT POWER COMES GREAT AMOUNTS OF SHIT YOU HAVE TO DEAL WITH.
AND THAT'S WHAT THIS IS.
GET THE FUCK OUT OF MY OFFICE!!

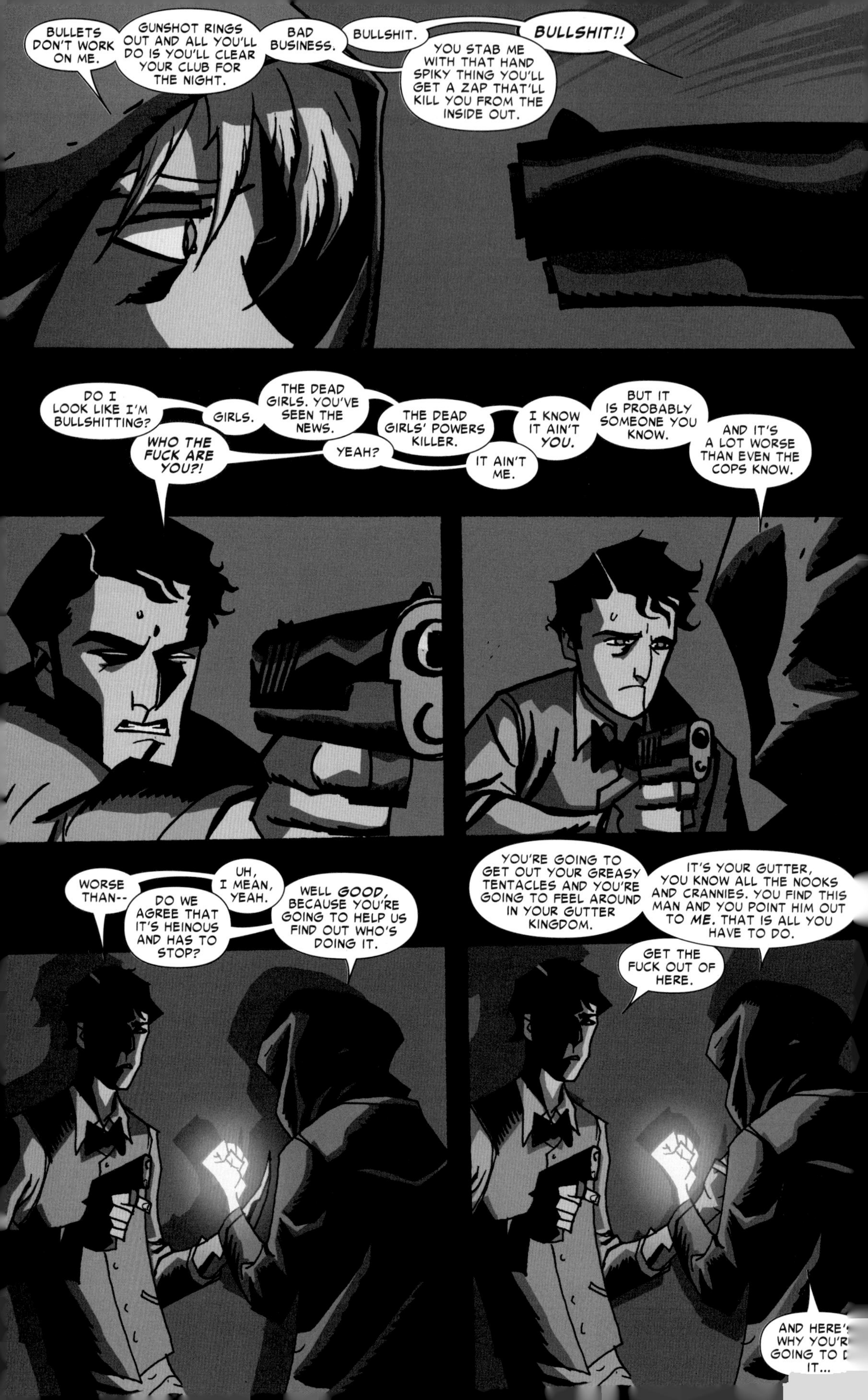
BULLETS DON'T WORK ON ME.
GUNSHOT RINGS OUT AND ALL YOU'LL DO IS YOU'LL CLEAR YOUR CLUB FOR THE NIGHT.
BAD BUSINESS.
BULLSHIT.
BULLSHIT!!
YOU STAB ME WITH THAT HAND SPIKY THING YOU'LL GET A ZAP THAT'LL KILL YOU FROM THE INSIDE OUT.
DO I LOOK LIKE I'M BULLSHITTING?
WHO THE FUCK ARE YOU?!
GIRLS.
THE DEAD GIRLS. YOU'VE SEEN THE NEWS.
YEAH?
THE DEAD GIRLS' POWERS KILLER.
IT AIN'T ME.
I KNOW IT AIN'T YOU.
BUT IT IS PROBABLY SOMEONE YOU KNOW.
AND IT'S A LOT WORSE THAN EVEN THE COPS KNOW.
WORSE THAN--
UH, I MEAN, YEAH.
DO WE AGREE THAT IT'S HEINOUS AND HAS TO STOP?
WELL GOOD, BECAUSE YOU'RE GOING TO HELP US FIND OUT WHO'S DOING IT.
YOU'RE GOING TO GET OUT YOUR GREASY TENTACLES AND YOU'RE GOING TO FEEL AROUND IN YOUR GUTTER KINGDOM.
IT'S YOUR GUTTER, YOU KNOW ALL THE NOOKS AND CRANNIES. YOU FIND THIS MAN AND YOU POINT HIM OUT TO ME. THAT IS ALL YOU HAVE TO DO.
GET THE FUCK OUT OF HERE.
AND HERE'S WHY YOU'RE GOING TO DO IT...

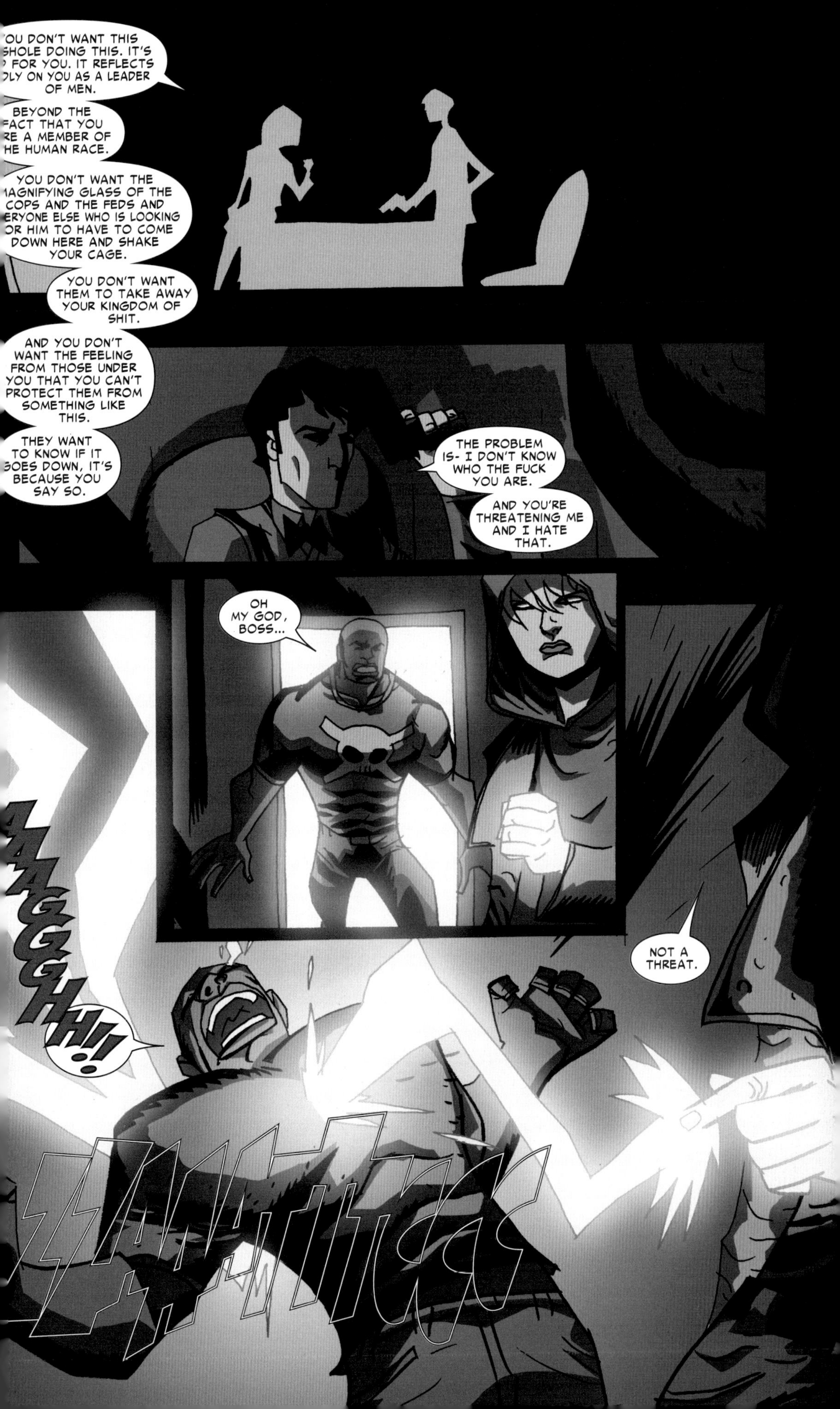

OU DON'T WANT THIS
SHOLE DOING THIS. IT'S
FOR YOU. IT REFLECTS
DLY ON YOU AS A LEADER OF MEN.
BEYOND THE FACT THAT YOU RE A MEMBER OF HE HUMAN RACE.
YOU DON'T WANT THE AGNIFYING GLASS OF THE COPS AND THE FEDS AND ERYONE ELSE WHO IS LOOKING OR HIM TO HAVE TO COME DOWN HERE AND SHAKE YOUR CAGE.
YOU DON'T WANT THEM TO TAKE AWAY YOUR KINGDOM OF SHIT.
AND YOU DON'T WANT THE FEELING FROM THOSE UNDER YOU THAT YOU CAN'T PROTECT THEM FROM SOMETHING LIKE THIS.
THEY WANT TO KNOW IF IT GOES DOWN, IT'S BECAUSE YOU SAY SO.
THE PROBLEM IS- I DON'T KNOW WHO THE FUCK YOU ARE.
AND YOU'RE THREATENING ME AND I HATE THAT.
OH MY GOD, BOSS...
NOT A THREAT.
AAAGGGHH!!

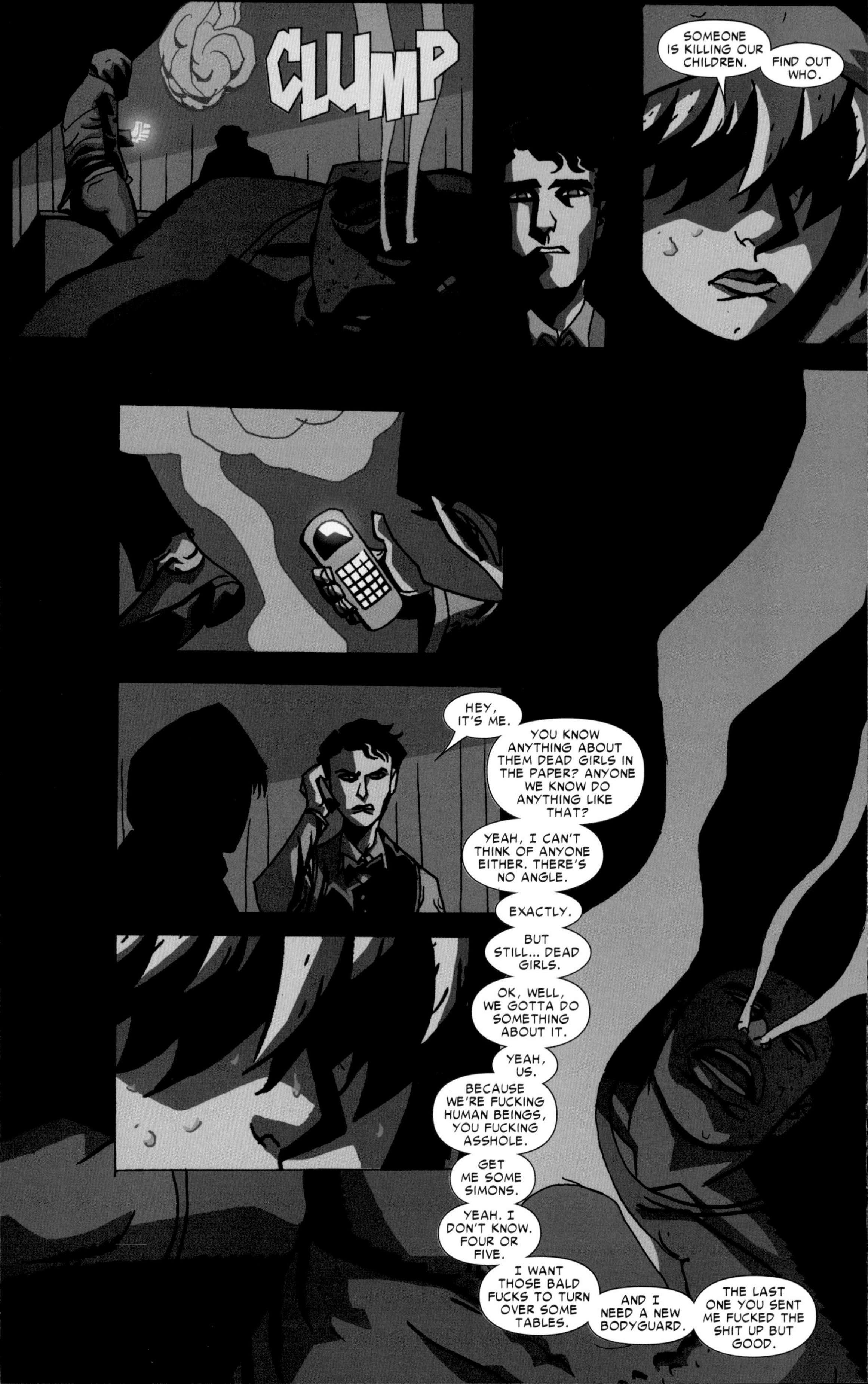
CLUMP
SOMEONE IS KILLING OUR CHILDREN.
FIND OUT WHO.
HEY, IT'S ME.
YOU KNOW ANYTHING ABOUT THEM DEAD GIRLS IN THE PAPER? ANYONE WE KNOW DO ANYTHING LIKE THAT?
YEAH, I CAN'T THINK OF ANYONE EITHER. THERE'S NO ANGLE.
EXACTLY.
BUT STILL... DEAD GIRLS.
OK, WELL, WE GOTTA DO SOMETHING ABOUT IT.
YEAH, US.
BECAUSE WE'RE FUCKING HUMAN BEINGS, YOU FUCKING ASSHOLE.
GET ME SOME SIMONS.
YEAH. I DON'T KNOW. FOUR OR FIVE.
I WANT THOSE BALD FUCKS TO TURN OVER SOME TABLES.
AND I NEED A NEW BODYGUARD.
THE LAST ONE YOU SENT ME FUCKED THE SHIT UP BUT GOOD.

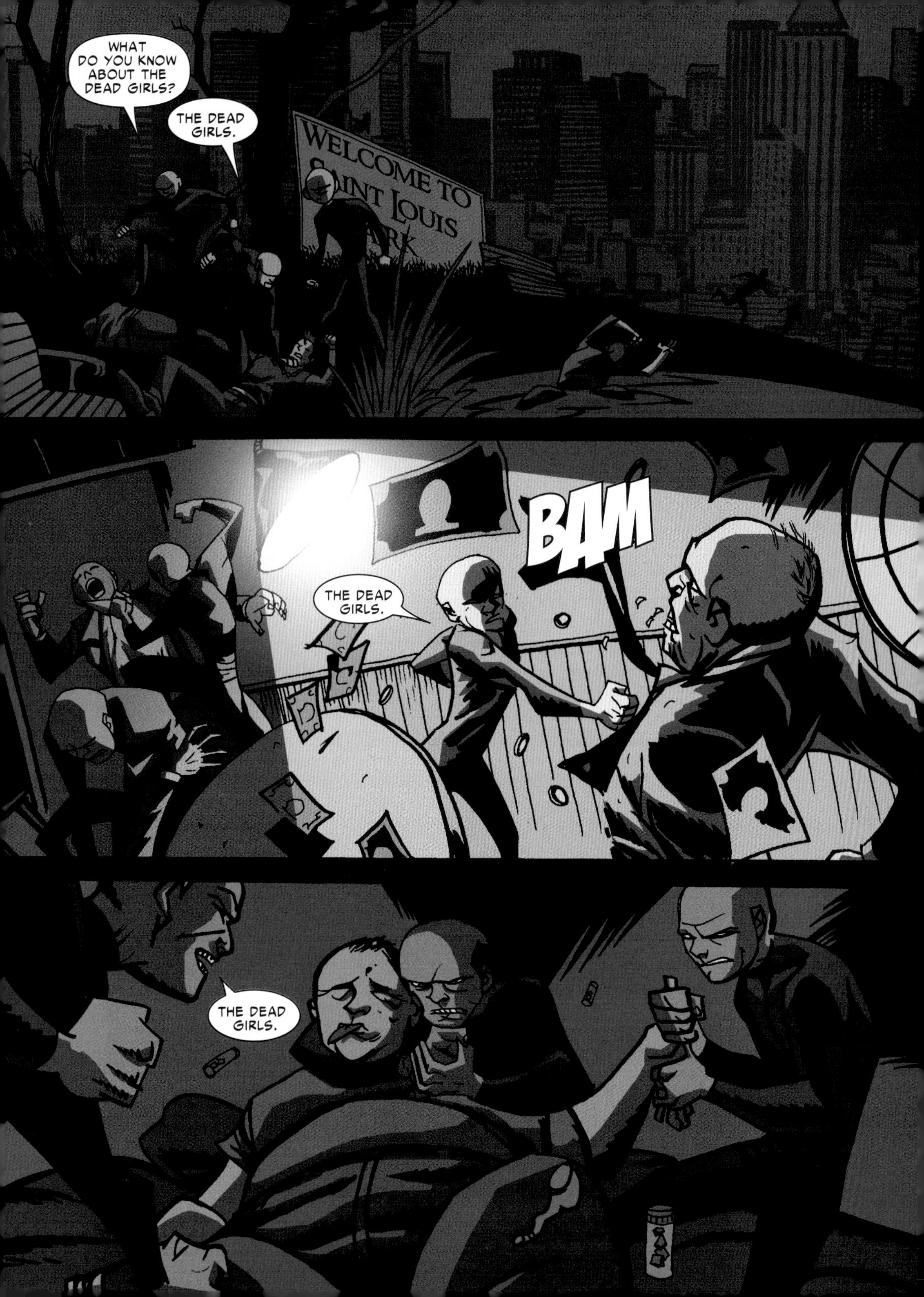
WHAT DO YOU KNOW ABOUT THE DEAD GIRLS?
THE DEAD GIRLS.
WELCOME TO SAINT LOUIS PARK
BAM
THE DEAD GIRLS.
THE DEAD GIRLS.

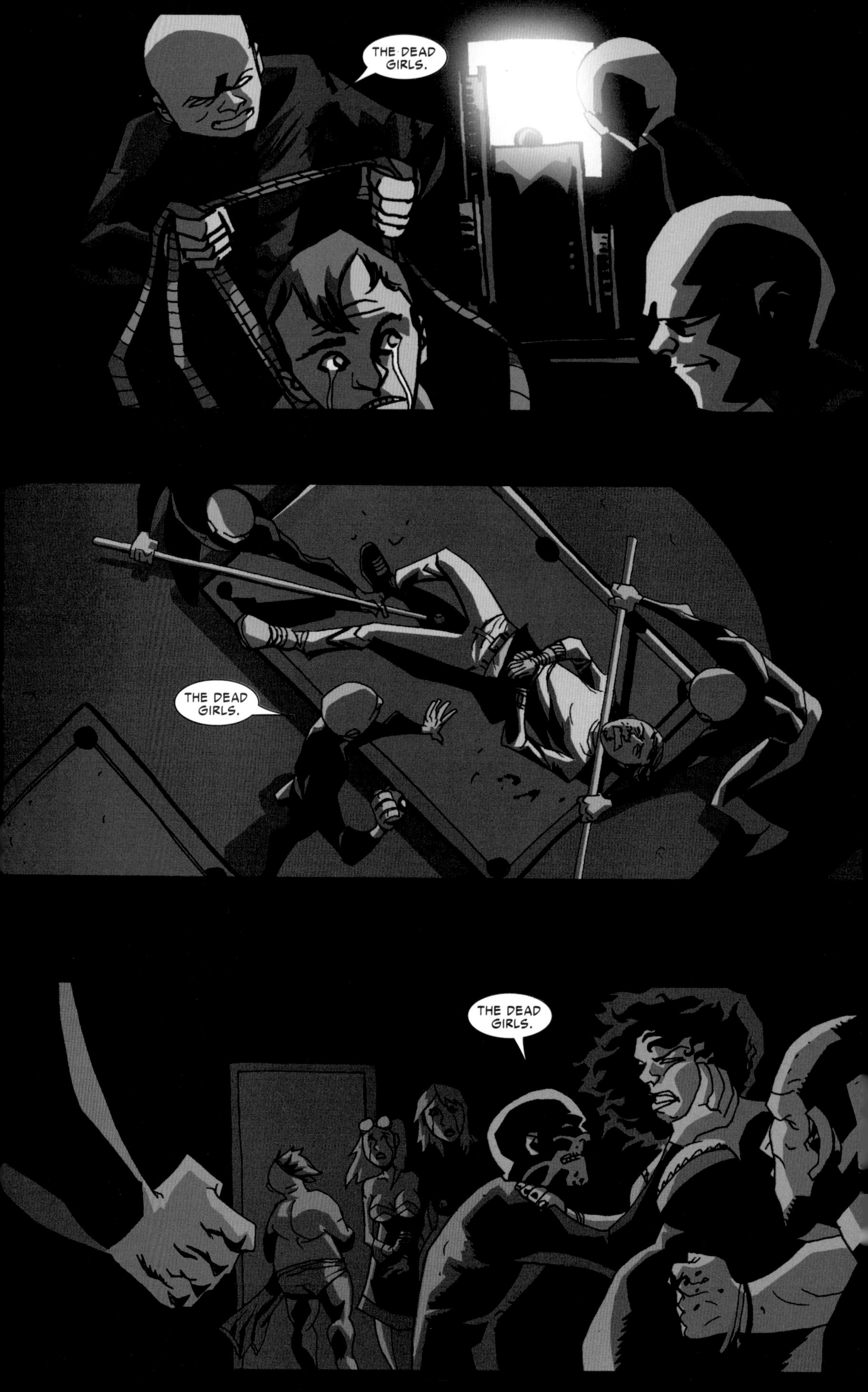
THE DEAD GIRLS.
THE DEAD GIRLS.
THE DEAD GIRLS.

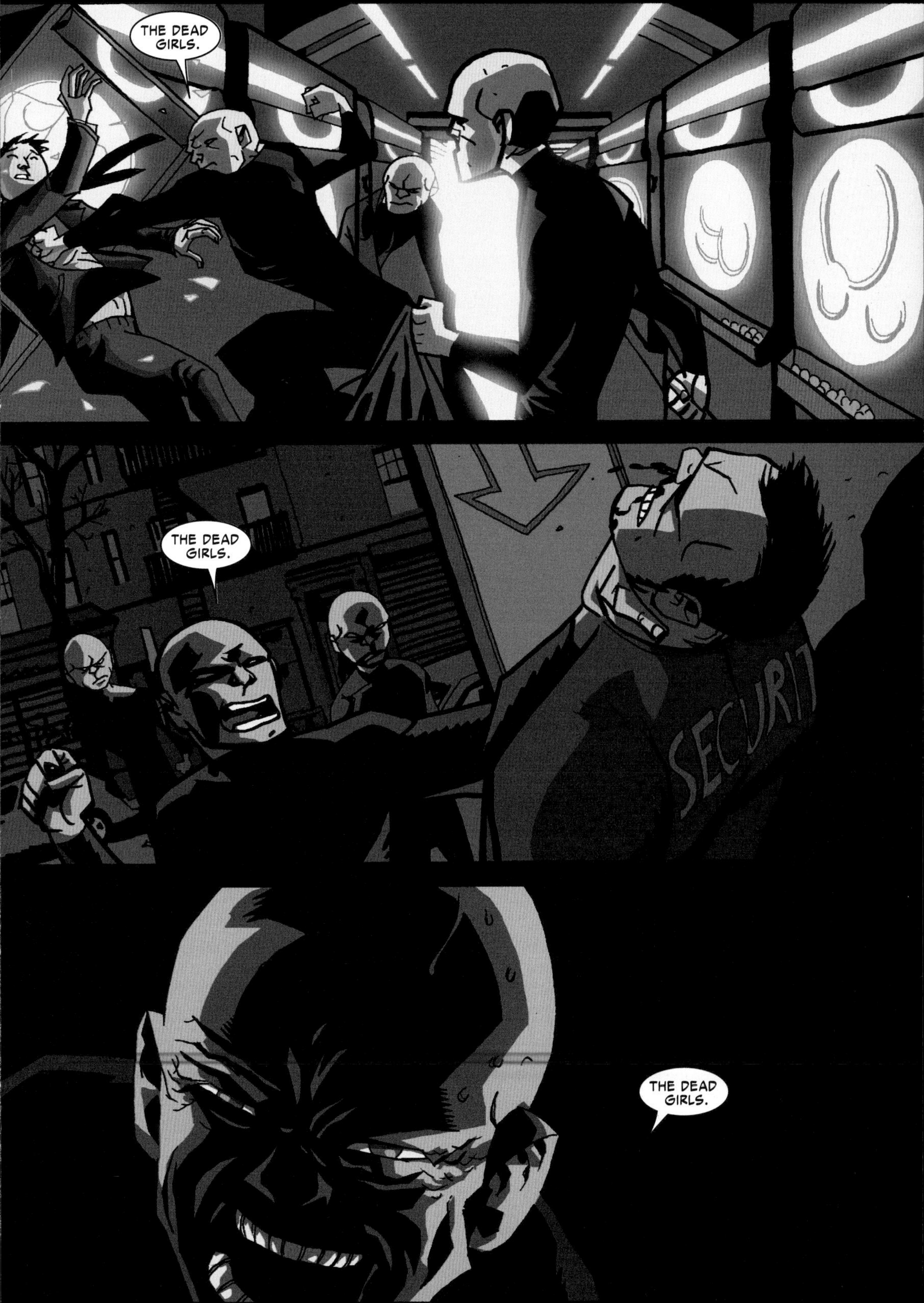
THE DEAD GIRLS.
THE DEAD GIRLS.
SECURIT
THE DEAD GIRLS.

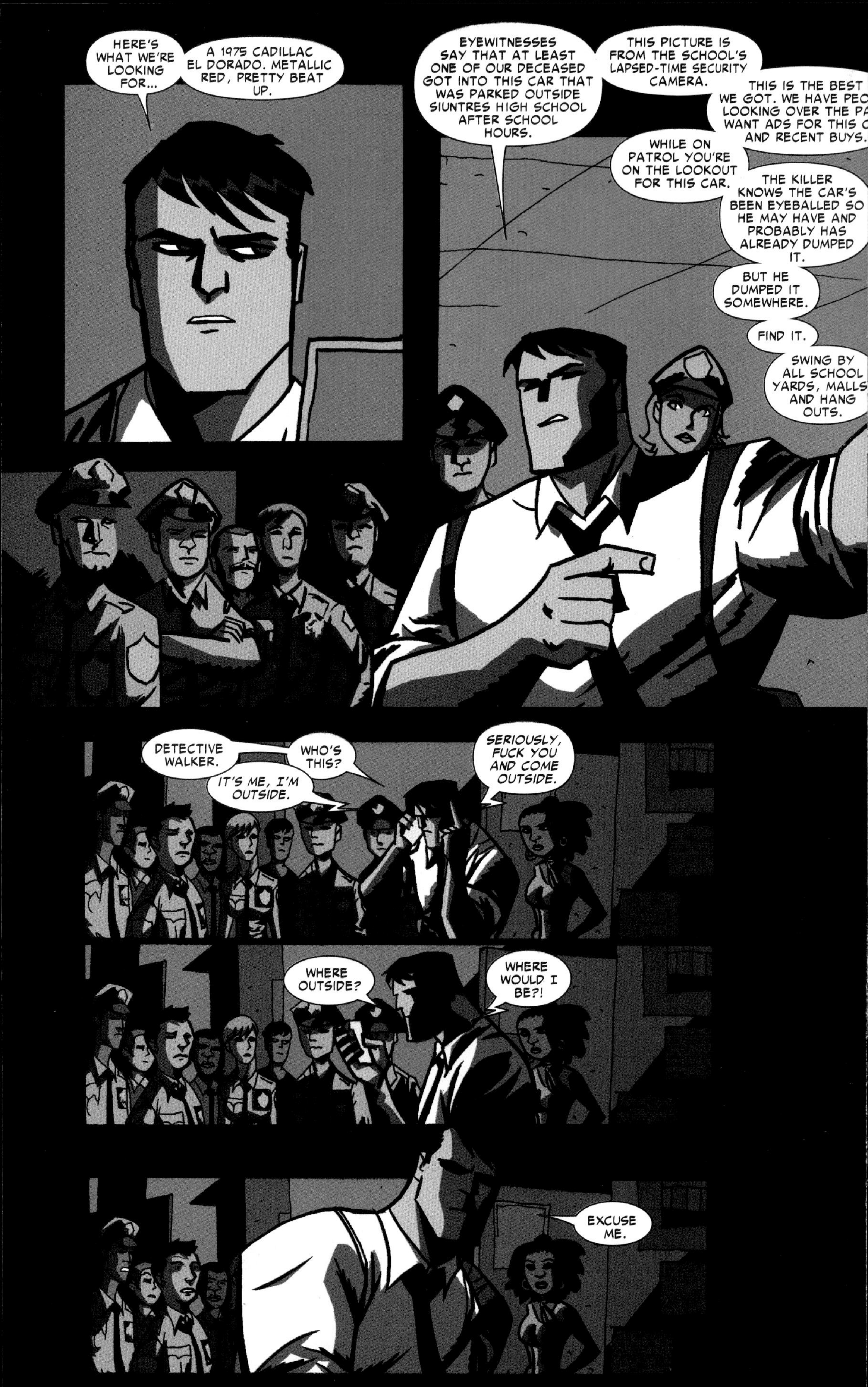
HERE'S WHAT WE'RE LOOKING FOR...
A 1975 CADILLAC EL DORADO. METALLIC RED, PRETTY BEAT UP.
EYEWITNESSES SAY THAT AT LEAST ONE OF OUR DECEASED GOT INTO THIS CAR THAT WAS PARKED OUTSIDE SIUNTRES HIGH SCHOOL AFTER SCHOOL HOURS.
THIS PICTURE IS FROM THE SCHOOL'S LAPSED-TIME SECURITY CAMERA.
THIS IS THE BEST WE GOT. WE HAVE PEO LOOKING OVER THE PA WANT ADS FOR THIS C AND RECENT BUYS.
WHILE ON PATROL YOU'RE ON THE LOOKOUT FOR THIS CAR.
THE KILLER KNOWS THE CAR'S BEEN EYEBALLED SO HE MAY HAVE AND PROBABLY HAS ALREADY DUMPED IT.
BUT HE DUMPED IT SOMEWHERE.
FIND IT.
SWING BY ALL SCHOOL YARDS, MALLS AND HANG OUTS.
DETECTIVE WALKER.
WHO'S THIS?
IT'S ME, I'M OUTSIDE.
SERIOUSLY, FUCK YOU AND COME OUTSIDE.
WHERE OUTSIDE?
WHERE WOULD I BE?!
EXCUSE ME.

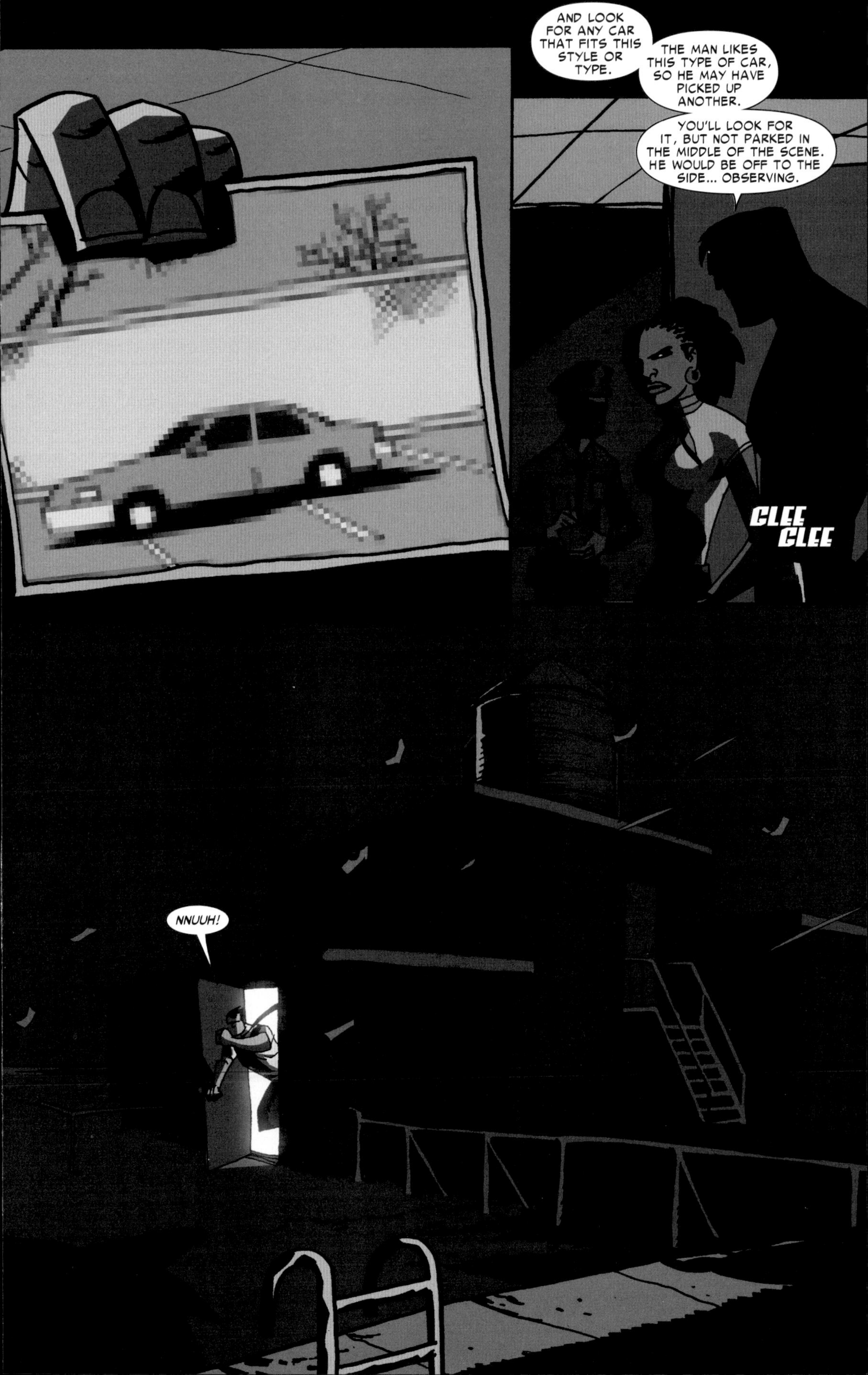
AND LOOK FOR ANY CAR THAT FITS THIS STYLE OR TYPE.
THE MAN LIKES THIS TYPE OF CAR, SO HE MAY HAVE PICKED UP ANOTHER.
YOU'LL LOOK FOR IT, BUT NOT PARKED IN THE MIDDLE OF THE SCENE. HE WOULD BE OFF TO THE SIDE... OBSERVING.
CLEE CLEE
NNUUH!

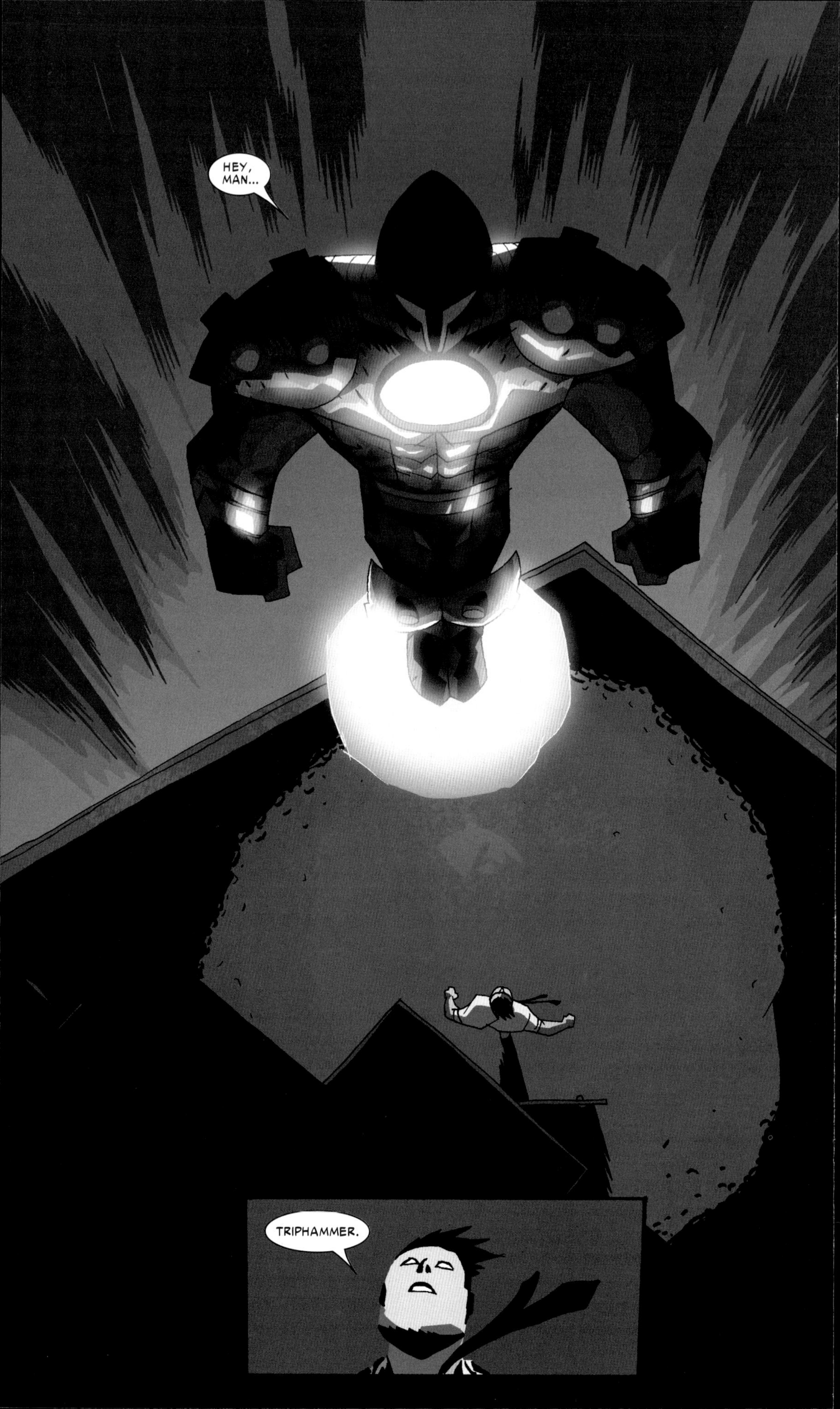

HEY, MAN...
TRIPHAMMER.

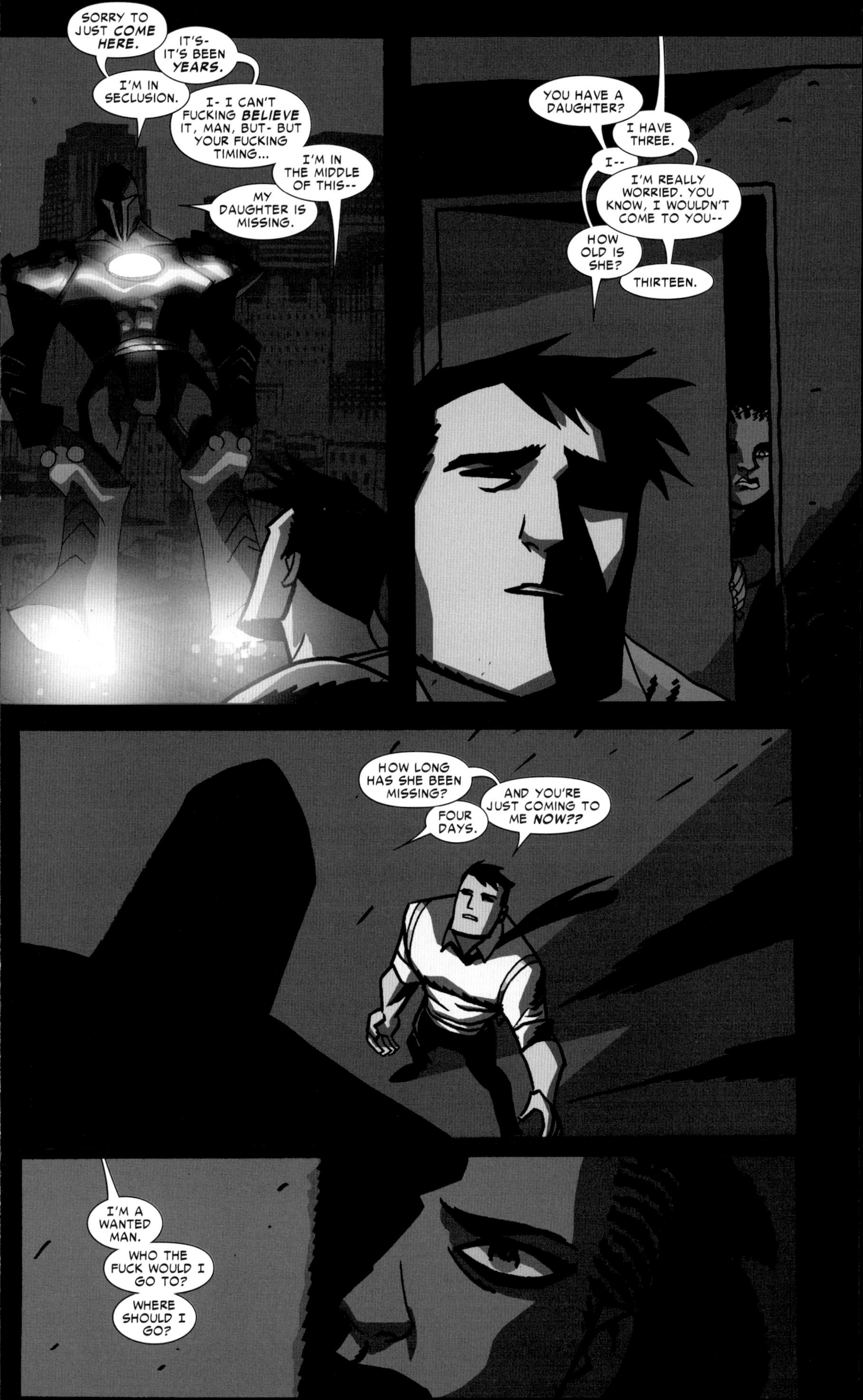
SORRY TO JUST COME HERE.
IT'S- IT'S BEEN YEARS.
I'M IN SECLUSION.
I- I CAN'T FUCKING BELIEVE IT, MAN, BUT- BUT YOUR FUCKING TIMING...
I'M IN THE MIDDLE OF THIS--
MY DAUGHTER IS MISSING.
YOU HAVE A DAUGHTER?
I HAVE THREE.
I--
I'M REALLY WORRIED. YOU KNOW, I WOULDN'T COME TO YOU--
HOW OLD IS SHE?
THIRTEEN.
HOW LONG HAS SHE BEEN MISSING?
FOUR DAYS.
AND YOU'RE JUST COMING TO ME NOW??
I'M A WANTED MAN.
WHO THE FUCK WOULD I GO TO?
WHERE SHOULD I GO?

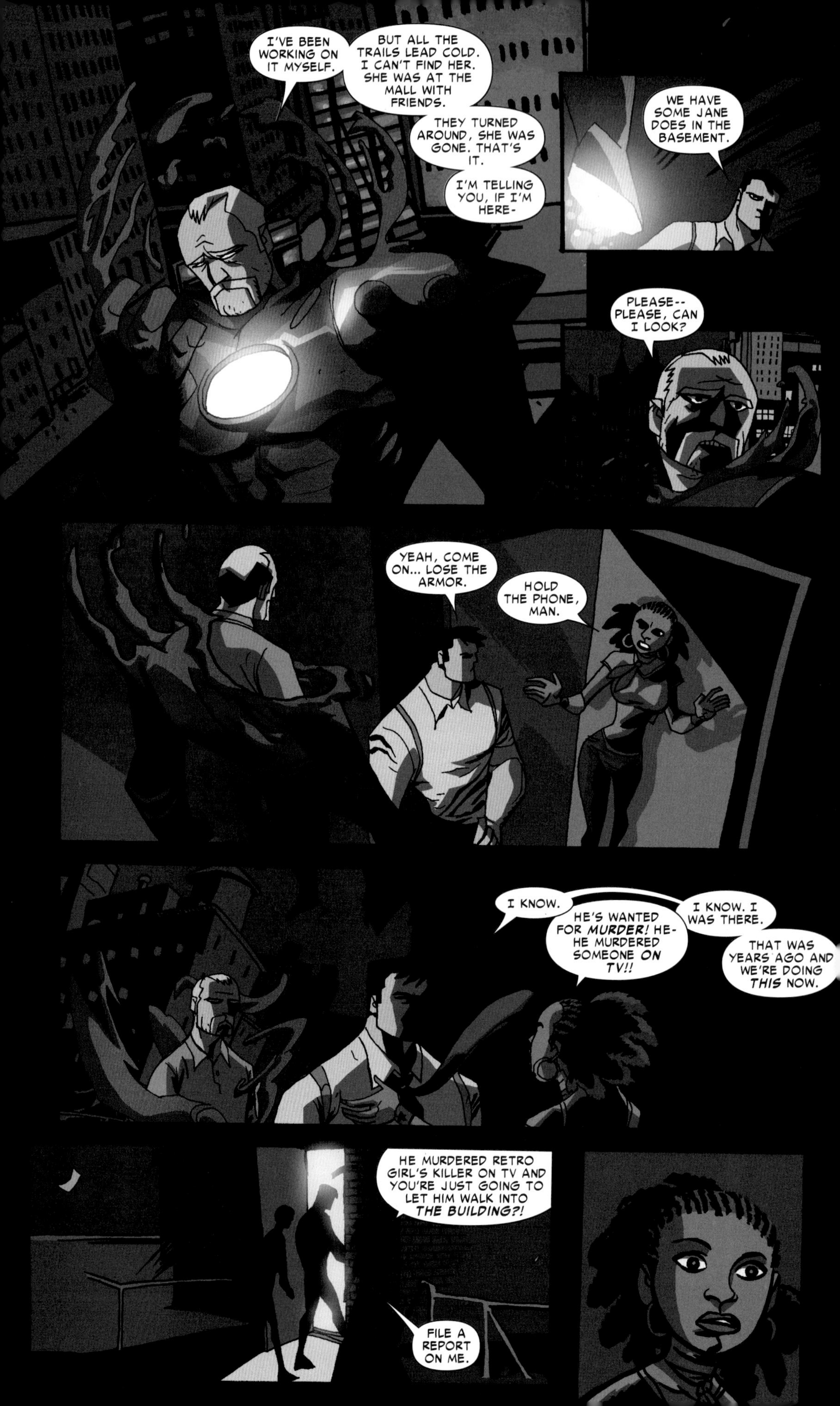

I'VE BEEN WORKING ON IT MYSELF.
BUT ALL THE TRAILS LEAD COLD. I CAN'T FIND HER. SHE WAS AT THE MALL WITH FRIENDS.
THEY TURNED AROUND, SHE WAS GONE. THAT'S IT.
I'M TELLING YOU, IF I'M HERE-
WE HAVE SOME JANE DOES IN THE BASEMENT.
PLEASE--PLEASE, CAN I LOOK?
YEAH, COME ON... LOSE THE ARMOR.
HOLD THE PHONE, MAN.
HE'S WANTED FOR MURDER! HE-HE MURDERED SOMEONE ON TV!!
I KNOW.
I KNOW. I WAS THERE.
THAT WAS YEARS AGO AND WE'RE DOING THIS NOW.
HE MURDERED RETRO GIRL'S KILLER ON TV AND YOU'RE JUST GOING TO LET HIM WALK INTO THE BUILDING?!
FILE A REPORT ON ME.

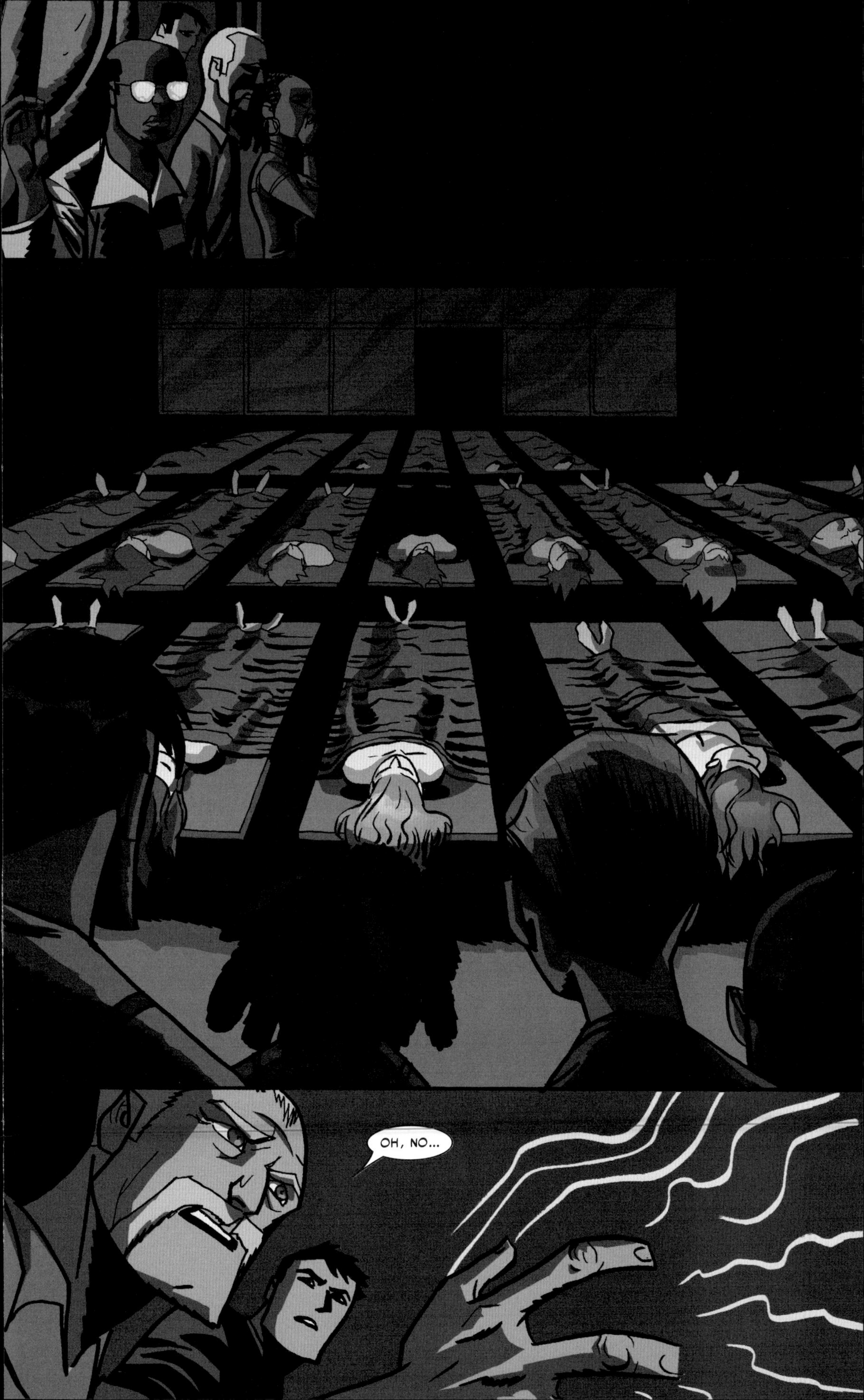
OH, NO...

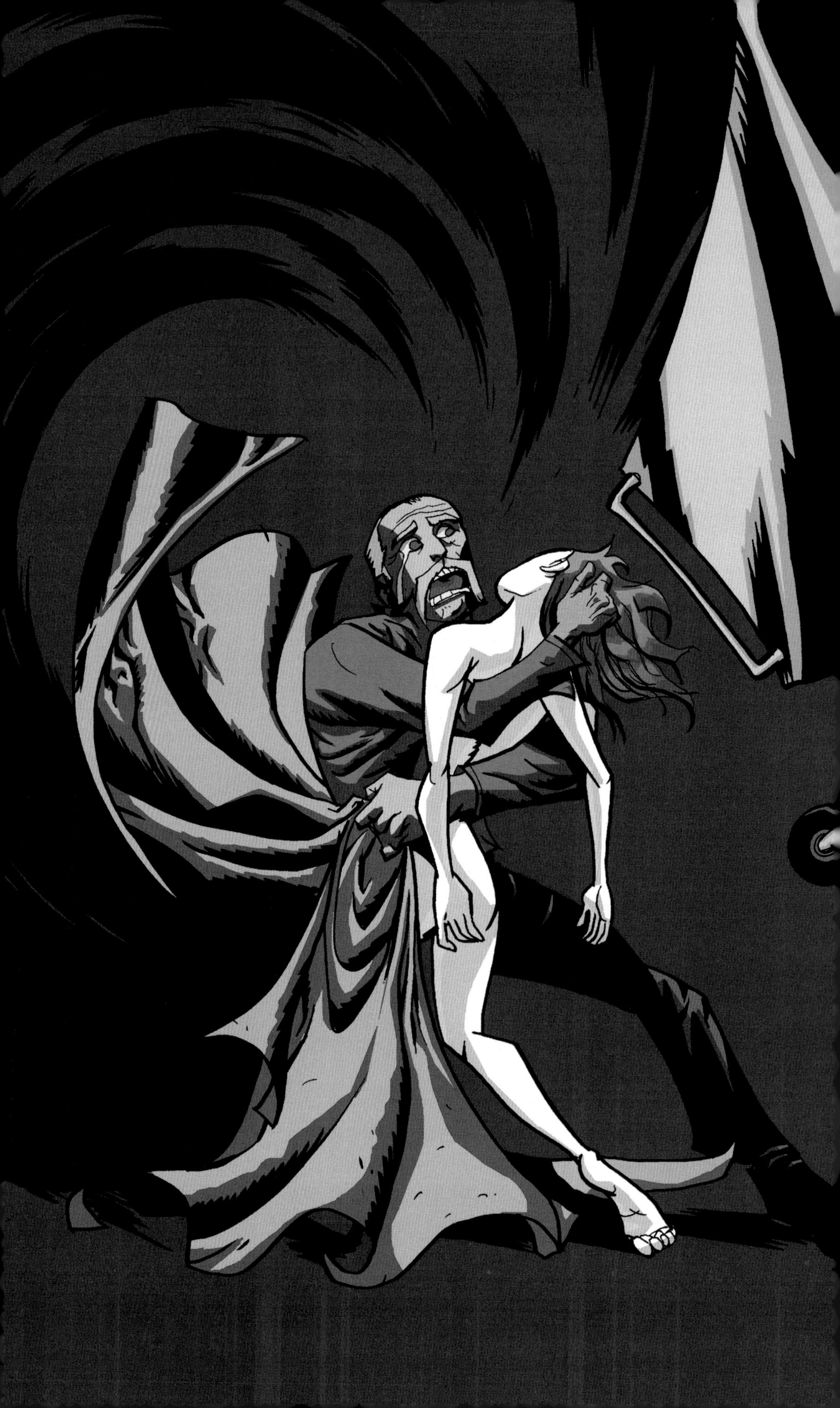

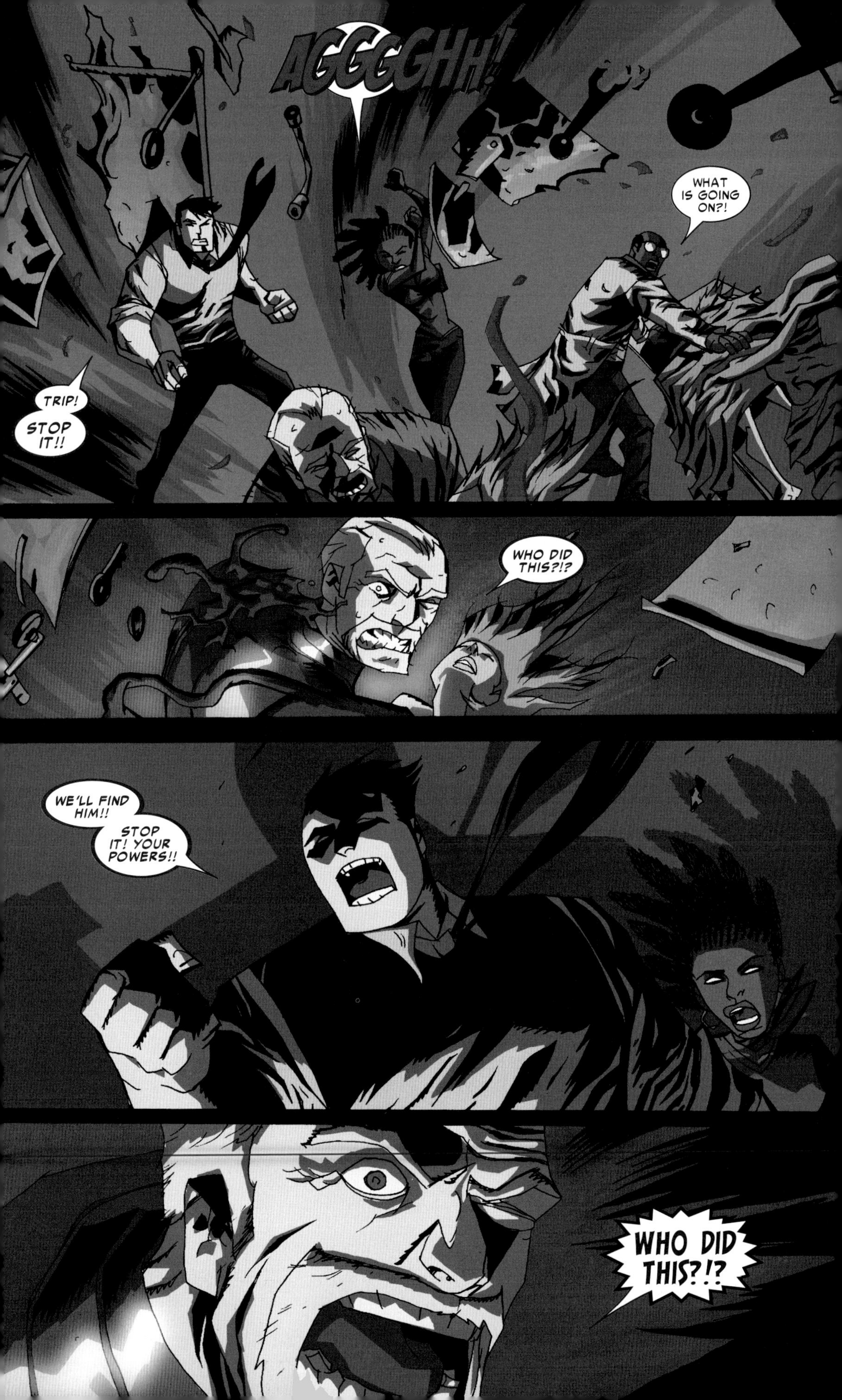
AGGGGHH!
WHAT IS GOING ON?!
TRIP!
STOP IT!!
WHO DID THIS?!?
WE'LL FIND HIM!!
STOP IT! YOUR POWERS!!
WHO DID THIS?!?

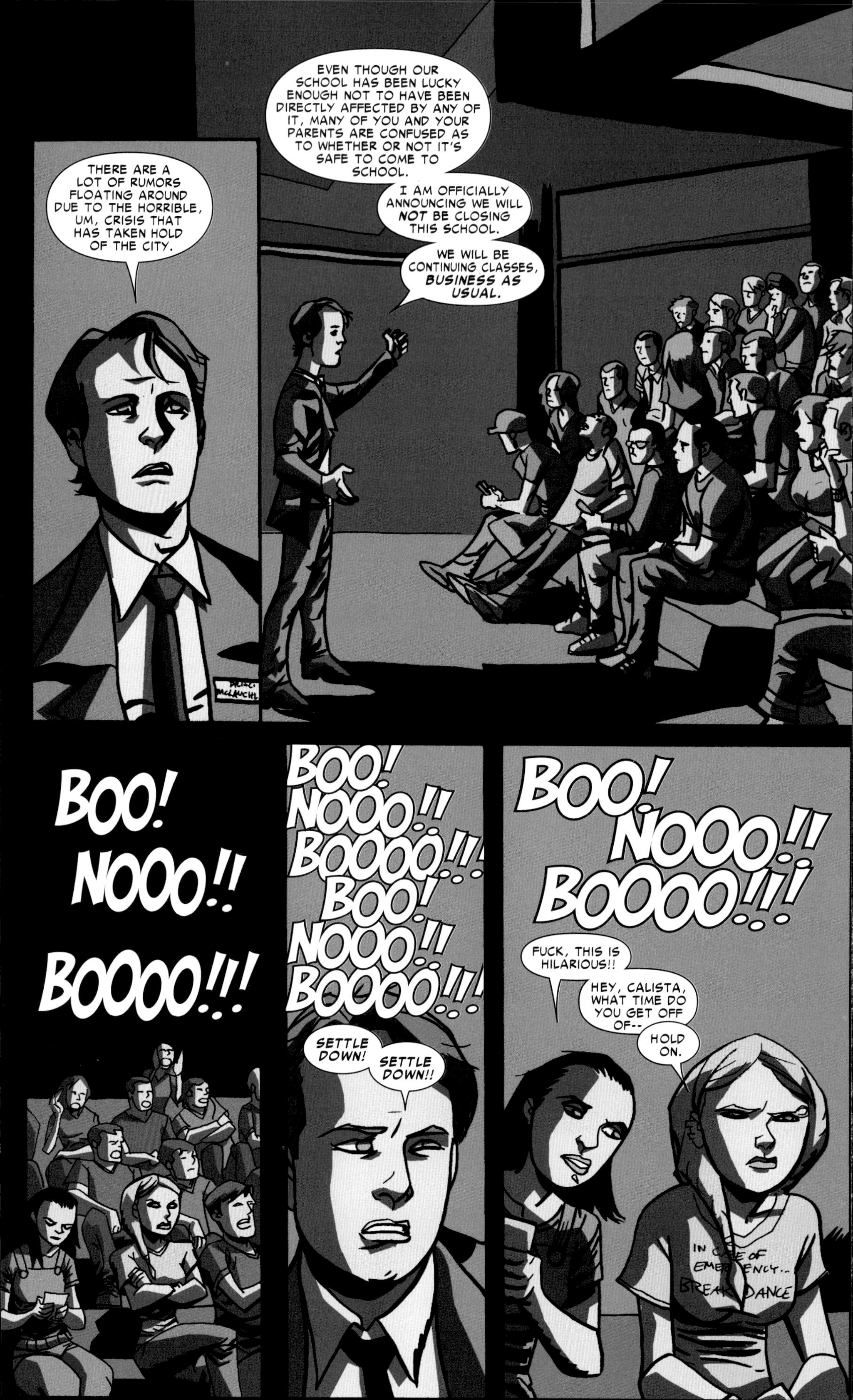
THERE ARE A LOT OF RUMORS FLOATING AROUND DUE TO THE HORRIBLE, UM, CRISIS THAT HAS TAKEN HOLD OF THE CITY.
EVEN THOUGH OUR SCHOOL HAS BEEN LUCKY ENOUGH NOT TO HAVE BEEN DIRECTLY AFFECTED BY ANY OF IT, MANY OF YOU AND YOUR PARENTS ARE CONFUSED AS TO WHETHER OR NOT IT'S SAFE TO COME TO SCHOOL.
I AM OFFICIALLY ANNOUNCING WE WILL NOT BE CLOSING THIS SCHOOL.
WE WILL BE CONTINUING CLASSES, BUSINESS AS USUAL.
BOO! NOOO!! BOOOO!!!
BOO! NOOO!! BOOOO!!! BOO! NOOO!! BOOOO!!!
SETTLE DOWN!
SETTLE DOWN!!
BOO! NOOO!! BOOOO!!!
FUCK, THIS IS HILARIOUS!!
HEY, CALISTA, WHAT TIME DO YOU GET OFF OF--
HOLD ON.
IN CASE OF EMERGENCY.. BREAK DANCE

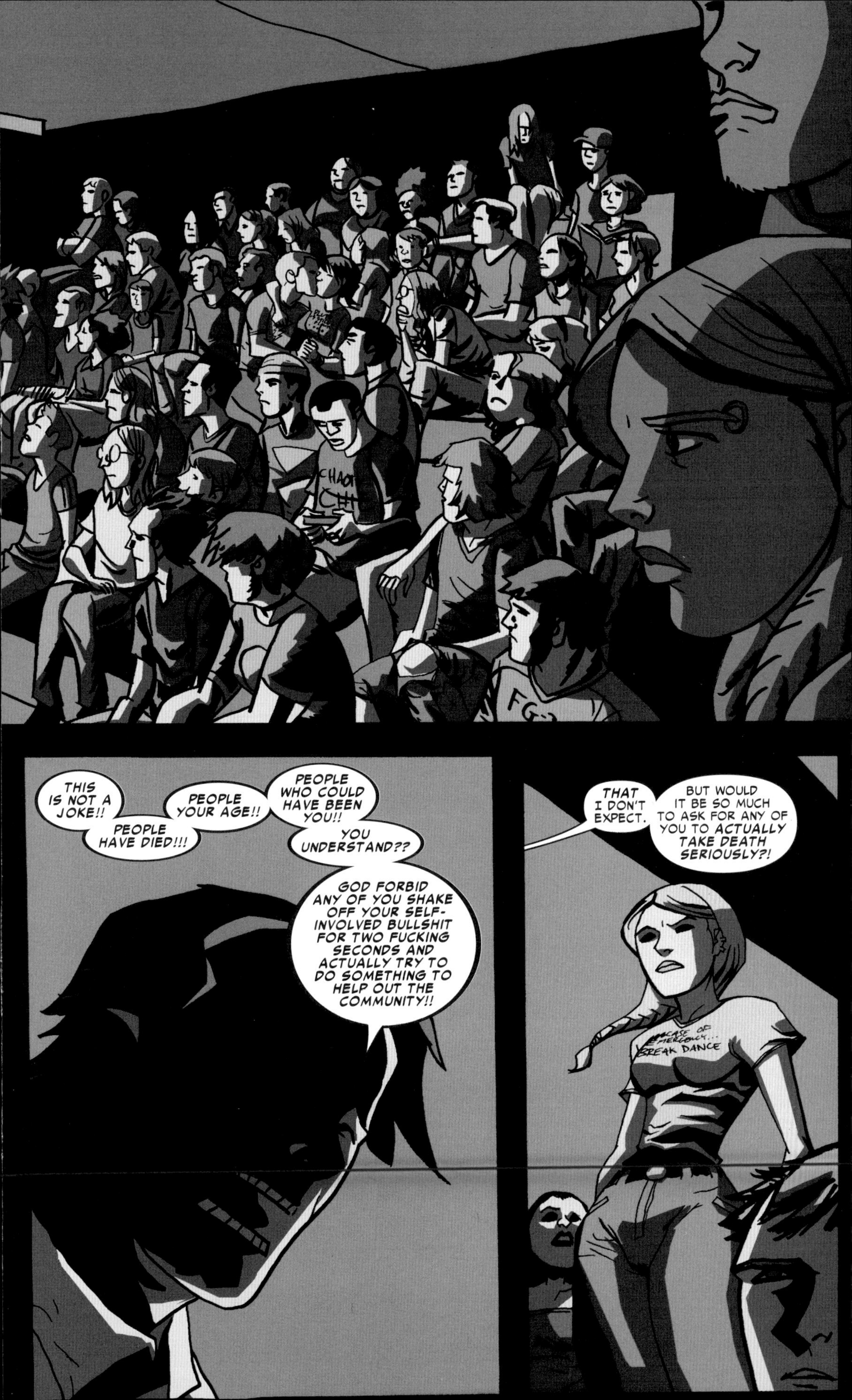
THIS IS NOT A JOKE!!
PEOPLE HAVE DIED!!!
PEOPLE YOUR AGE!!
PEOPLE WHO COULD HAVE BEEN YOU!!
YOU UNDERSTAND??
GOD FORBID ANY OF YOU SHAKE OFF YOUR SELF-INVOLVED BULLSHIT FOR TWO FUCKING SECONDS AND ACTUALLY TRY TO DO SOMETHING TO HELP OUT THE COMMUNITY!!
THAT I DON'T EXPECT.
BUT WOULD IT BE SO MUCH TO ASK FOR ANY OF YOU TO ACTUALLY TAKE DEATH SERIOUSLY?!
IN CASE OF EMERGENCY... BREAK DANCE

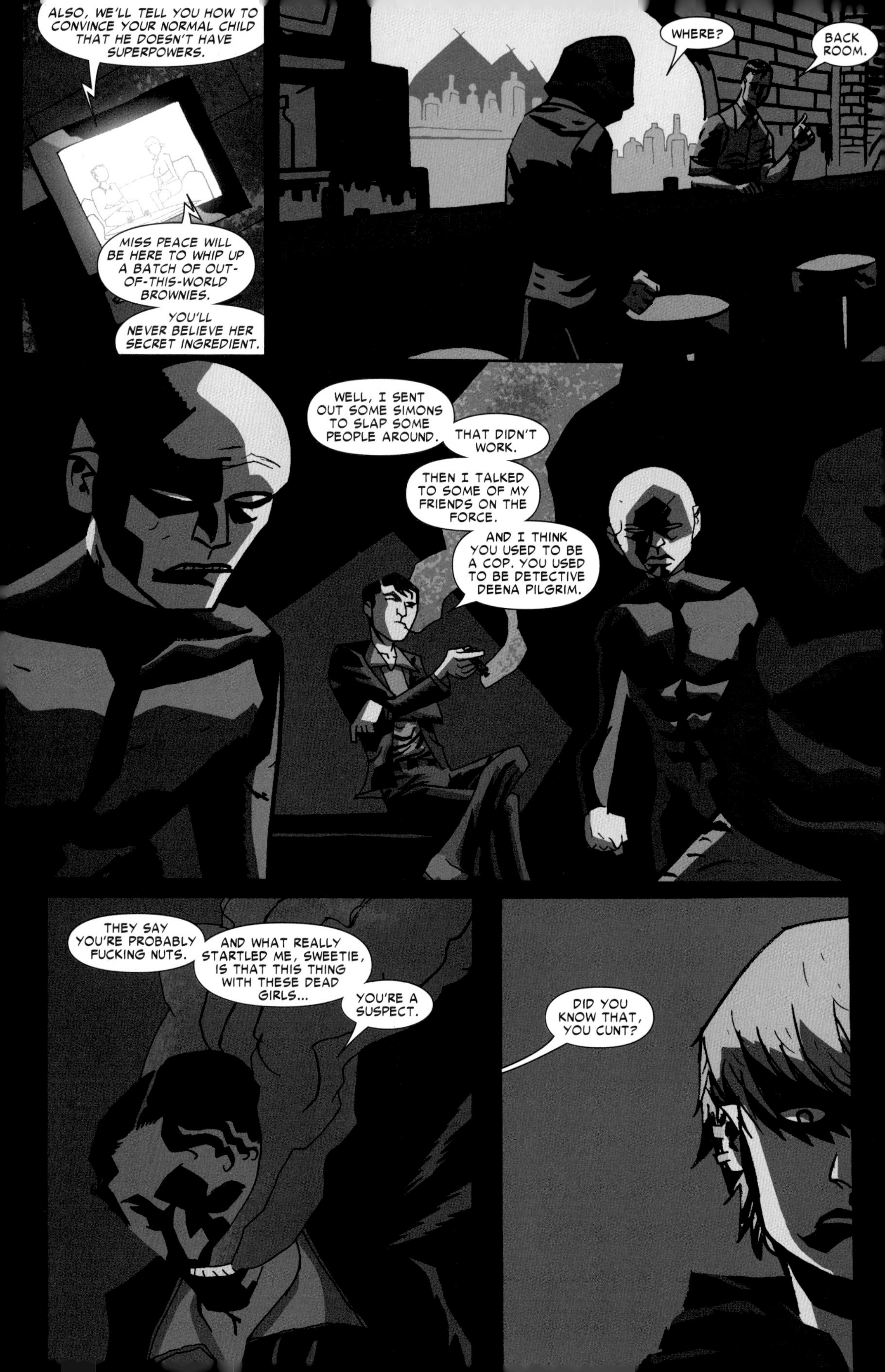
ALSO, WE'LL TELL YOU HOW TO CONVINCE YOUR NORMAL CHILD THAT HE DOESN'T HAVE SUPERPOWERS.
MISS PEACE WILL BE HERE TO WHIP UP A BATCH OF OUT-OF-THIS-WORLD BROWNIES.
YOU'LL NEVER BELIEVE HER SECRET INGREDIENT.
WHERE?
BACK ROOM.
WELL, I SENT OUT SOME SIMONS TO SLAP SOME PEOPLE AROUND.
THAT DIDN'T WORK.
THEN I TALKED TO SOME OF MY FRIENDS ON THE FORCE.
AND I THINK YOU USED TO BE A COP. YOU USED TO BE DETECTIVE DEENA PILGRIM.
THEY SAY YOU'RE PROBABLY FUCKING NUTS.
AND WHAT REALLY STARTLED ME, SWEETIE, IS THAT THIS THING WITH THESE DEAD GIRLS...
YOU'RE A SUSPECT.
DID YOU KNOW THAT, YOU CUNT?

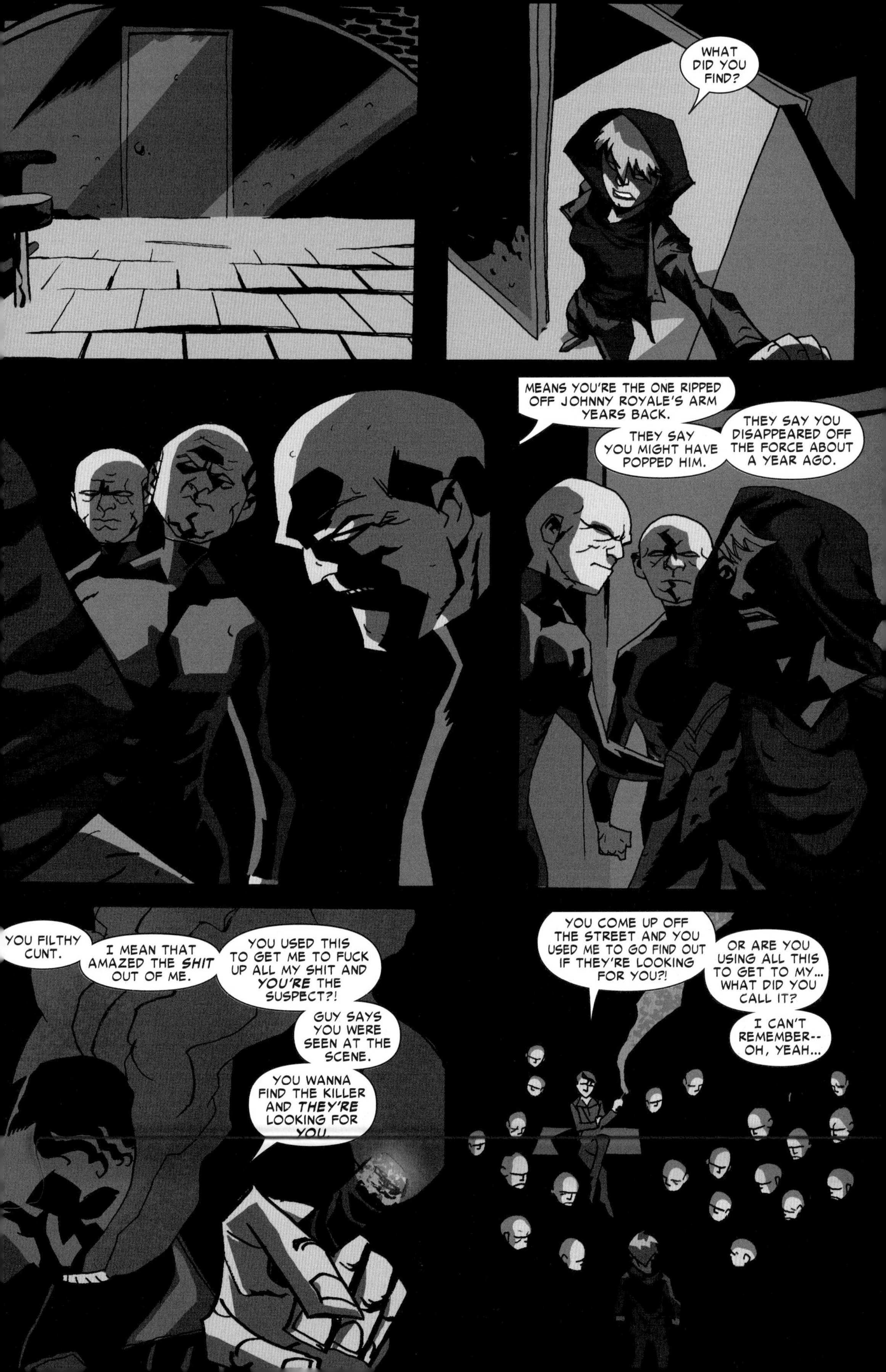
WHAT DID YOU FIND?
MEANS YOU'RE THE ONE RIPPED OFF JOHNNY ROYALE'S ARM YEARS BACK.
THEY SAY YOU MIGHT HAVE POPPED HIM.
THEY SAY YOU DISAPPEARED OFF THE FORCE ABOUT A YEAR AGO.
YOU FILTHY CUNT.
I MEAN THAT AMAZED THE *SHIT* OUT OF ME.
YOU USED THIS TO GET ME TO FUCK UP ALL MY SHIT AND *YOU'RE* THE SUSPECT?!
GUY SAYS YOU WERE SEEN AT THE SCENE.
YOU WANNA FIND THE KILLER AND *THEY'RE* LOOKING FOR *YOU*.
YOU COME UP OFF THE STREET AND YOU USED ME TO GO FIND OUT IF THEY'RE LOOKING FOR YOU?!
OR ARE YOU USING ALL THIS TO GET TO MY... WHAT DID YOU CALL IT?
I CAN'T REMEMBER-- OH, YEAH...

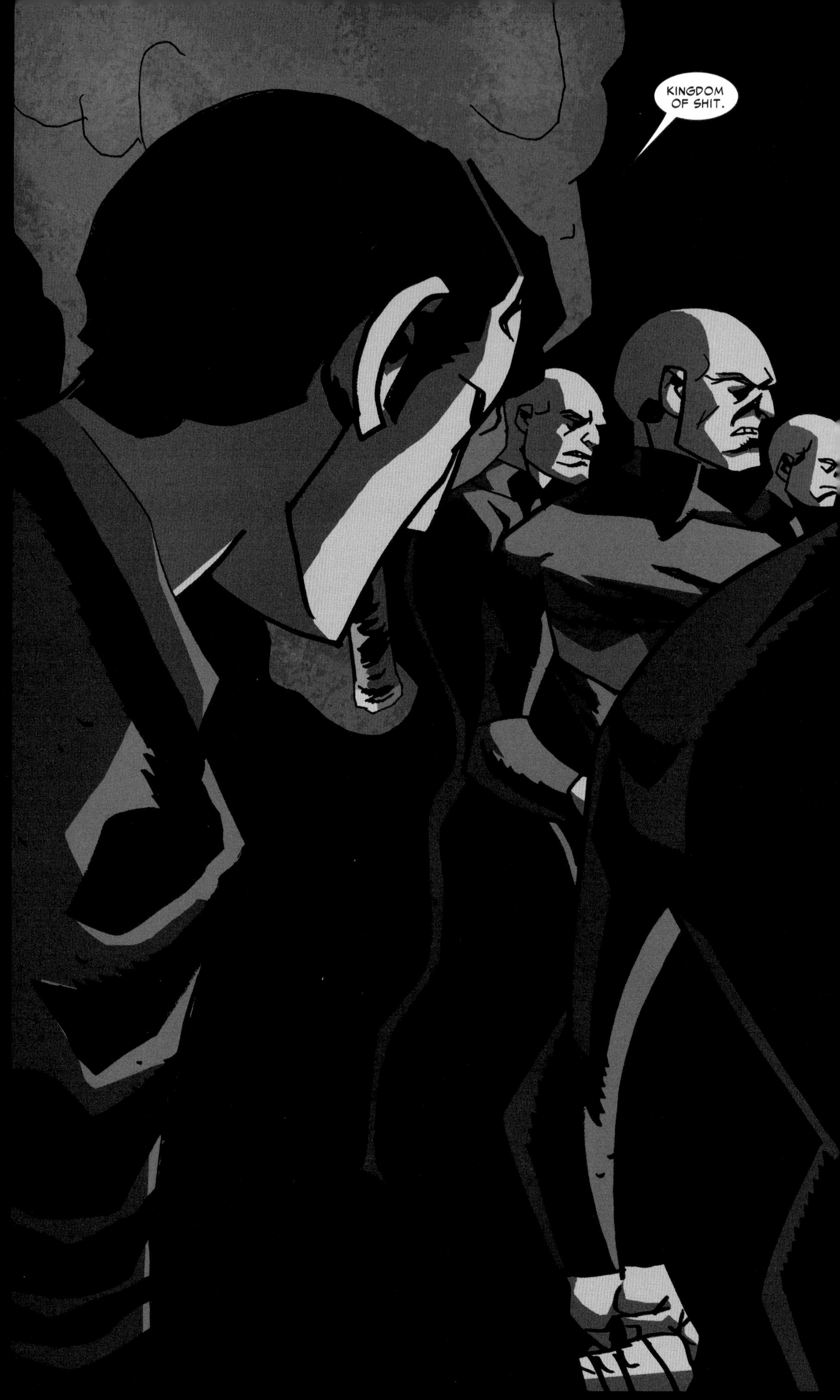
KINGDOM OF SHIT.

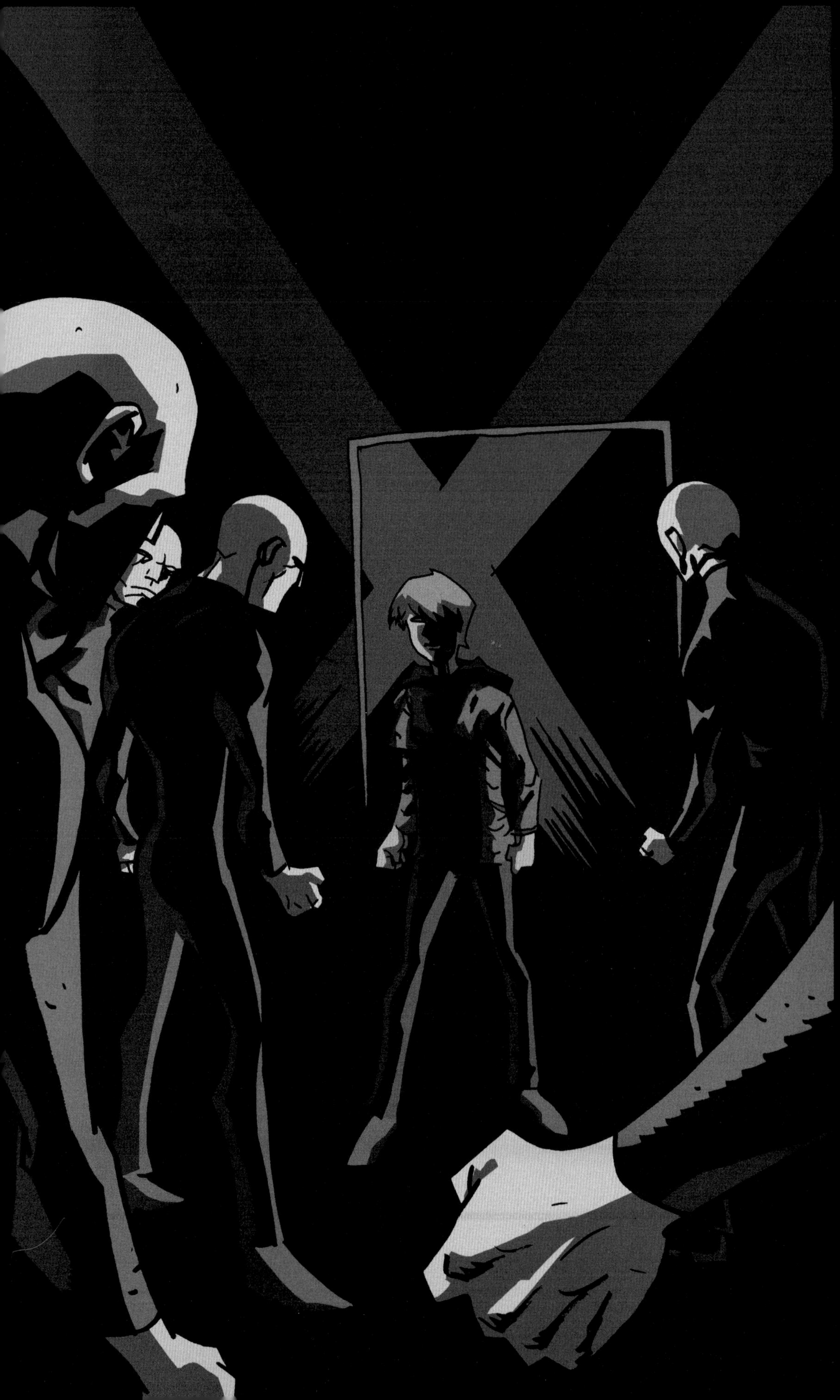

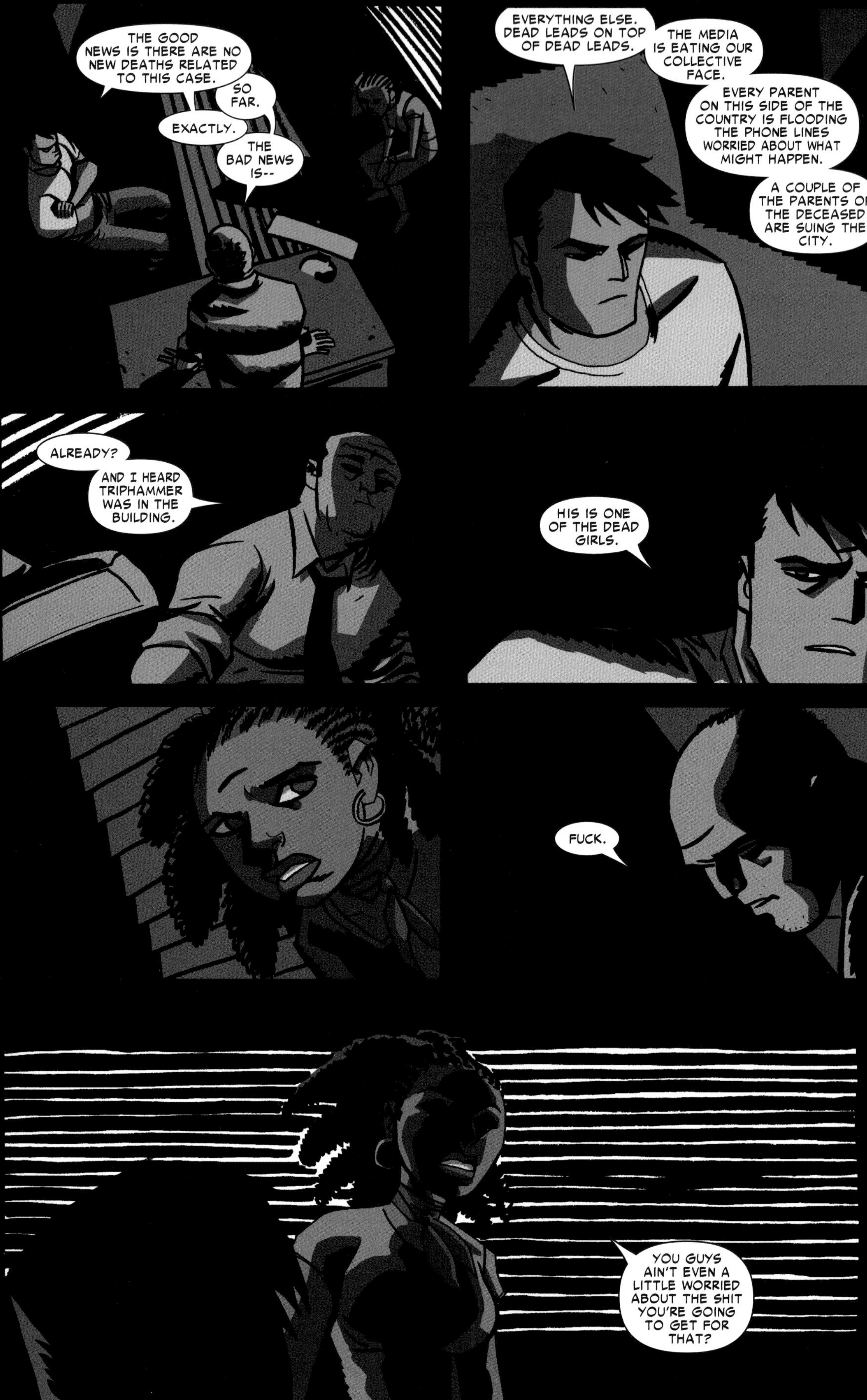
THE GOOD NEWS IS THERE ARE NO NEW DEATHS RELATED TO THIS CASE.
SO FAR.
EXACTLY.
THE BAD NEWS IS--
EVERYTHING ELSE. DEAD LEADS ON TOP OF DEAD LEADS.
THE MEDIA IS EATING OUR COLLECTIVE FACE.
EVERY PARENT ON THIS SIDE OF THE COUNTRY IS FLOODING THE PHONE LINES WORRIED ABOUT WHAT MIGHT HAPPEN.
A COUPLE OF THE PARENTS OF THE DECEASED ARE SUING THE CITY.
ALREADY?
AND I HEARD TRIPHAMMER WAS IN THE BUILDING.
HIS IS ONE OF THE DEAD GIRLS.
FUCK.
YOU GUYS AIN'T EVEN A LITTLE WORRIED ABOUT THE SHIT YOU'RE GOING TO GET FOR THAT?

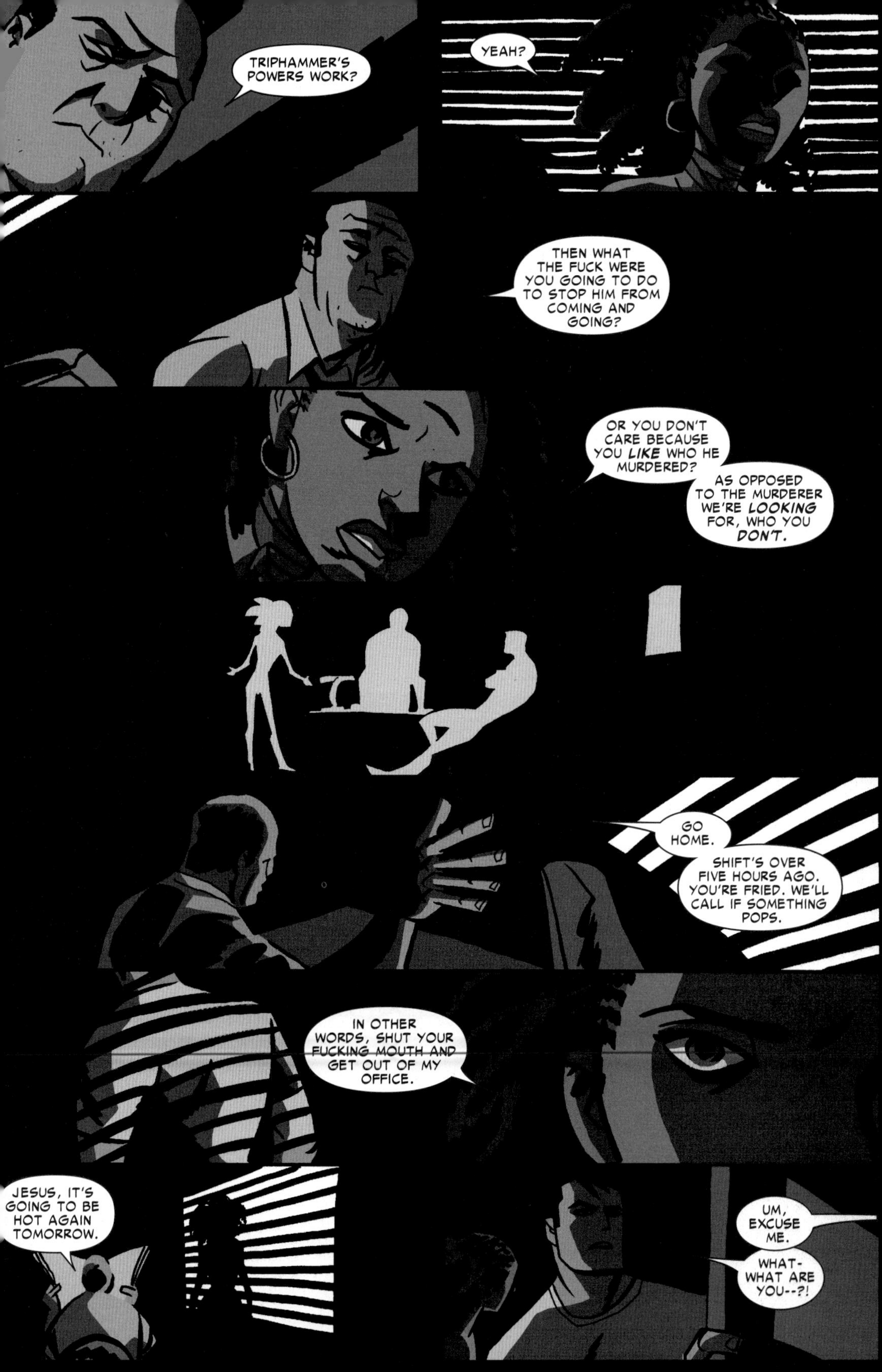
TRIPHAMMER'S POWERS WORK?
YEAH?
THEN WHAT THE FUCK WERE YOU GOING TO DO TO STOP HIM FROM COMING AND GOING?
OR YOU DON'T CARE BECAUSE YOU LIKE WHO HE MURDERED?
AS OPPOSED TO THE MURDERER WE'RE LOOKING FOR, WHO YOU DON'T.
GO HOME.
SHIFT'S OVER FIVE HOURS AGO. YOU'RE FRIED. WE'LL CALL IF SOMETHING POPS.
IN OTHER WORDS, SHUT YOUR FUCKING MOUTH AND GET OUT OF MY OFFICE.
JESUS, IT'S GOING TO BE HOT AGAIN TOMORROW.
UM, EXCUSE ME.
WHAT-WHAT ARE YOU--?!

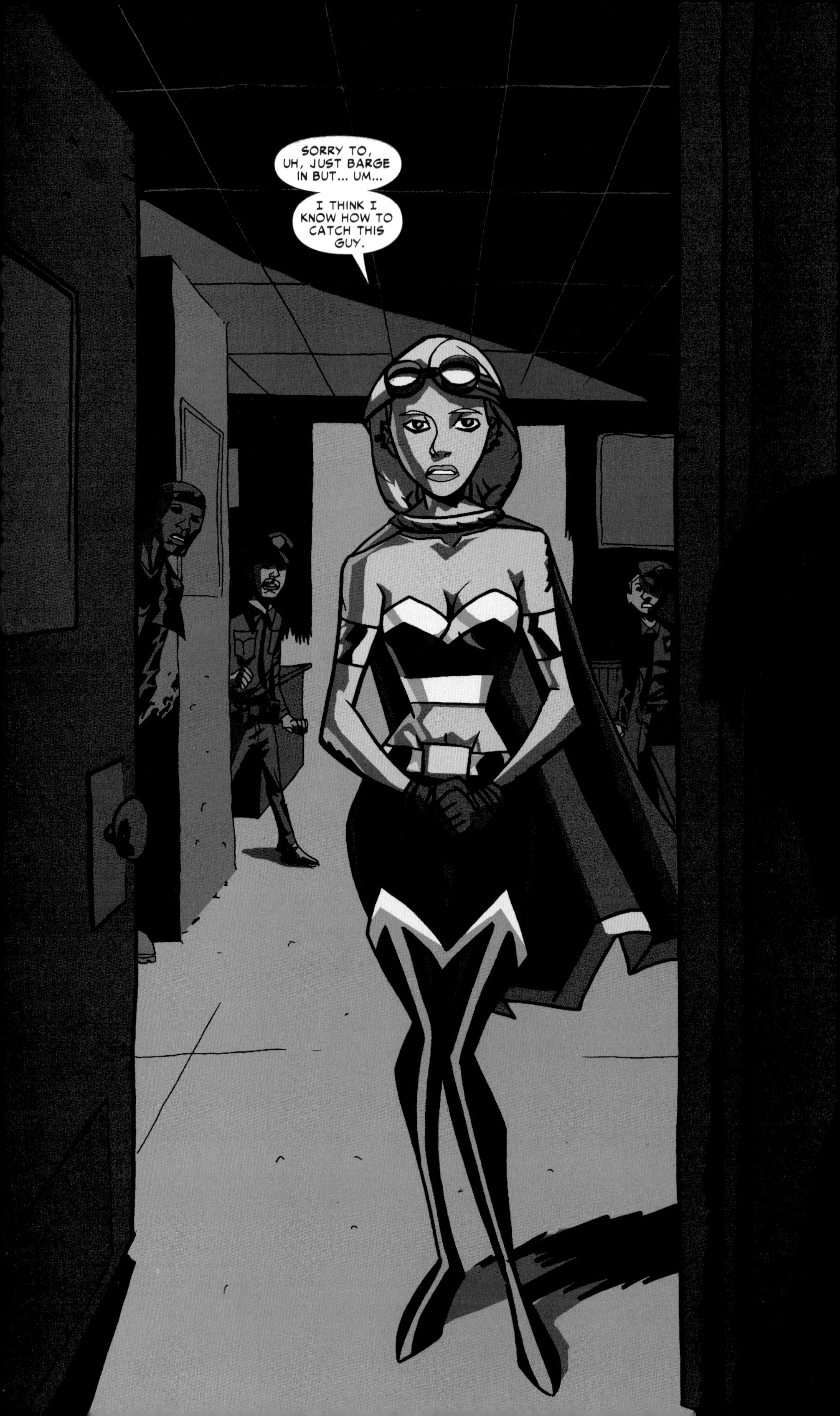
SORRY TO, UH, JUST BARGE IN BUT... UM...
I THINK I KNOW HOW TO CATCH THIS GUY.

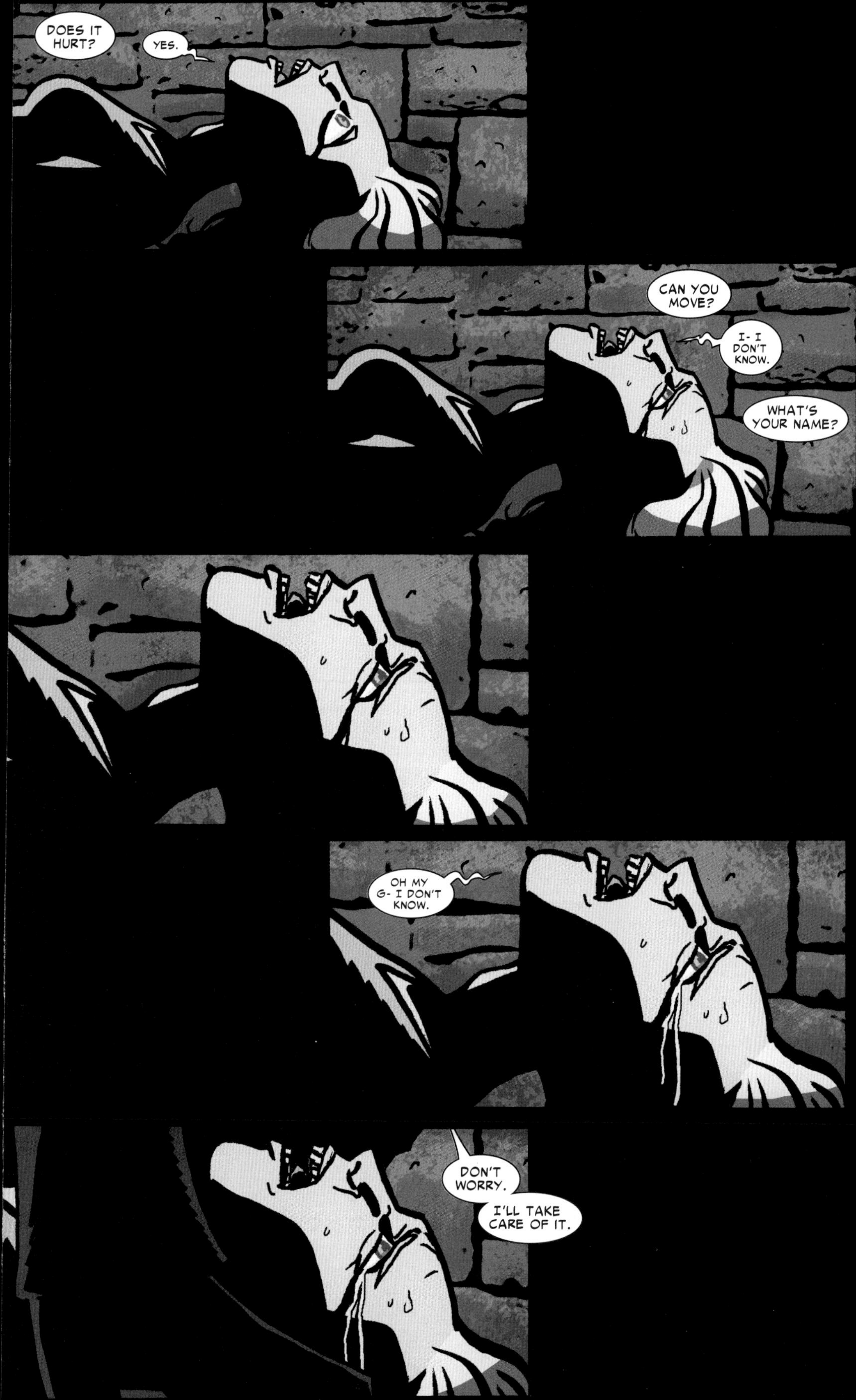
DOES IT HURT?
YES.
CAN YOU MOVE?
I- I DON'T KNOW.
WHAT'S YOUR NAME?
OH MY G- I DON'T KNOW.
DON'T WORRY.
I'LL TAKE CARE OF IT.

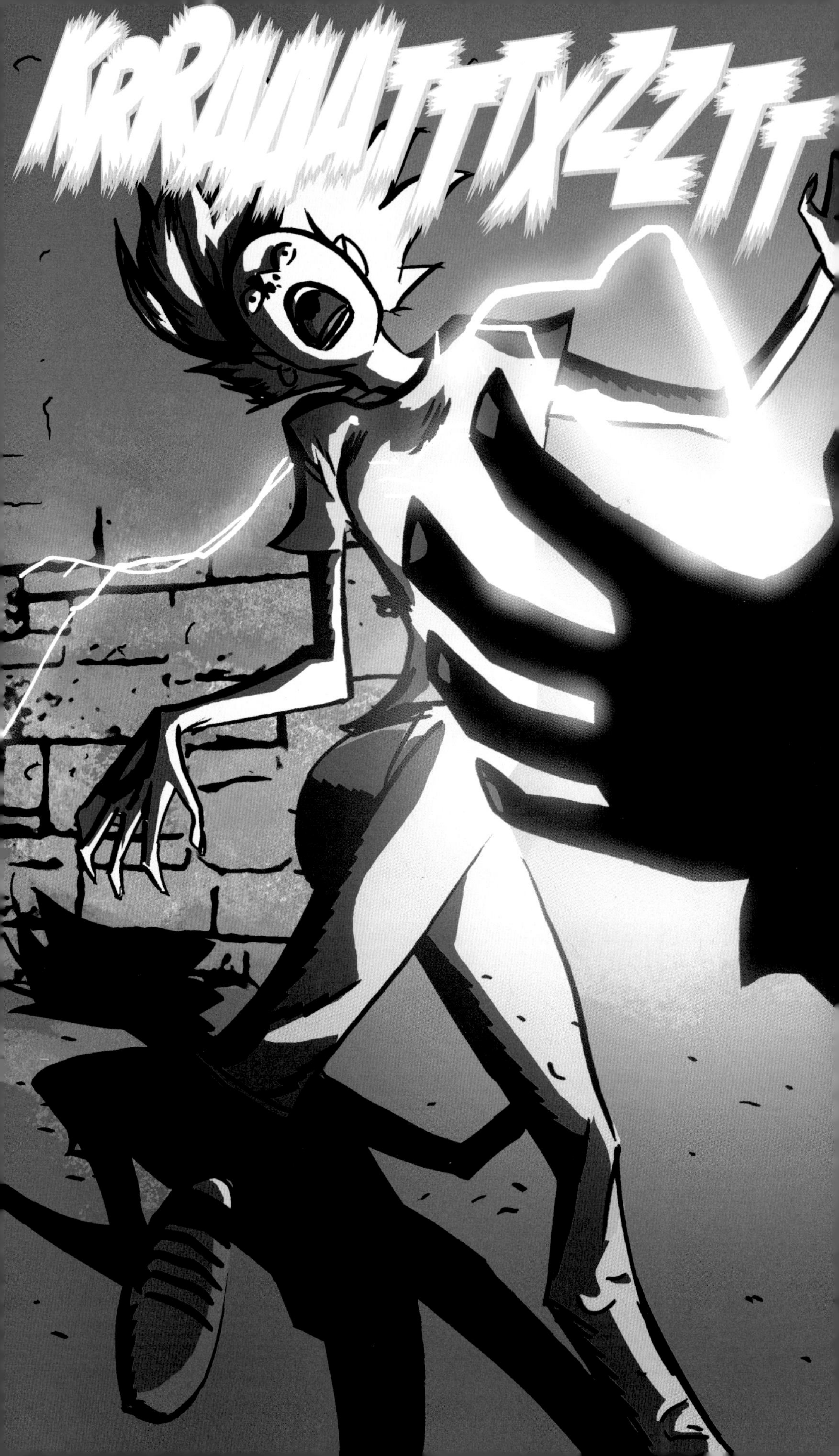
KRRAAATTTXZZTT

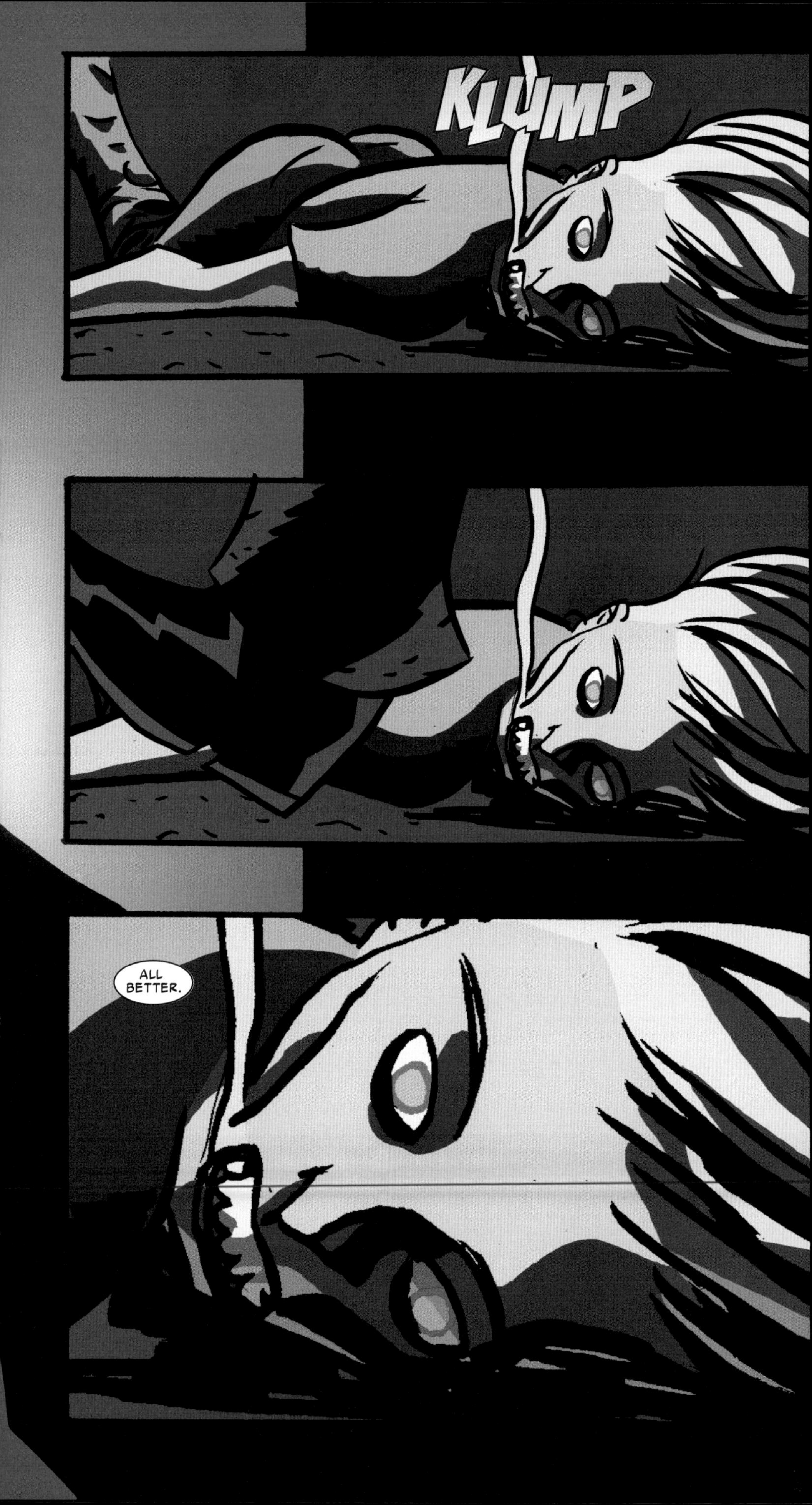
KLUMP
ALL BETTER.

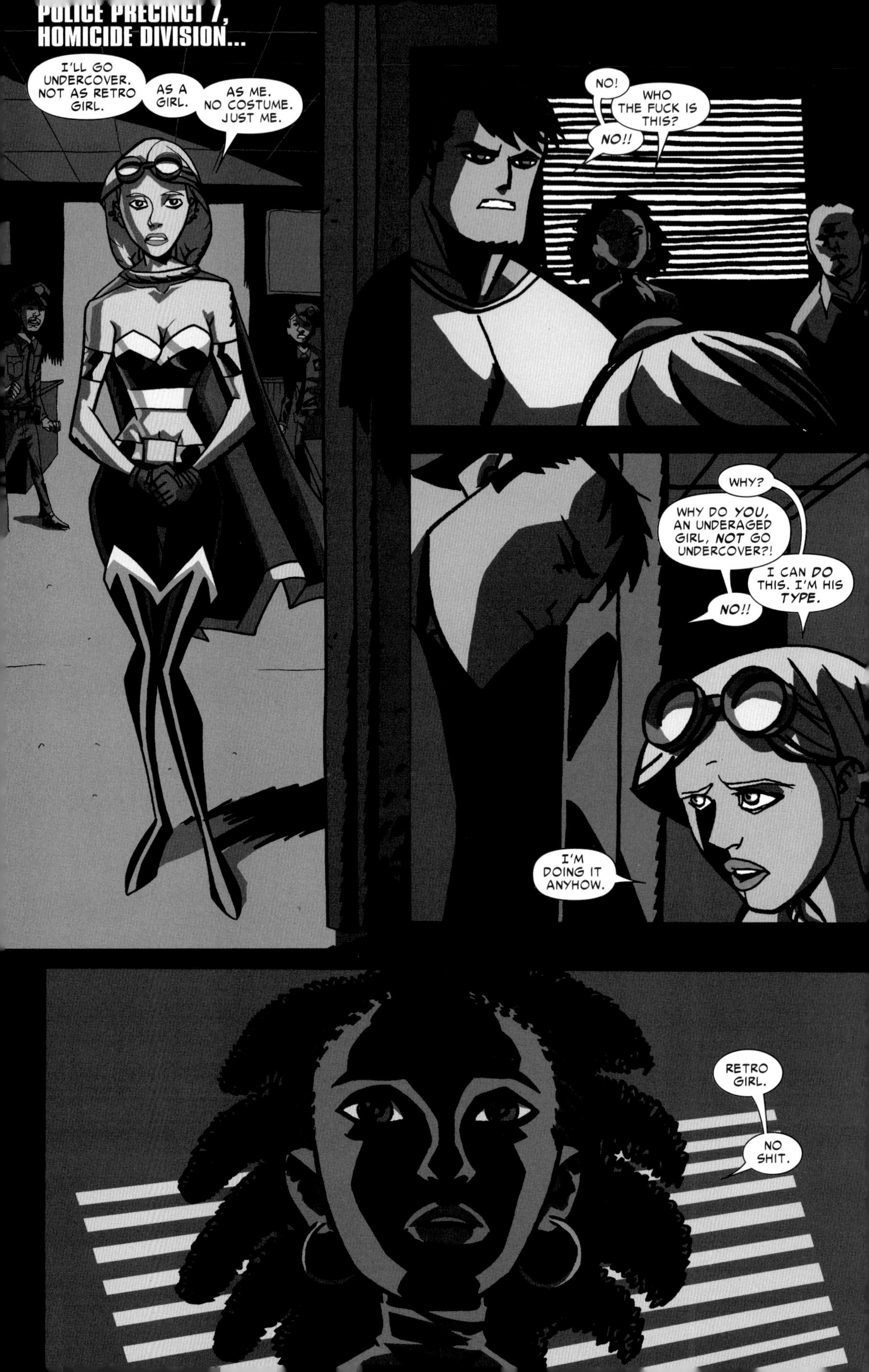
POLICE PRECINCT 7, HOMICIDE DIVISION...
I'LL GO UNDERCOVER. NOT AS RETRO GIRL.
AS A GIRL.
AS ME. NO COSTUME. JUST ME.
NO!
WHO THE FUCK IS THIS?
NO!!
WHY?
WHY DO YOU, AN UNDERAGED GIRL, NOT GO UNDERCOVER?!
NO!!
I CAN DO THIS. I'M HIS TYPE.
I'M DOING IT ANYHOW.
RETRO GIRL.
NO SHIT.

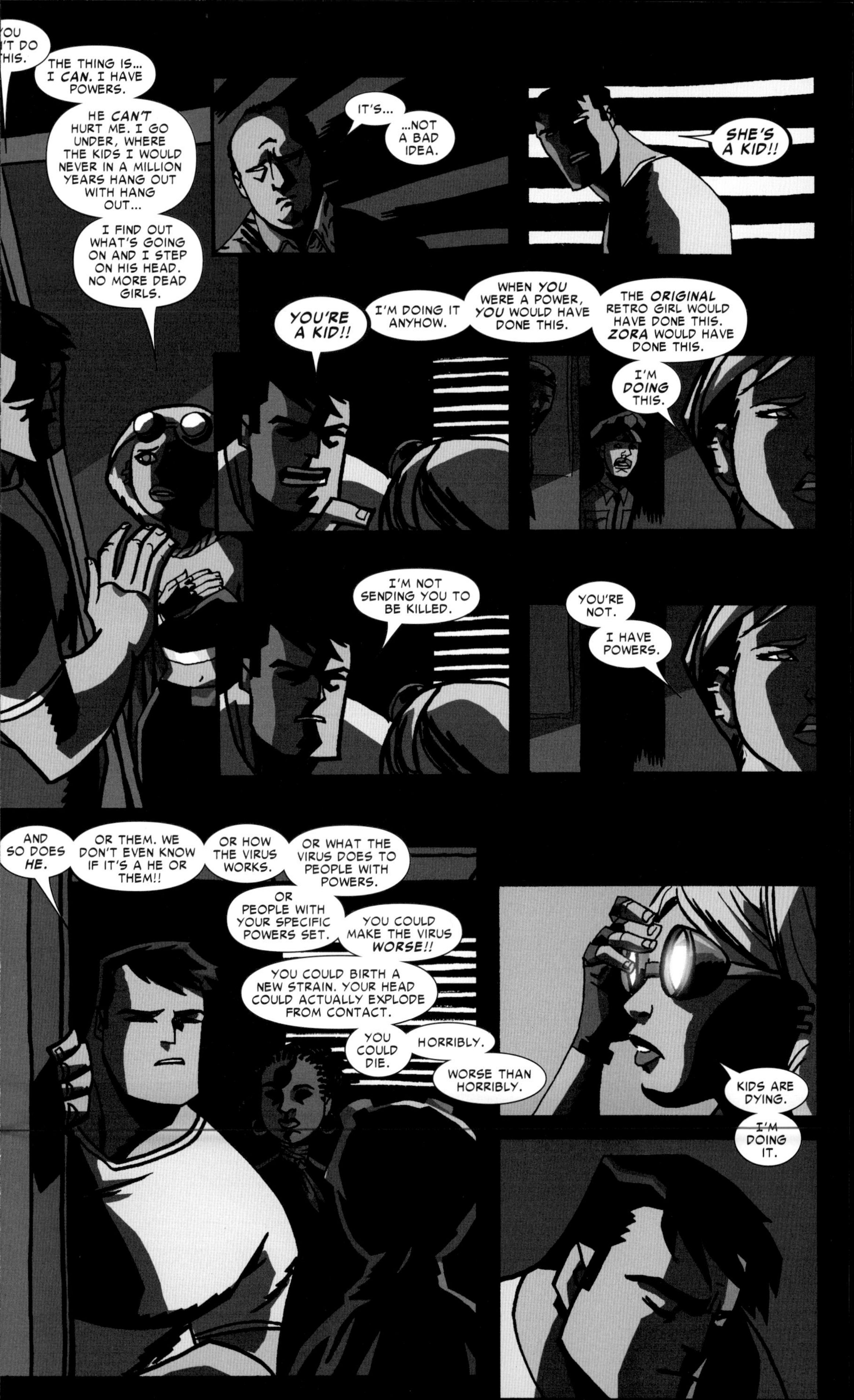

YOU 'T DO THIS.
THE THING IS... I CAN. I HAVE POWERS.
HE CAN'T HURT ME. I GO UNDER, WHERE THE KIDS I WOULD NEVER IN A MILLION YEARS HANG OUT WITH HANG OUT...
I FIND OUT WHAT'S GOING ON AND I STEP ON HIS HEAD. NO MORE DEAD GIRLS.
IT'S...
...NOT A BAD IDEA.
SHE'S A KID!!
YOU'RE A KID!!
I'M DOING IT ANYHOW.
WHEN YOU WERE A POWER, YOU WOULD HAVE DONE THIS.
THE ORIGINAL RETRO GIRL WOULD HAVE DONE THIS. ZORA WOULD HAVE DONE THIS.
I'M DOING THIS.
I'M NOT SENDING YOU TO BE KILLED.
YOU'RE NOT.
I HAVE POWERS.
AND SO DOES HE.
OR THEM. WE DON'T EVEN KNOW IF IT'S A HE OR THEM!!
OR HOW THE VIRUS WORKS.
OR WHAT THE VIRUS DOES TO PEOPLE WITH POWERS.
OR PEOPLE WITH YOUR SPECIFIC POWERS SET.
YOU COULD MAKE THE VIRUS WORSE!!
YOU COULD BIRTH A NEW STRAIN. YOUR HEAD COULD ACTUALLY EXPLODE FROM CONTACT.
YOU COULD DIE.
HORRIBLY.
WORSE THAN HORRIBLY.
KIDS ARE DYING.
I'M DOING IT.

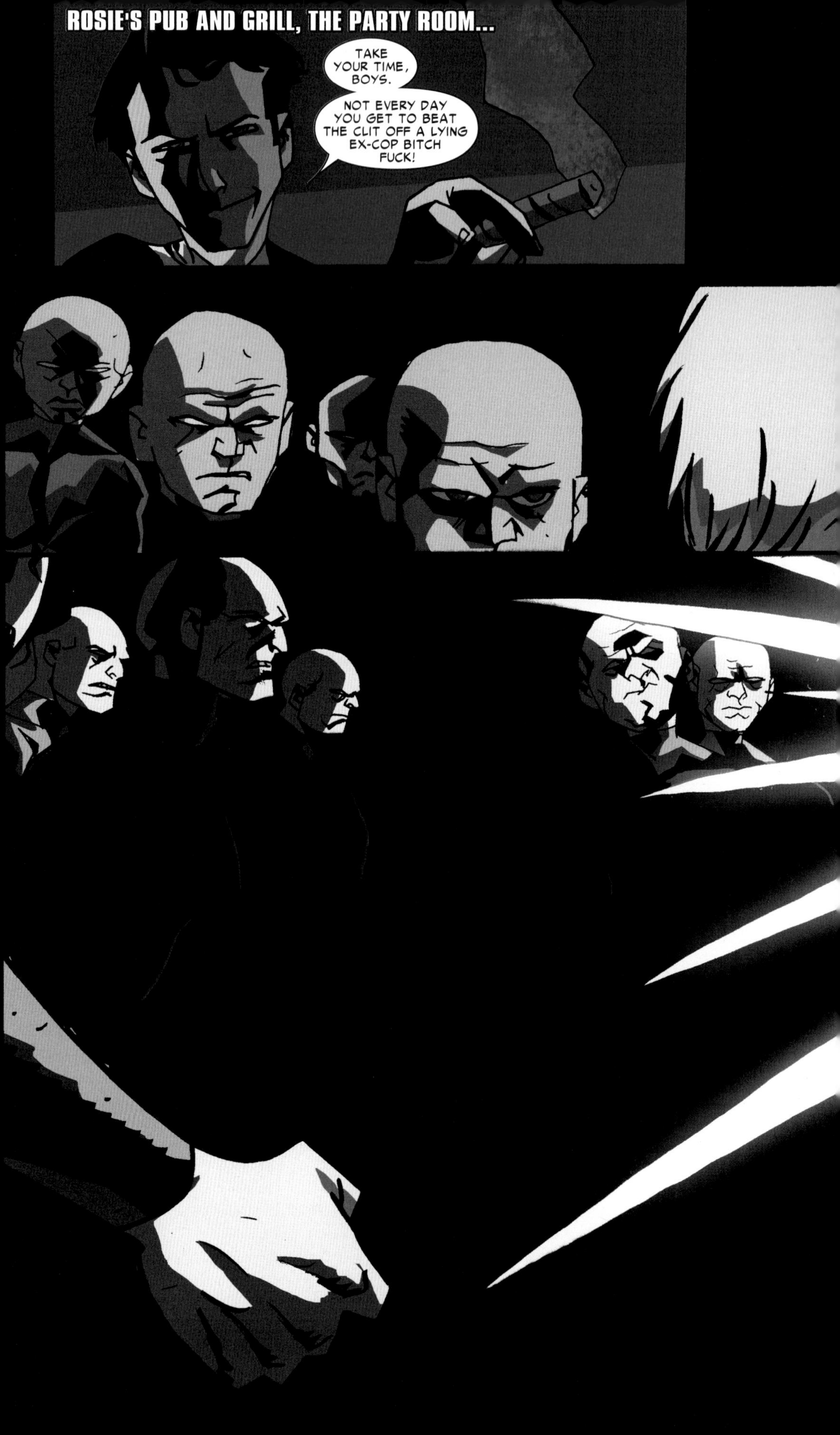
ROSIE'S PUB AND GRILL, THE PARTY ROOM...
TAKE YOUR TIME, BOYS.
NOT EVERY DAY YOU GET TO BEAT THE CLIT OFF A LYING EX-COP BITCH FUCK!

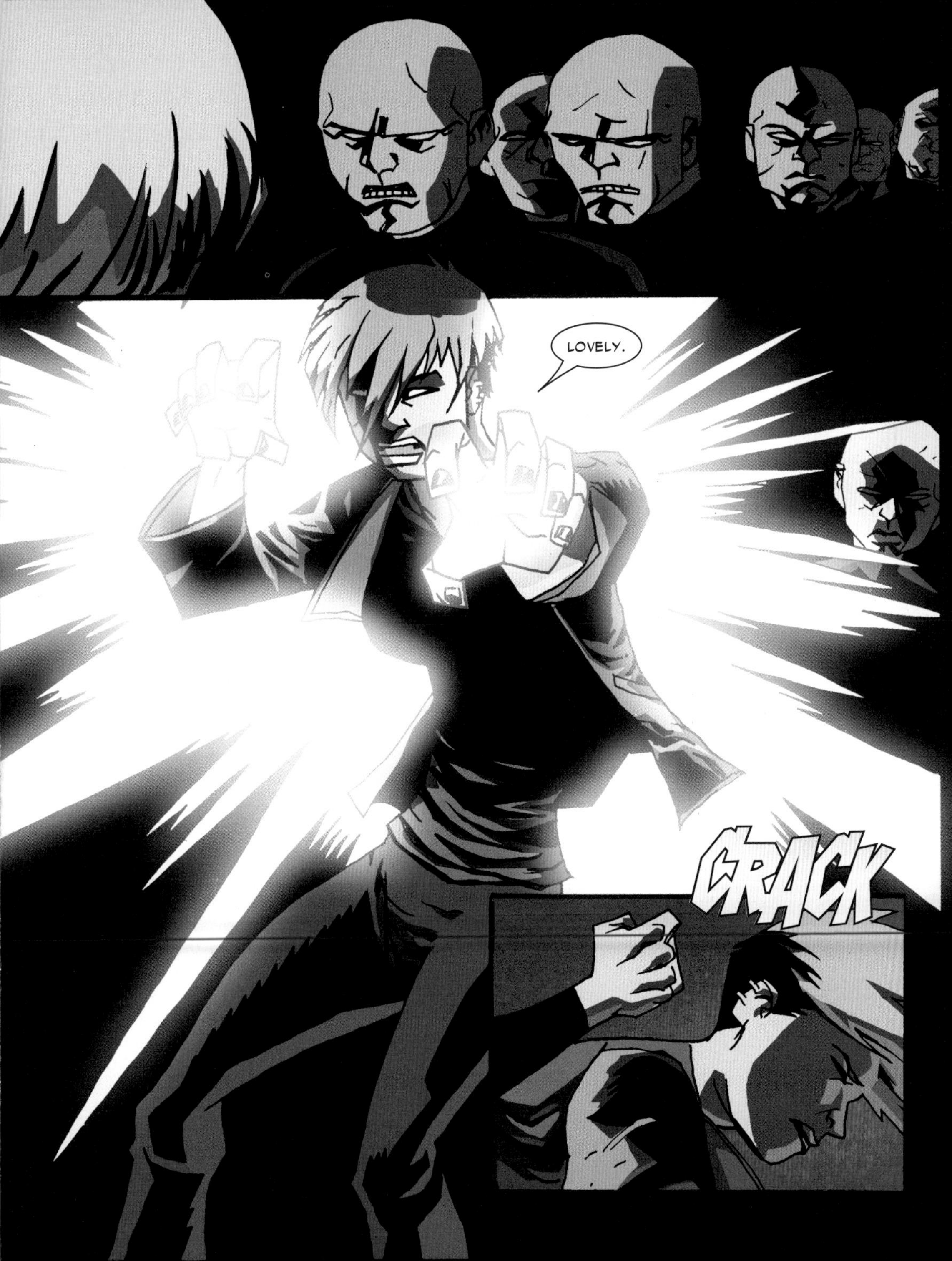
LOVELY.
CRACK

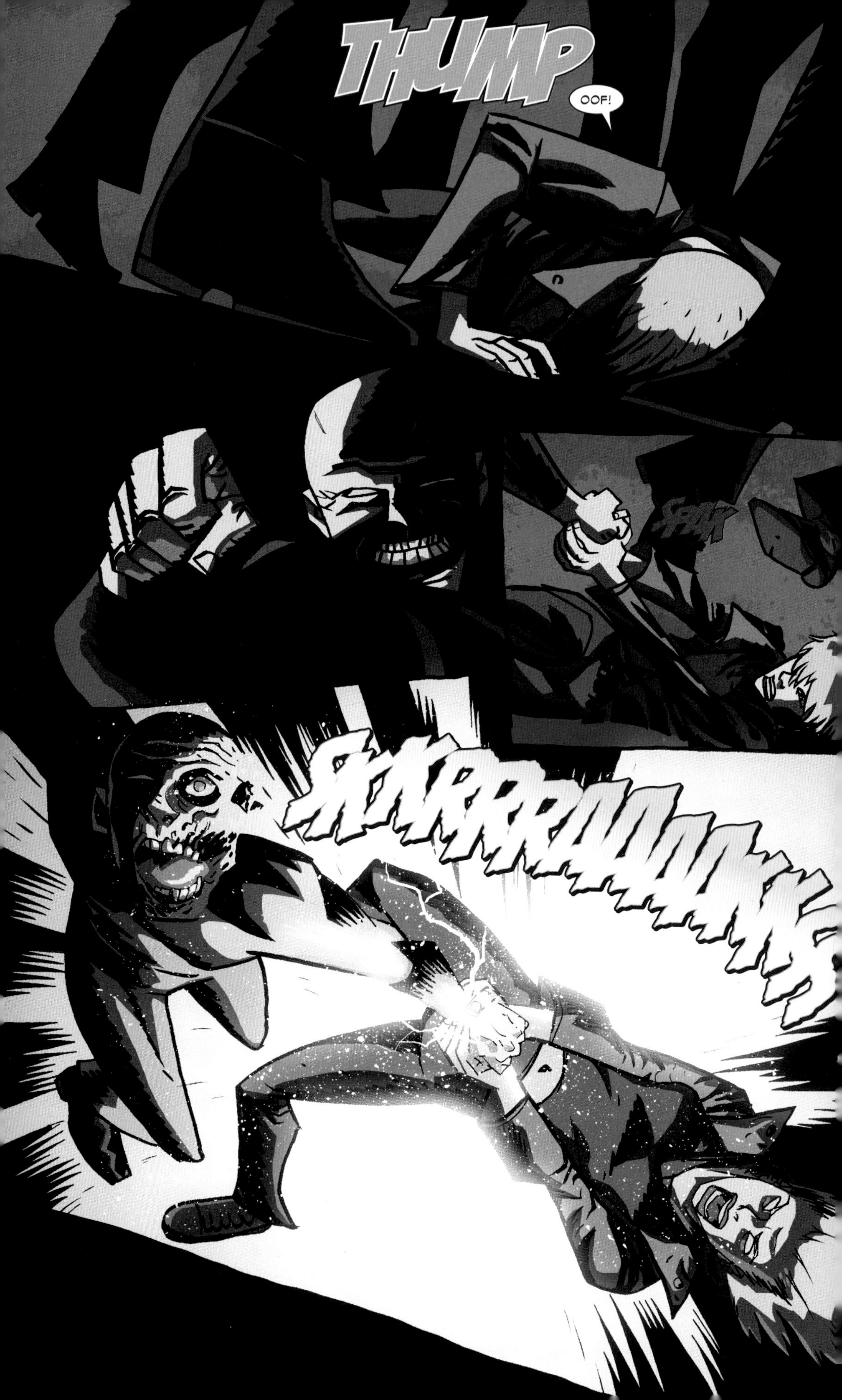
THUMP
OOF!
SPAK

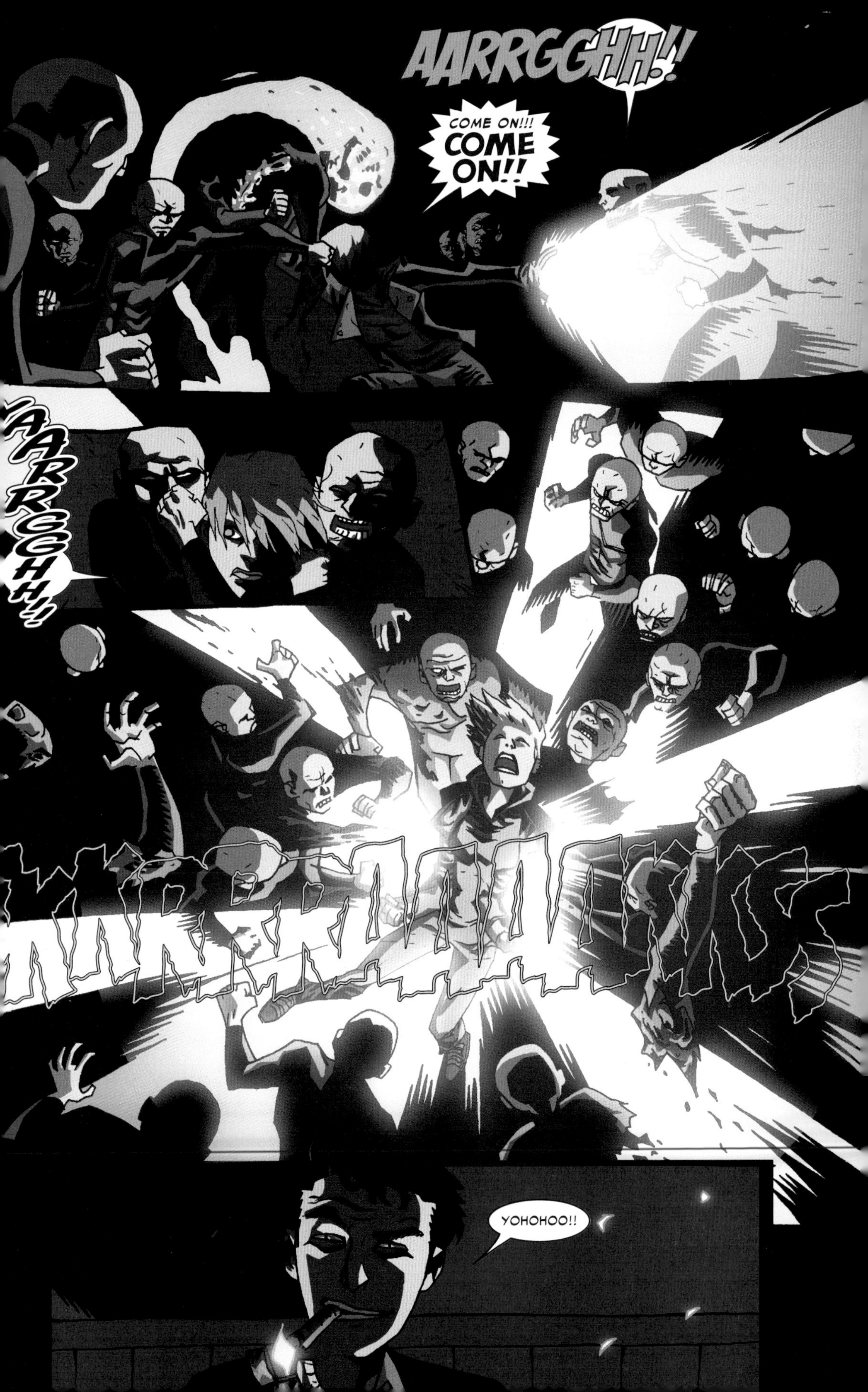
AARRGGHH!!
COME ON!!! COME ON!!
AARRGGHH!!
YOHOHOO!!

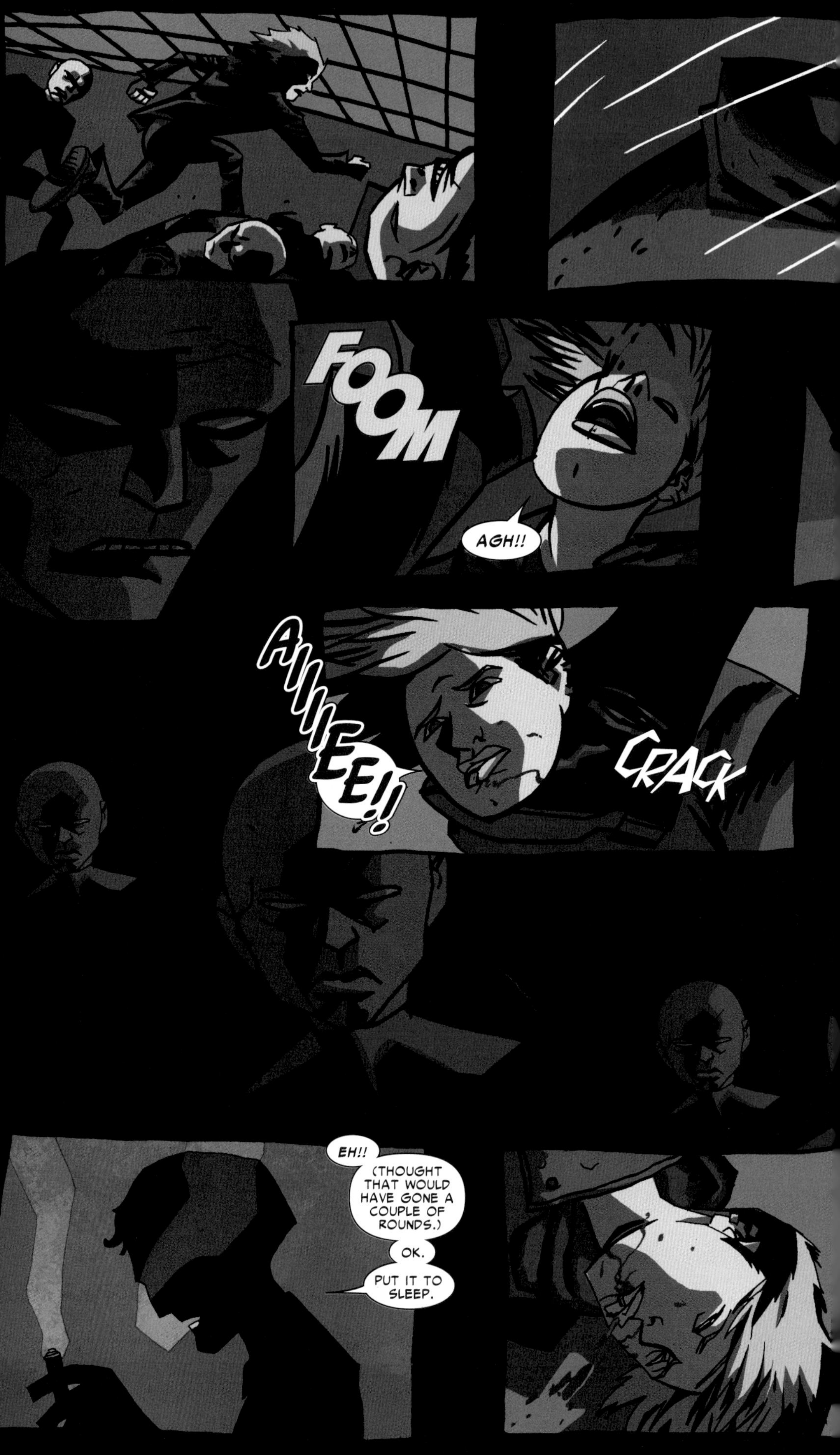
FOOM
AGH!!
AIIIEEE!!
CRACK
EH!!
(THOUGHT THAT WOULD HAVE GONE A COUPLE OF ROUNDS.)
OK.
PUT IT TO SLEEP.

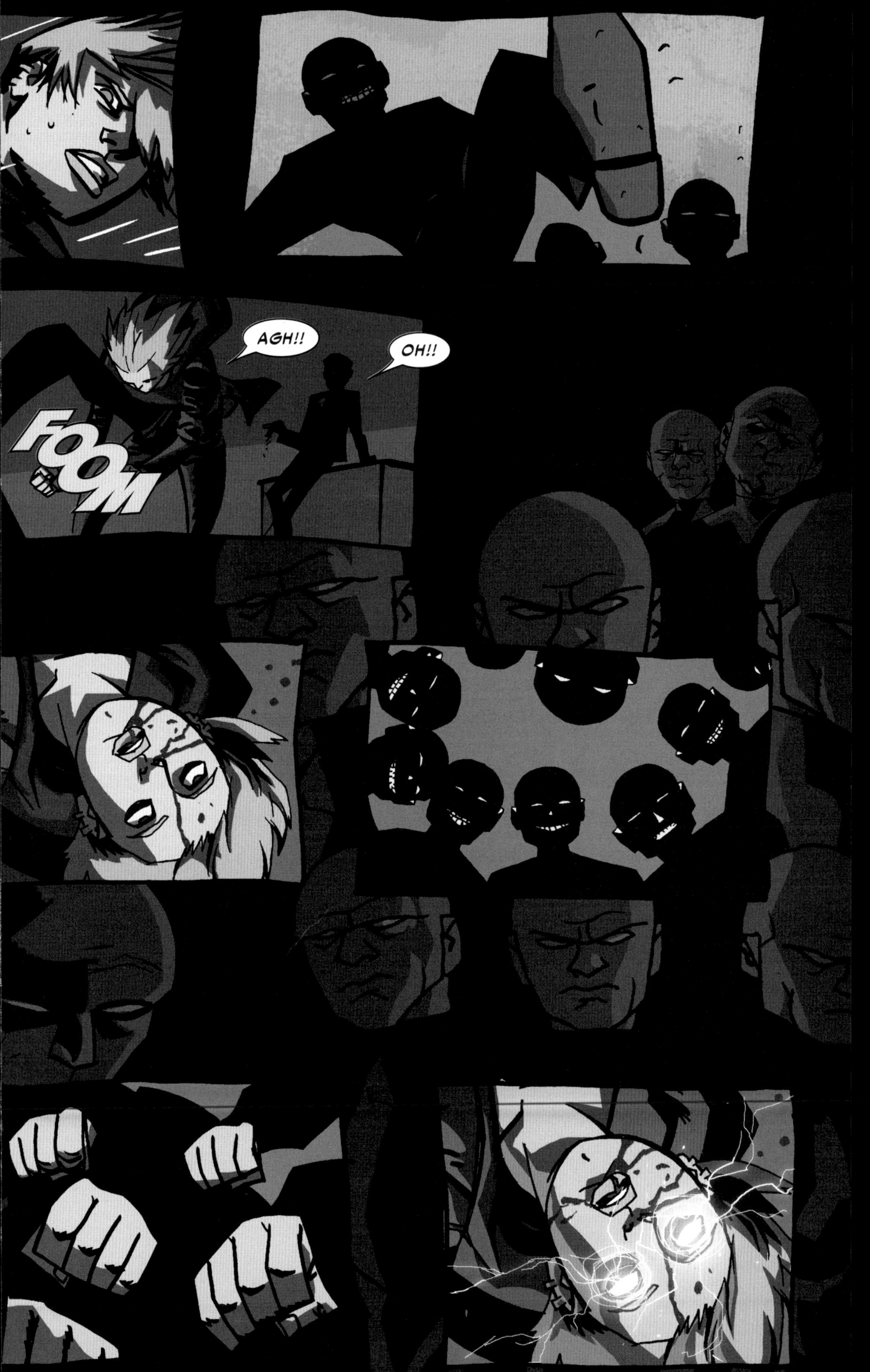
AGH!!
OH!!
FOOM

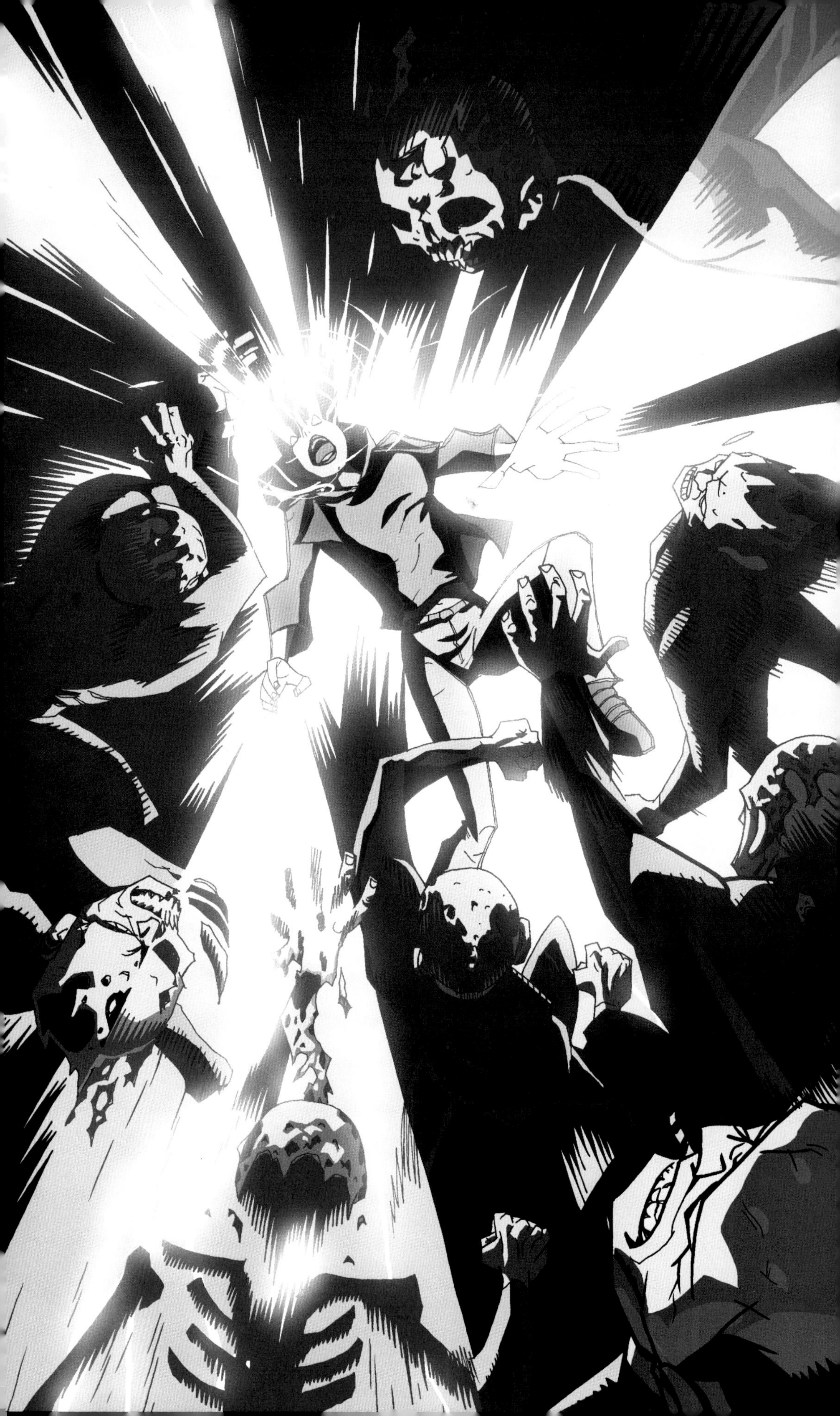

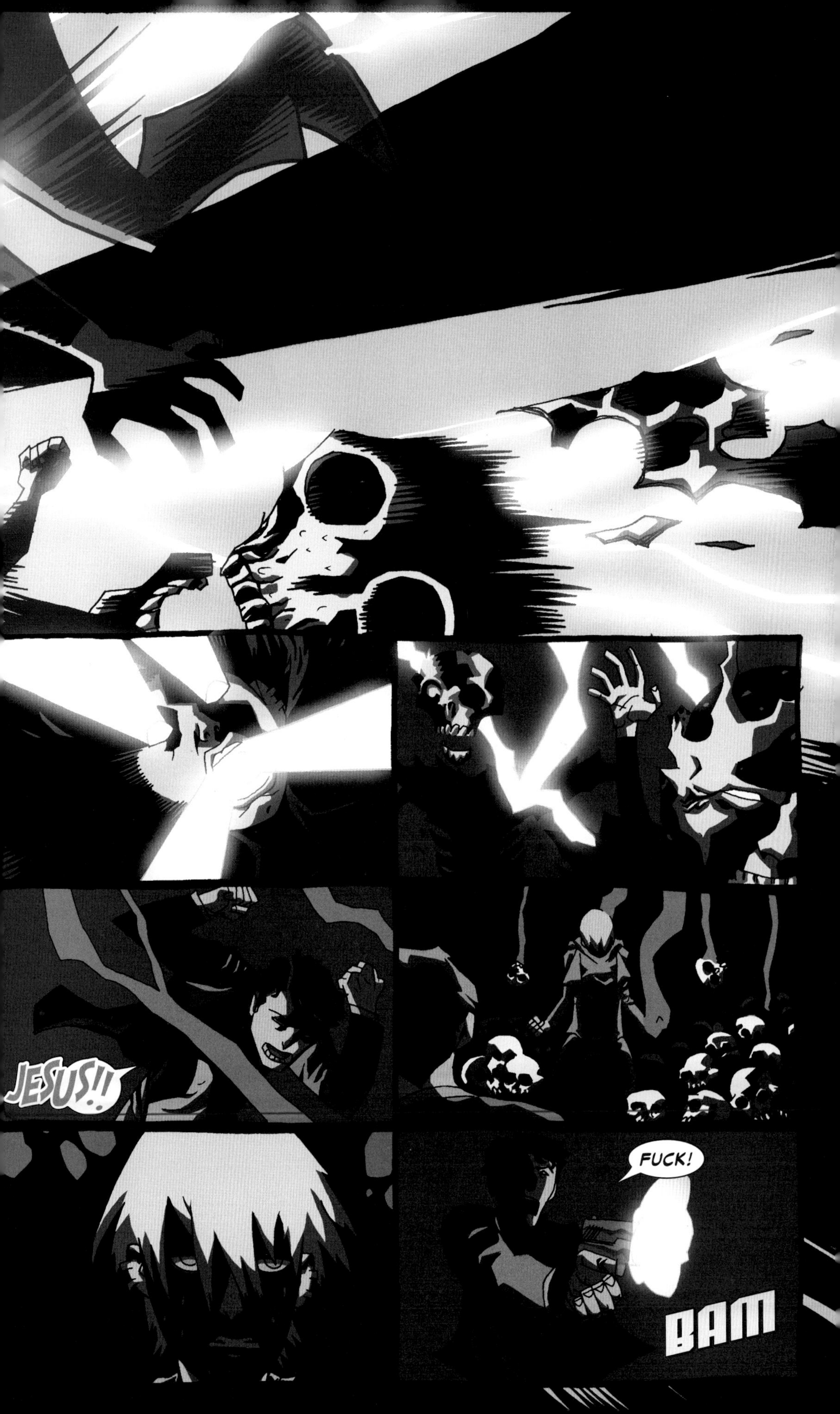
JESUS!!
FUCK!
BAM

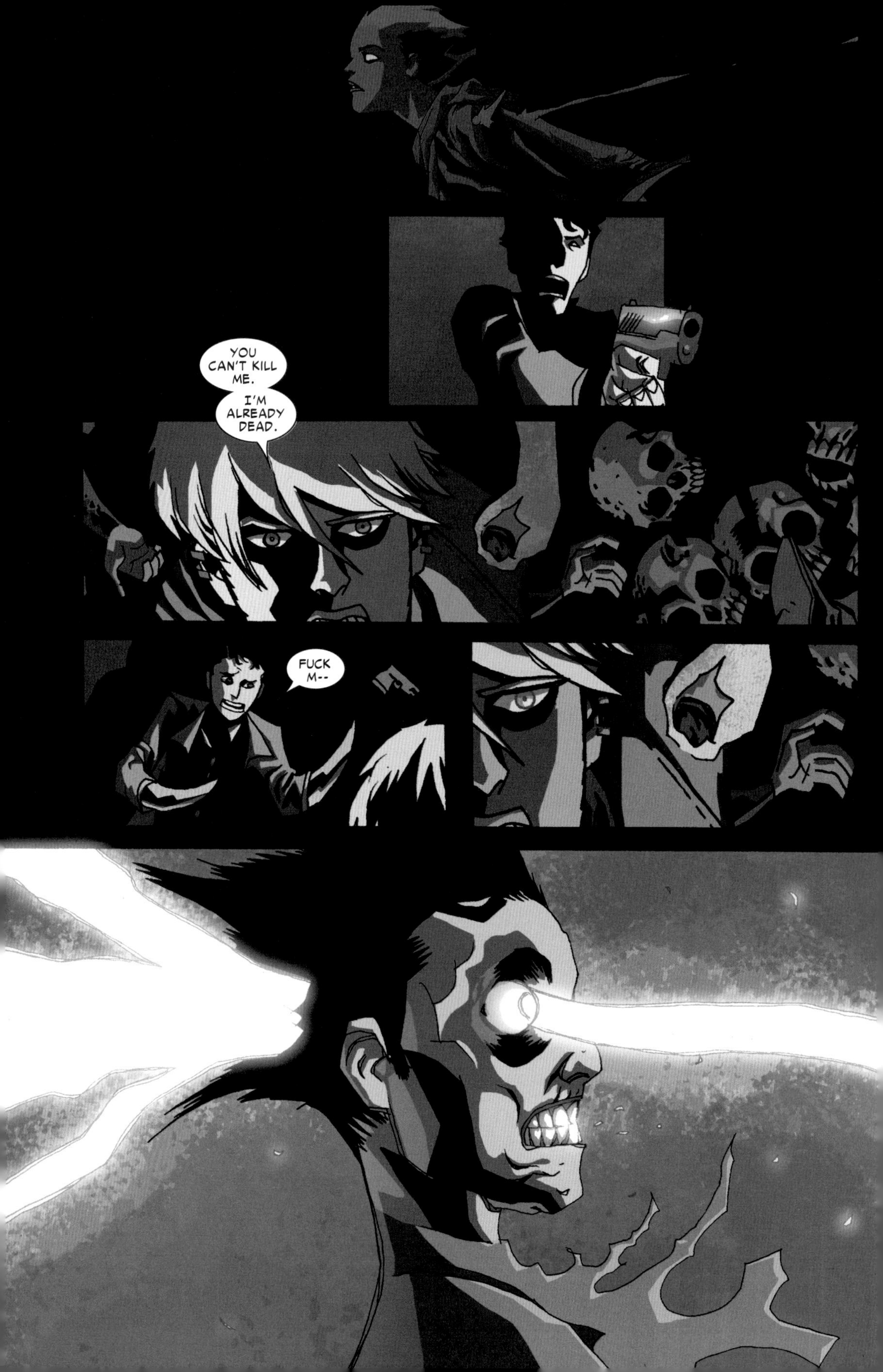

YOU CAN'T KILL ME.
I'M ALREADY DEAD.
FUCK M--

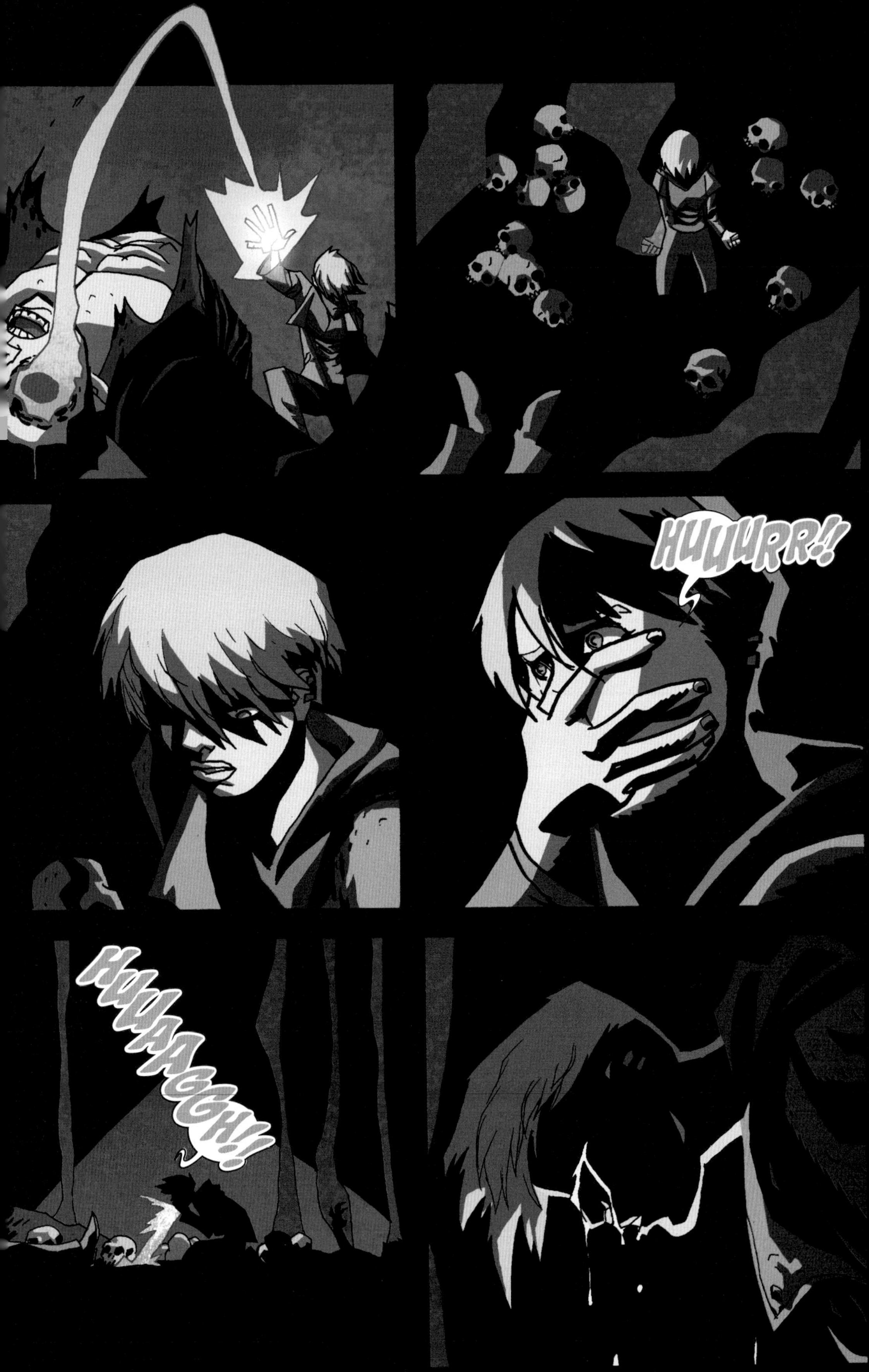
HUUURR!!
HUUAAGGH!!

POLICE VAN, CORNER OF SIMONSON AND WARE...

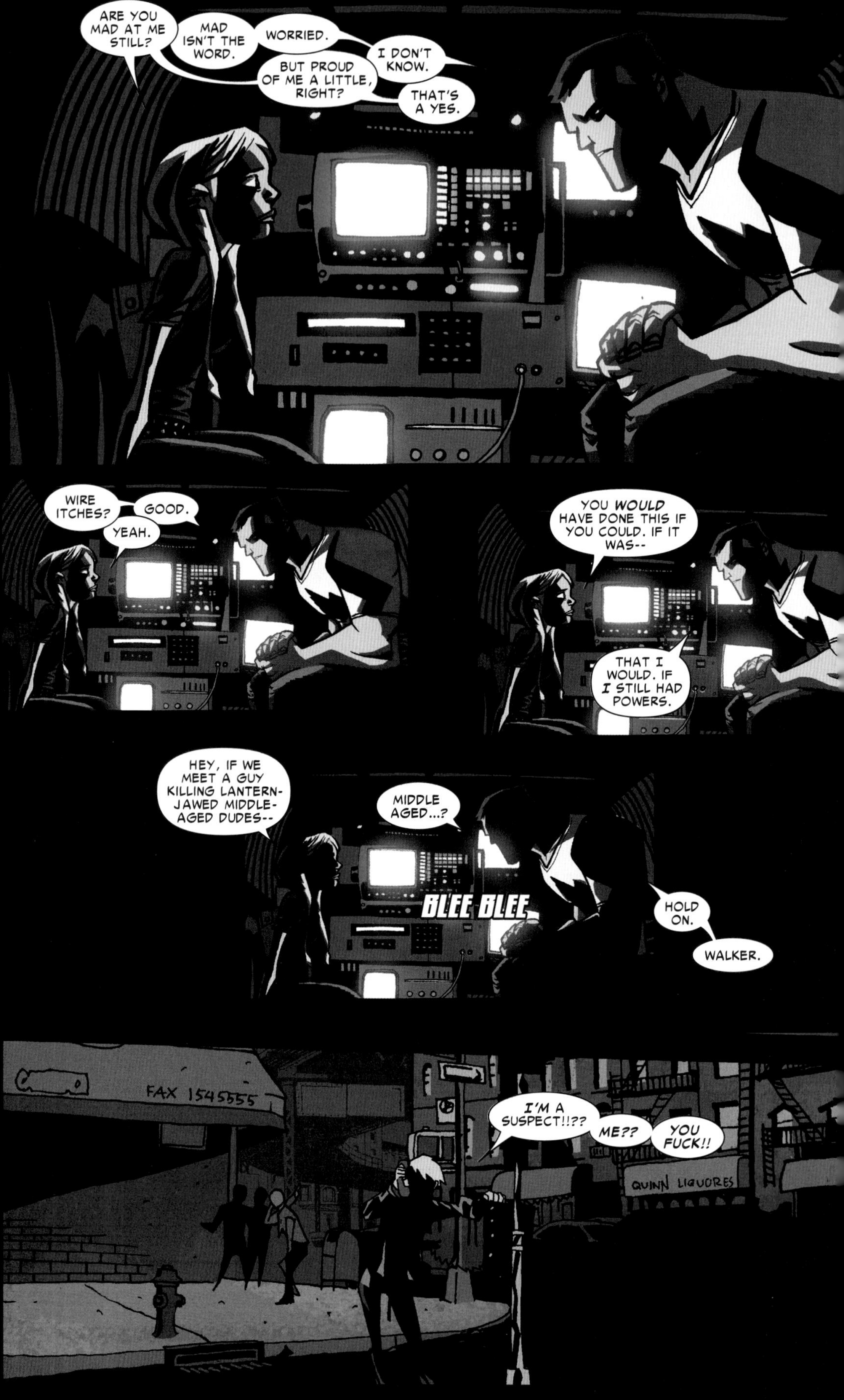
ARE YOU MAD AT ME STILL?
MAD ISN'T THE WORD.
WORRIED.
I DON'T KNOW.
BUT PROUD OF ME A LITTLE, RIGHT?
THAT'S A YES.
WIRE ITCHES?
GOOD.
YEAH.
YOU WOULD HAVE DONE THIS IF YOU COULD. IF IT WAS--
THAT I WOULD. IF I STILL HAD POWERS.
HEY, IF WE MEET A GUY KILLING LANTERN-JAWED MIDDLE-AGED DUDES--
MIDDLE AGED...?
BLEE BLEE
HOLD ON.
WALKER.
FAX 1545555
I'M A SUSPECT!!??
ME??
YOU FUCK!!
QUINN LIQUORES

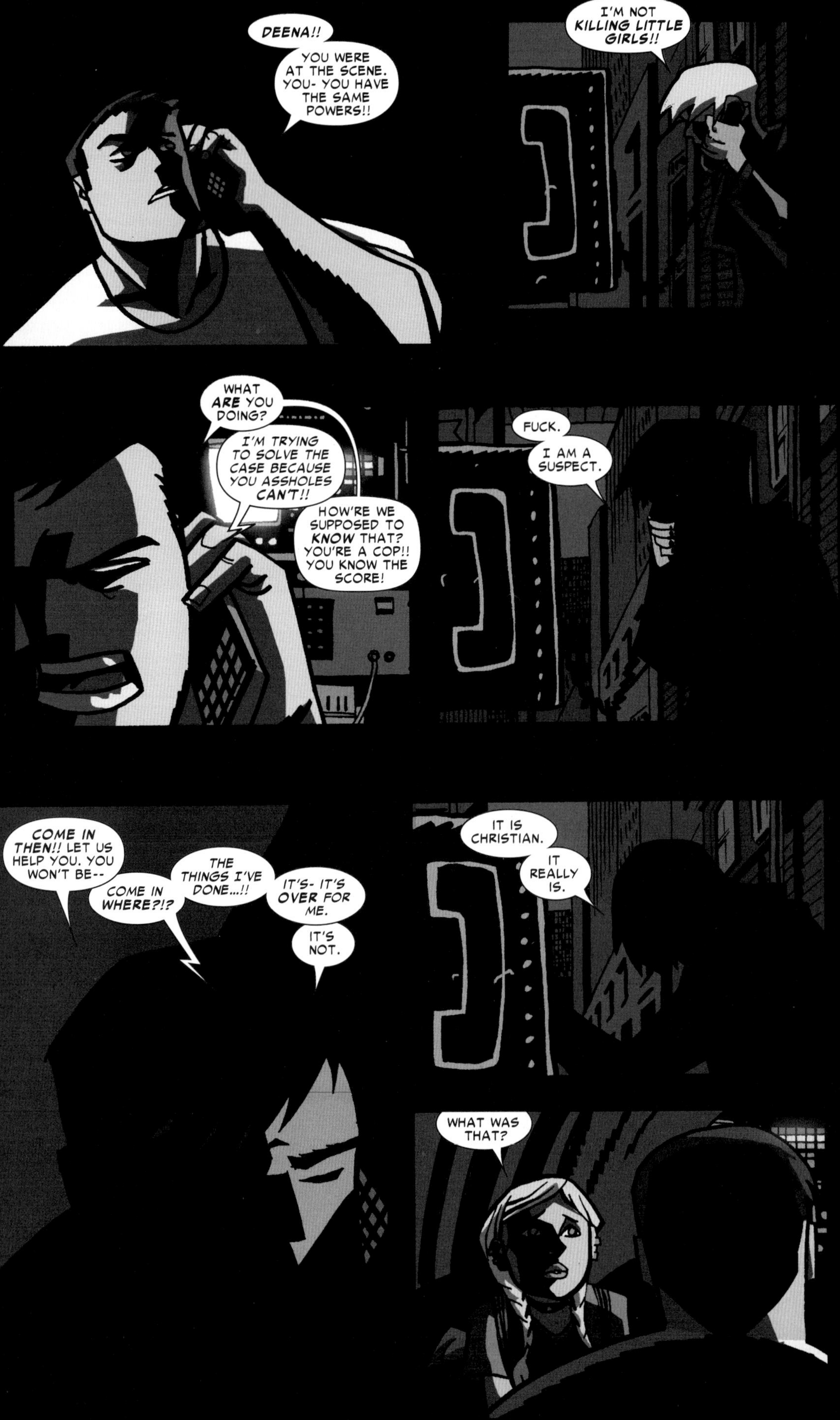
DEENA!!
YOU WERE AT THE SCENE. YOU- YOU HAVE THE SAME POWERS!!
I'M NOT KILLING LITTLE GIRLS!!
WHAT ARE YOU DOING?
I'M TRYING TO SOLVE THE CASE BECAUSE YOU ASSHOLES CAN'T!!
HOW'RE WE SUPPOSED TO KNOW THAT? YOU'RE A COP!! YOU KNOW THE SCORE!
FUCK.
I AM A SUSPECT.
COME IN THEN!! LET US HELP YOU. YOU WON'T BE--
COME IN WHERE?!?
THE THINGS I'VE DONE...!!
IT'S- IT'S OVER FOR ME.
IT'S NOT.
IT IS CHRISTIAN.
IT REALLY IS.
WHAT WAS THAT?

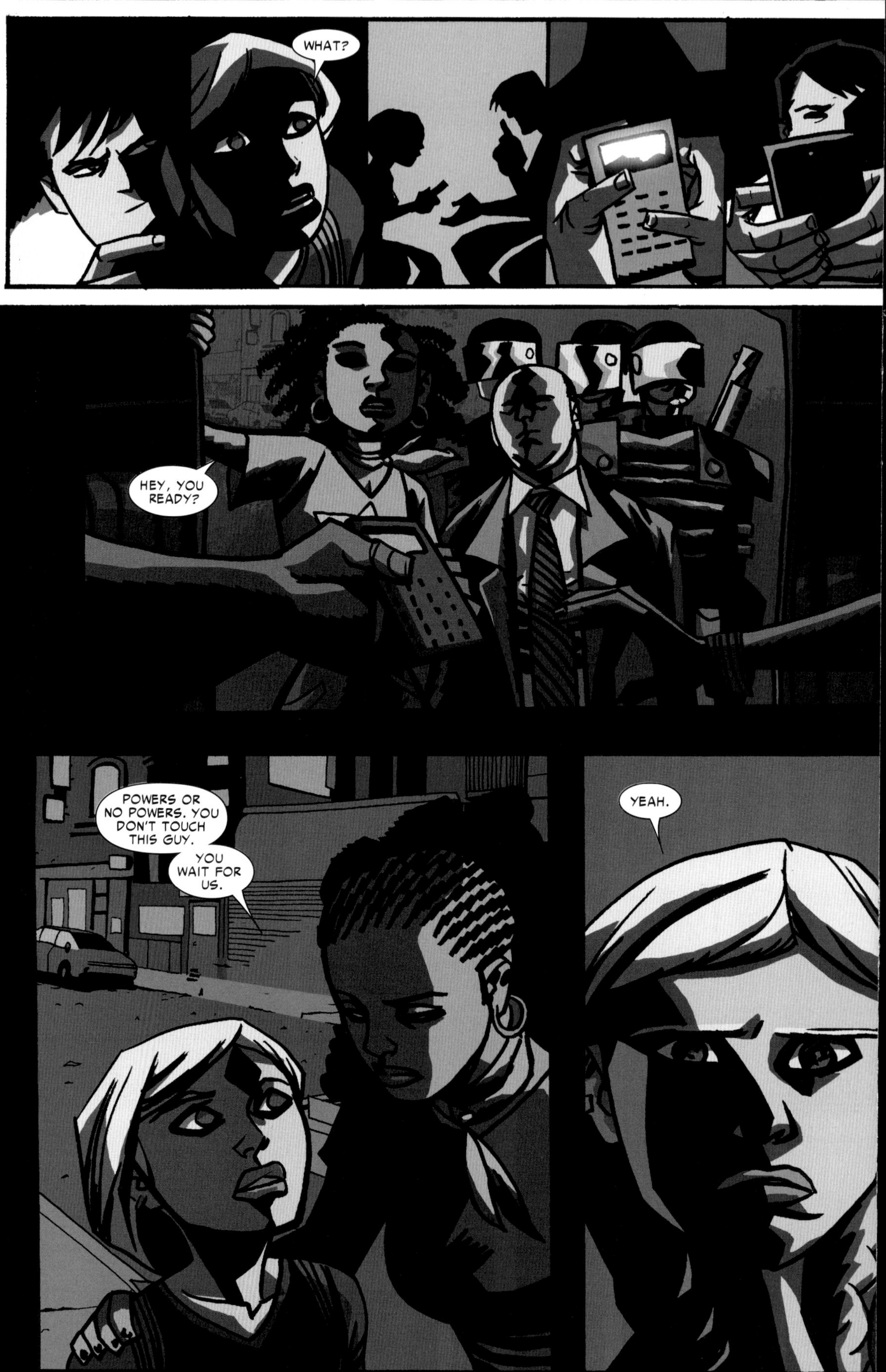
WHAT?
HEY, YOU READY?
POWERS OR NO POWERS. YOU DON'T TOUCH THIS GUY.
YOU WAIT FOR US.
YEAH.

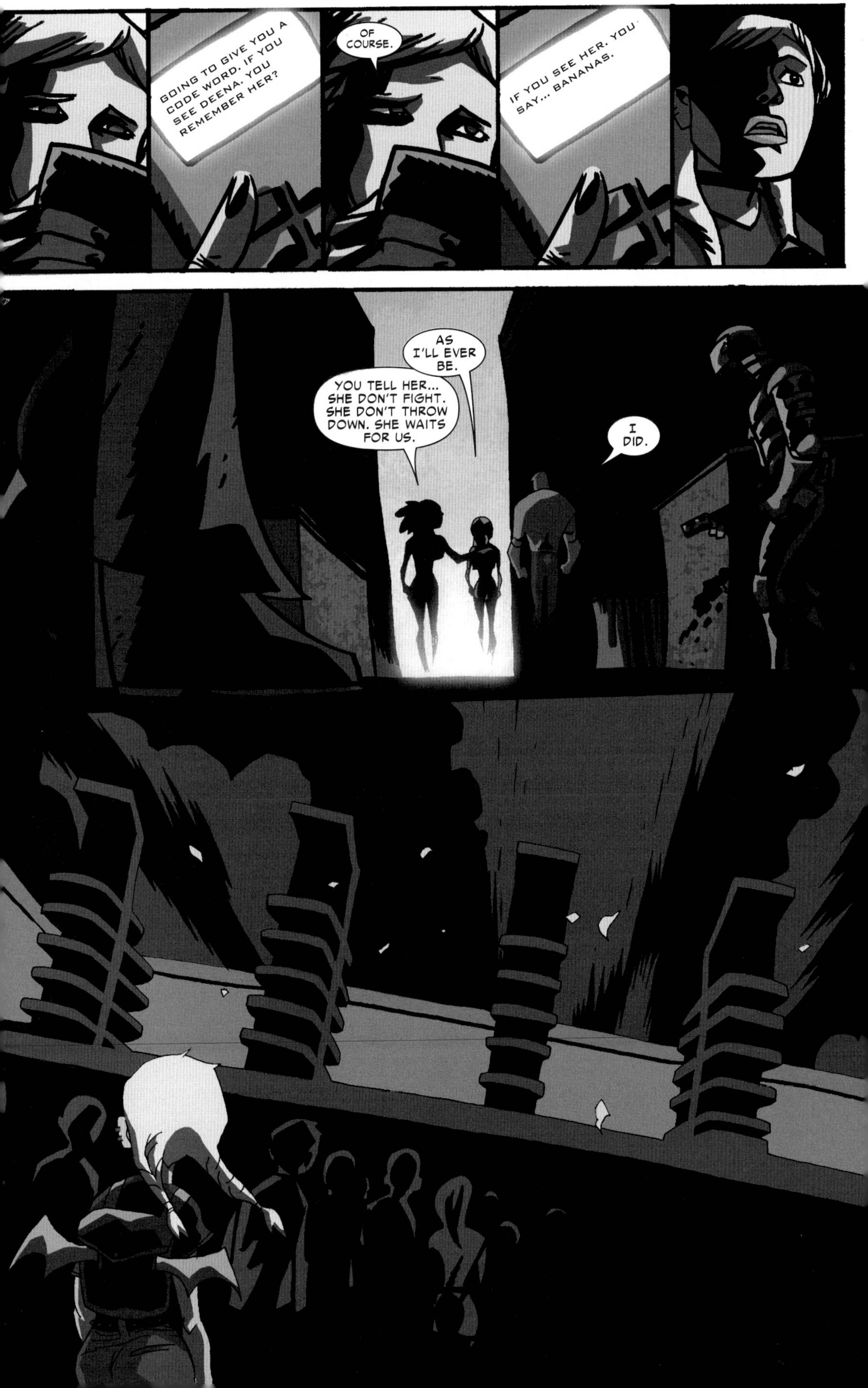
GOING TO GIVE YOU A CODE WORD. IF YOU SEE DEENA. YOU REMEMBER HER?
OF COURSE.
IF YOU SEE HER. YOU SAY... BANANAS.
YOU TELL HER... SHE DON'T FIGHT. SHE DON'T THROW DOWN. SHE WAITS FOR US.
AS I'LL EVER BE.
I DID.

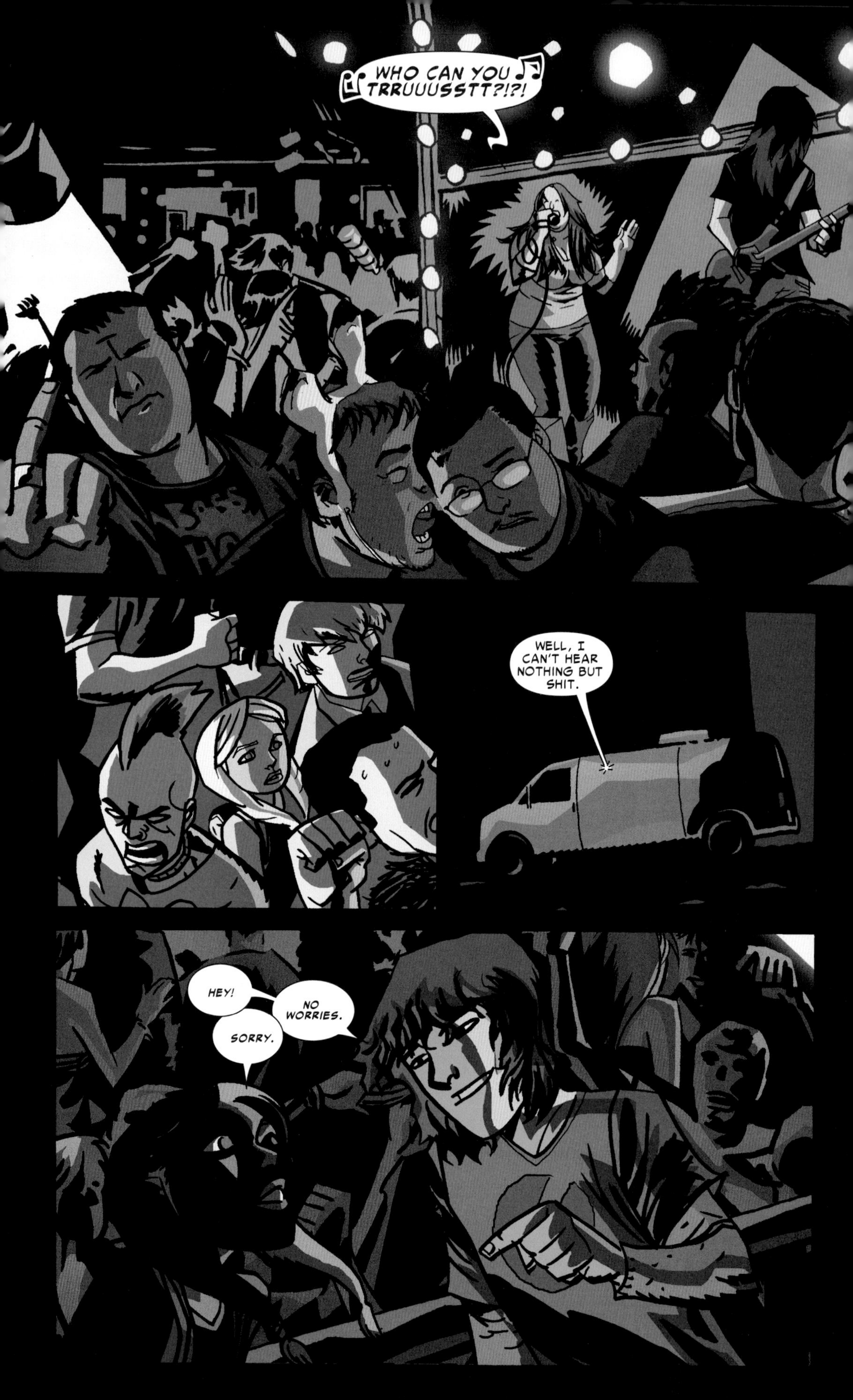
WHO CAN YOU TRRUUUSSTT?!?!
WELL, I CAN'T HEAR NOTHING BUT SHIT.
HEY!
SORRY.
NO WORRIES.

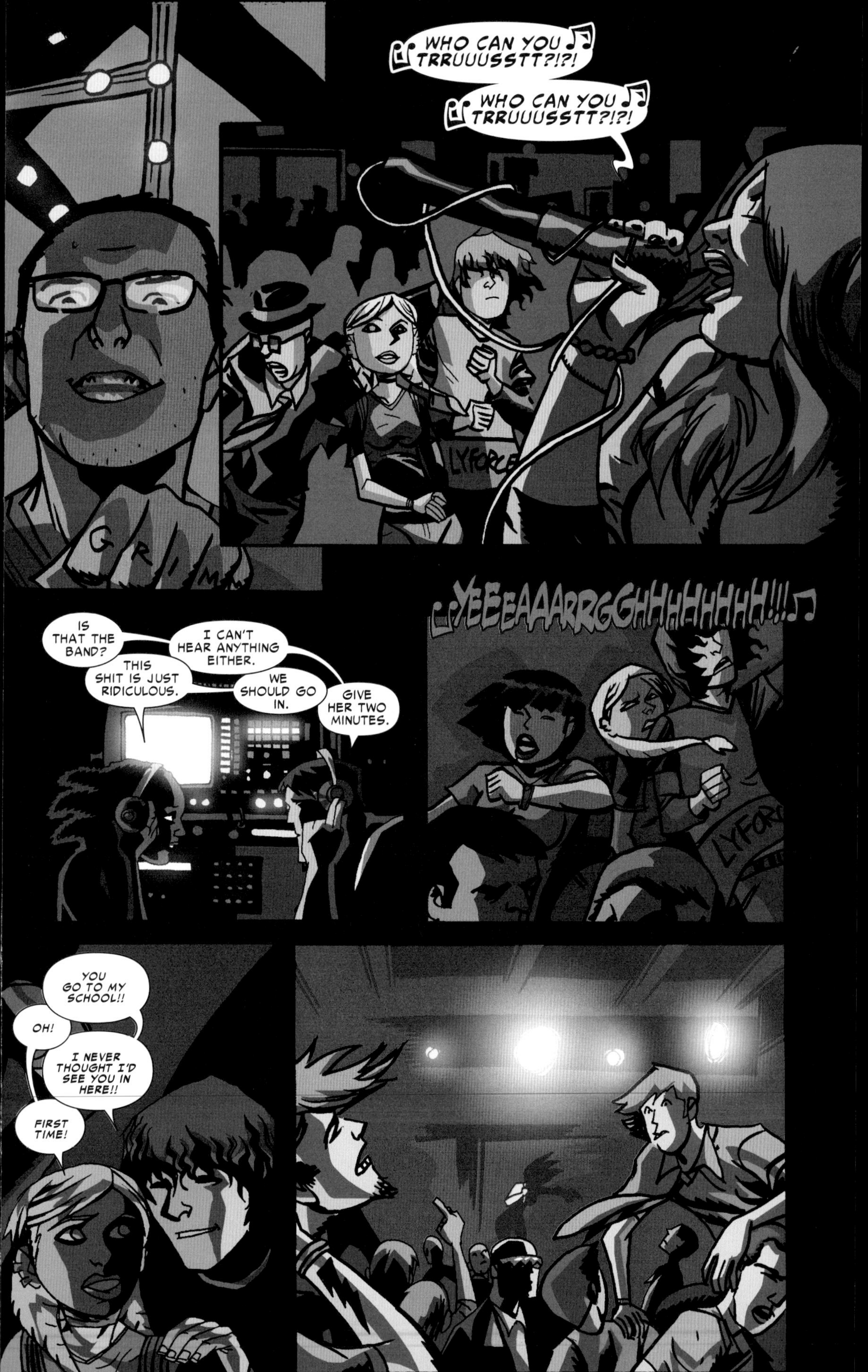

WHO CAN YOU TRRUUUSSTT?!?!
WHO CAN YOU TRRUUUSSTT?!?!
LYFORCE
GRIM
IS THAT THE BAND?
I CAN'T HEAR ANYTHING EITHER.
THIS SHIT IS JUST RIDICULOUS.
WE SHOULD GO IN.
GIVE HER TWO MINUTES.
YEEEAAARRGGHHHHHHH!!!
LYFORCE
YOU GO TO MY SCHOOL!!
OH!
I NEVER THOUGHT I'D SEE YOU IN HERE!!
FIRST TIME!

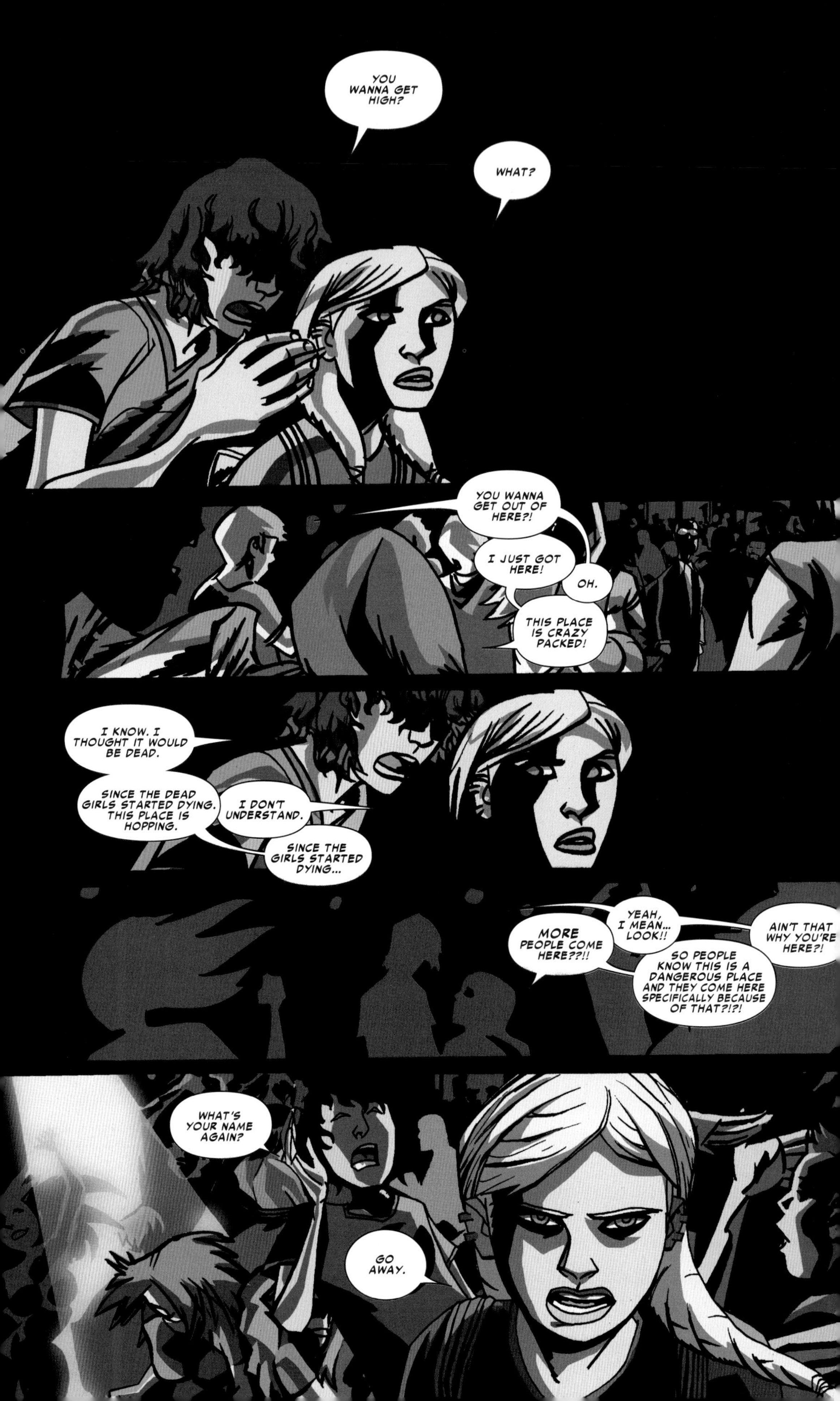
YOU WANNA GET HIGH?
WHAT?
YOU WANNA GET OUT OF HERE?!
I JUST GOT HERE!
OH.
THIS PLACE IS CRAZY PACKED!
I KNOW. I THOUGHT IT WOULD BE DEAD.
SINCE THE DEAD GIRLS STARTED DYING. THIS PLACE IS HOPPING.
I DON'T UNDERSTAND.
SINCE THE GIRLS STARTED DYING...
MORE PEOPLE COME HERE??!!
YEAH, I MEAN... LOOK!!
AIN'T THAT WHY YOU'RE HERE?!
SO PEOPLE KNOW THIS IS A DANGEROUS PLACE AND THEY COME HERE SPECIFICALLY BECAUSE OF THAT?!?!
WHAT'S YOUR NAME AGAIN?
GO AWAY.

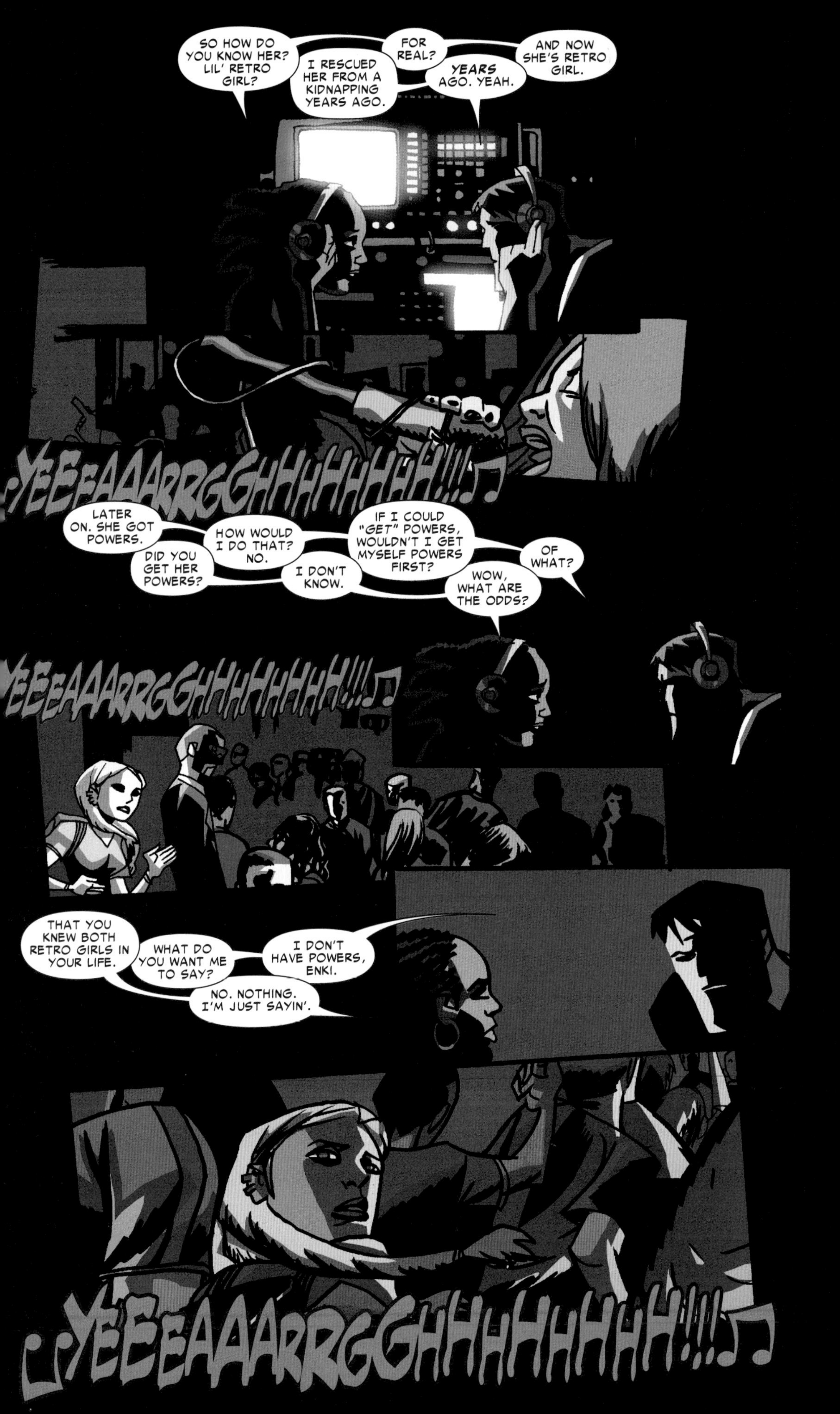

SO HOW DO YOU KNOW HER? LIL' RETRO GIRL?
I RESCUED HER FROM A KIDNAPPING YEARS AGO.
FOR REAL?
YEARS AGO. YEAH.
AND NOW SHE'S RETRO GIRL.
YEEEAAARRGGHHHHHHHH!!!
LATER ON. SHE GOT POWERS.
DID YOU GET HER POWERS?
HOW WOULD I DO THAT? NO.
I DON'T KNOW.
IF I COULD "*GET*" POWERS, WOULDN'T I GET MYSELF POWERS FIRST?
OF WHAT?
WOW, WHAT ARE THE ODDS?
YEEEAAARRGGHHHHHHHH!!!
THAT YOU KNEW BOTH RETRO GIRLS IN YOUR LIFE.
WHAT DO YOU WANT ME TO SAY?
I DON'T HAVE POWERS, ENKI.
NO. NOTHING. I'M JUST SAYIN'.
YEEEAAARRGGHHHHHHHH!!!

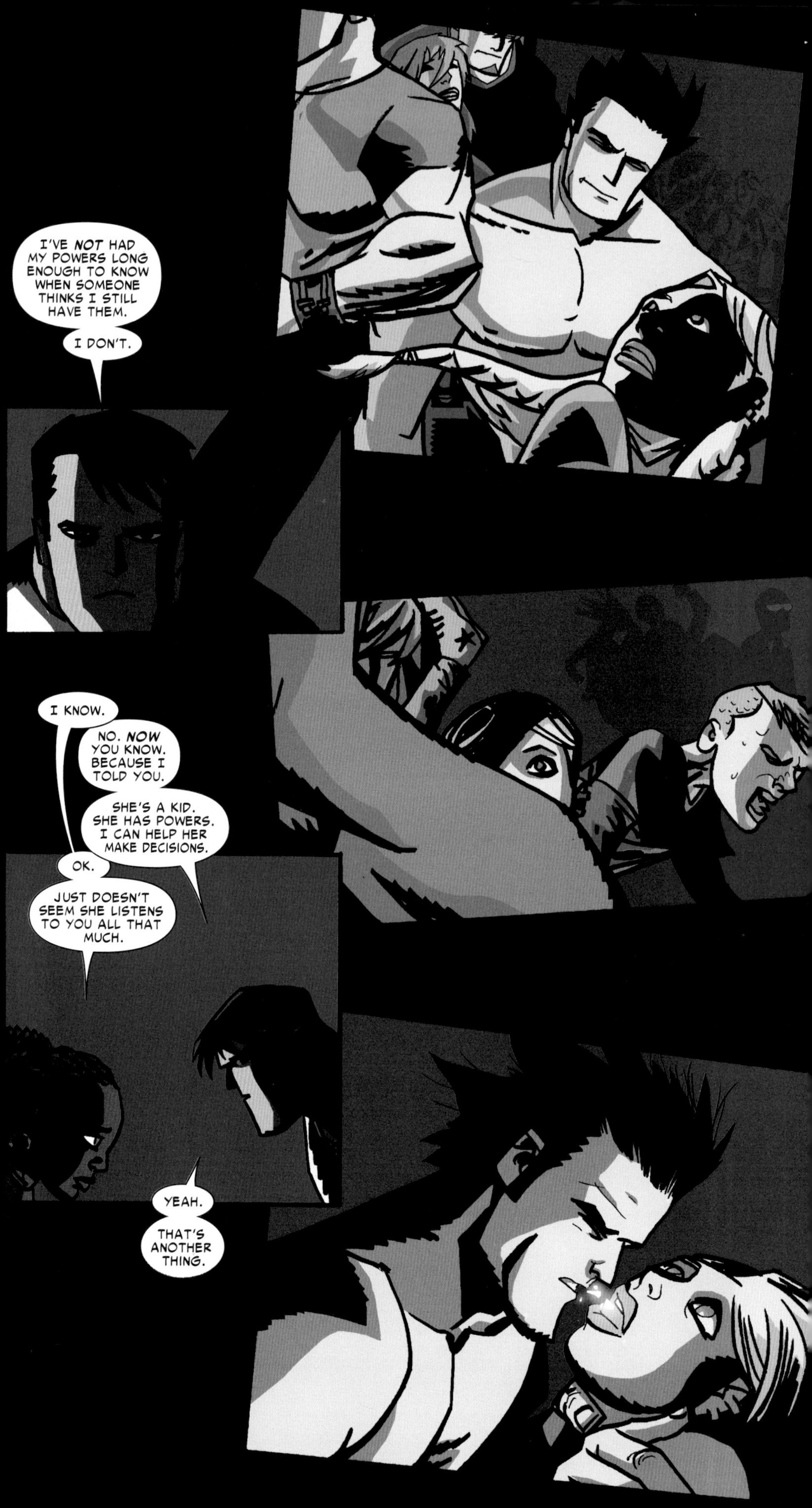
I'VE NOT HAD MY POWERS LONG ENOUGH TO KNOW WHEN SOMEONE THINKS I STILL HAVE THEM.
I DON'T.
I KNOW.
NO. NOW YOU KNOW. BECAUSE I TOLD YOU.
SHE'S A KID. SHE HAS POWERS. I CAN HELP HER MAKE DECISIONS.
OK.
JUST DOESN'T SEEM SHE LISTENS TO YOU ALL THAT MUCH.
YEAH.
THAT'S ANOTHER THING.

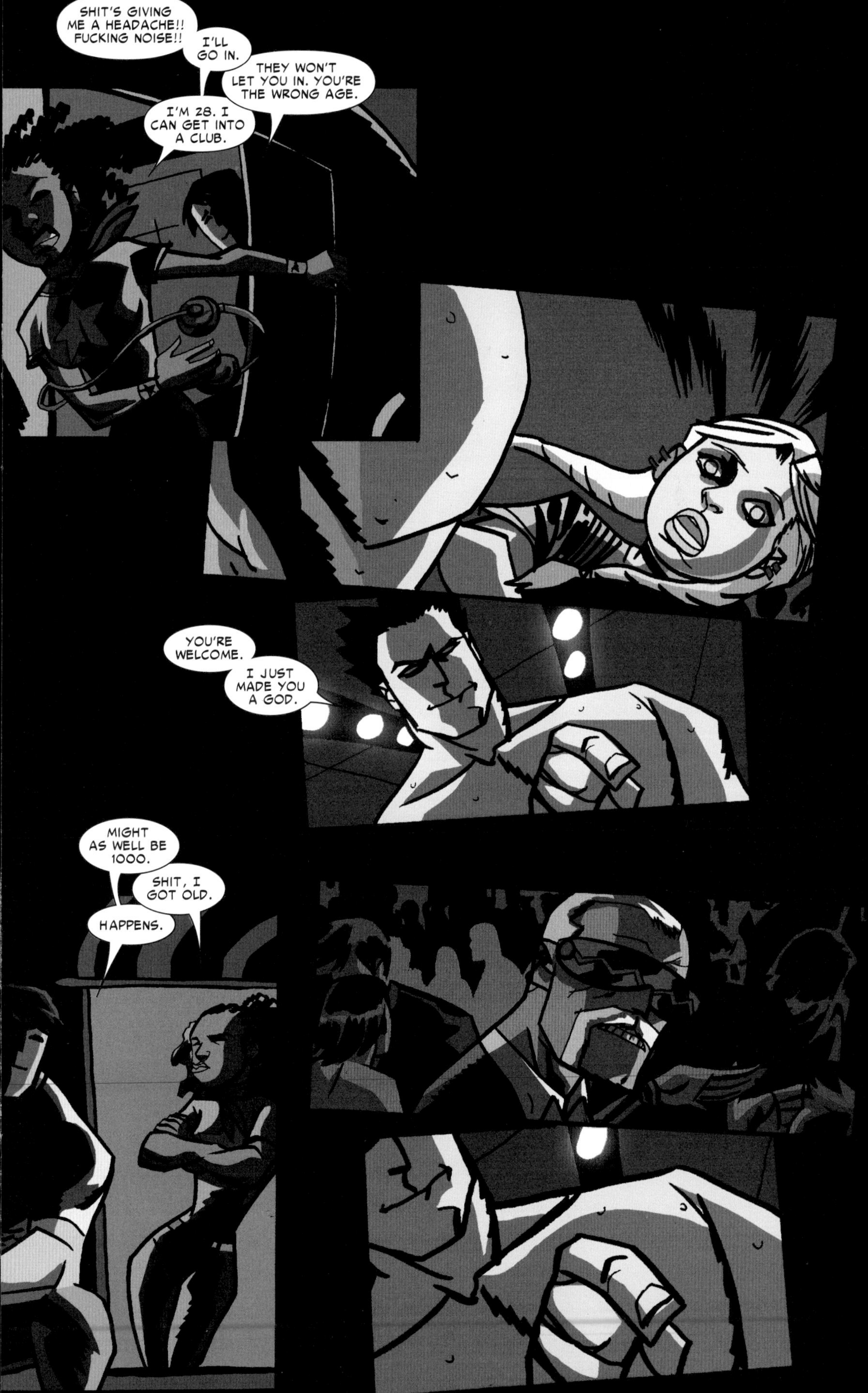
SHIT'S GIVING ME A HEADACHE!! FUCKING NOISE!!
I'LL GO IN.
THEY WON'T LET YOU IN. YOU'RE THE WRONG AGE.
I'M 28. I CAN GET INTO A CLUB.
YOU'RE WELCOME.
I JUST MADE YOU A GOD.
MIGHT AS WELL BE 1000.
SHIT, I GOT OLD.
HAPPENS.

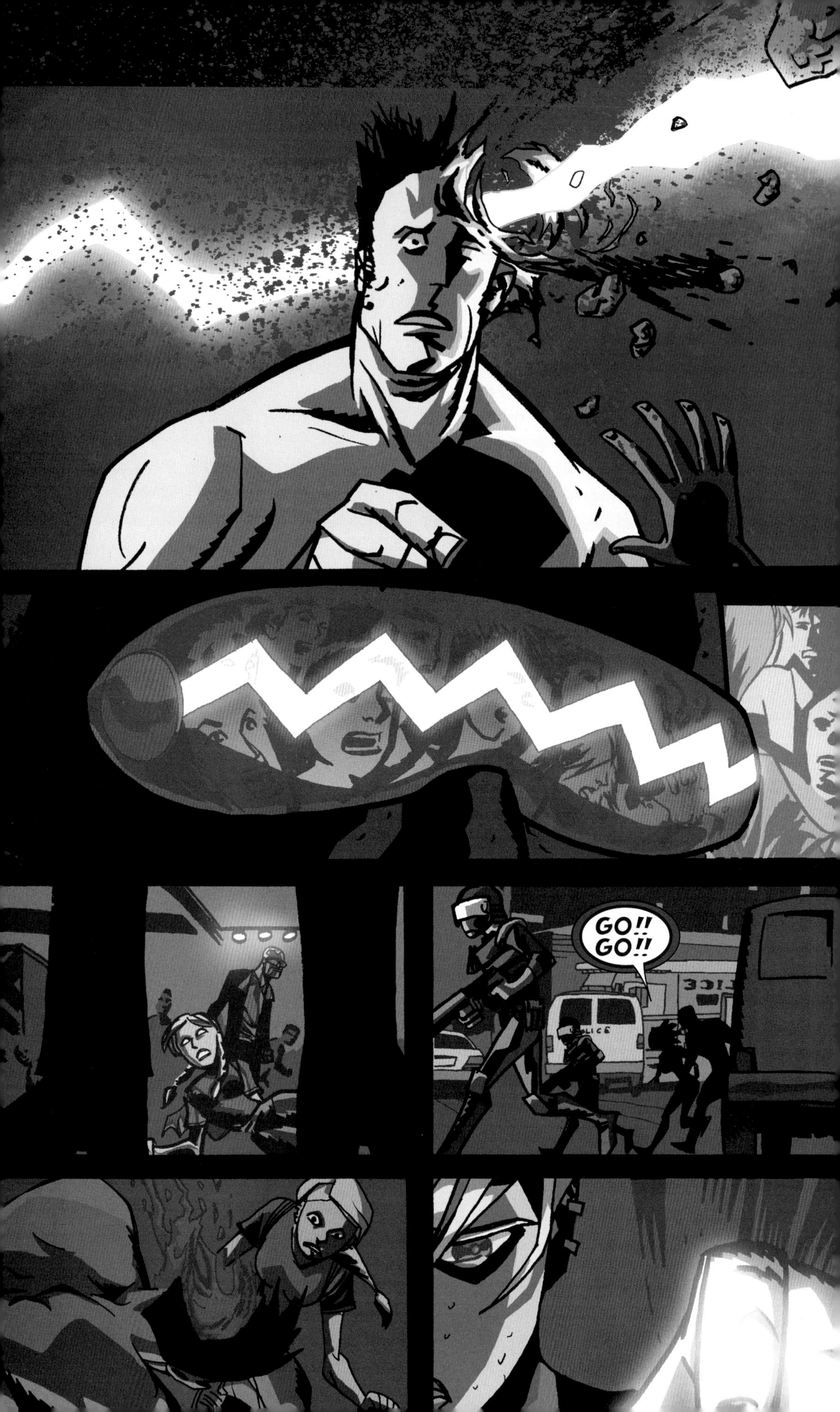
GO!! GO!!

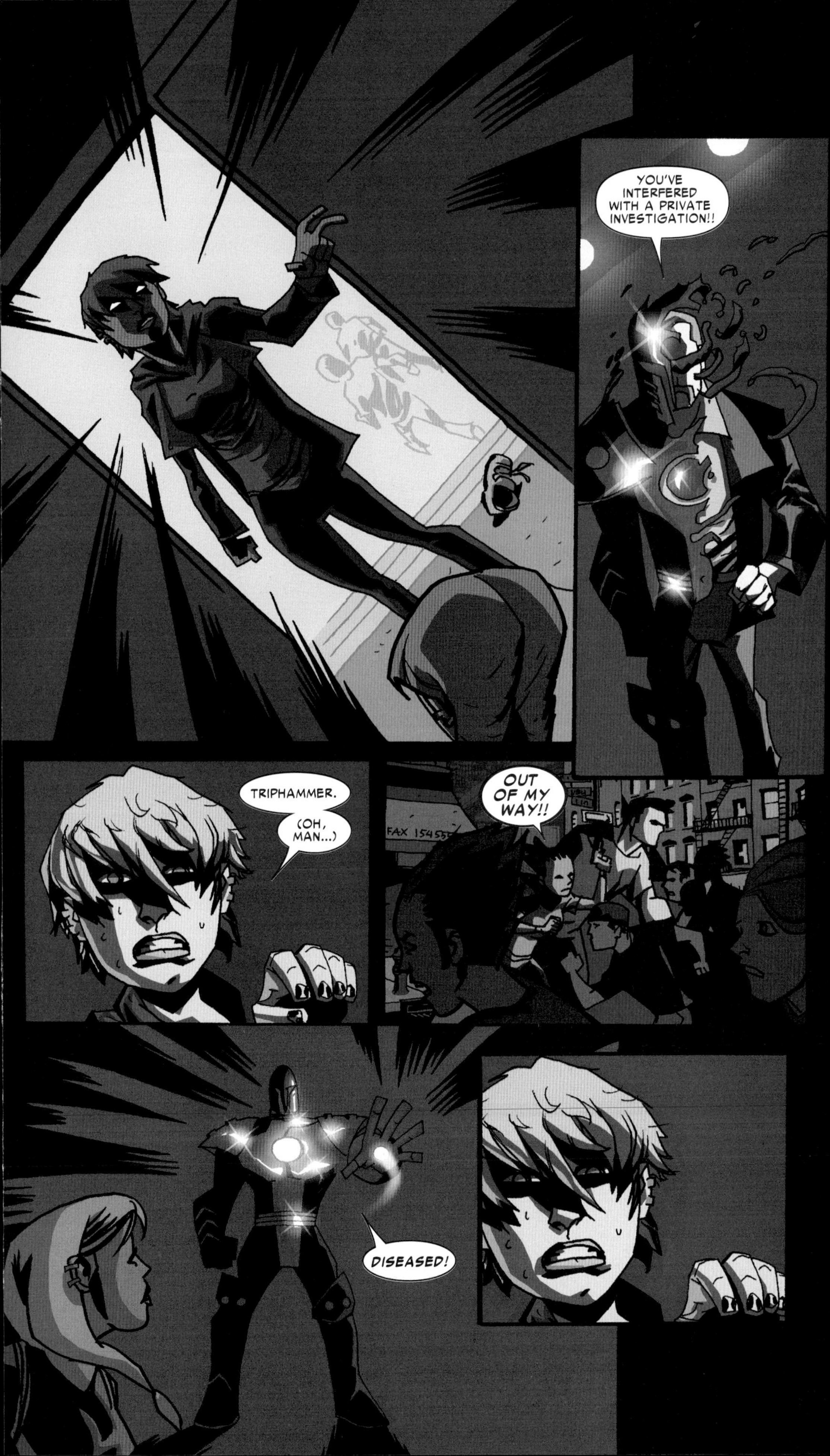
YOU'VE INTERFERED WITH A PRIVATE INVESTIGATION!!
TRIPHAMMER.
(OH, MAN...)
OUT OF MY WAY!!
FAX 15455
DISEASED!

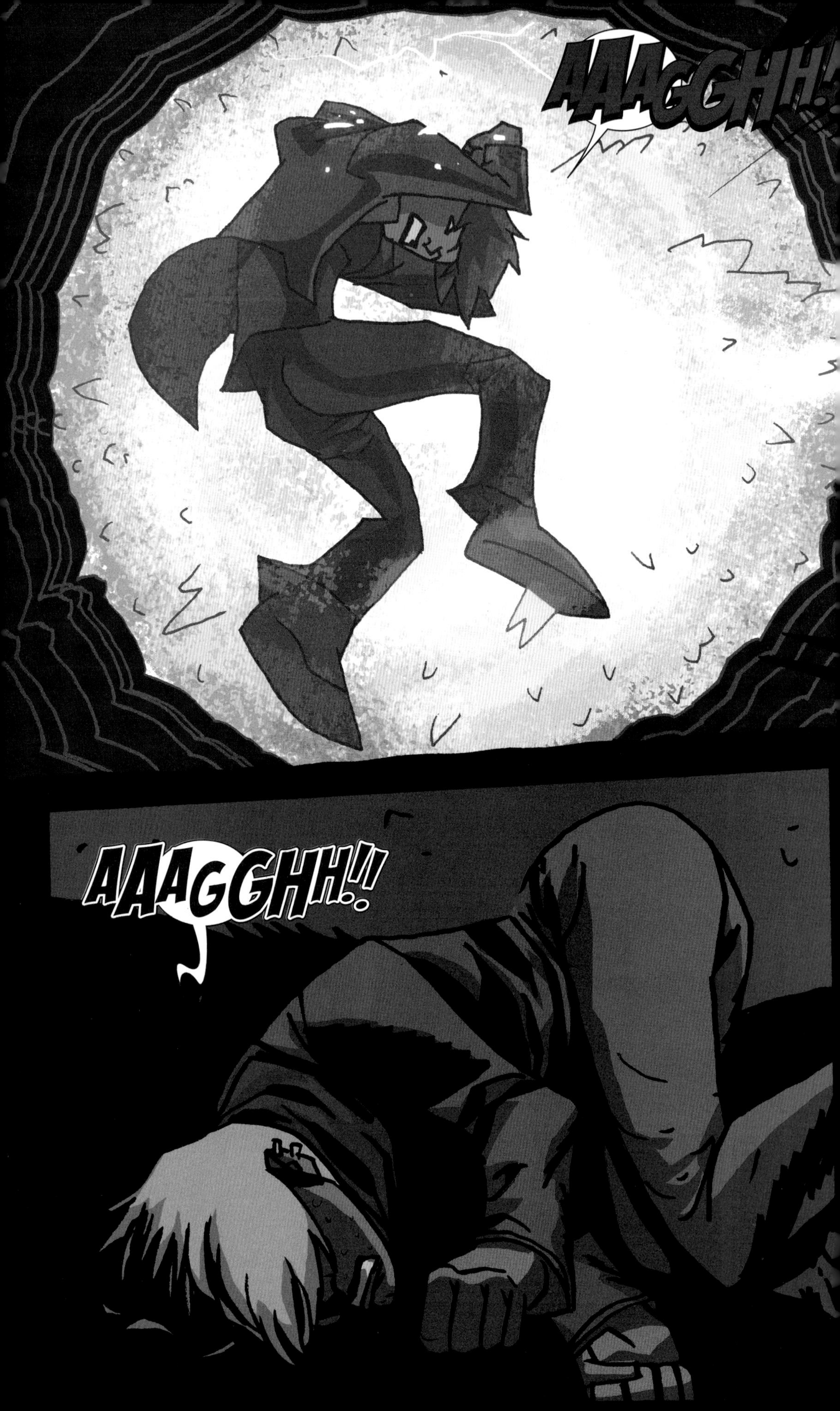
AAAGGHH!!
AAAGGHH!!

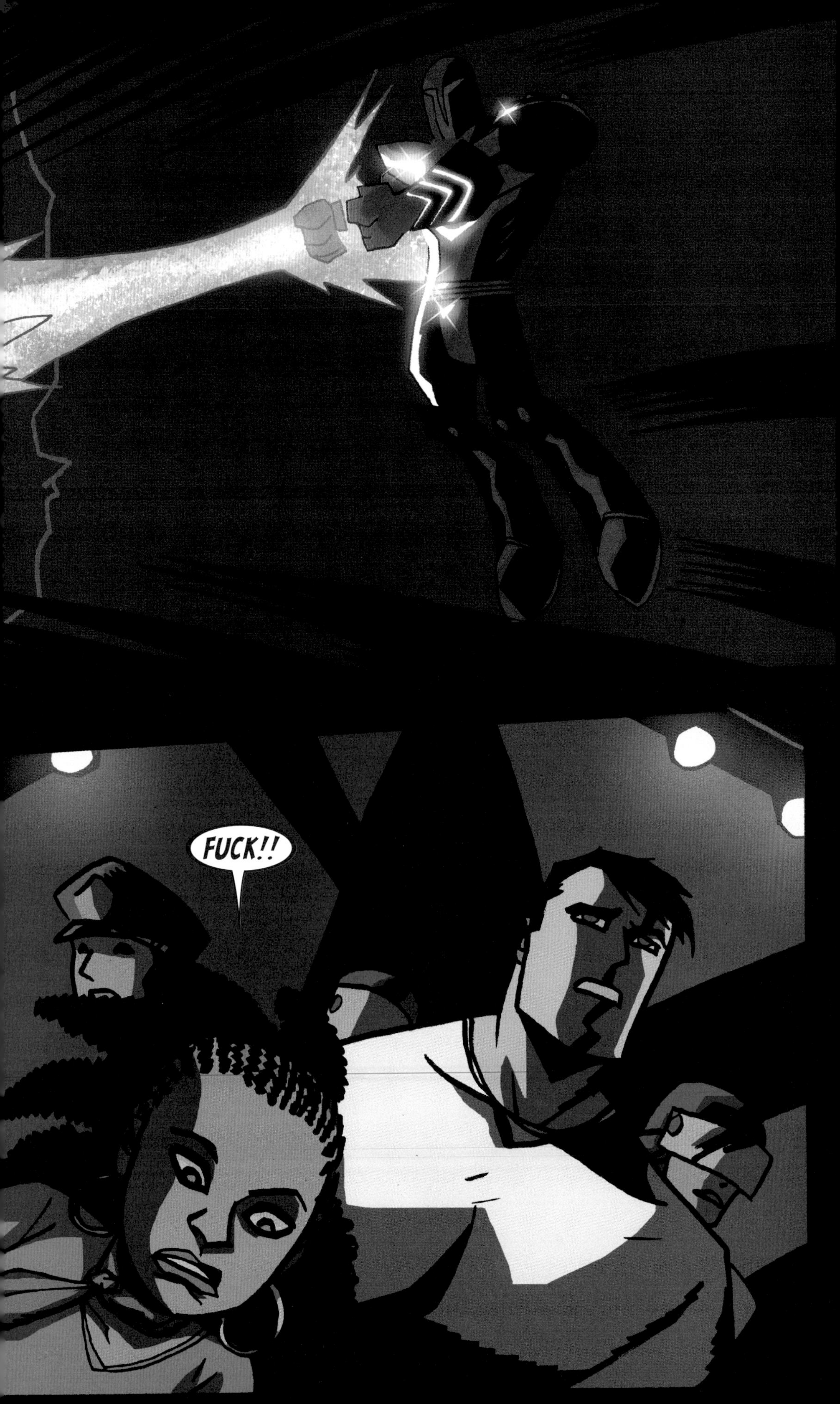
FUCK!!

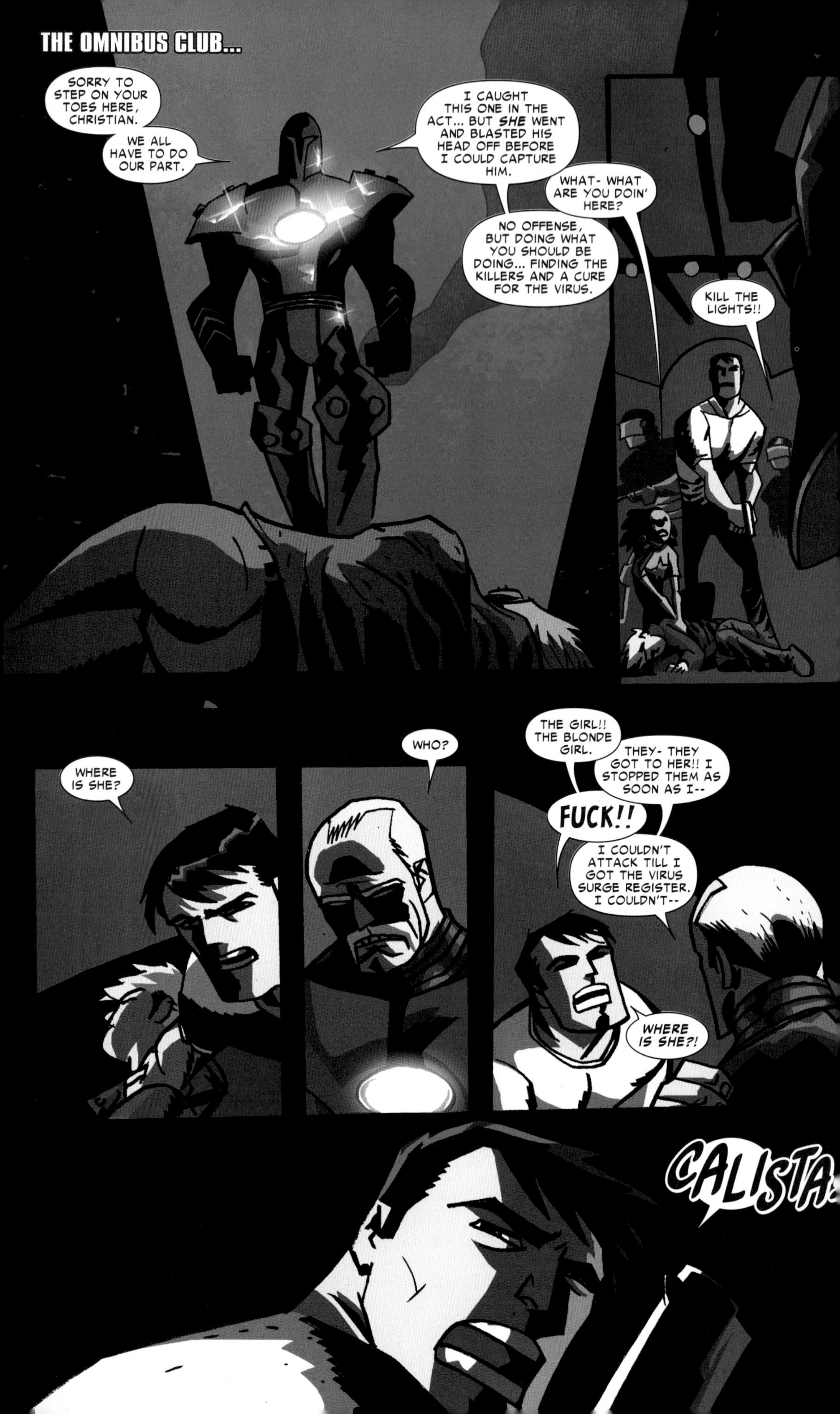
THE OMNIBUS CLUB...
SORRY TO STEP ON YOUR TOES HERE, CHRISTIAN.
WE ALL HAVE TO DO OUR PART.
I CAUGHT THIS ONE IN THE ACT... BUT SHE WENT AND BLASTED HIS HEAD OFF BEFORE I COULD CAPTURE HIM.
WHAT- WHAT ARE YOU DOIN' HERE?
NO OFFENSE, BUT DOING WHAT YOU SHOULD BE DOING... FINDING THE KILLERS AND A CURE FOR THE VIRUS.
KILL THE LIGHTS!!
WHERE IS SHE?
WHO?
THE GIRL!! THE BLONDE GIRL.
THEY- THEY GOT TO HER!! I STOPPED THEM AS SOON AS I--
FUCK!!
I COULDN'T ATTACK TILL I GOT THE VIRUS SURGE REGISTER. I COULDN'T--
WHERE IS SHE?!
CALISTA

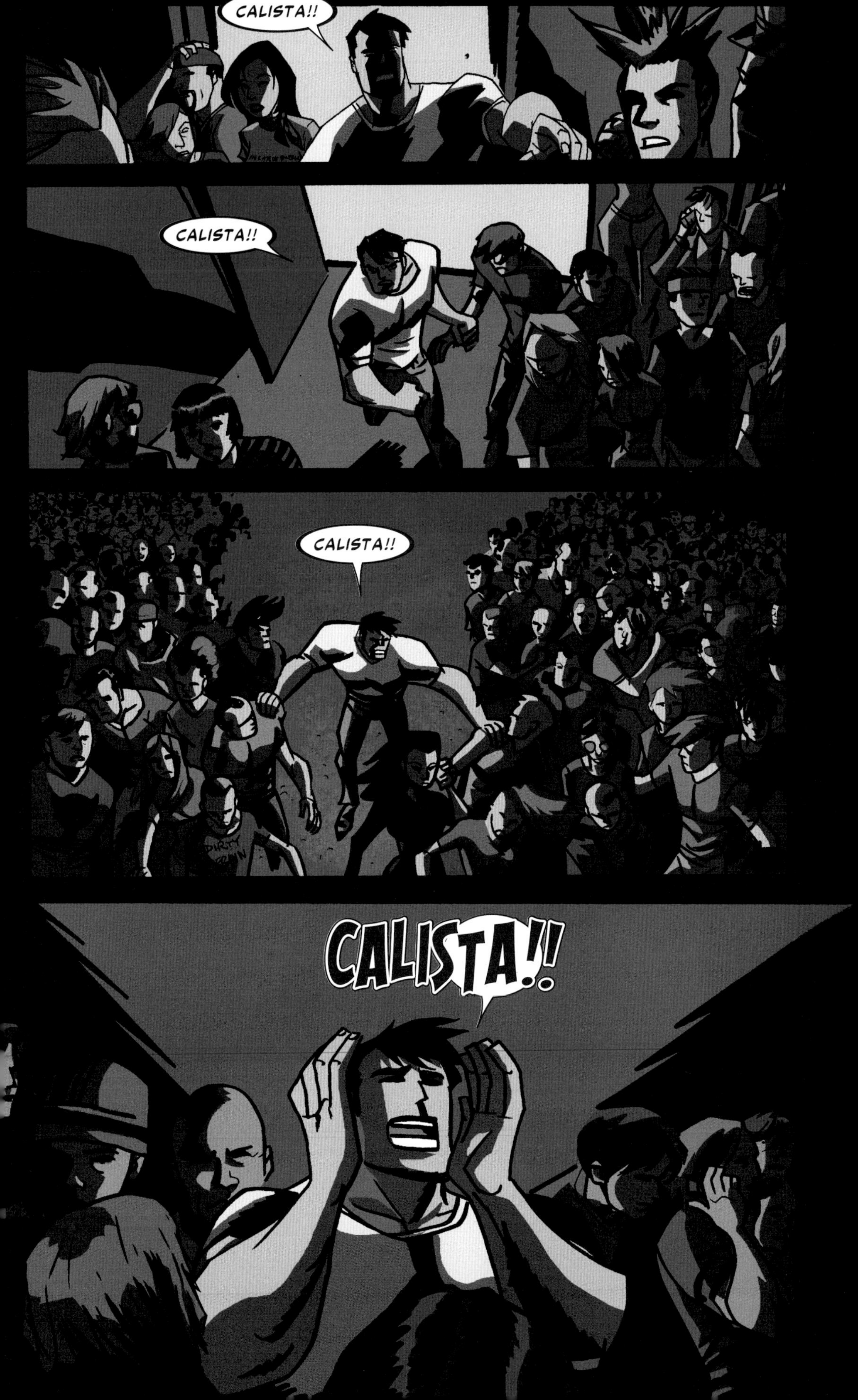
CALISTA!!
CALISTA!!
CALISTA!!
CALISTA!!

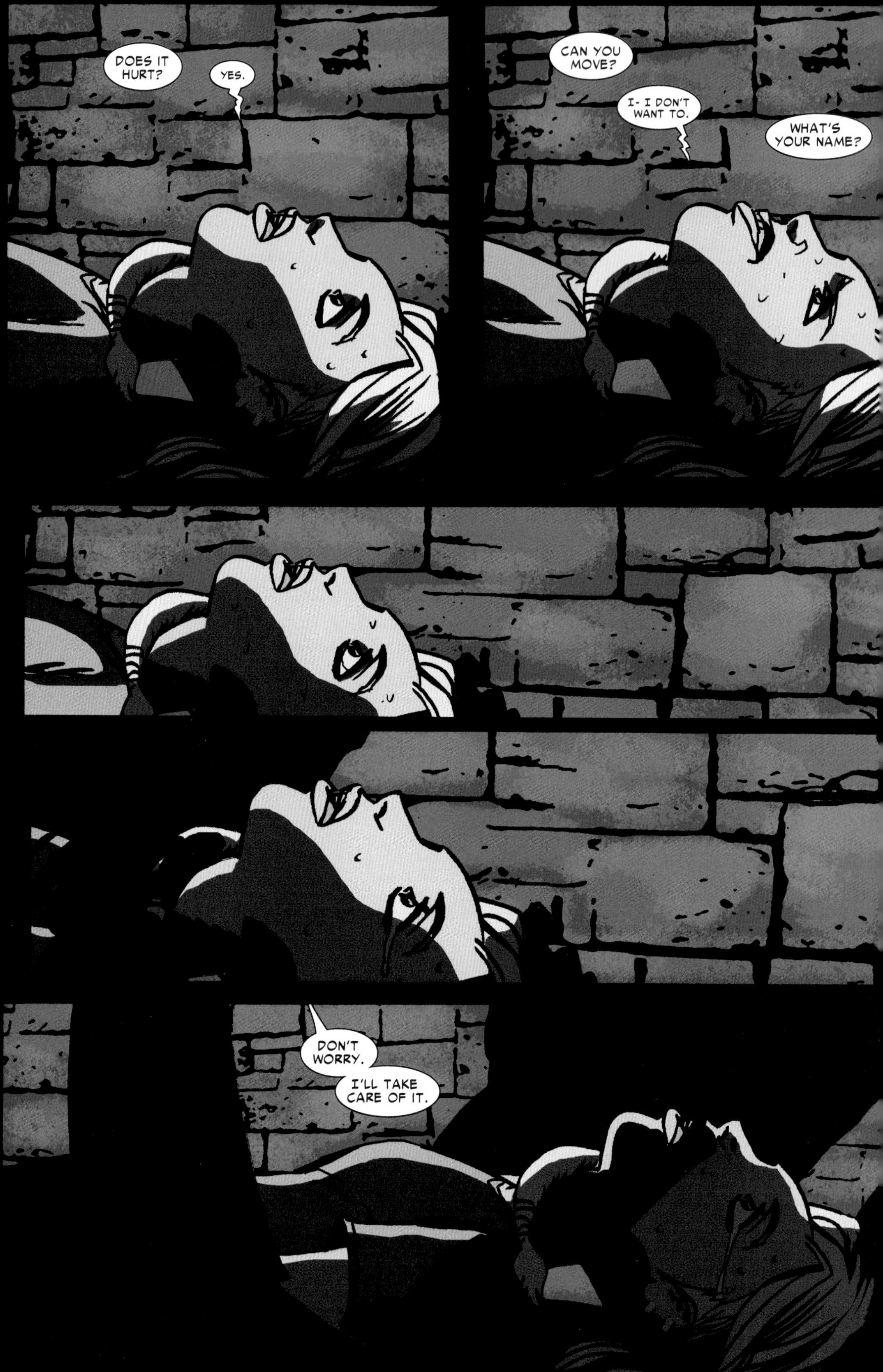
DOES IT HURT?
YES.
CAN YOU MOVE?
I- I DON'T WANT TO.
WHAT'S YOUR NAME?
DON'T WORRY.
I'LL TAKE CARE OF IT.

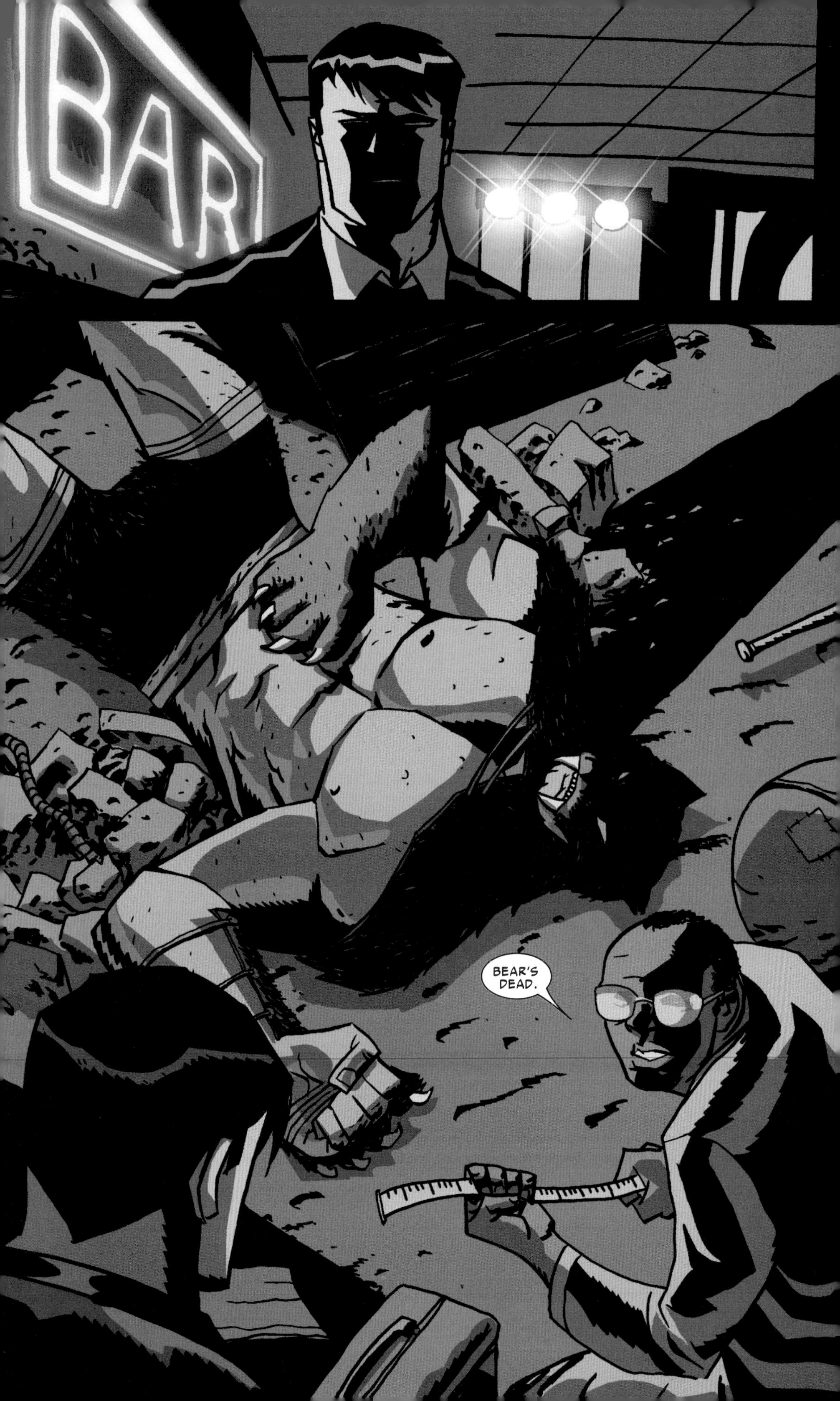
BAR
BEAR'S DEAD.

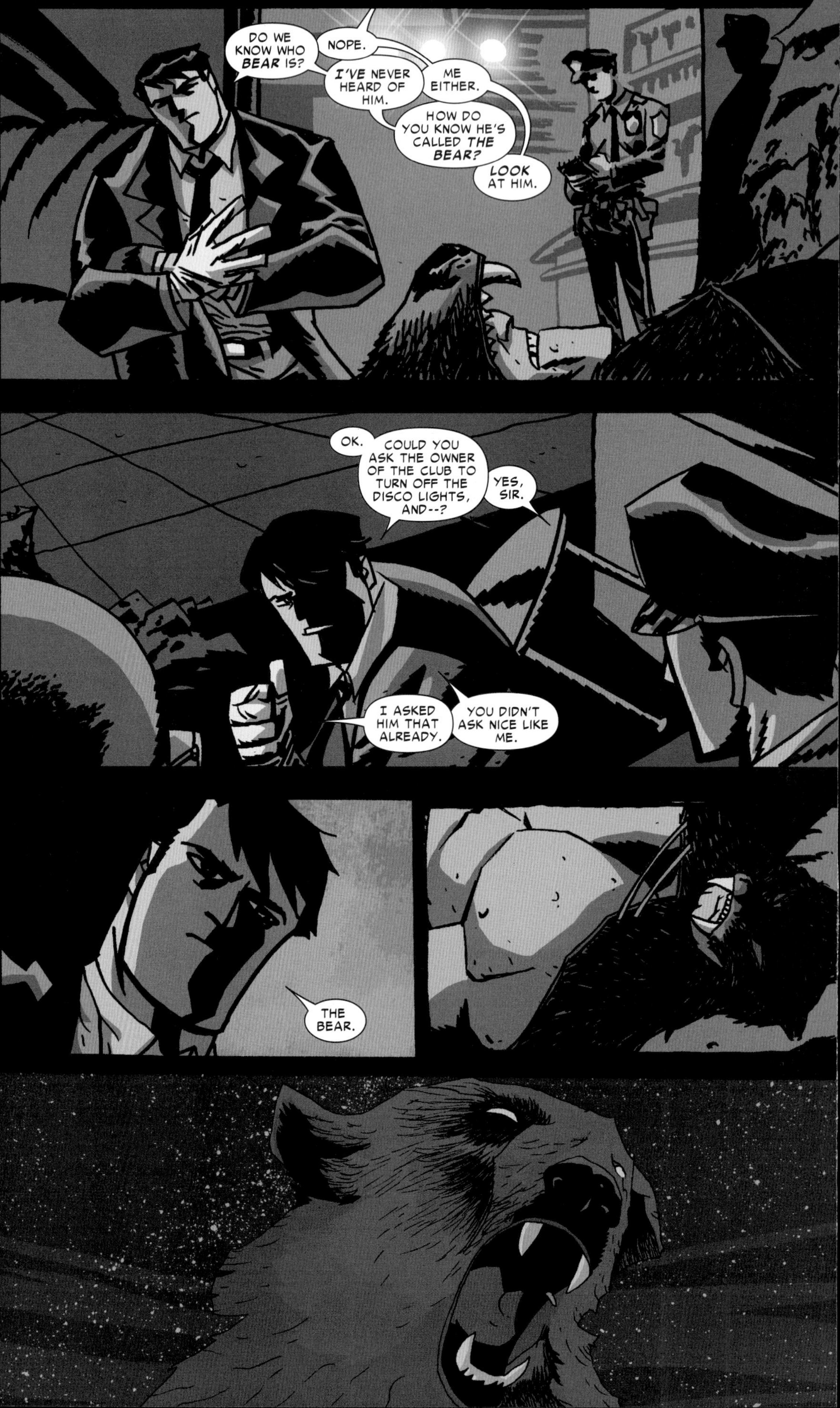
DO WE KNOW WHO BEAR IS?
NOPE.
I'VE NEVER HEARD OF HIM.
ME EITHER.
HOW DO YOU KNOW HE'S CALLED THE BEAR?
LOOK AT HIM.
OK.
COULD YOU ASK THE OWNER OF THE CLUB TO TURN OFF THE DISCO LIGHTS, AND--?
YES, SIR.
I ASKED HIM THAT ALREADY.
YOU DIDN'T ASK NICE LIKE ME.
THE BEAR.

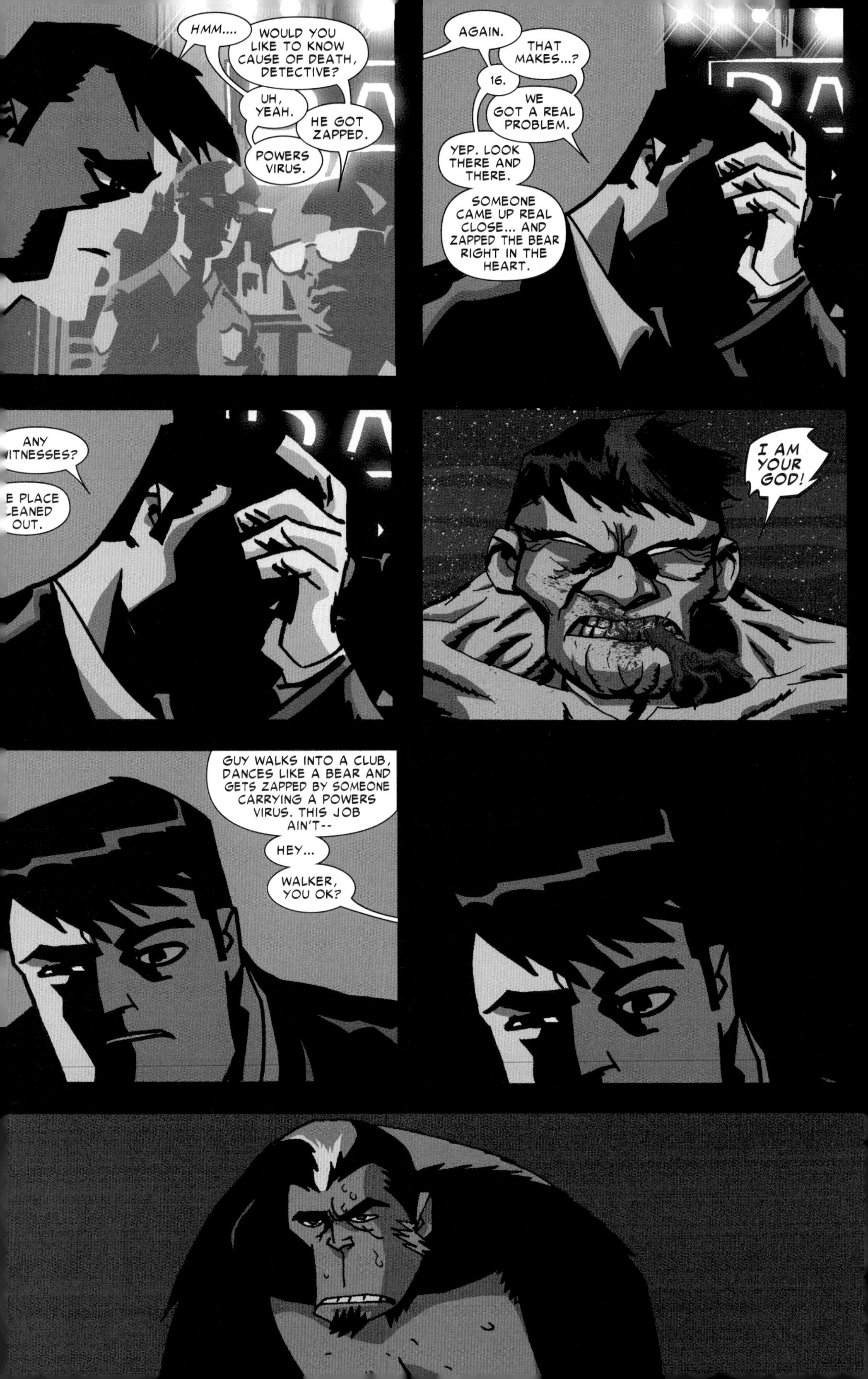
HMM....
WOULD YOU LIKE TO KNOW CAUSE OF DEATH, DETECTIVE?
UH, YEAH.
HE GOT ZAPPED.
POWERS VIRUS.
AGAIN.
THAT MAKES...?
16.
WE GOT A REAL PROBLEM.
YEP. LOOK THERE AND THERE.
SOMEONE CAME UP REAL CLOSE... AND ZAPPED THE BEAR RIGHT IN THE HEART.
ANY WITNESSES?
I AM YOUR GOD!
GUY WALKS INTO A CLUB, DANCES LIKE A BEAR AND GETS ZAPPED BY SOMEONE CARRYING A POWERS VIRUS. THIS JOB AIN'T--
HEY...
WALKER, YOU OK?

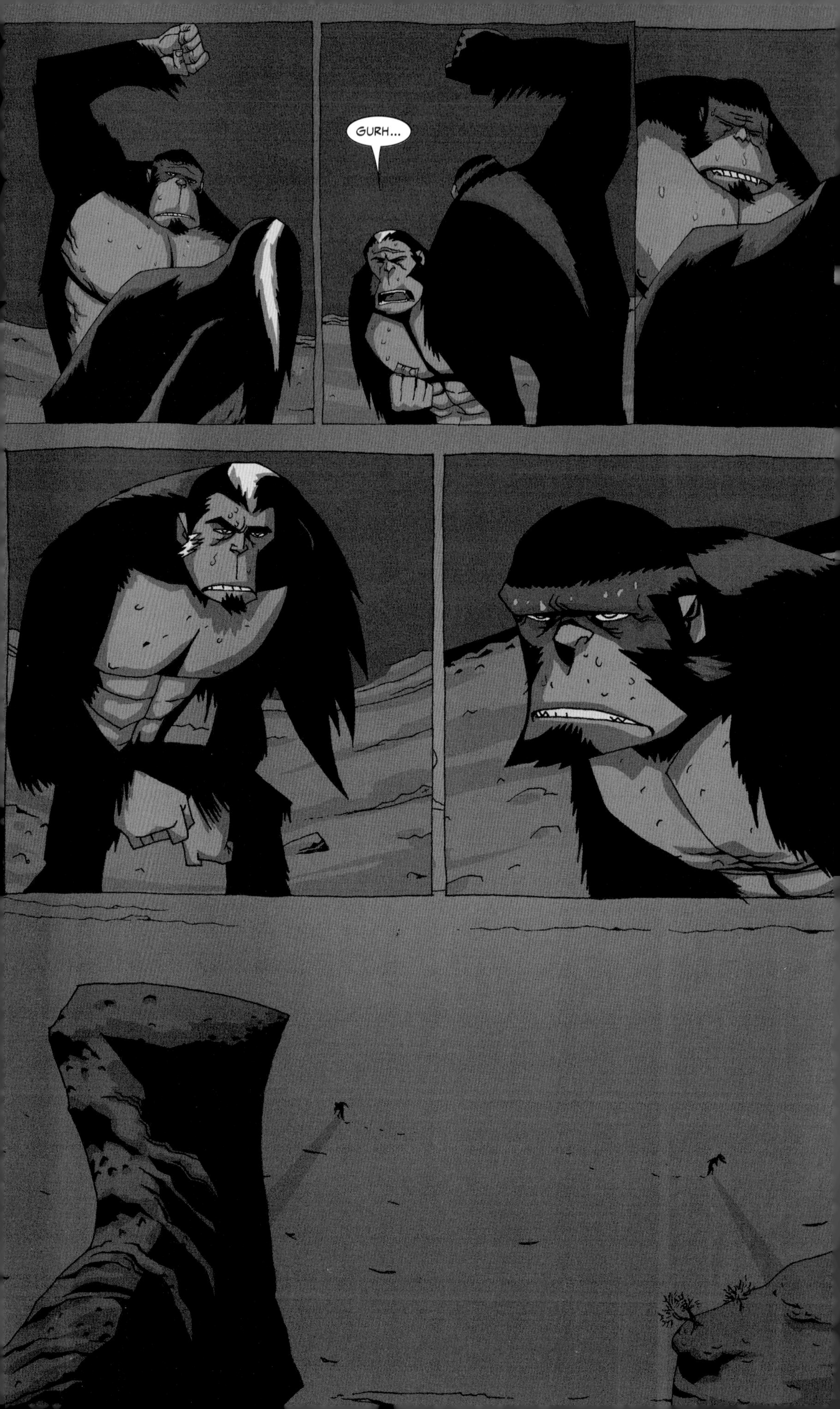
GURH...

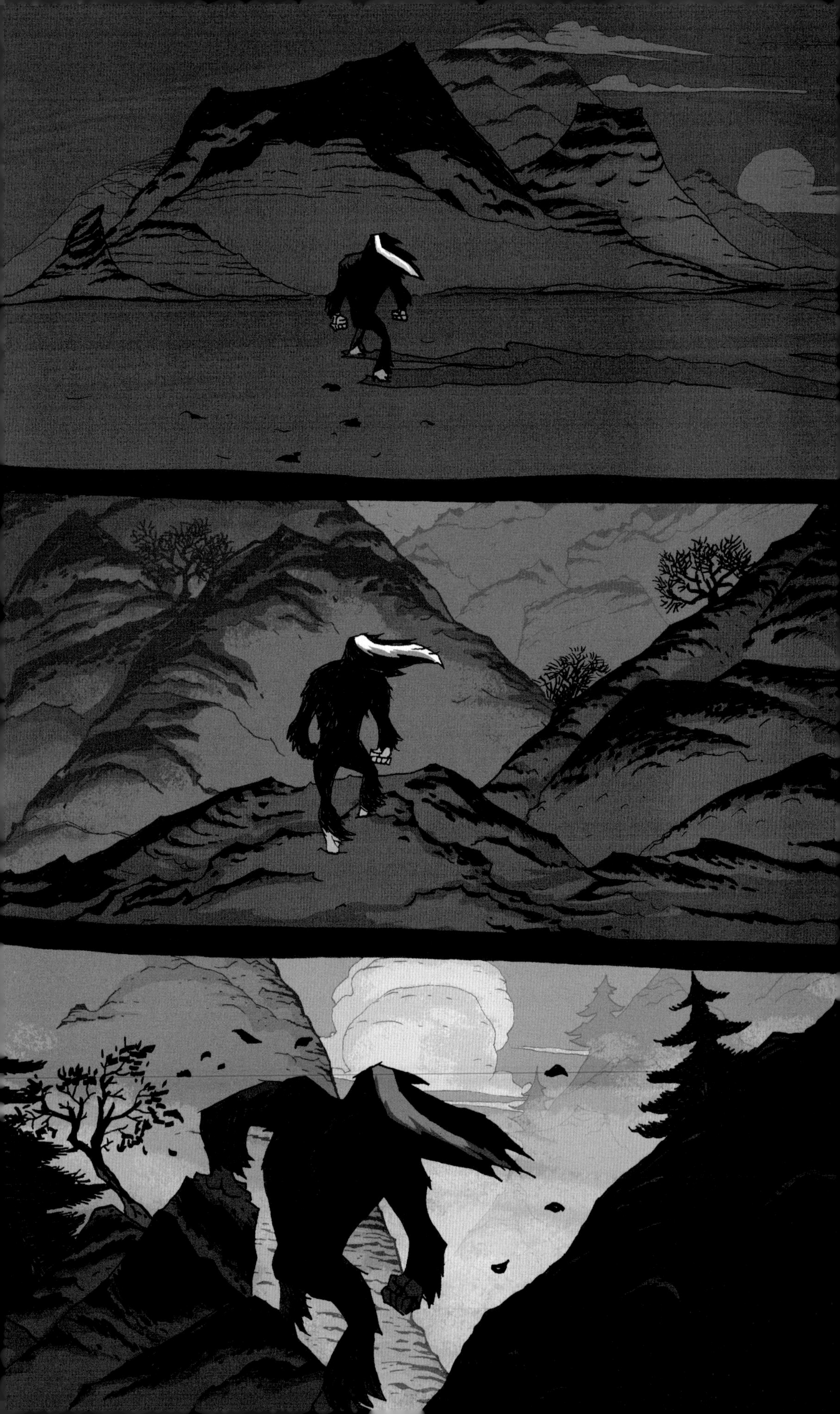

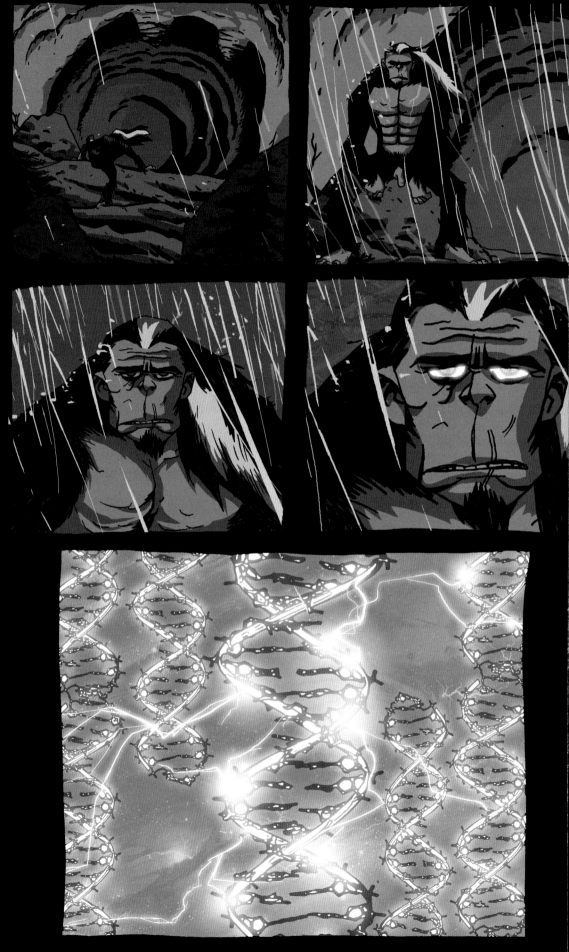

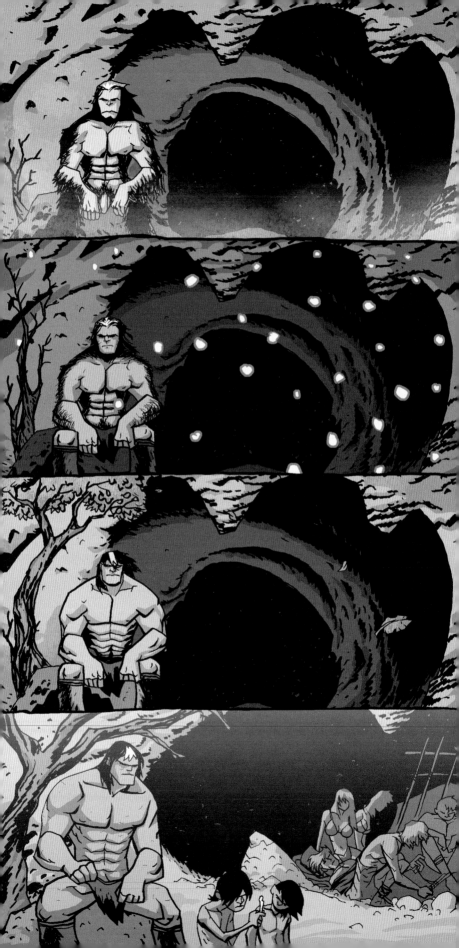

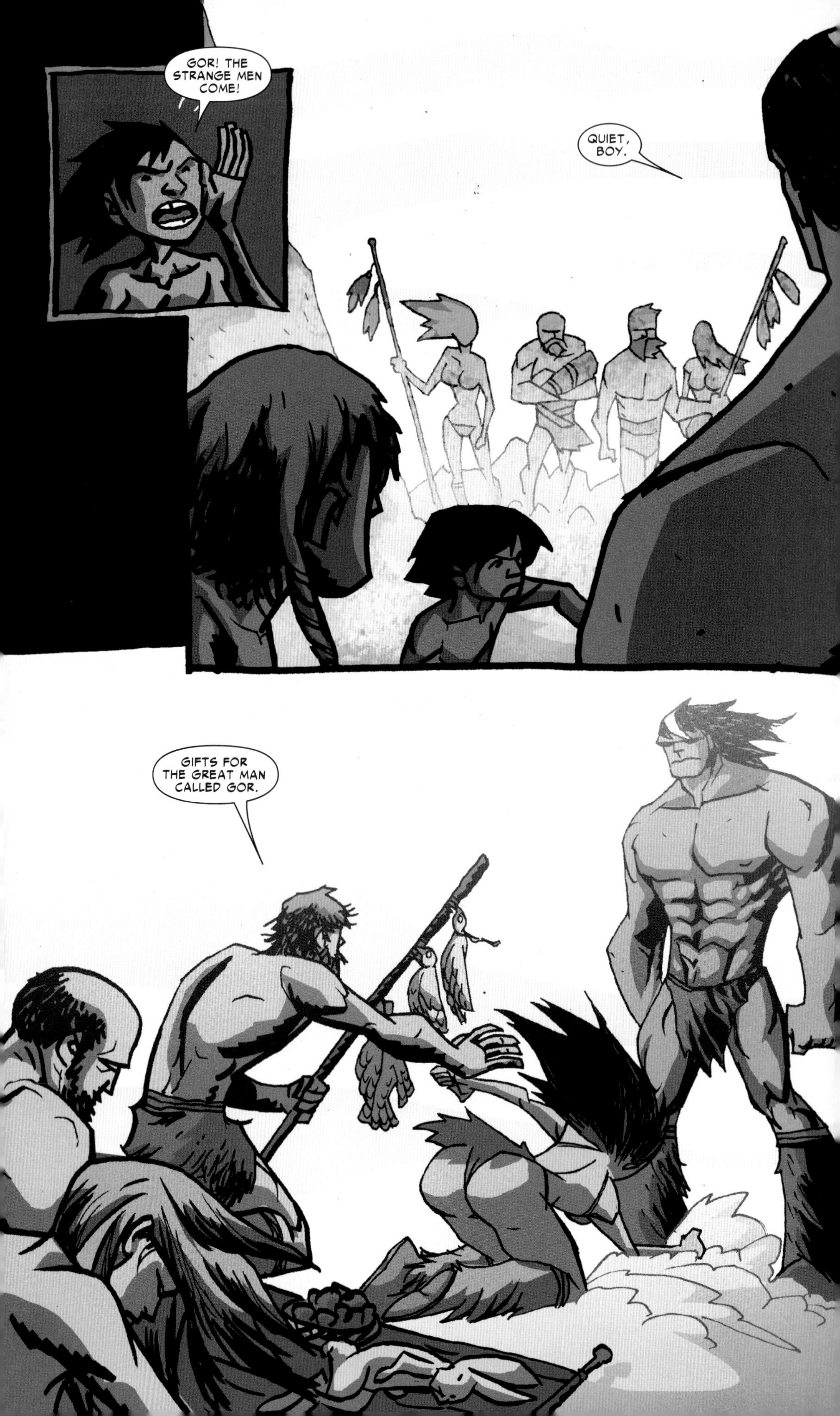
GOR! THE STRANGE MEN COME!
QUIET, BOY.
GIFTS FOR THE GREAT MAN CALLED GOR.

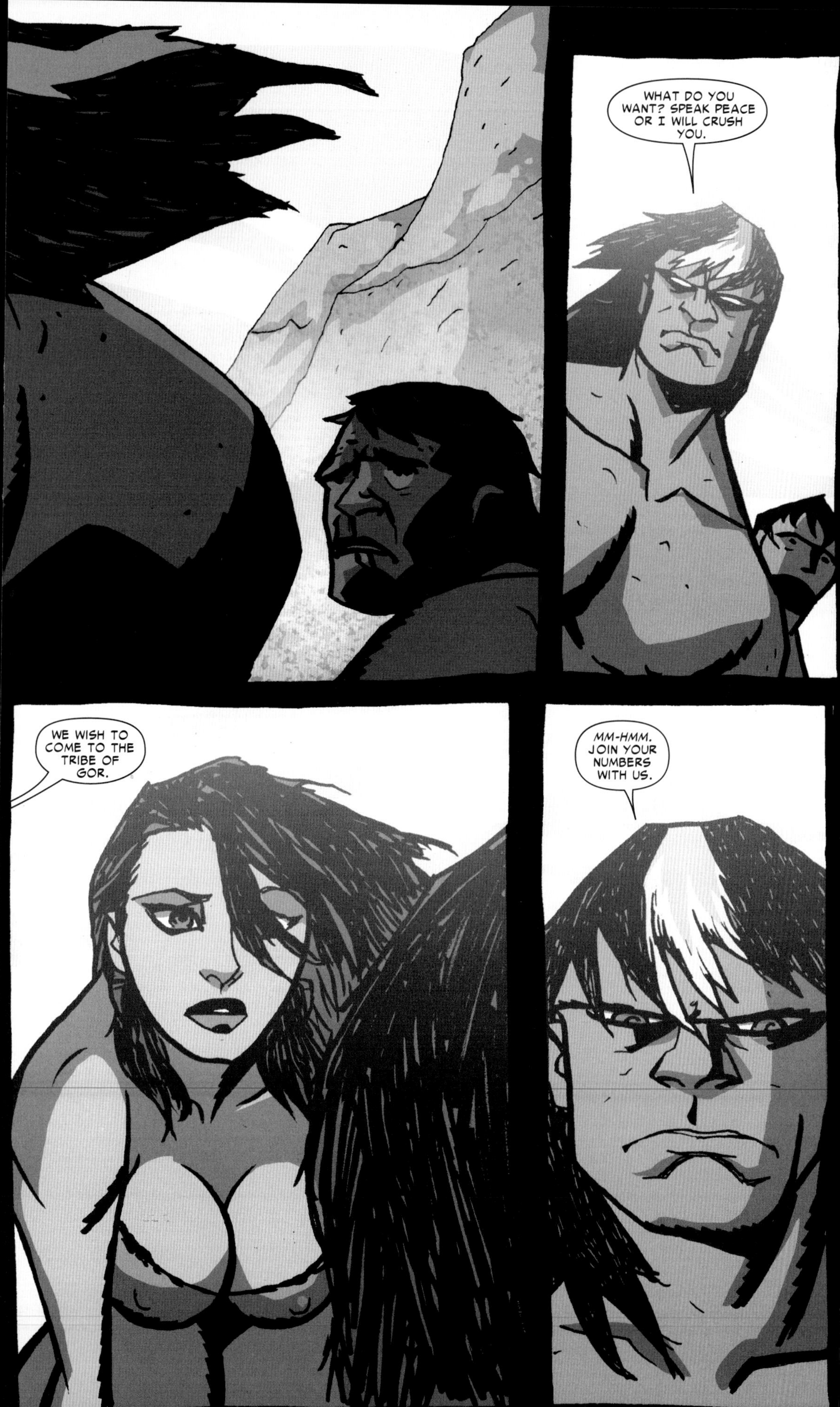
WHAT DO YOU WANT? SPEAK PEACE OR I WILL CRUSH YOU.
WE WISH TO COME TO THE TRIBE OF GOR.
MM-HMM. JOIN YOUR NUMBERS WITH US.

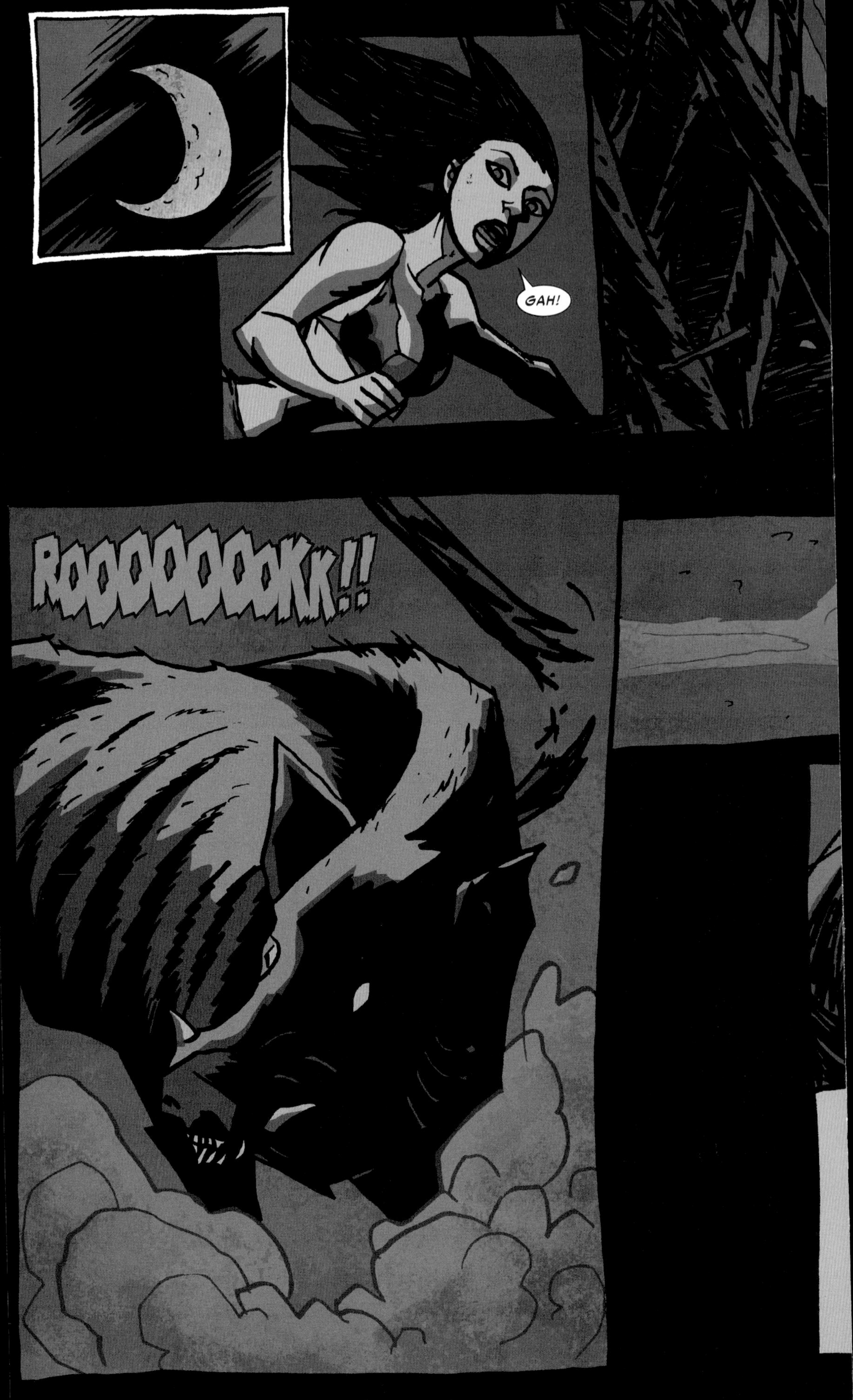
GAH!
ROOOOOOOKK!!

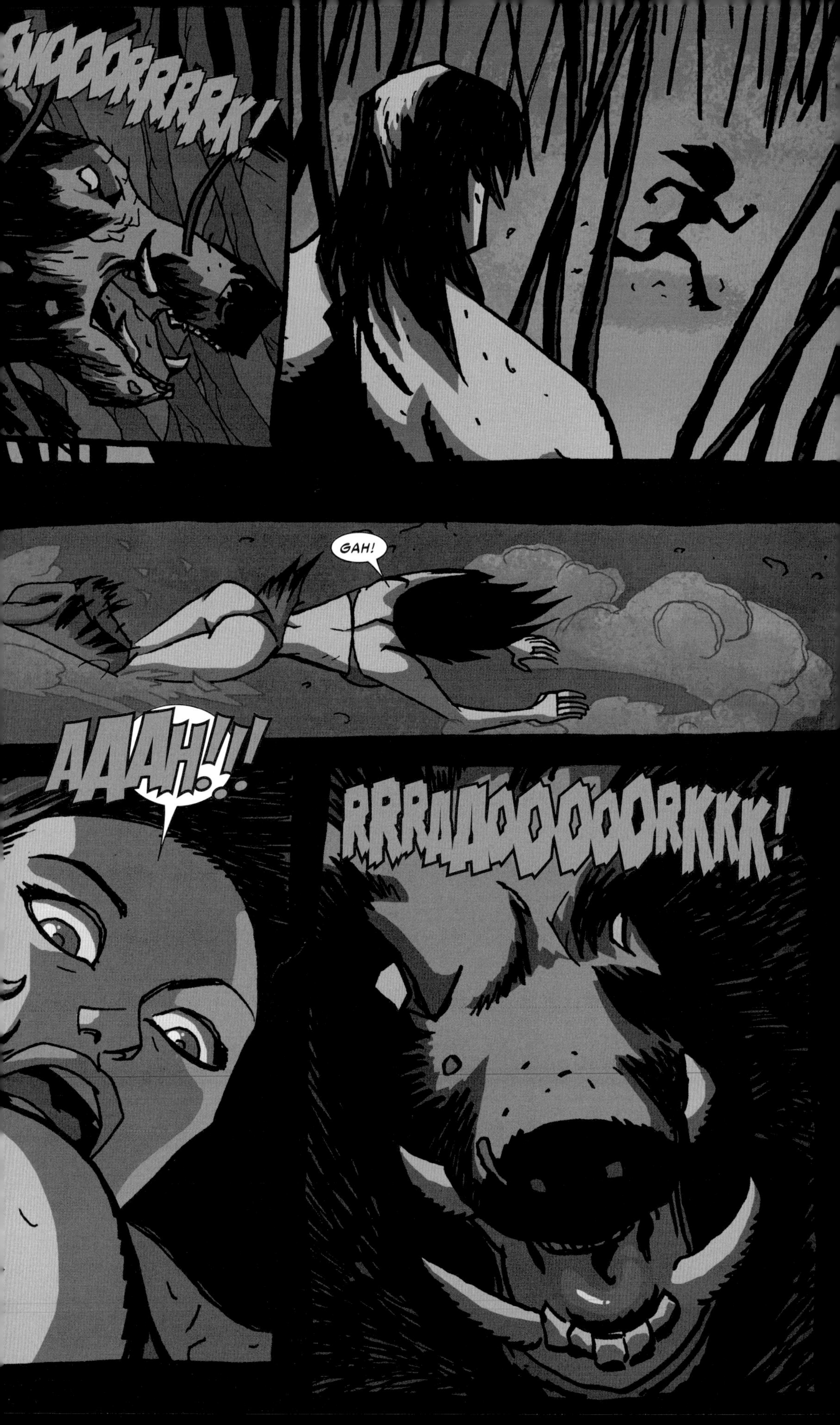
WOOORRRRK!
GAH!
AAAH!!!
RRRAAOOOOORKKK!

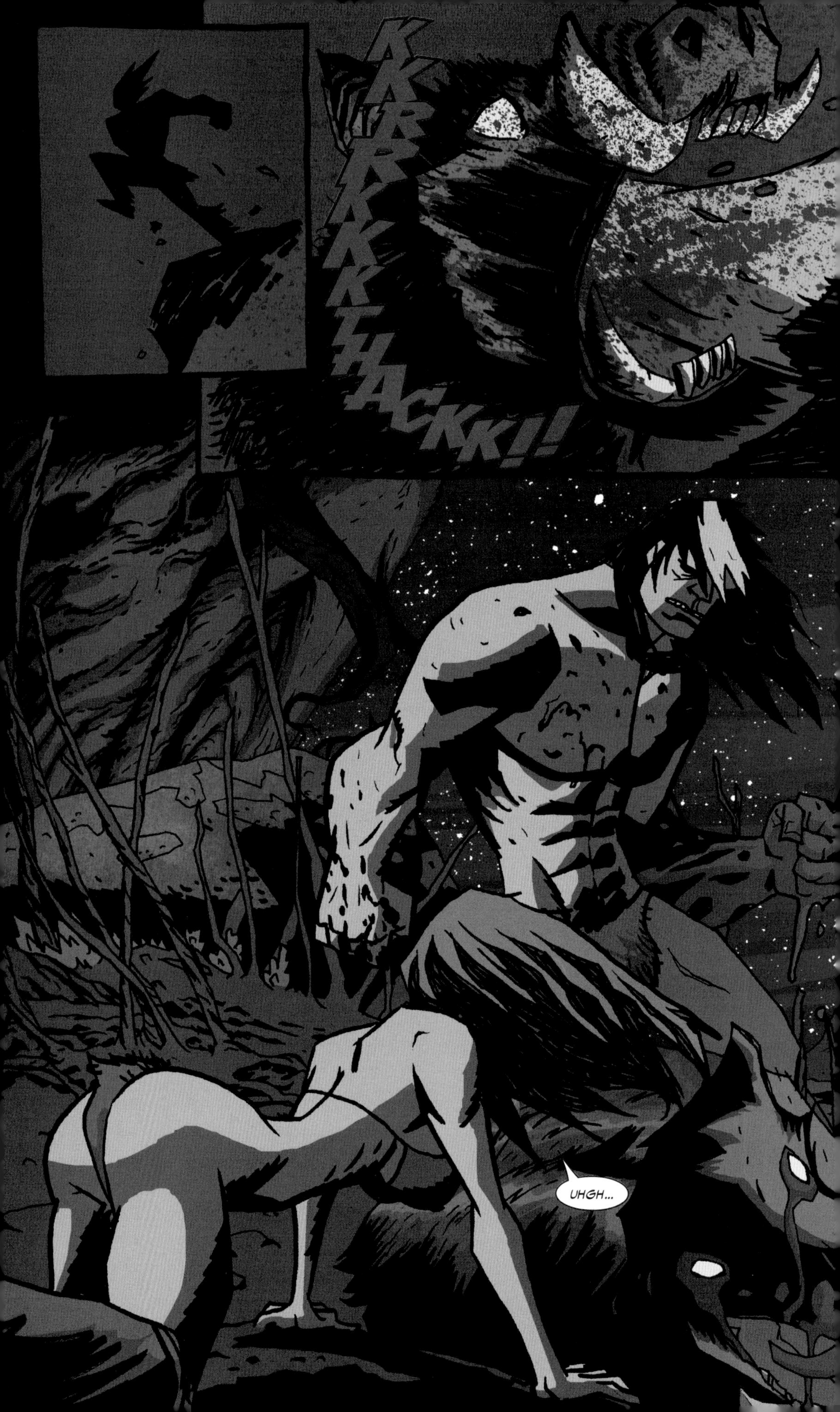
KRRAKKKTHACKK!!
UHGH...

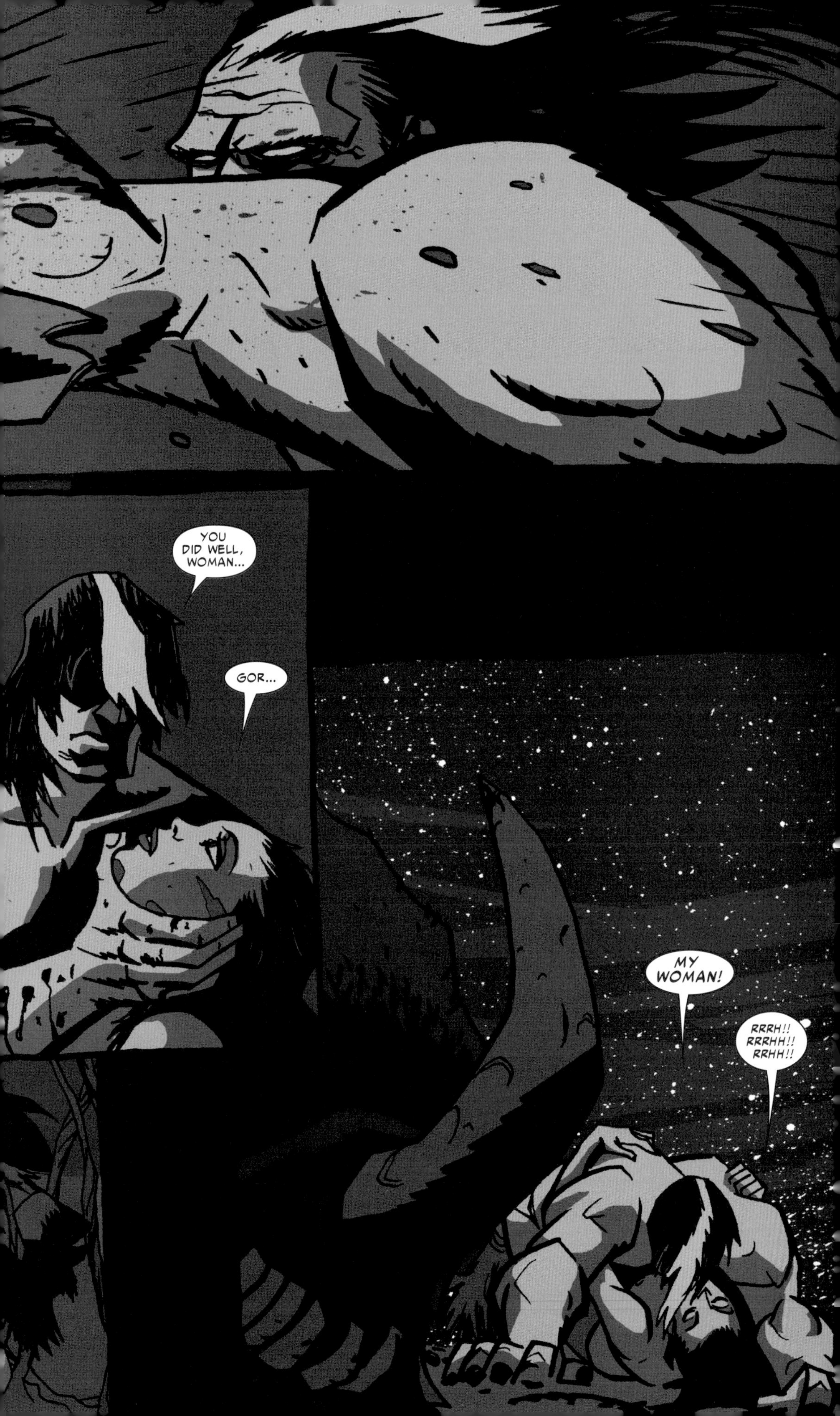
YOU DID WELL, WOMAN...
GOR...
MY WOMAN!
RRRH!! RRRHH!! RRHH!!

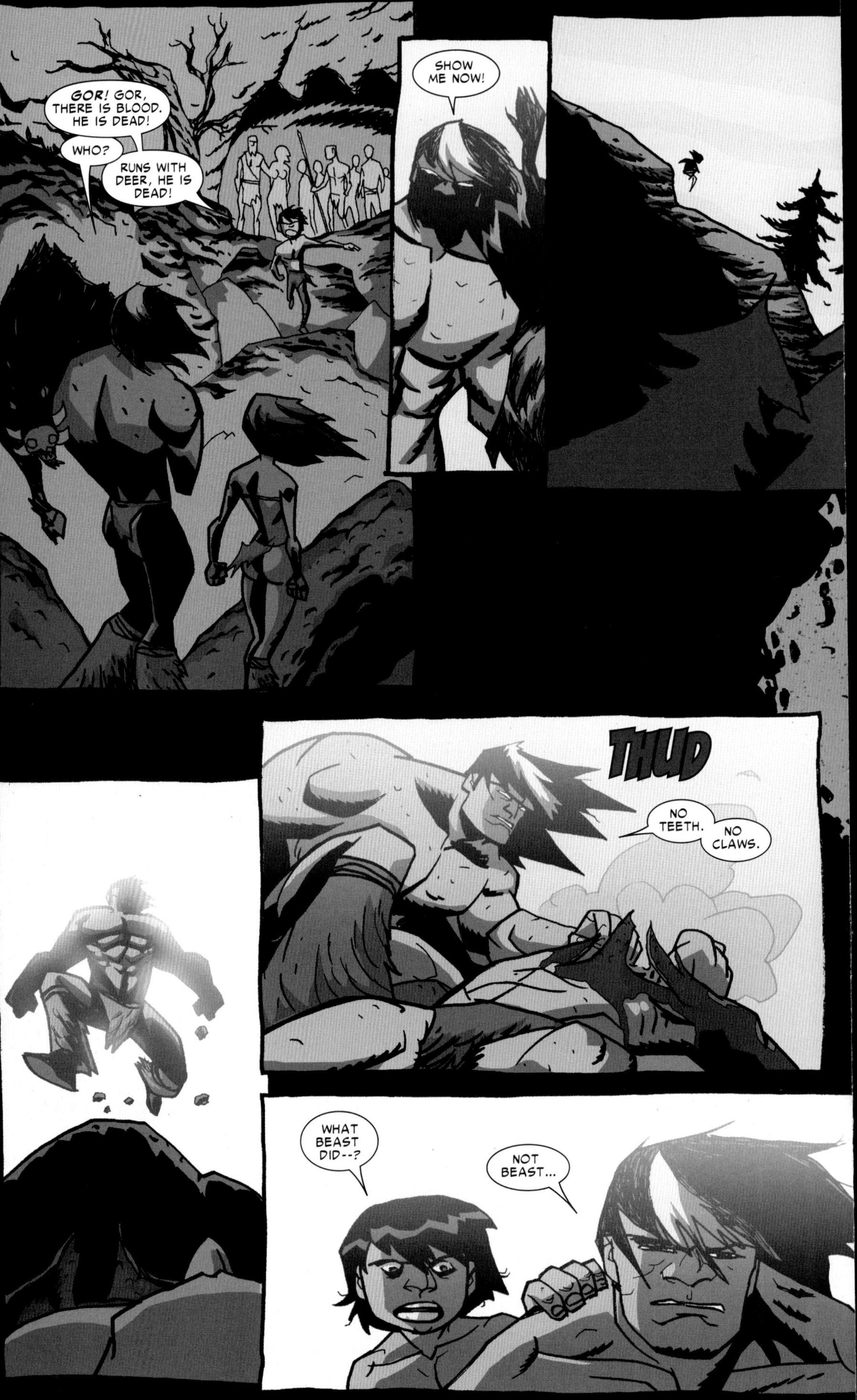
GOR! GOR, THERE IS BLOOD. HE IS DEAD!
WHO?
RUNS WITH DEER, HE IS DEAD!
SHOW ME NOW!
THUD
NO TEETH.
NO CLAWS.
WHAT BEAST DID--?
NOT BEAST...

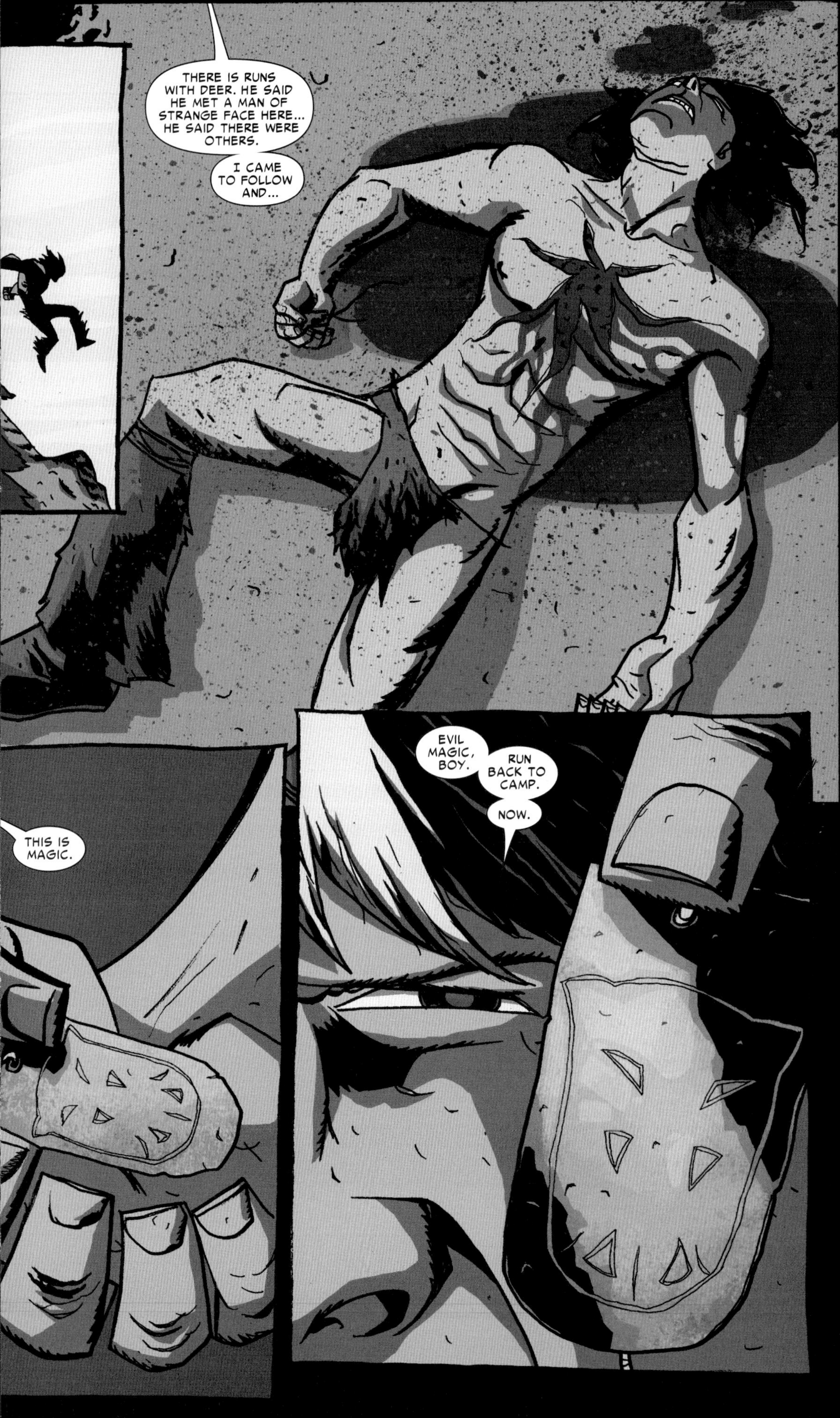

THERE IS RUNS WITH DEER. HE SAID HE MET A MAN OF STRANGE FACE HERE... HE SAID THERE WERE OTHERS.
I CAME TO FOLLOW AND...
THIS IS MAGIC.
EVIL MAGIC, BOY.
RUN BACK TO CAMP.
NOW.

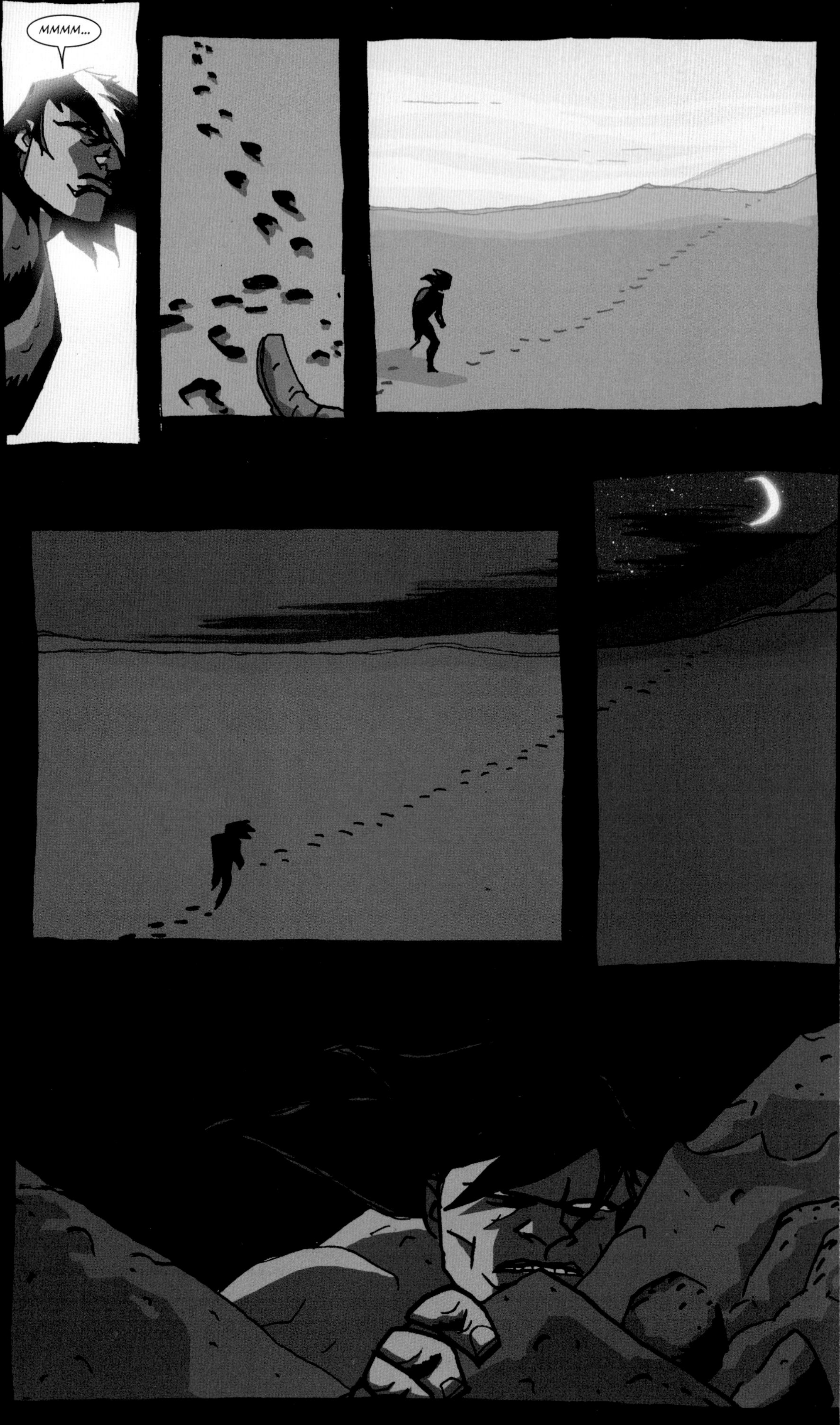
MMMM...

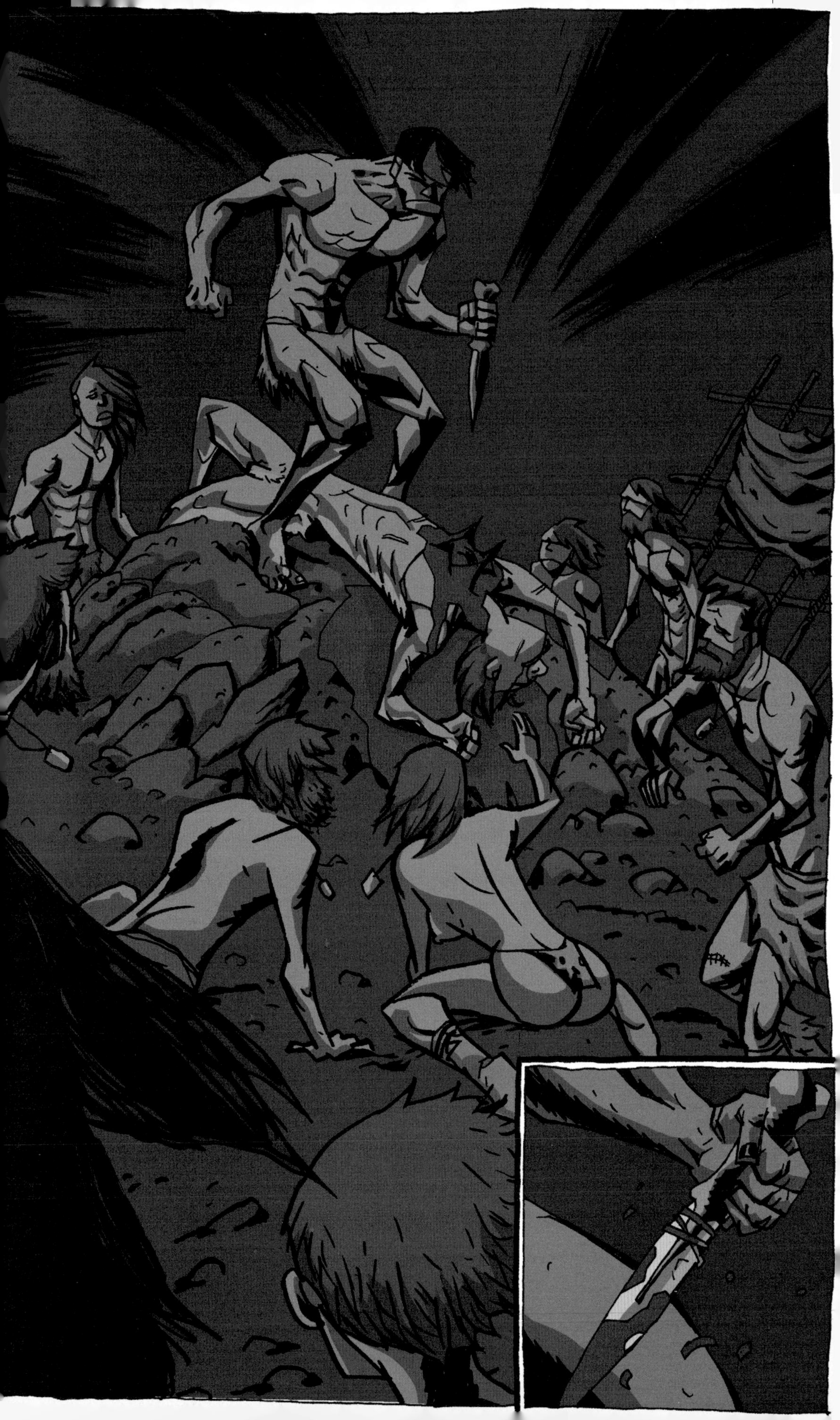

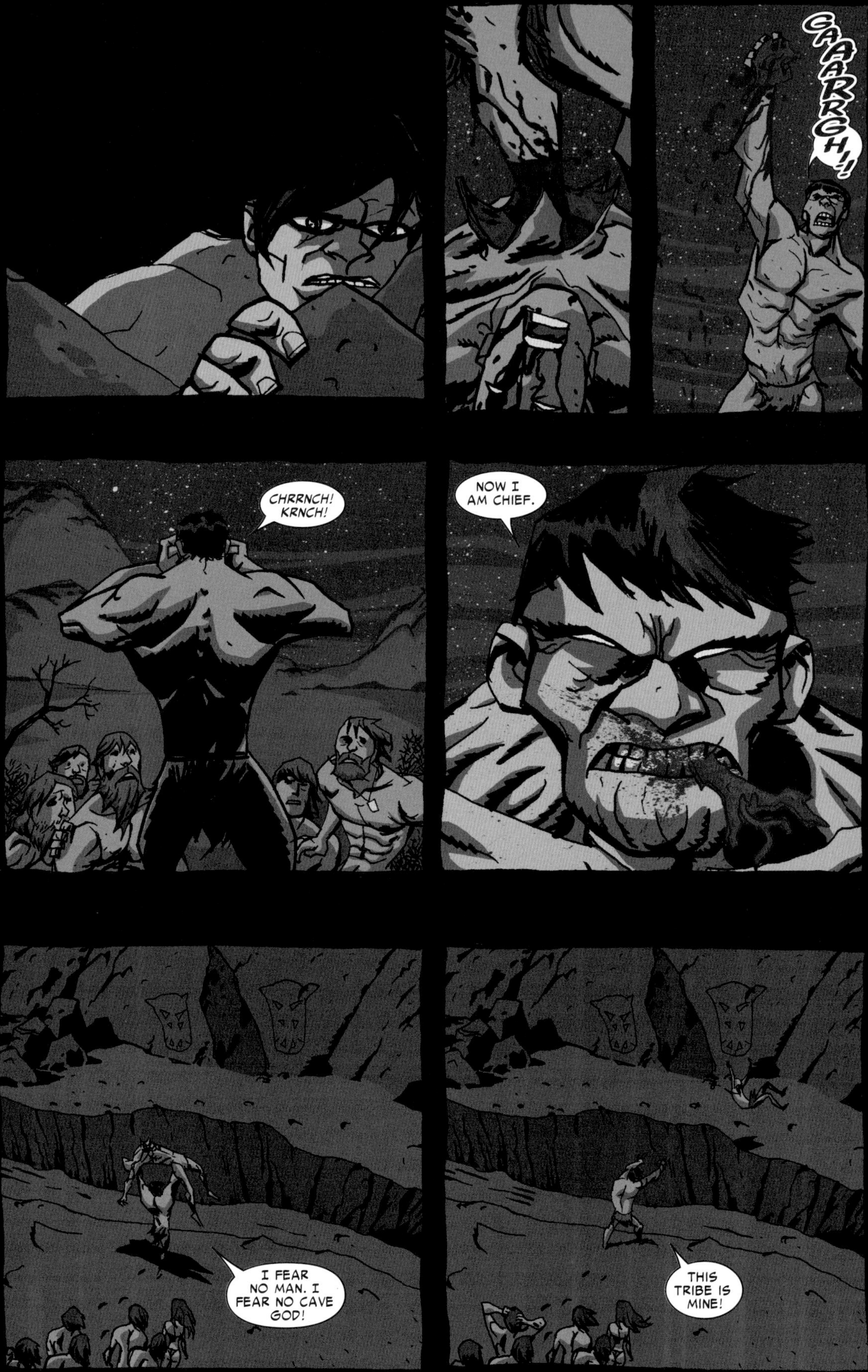
GAAARRGH!!
CHRRNCH! KRNCH!
NOW I AM CHIEF.
I FEAR NO MAN. I FEAR NO CAVE GOD!
THIS TRIBE IS MINE!

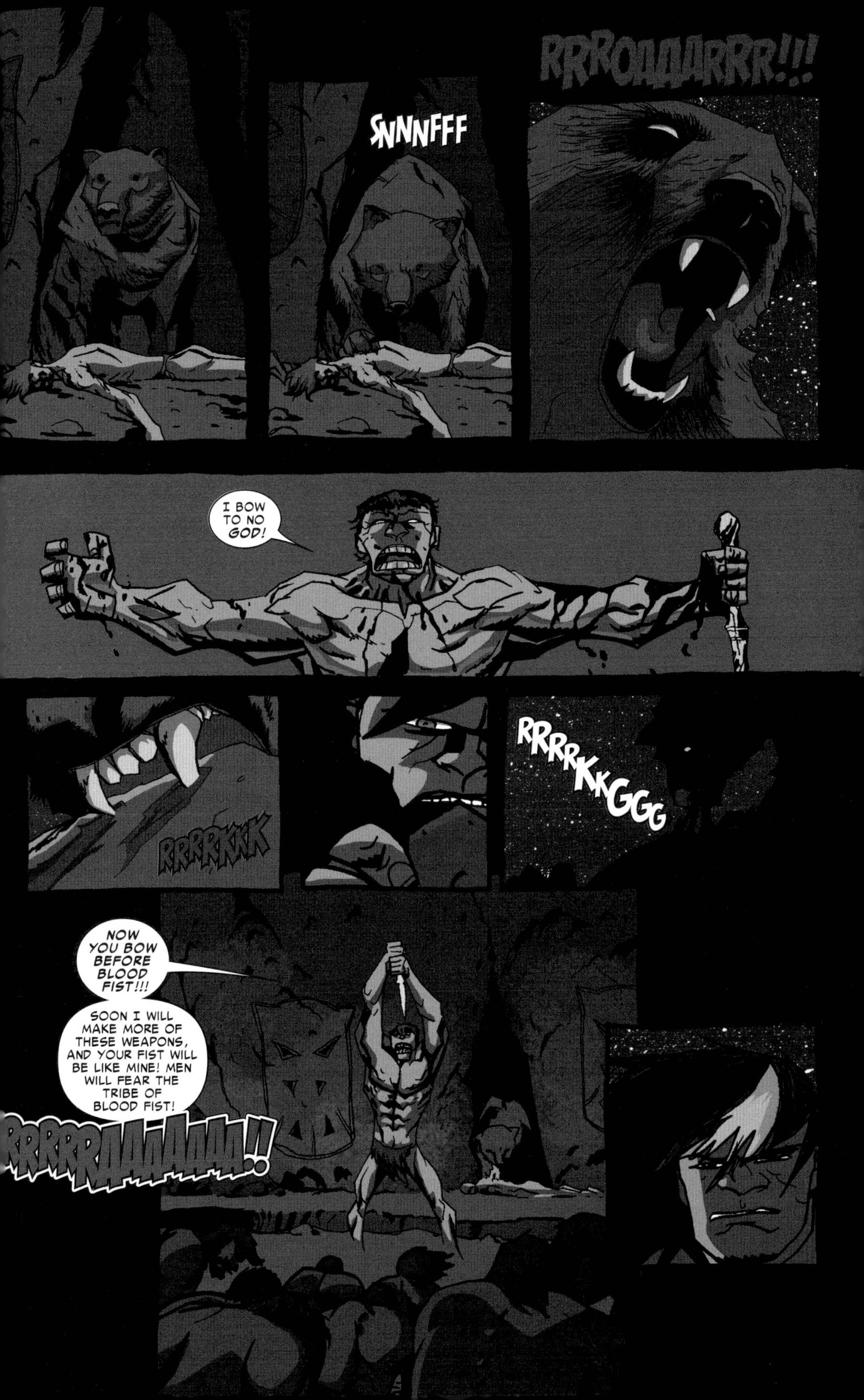
RRROAAARRRR!!!
SNNNFFF
I BOW TO NO GOD!
RRRRKKK
RRRRKKGGG
NOW YOU BOW BEFORE BLOOD FIST!!!
SOON I WILL MAKE MORE OF THESE WEAPONS, AND YOUR FIST WILL BE LIKE MINE! MEN WILL FEAR THE TRIBE OF BLOOD FIST!
RRRRRAAAAAAA!!

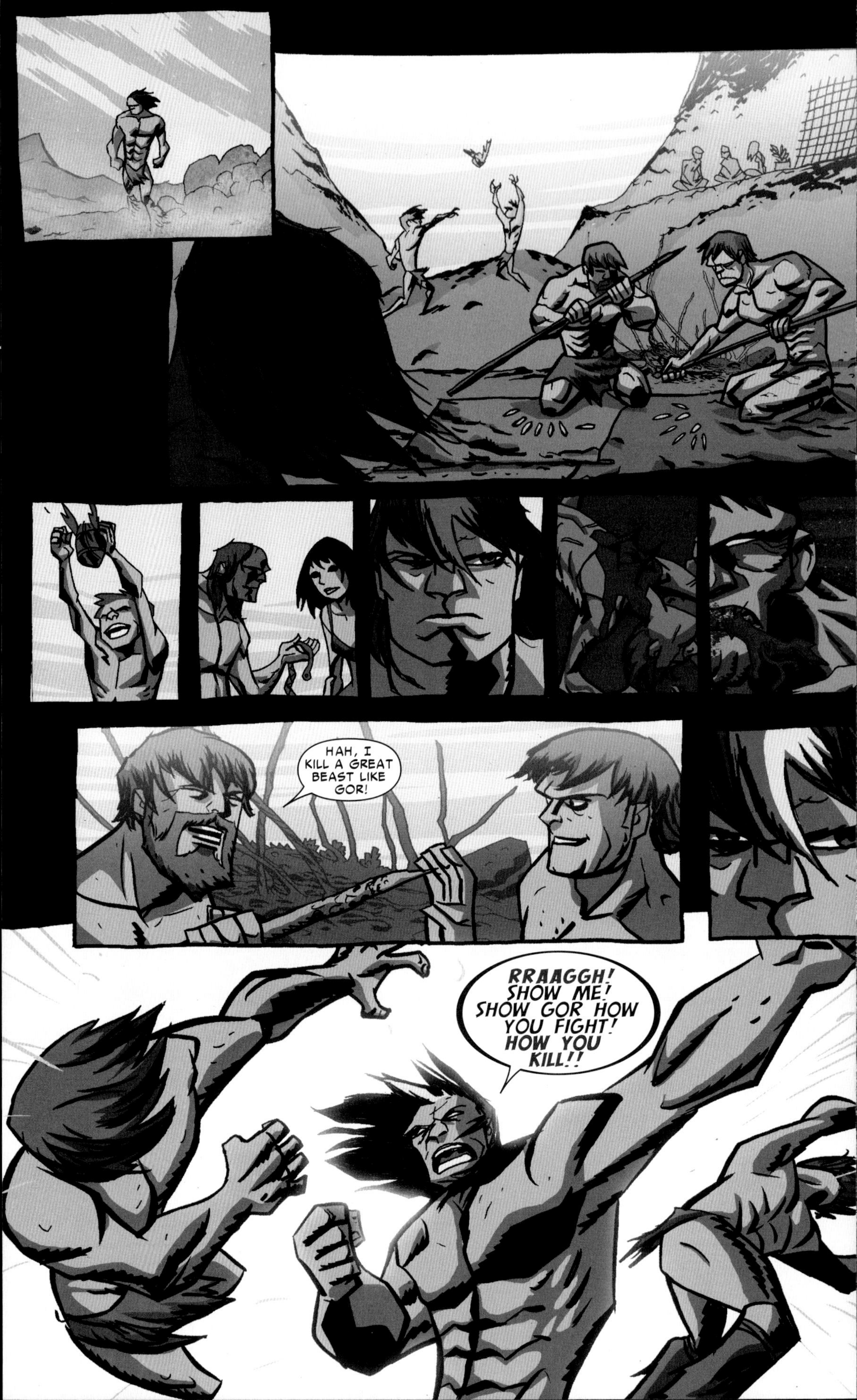
HAH, I KILL A GREAT BEAST LIKE GOR!
RRAAGGH! SHOW ME! SHOW GOR HOW YOU FIGHT! HOW YOU KILL!!

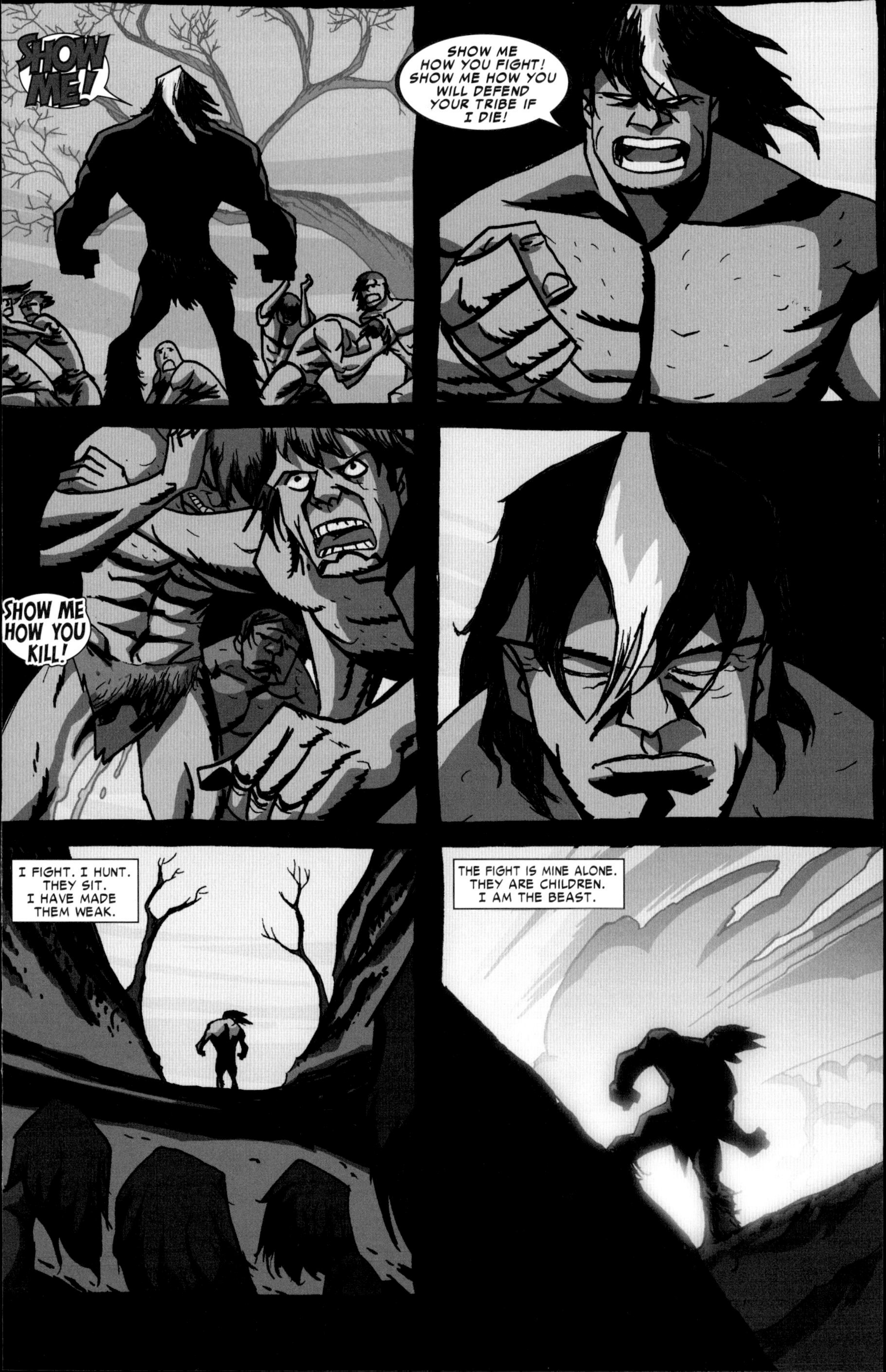
SHOW ME!
SHOW ME HOW YOU FIGHT! SHOW ME HOW YOU WILL DEFEND YOUR TRIBE IF I DIE!
SHOW ME HOW YOU KILL!
I FIGHT. I HUNT. THEY SIT. I HAVE MADE THEM WEAK.
THE FIGHT IS MINE ALONE. THEY ARE CHILDREN. I AM THE BEAST.

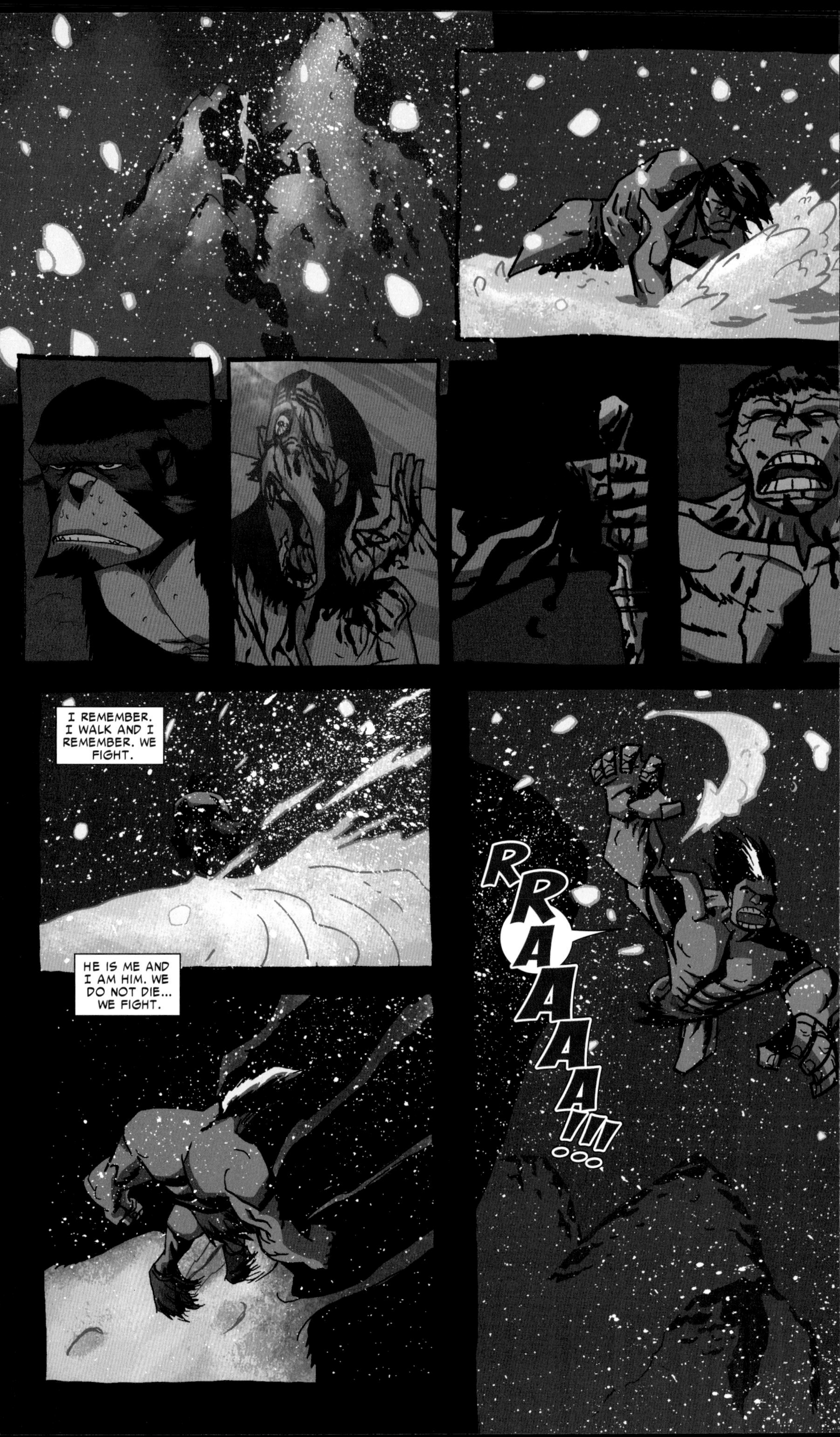
I REMEMBER. I WALK AND I REMEMBER. WE FIGHT.
HE IS ME AND I AM HIM. WE DO NOT DIE... WE FIGHT.
RRAAAA!!!...

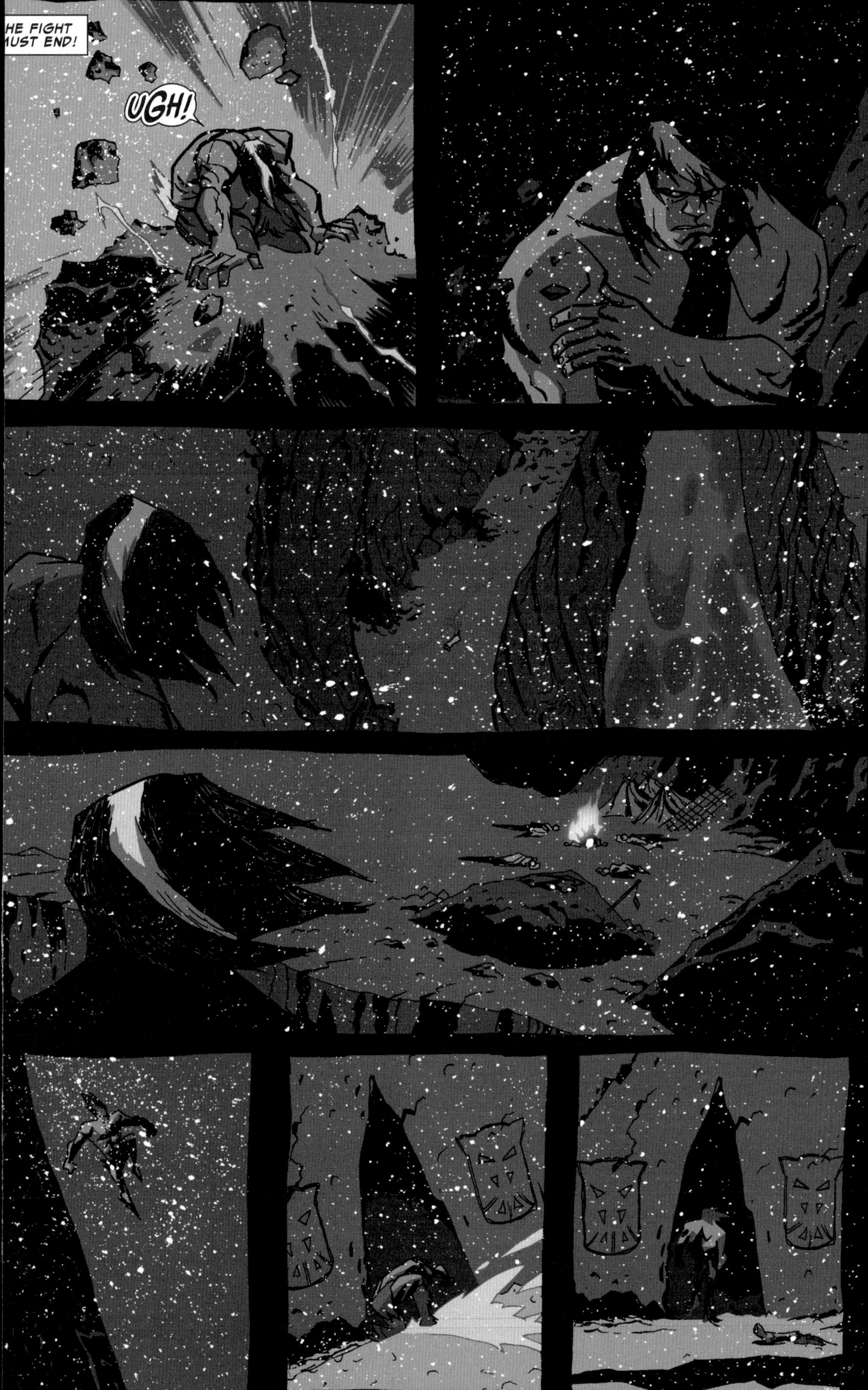
HE FIGHT MUST END!
UGH!

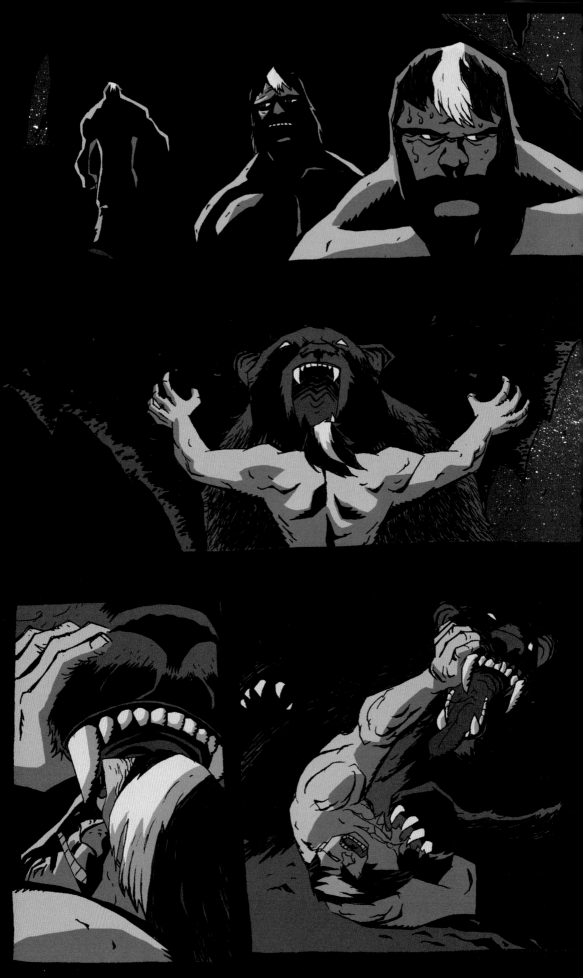

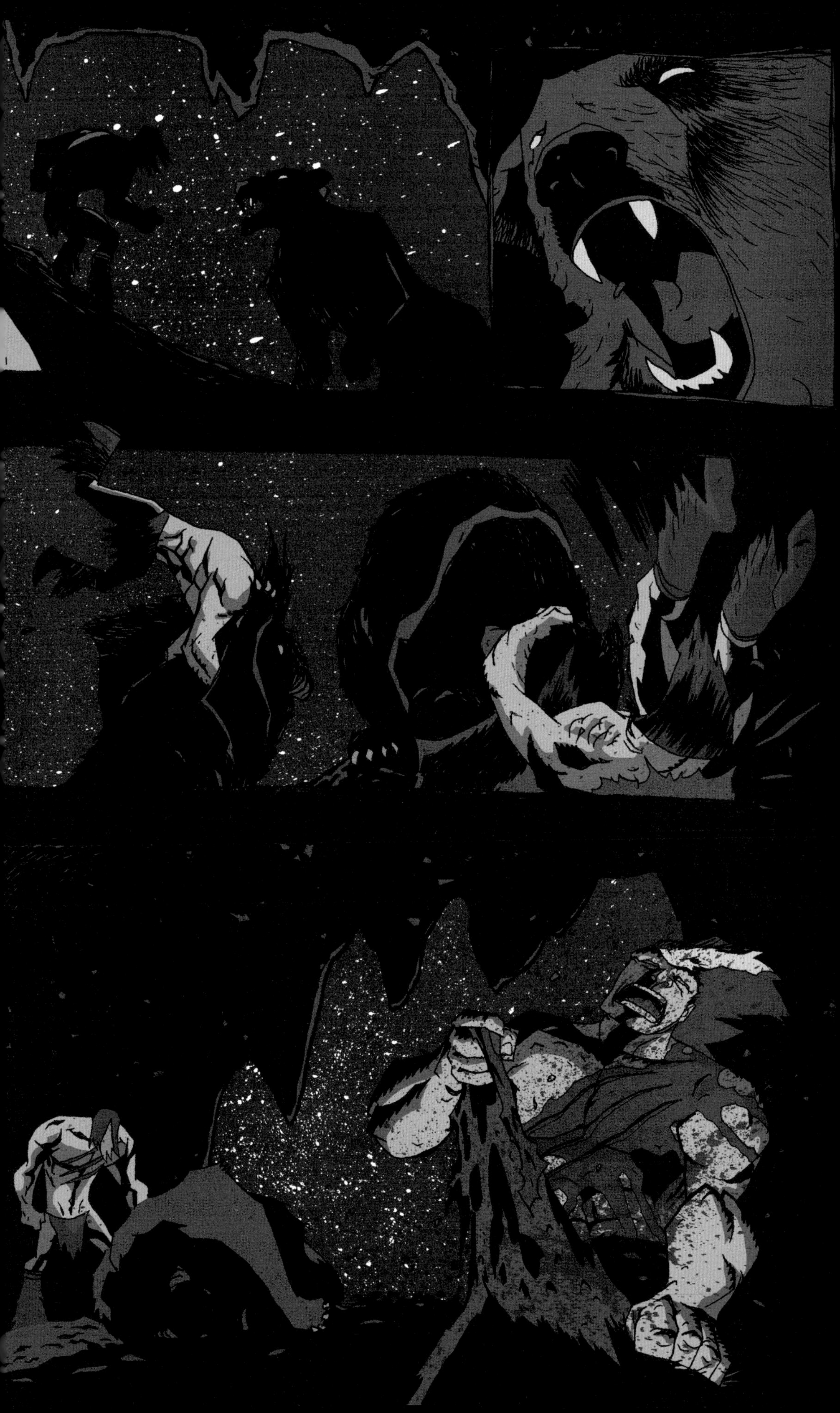

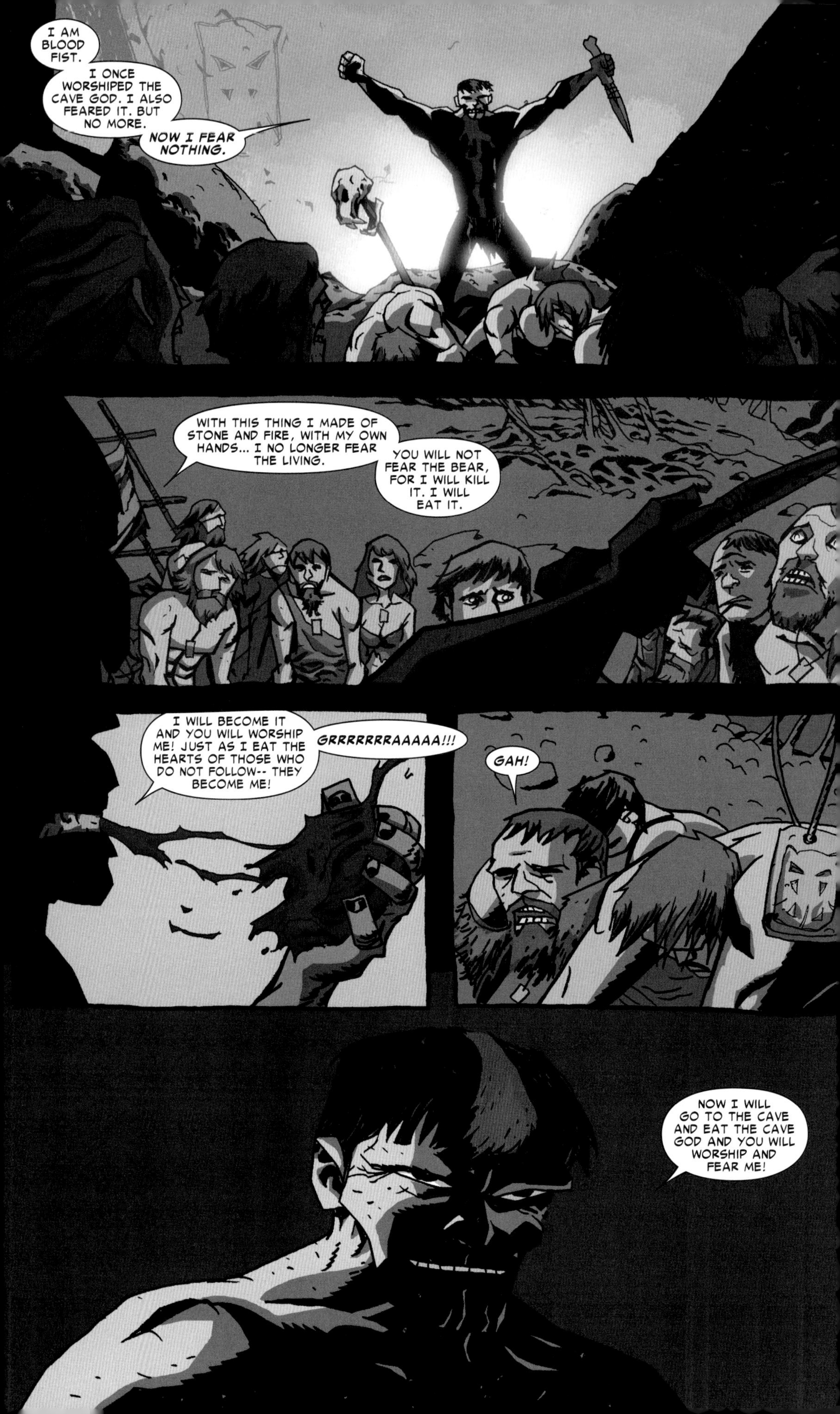
I AM BLOOD FIST.
I ONCE WORSHIPED THE CAVE GOD. I ALSO FEARED IT. BUT NO MORE.
NOW I FEAR NOTHING.
WITH THIS THING I MADE OF STONE AND FIRE, WITH MY OWN HANDS... I NO LONGER FEAR THE LIVING.
YOU WILL NOT FEAR THE BEAR, FOR I WILL KILL IT. I WILL EAT IT.
I WILL BECOME IT AND YOU WILL WORSHIP ME! JUST AS I EAT THE HEARTS OF THOSE WHO DO NOT FOLLOW-- THEY BECOME ME!
GRRRRRRRAAAAAA!!!
GAH!
NOW I WILL GO TO THE CAVE AND EAT THE CAVE GOD AND YOU WILL WORSHIP AND FEAR ME!

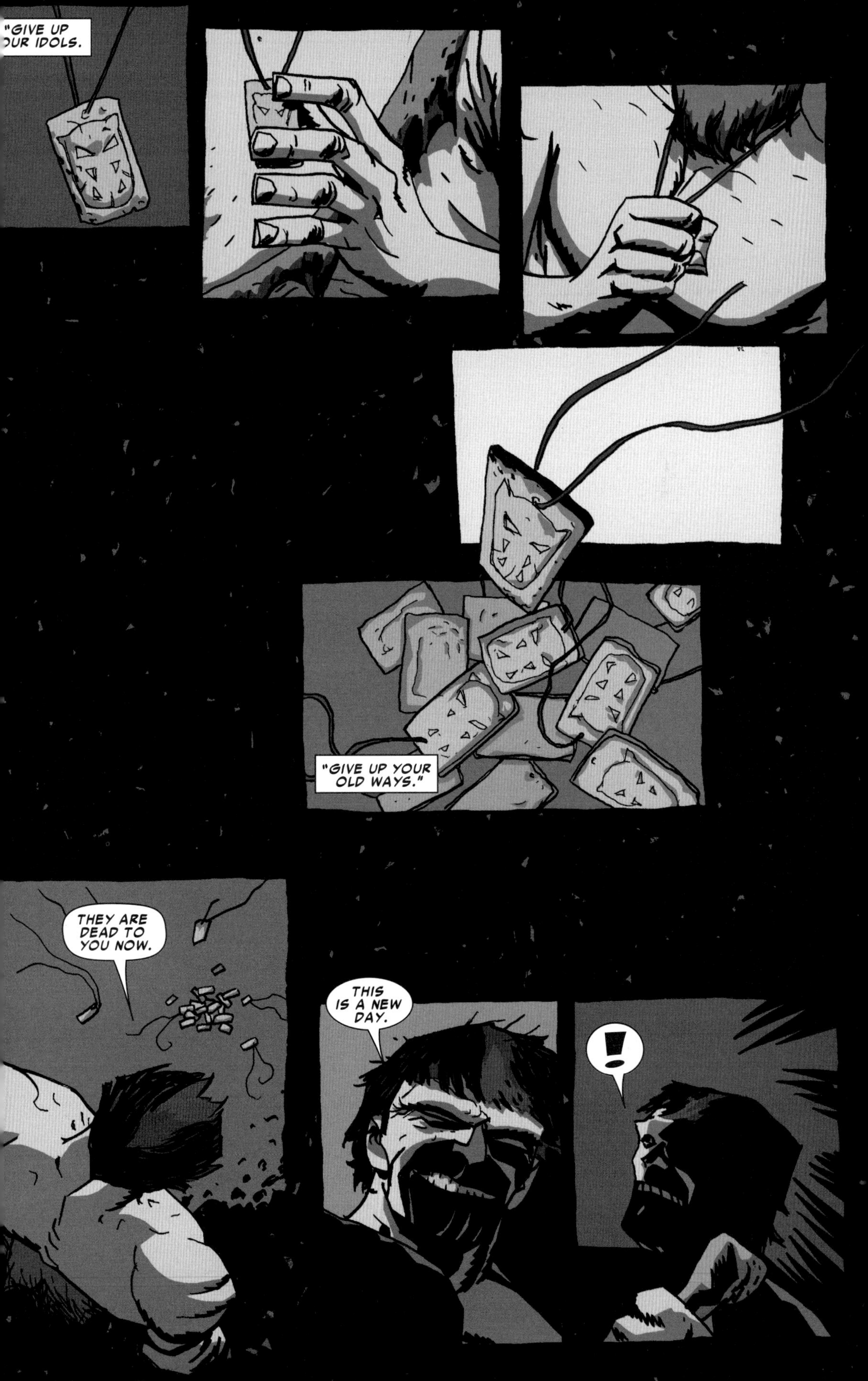
"GIVE UP
OUR IDOLS.
"GIVE UP YOUR OLD WAYS."
THEY ARE DEAD TO YOU NOW.
THIS IS A NEW DAY.
!

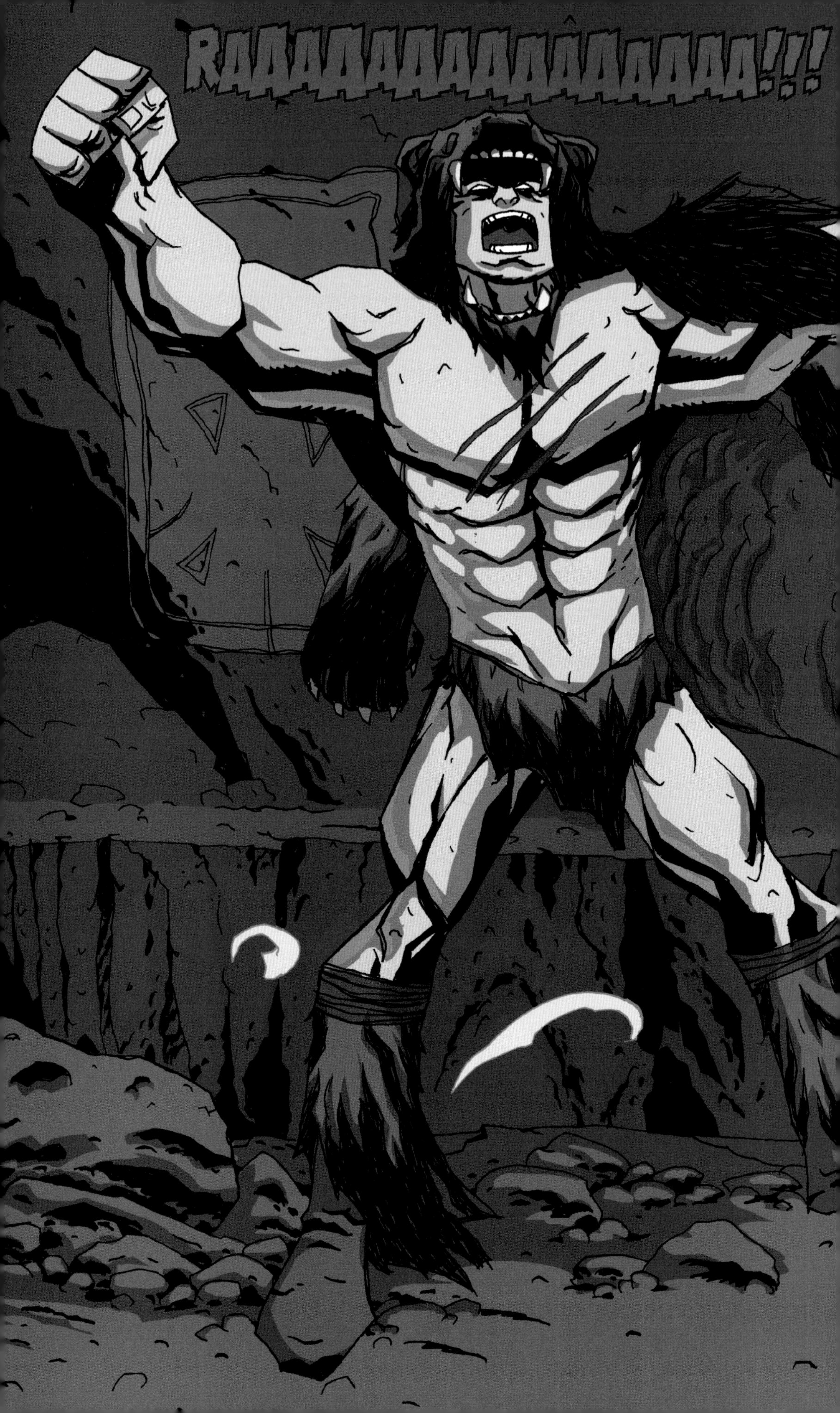
RAAAAAAAAAAAAAAA!!!

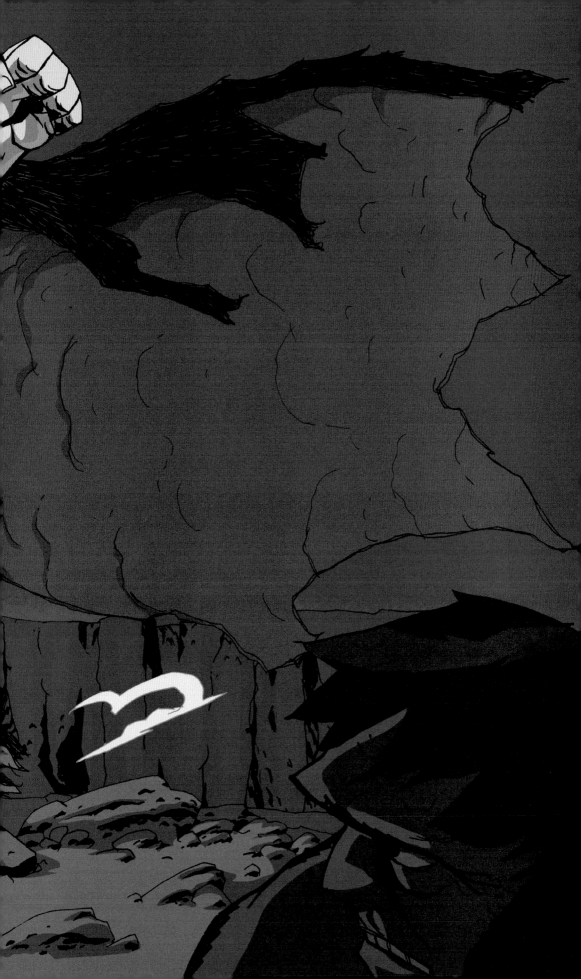

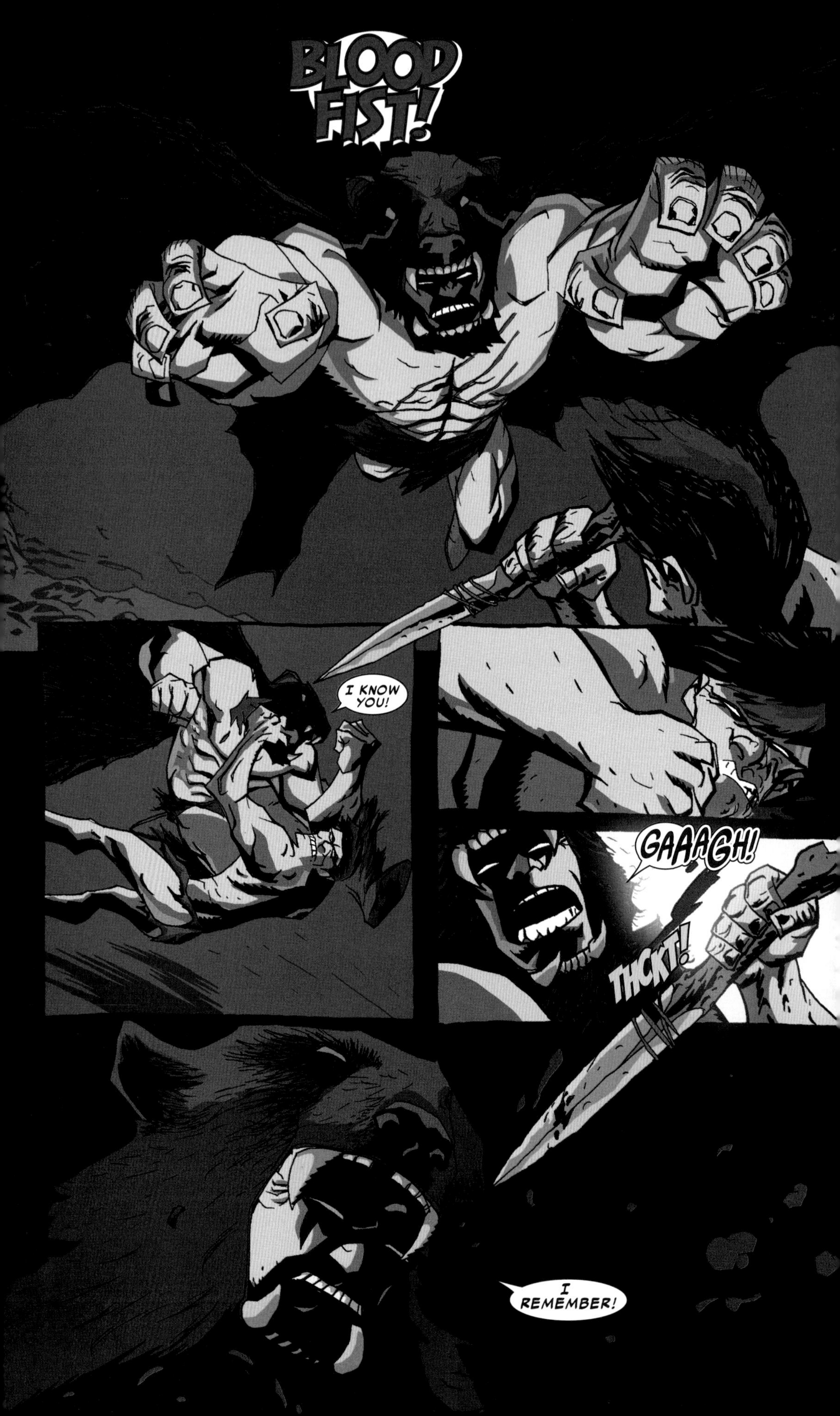
BLOOD FIST!
I KNOW YOU!
GAAAGH!
THCKT!
I REMEMBER!

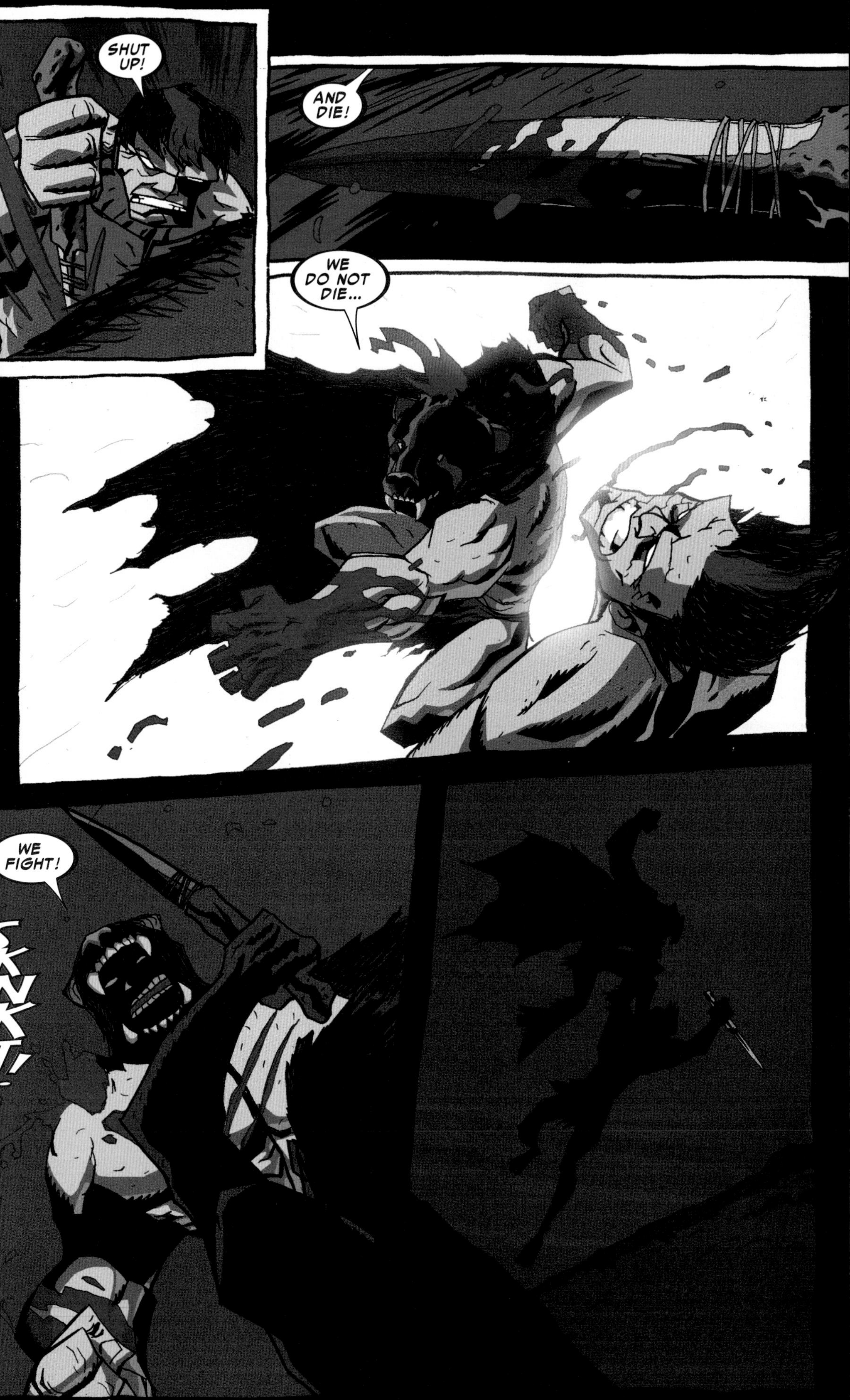
SHUT UP!
AND DIE!
WE DO NOT DIE...
WE FIGHT!

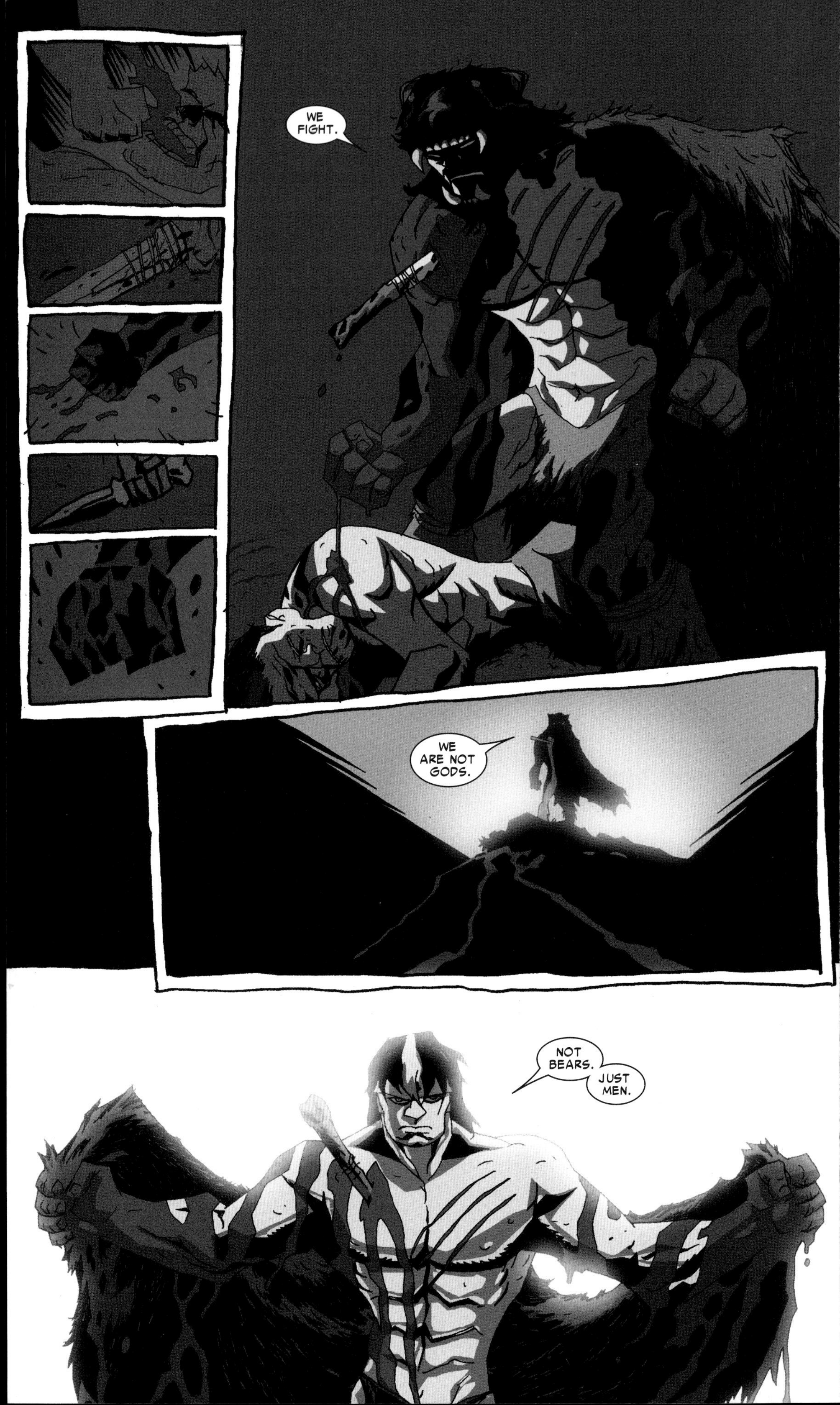
WE FIGHT.
WE ARE NOT GODS.
NOT BEARS.
JUST MEN.

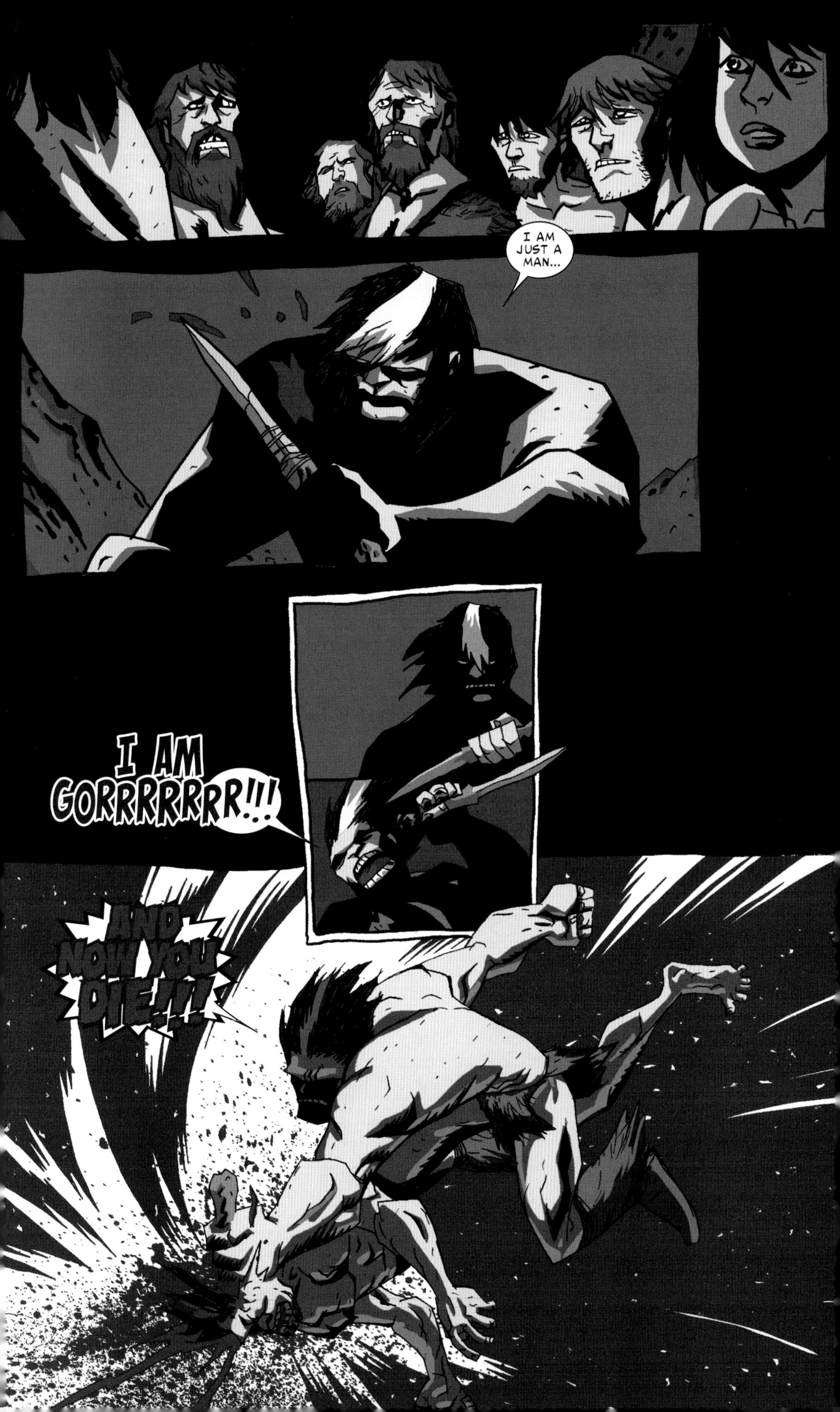
I AM JUST A MAN...
I AM GORRRRRRR!!!
AND NOW YOU DIE!!!

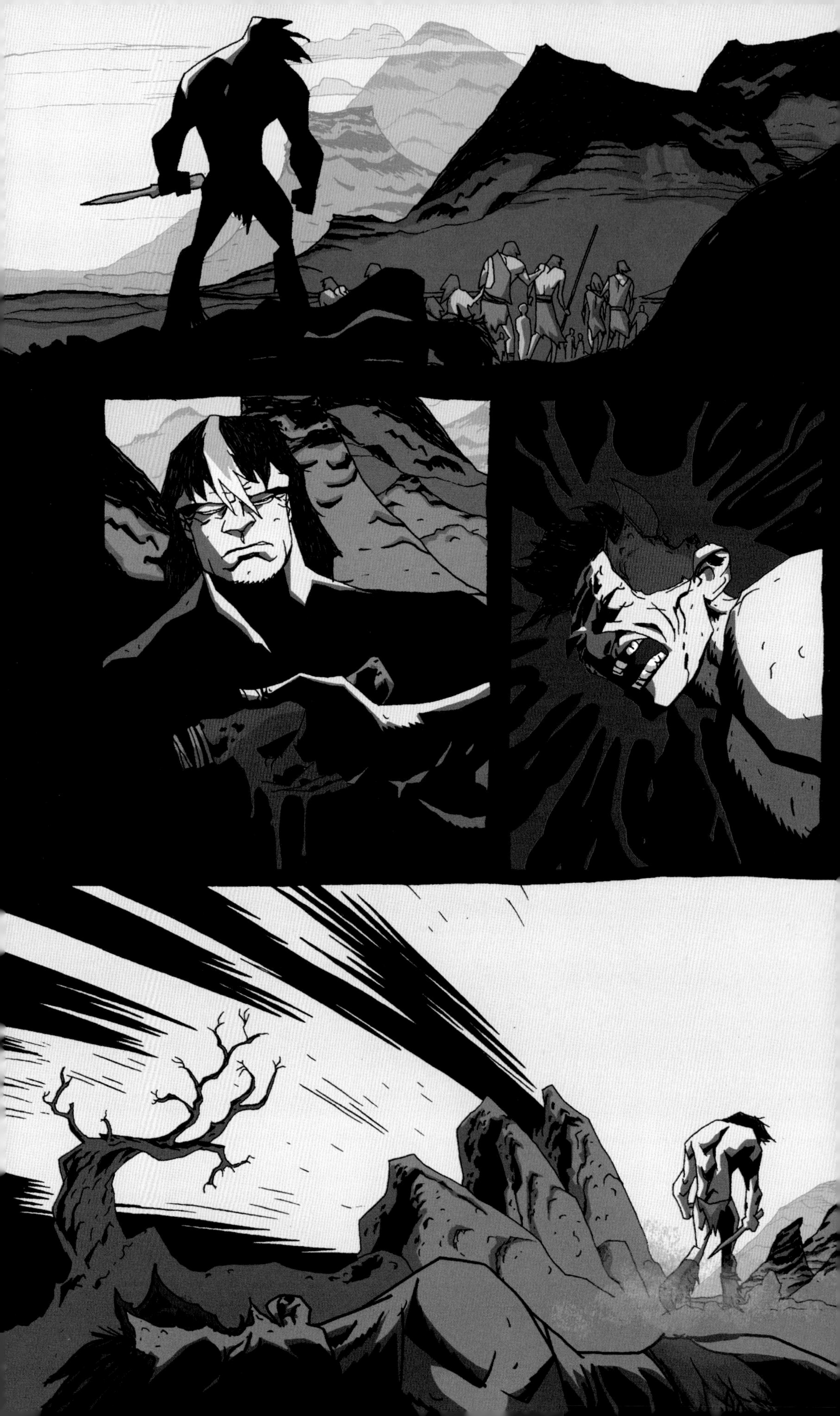

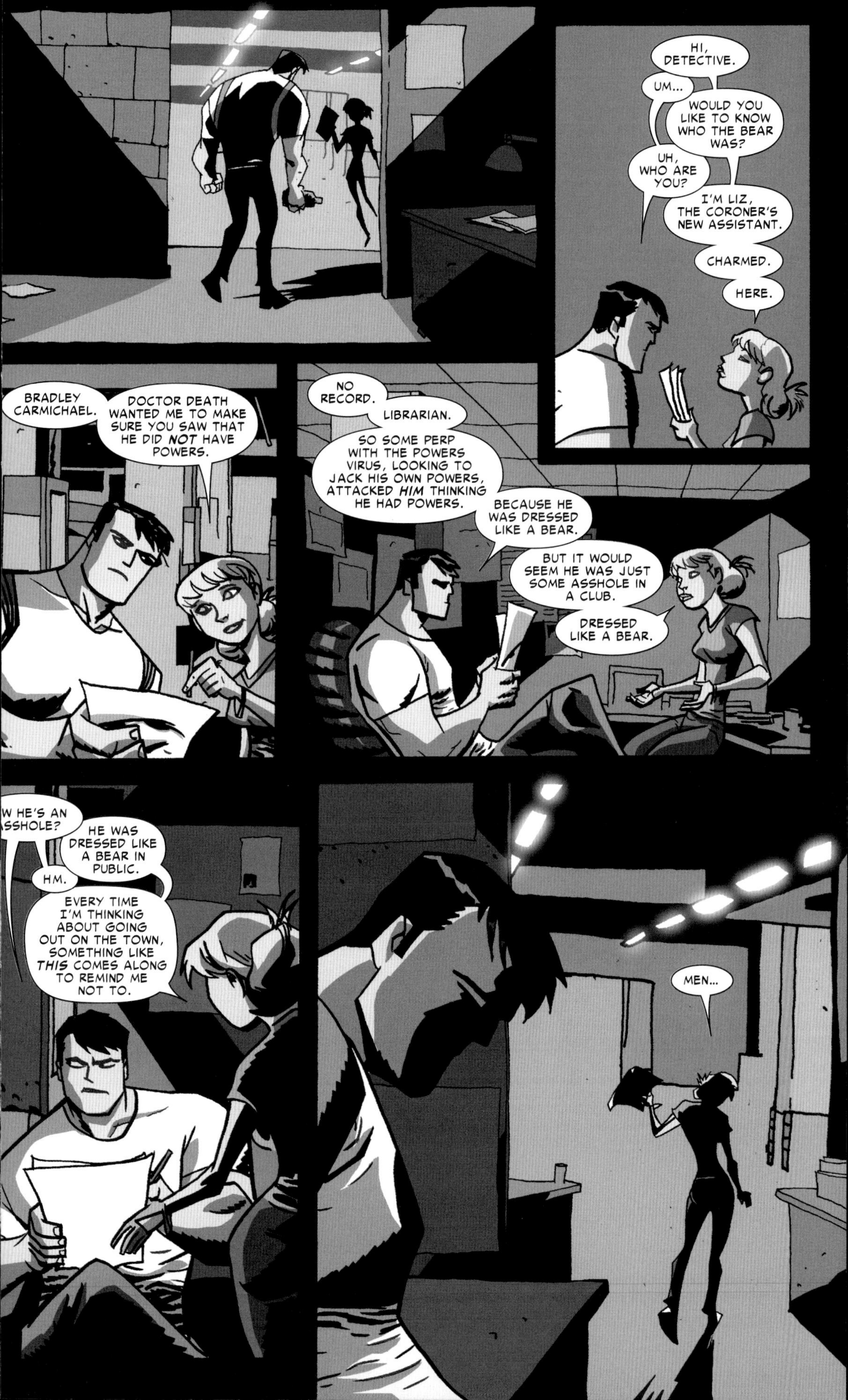
HI, DETECTIVE.
UM...
WOULD YOU LIKE TO KNOW WHO THE BEAR WAS?
UH, WHO ARE YOU?
I'M LIZ, THE CORONER'S NEW ASSISTANT.
CHARMED.
HERE.
BRADLEY CARMICHAEL.
DOCTOR DEATH WANTED ME TO MAKE SURE YOU SAW THAT HE DID NOT HAVE POWERS.
NO RECORD.
LIBRARIAN.
SO SOME PERP WITH THE POWERS VIRUS, LOOKING TO JACK HIS OWN POWERS, ATTACKED HIM THINKING HE HAD POWERS.
BECAUSE HE WAS DRESSED LIKE A BEAR.
BUT IT WOULD SEEM HE WAS JUST SOME ASSHOLE IN A CLUB.
DRESSED LIKE A BEAR.
W HE'S AN SSHOLE?
HE WAS DRESSED LIKE A BEAR IN PUBLIC.
HM.
EVERY TIME I'M THINKING ABOUT GOING OUT ON THE TOWN, SOMETHING LIKE THIS COMES ALONG TO REMIND ME NOT TO.
MEN...

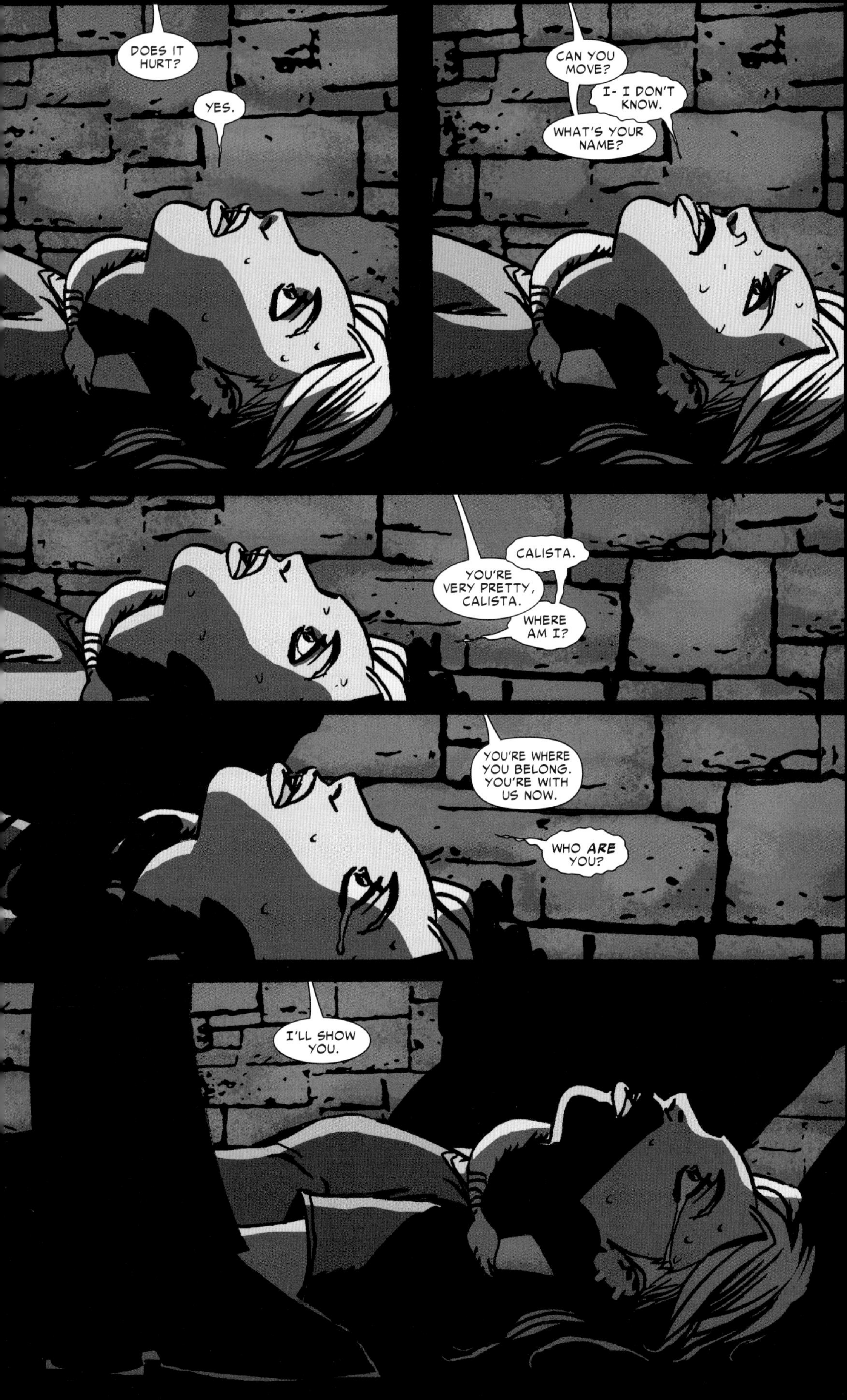
DOES IT HURT?
YES.
CAN YOU MOVE?
I- I DON'T KNOW.
WHAT'S YOUR NAME?
CALISTA.
YOU'RE VERY PRETTY, CALISTA.
WHERE AM I?
YOU'RE WHERE YOU BELONG. YOU'RE WITH US NOW.
WHO **ARE** YOU?
I'LL SHOW YOU.

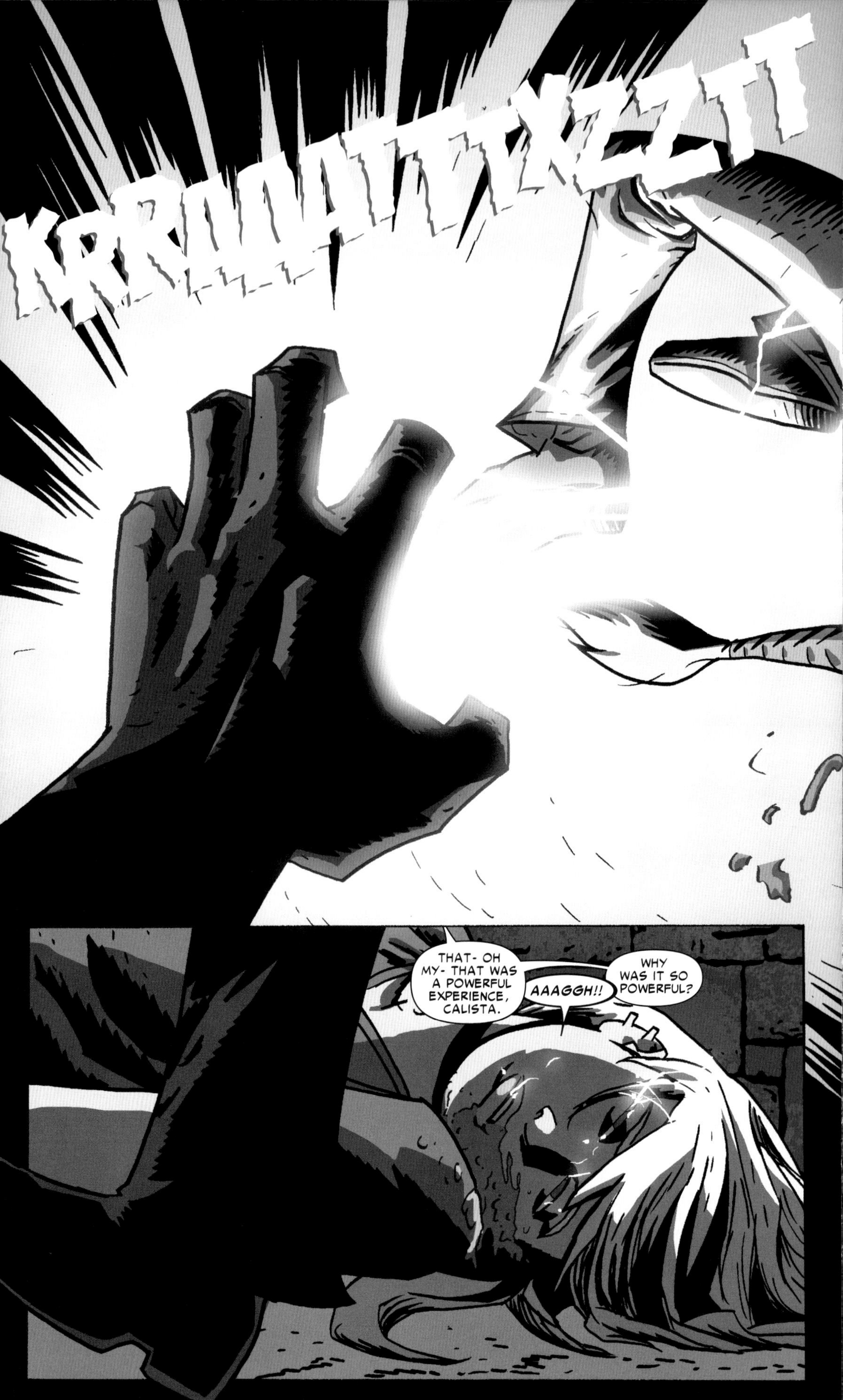
KRRAAATTTXZZTT
THAT- OH MY- THAT WAS A POWERFUL EXPERIENCE, CALISTA.
AAAGGH!!
WHY WAS IT SO POWERFUL?

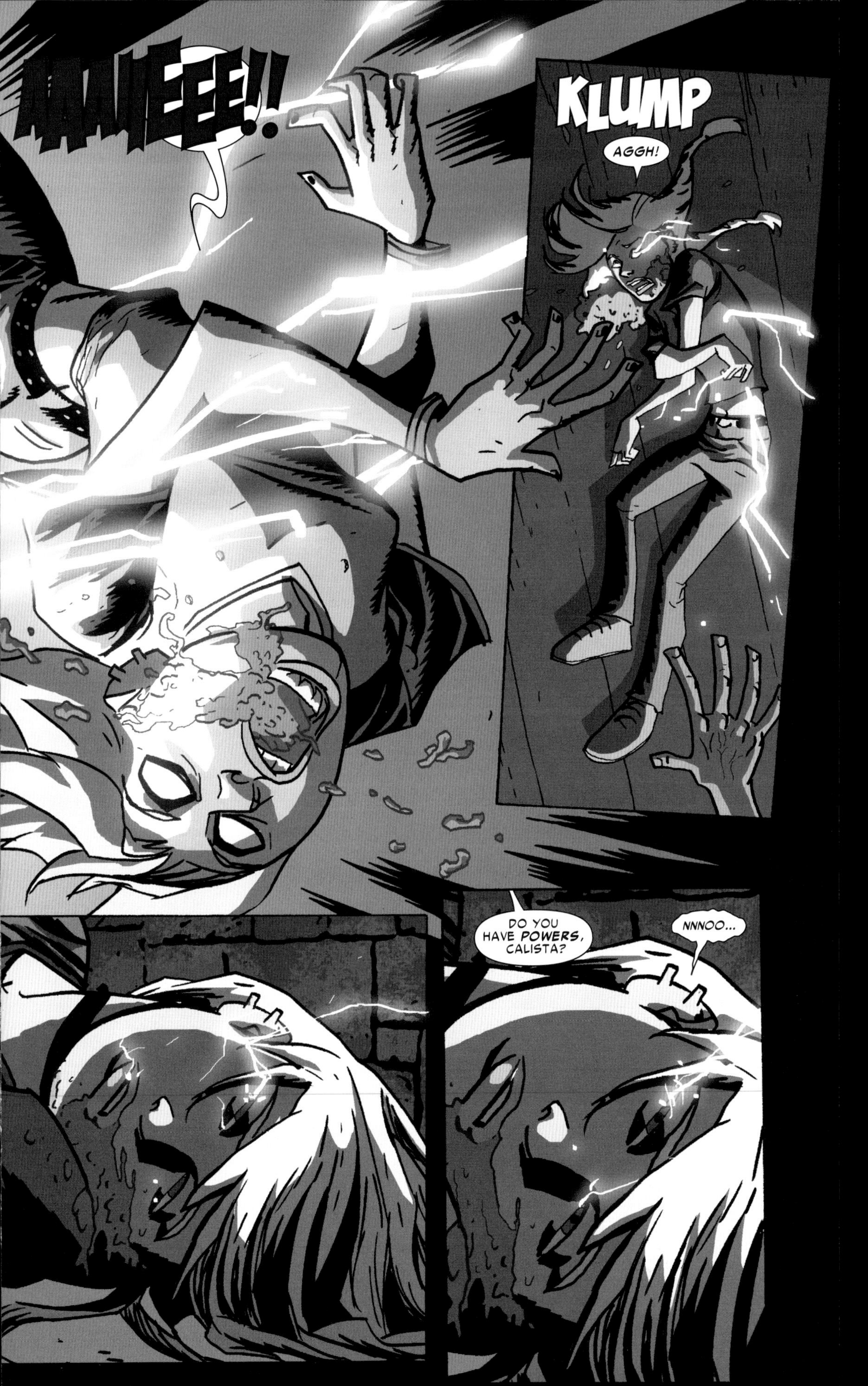
AAAIEEE!!
KLUMP
AGGH!
DO YOU HAVE POWERS, CALISTA?
NNNOO...

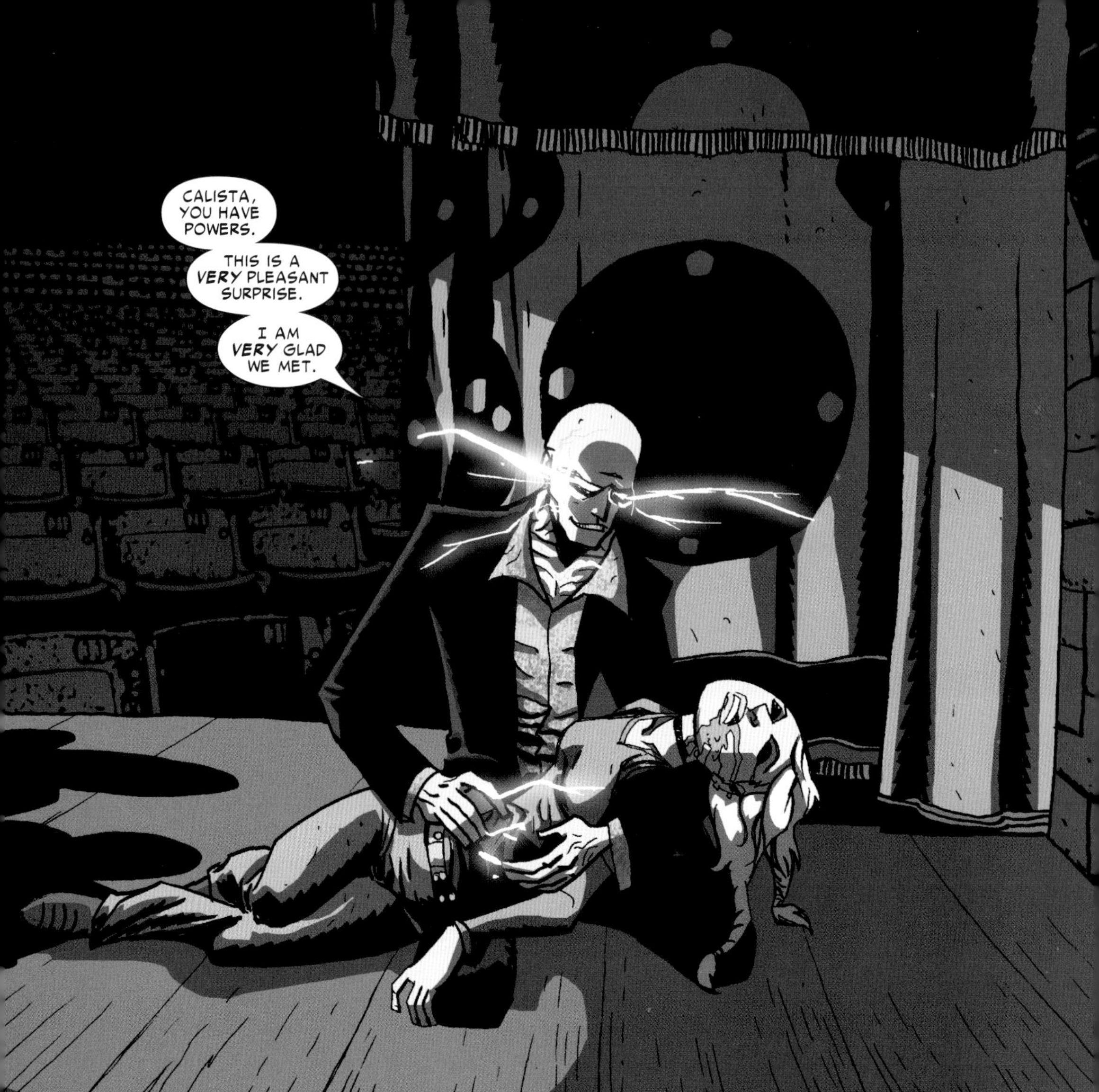
CALISTA, YOU HAVE POWERS.
THIS IS A VERY PLEASANT SURPRISE.
I AM VERY GLAD WE MET.

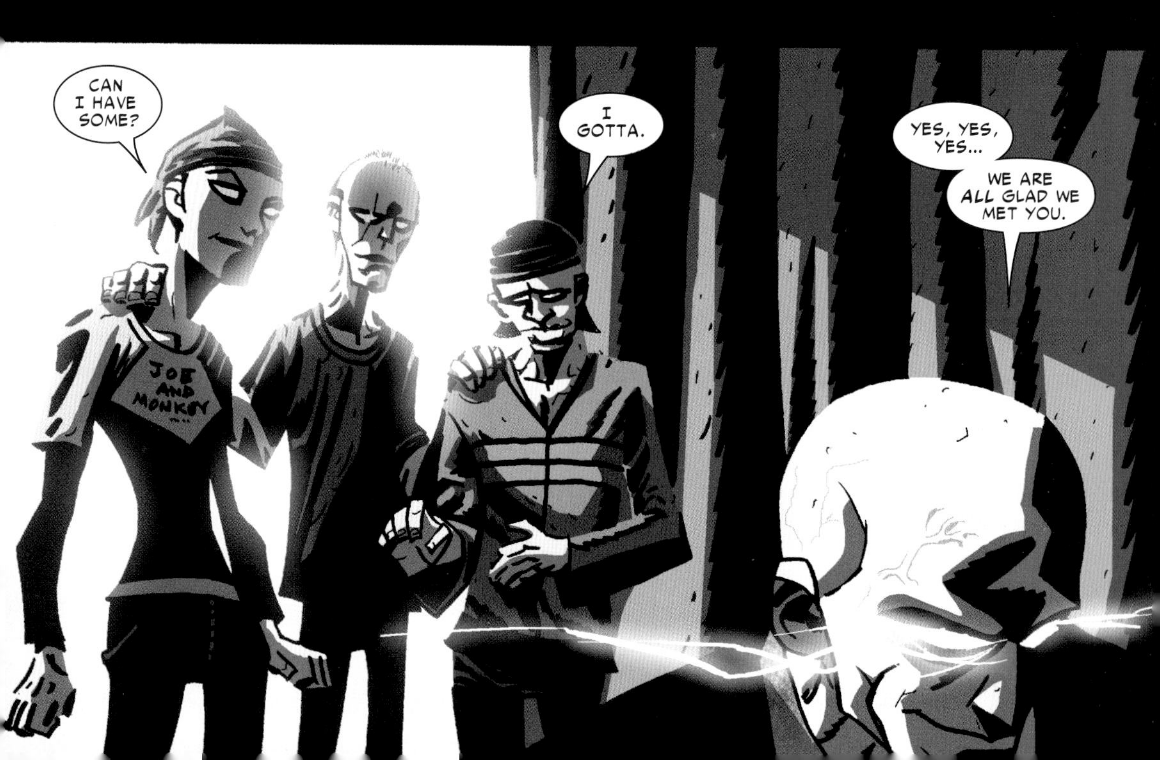
CAN I HAVE SOME?
JOE AND MONKEY
I GOTTA.
YES, YES, YES...
WE ARE ALL GLAD WE MET YOU.

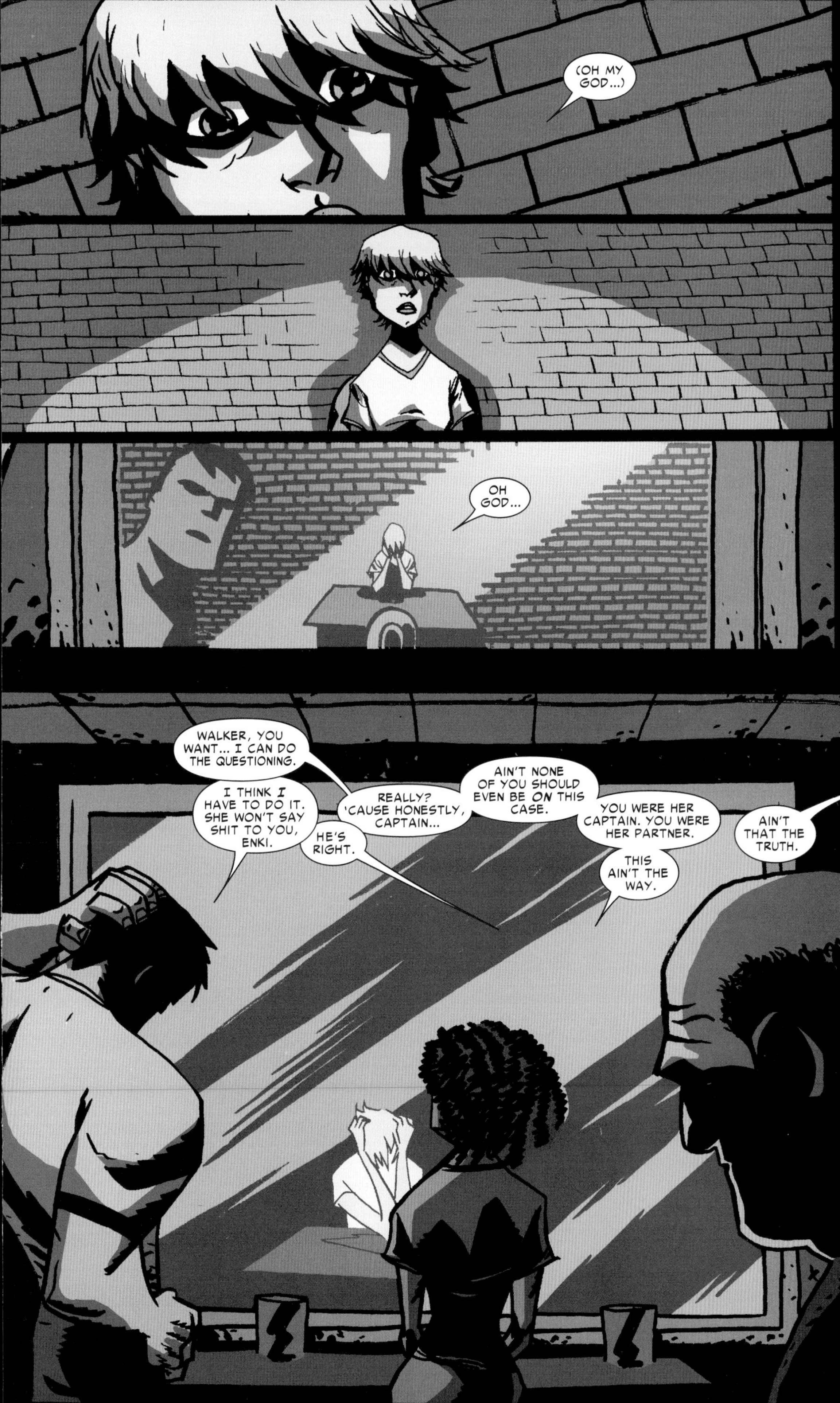
(OH MY GOD...)
OH GOD...
WALKER, YOU WANT... I CAN DO THE QUESTIONING.
I THINK *I* HAVE TO DO IT. SHE WON'T SAY SHIT TO YOU, ENKI.
HE'S RIGHT.
REALLY? 'CAUSE HONESTLY, CAPTAIN...
AIN'T NONE OF YOU SHOULD EVEN BE *ON* THIS CASE.
YOU WERE HER CAPTAIN. YOU WERE HER PARTNER.
THIS AIN'T THE WAY.
AIN'T THAT THE TRUTH.

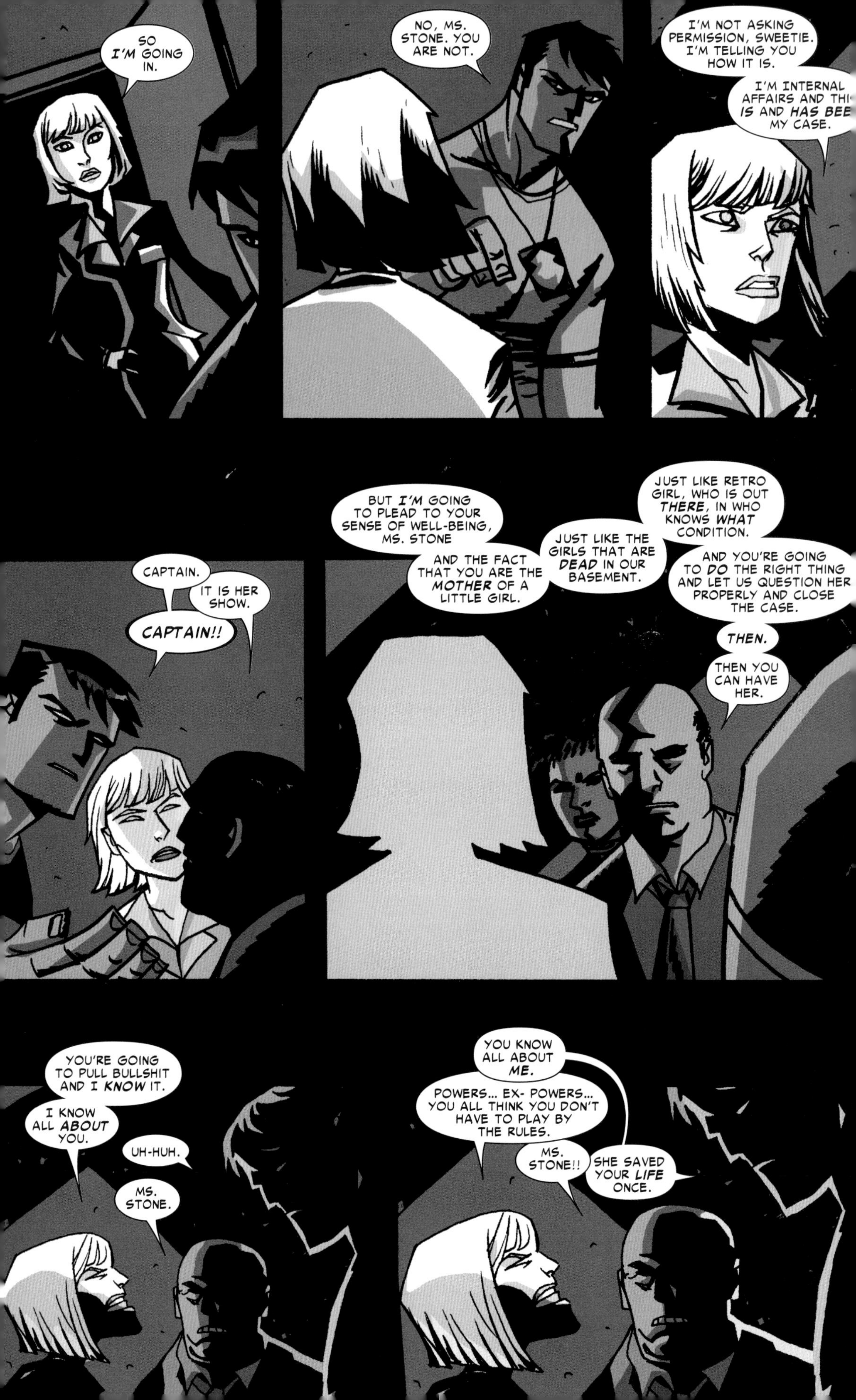
SO I'M GOING IN.
NO, MS. STONE. YOU ARE NOT.
I'M NOT ASKING PERMISSION, SWEETIE. I'M TELLING YOU HOW IT IS.
I'M INTERNAL AFFAIRS AND THI IS AND HAS BEE MY CASE.
CAPTAIN.
IT IS HER SHOW.
CAPTAIN!!
BUT I'M GOING TO PLEAD TO YOUR SENSE OF WELL-BEING, MS. STONE
AND THE FACT THAT YOU ARE THE MOTHER OF A LITTLE GIRL.
JUST LIKE THE GIRLS THAT ARE DEAD IN OUR BASEMENT.
JUST LIKE RETRO GIRL, WHO IS OUT THERE, IN WHO KNOWS WHAT CONDITION.
AND YOU'RE GOING TO DO THE RIGHT THING AND LET US QUESTION HER PROPERLY AND CLOSE THE CASE.
THEN.
THEN YOU CAN HAVE HER.
YOU'RE GOING TO PULL BULLSHIT AND I KNOW IT.
I KNOW ALL ABOUT YOU.
UH-HUH.
MS. STONE.
YOU KNOW ALL ABOUT ME.
POWERS... EX- POWERS... YOU ALL THINK YOU DON'T HAVE TO PLAY BY THE RULES.
MS. STONE!!
SHE SAVED YOUR LIFE ONCE.

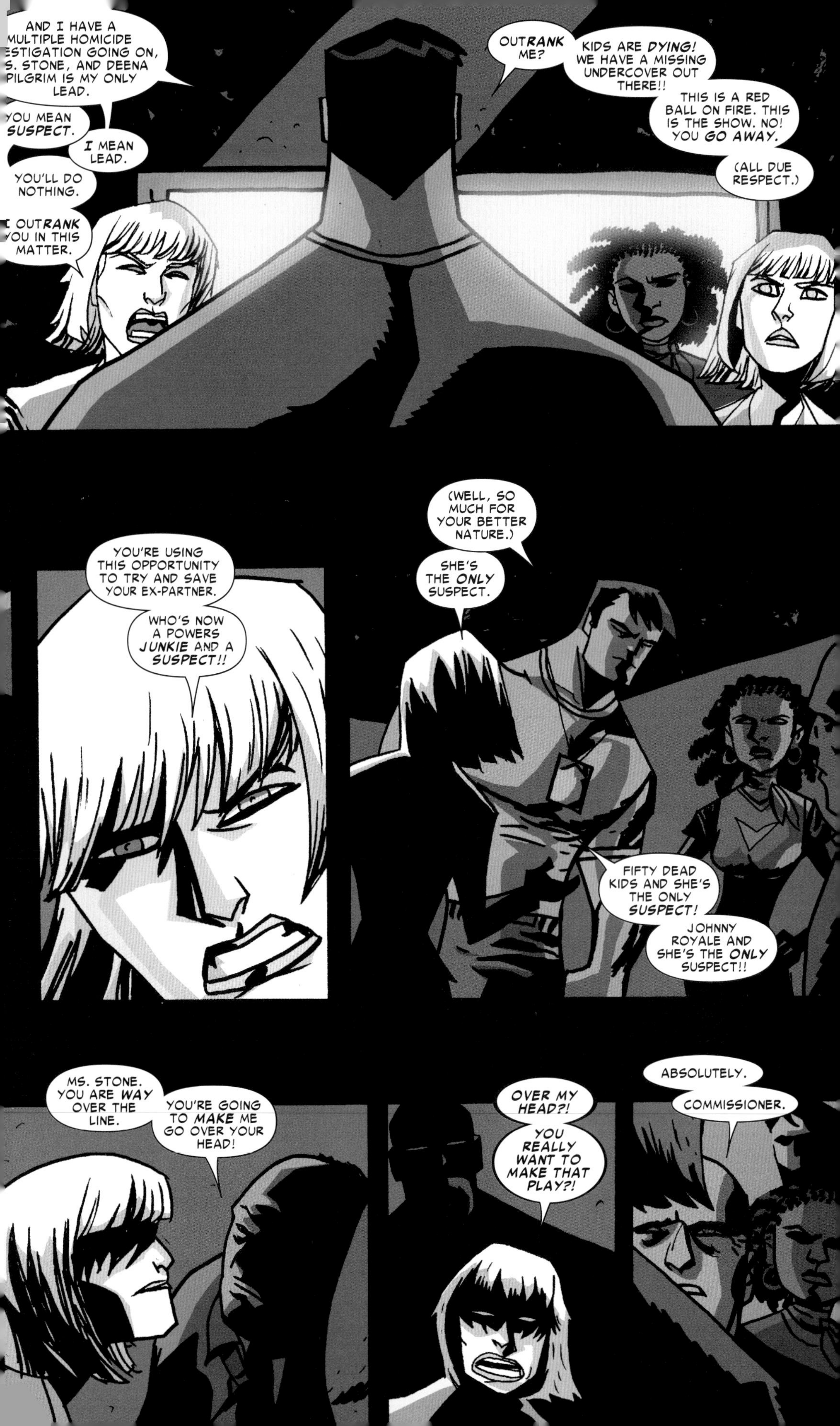
AND I HAVE A MULTIPLE HOMICIDE ESTIGATION GOING ON, S. STONE, AND DEENA PILGRIM IS MY ONLY LEAD.
YOU MEAN SUSPECT.
I MEAN LEAD.
YOU'LL DO NOTHING.
I OUTRANK YOU IN THIS MATTER.
OUTRANK ME?
KIDS ARE DYING! WE HAVE A MISSING UNDERCOVER OUT THERE!!
THIS IS A RED BALL ON FIRE. THIS IS THE SHOW. NO! YOU GO AWAY.
(ALL DUE RESPECT.)
YOU'RE USING THIS OPPORTUNITY TO TRY AND SAVE YOUR EX-PARTNER.
WHO'S NOW A POWERS JUNKIE AND A SUSPECT!!
(WELL, SO MUCH FOR YOUR BETTER NATURE.)
SHE'S THE ONLY SUSPECT.
FIFTY DEAD KIDS AND SHE'S THE ONLY SUSPECT!
JOHNNY ROYALE AND SHE'S THE ONLY SUSPECT!!
MS. STONE. YOU ARE WAY OVER THE LINE.
YOU'RE GOING TO MAKE ME GO OVER YOUR HEAD!
OVER MY HEAD?!
YOU REALLY WANT TO MAKE THAT PLAY?!
ABSOLUTELY.
COMMISSIONER.

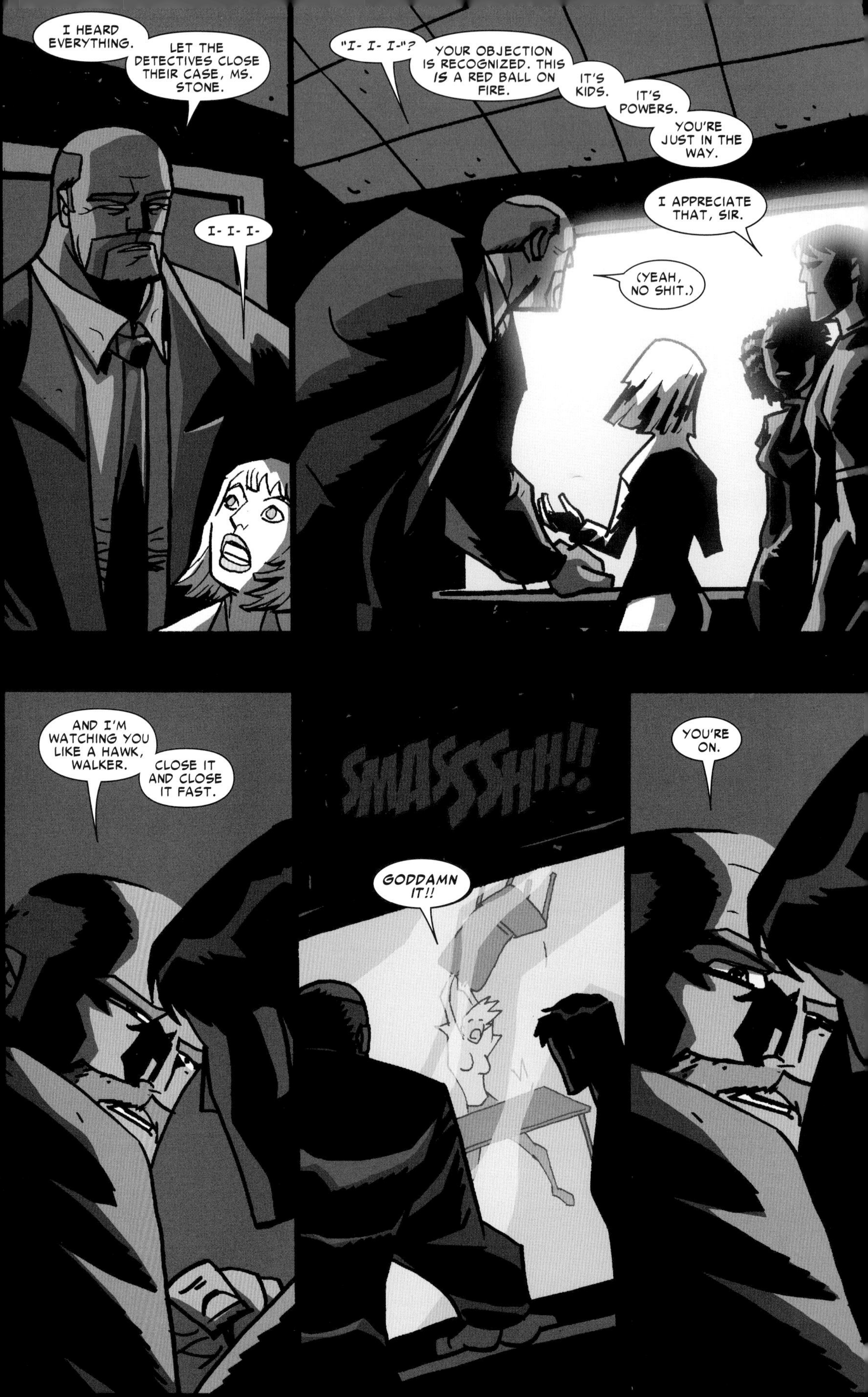
I HEARD EVERYTHING.
LET THE DETECTIVES CLOSE THEIR CASE, MS. STONE.
I- I- I-
"I- I- I-"?
YOUR OBJECTION IS RECOGNIZED. THIS *IS* A RED BALL ON FIRE.
IT'S KIDS.
IT'S POWERS.
YOU'RE JUST IN THE WAY.
I APPRECIATE THAT, SIR.
(YEAH, NO SHIT.)
AND I'M WATCHING YOU LIKE A HAWK, WALKER.
CLOSE IT AND CLOSE IT FAST.
SMASSSHH!!
GODDAMN IT!!
YOU'RE ON.

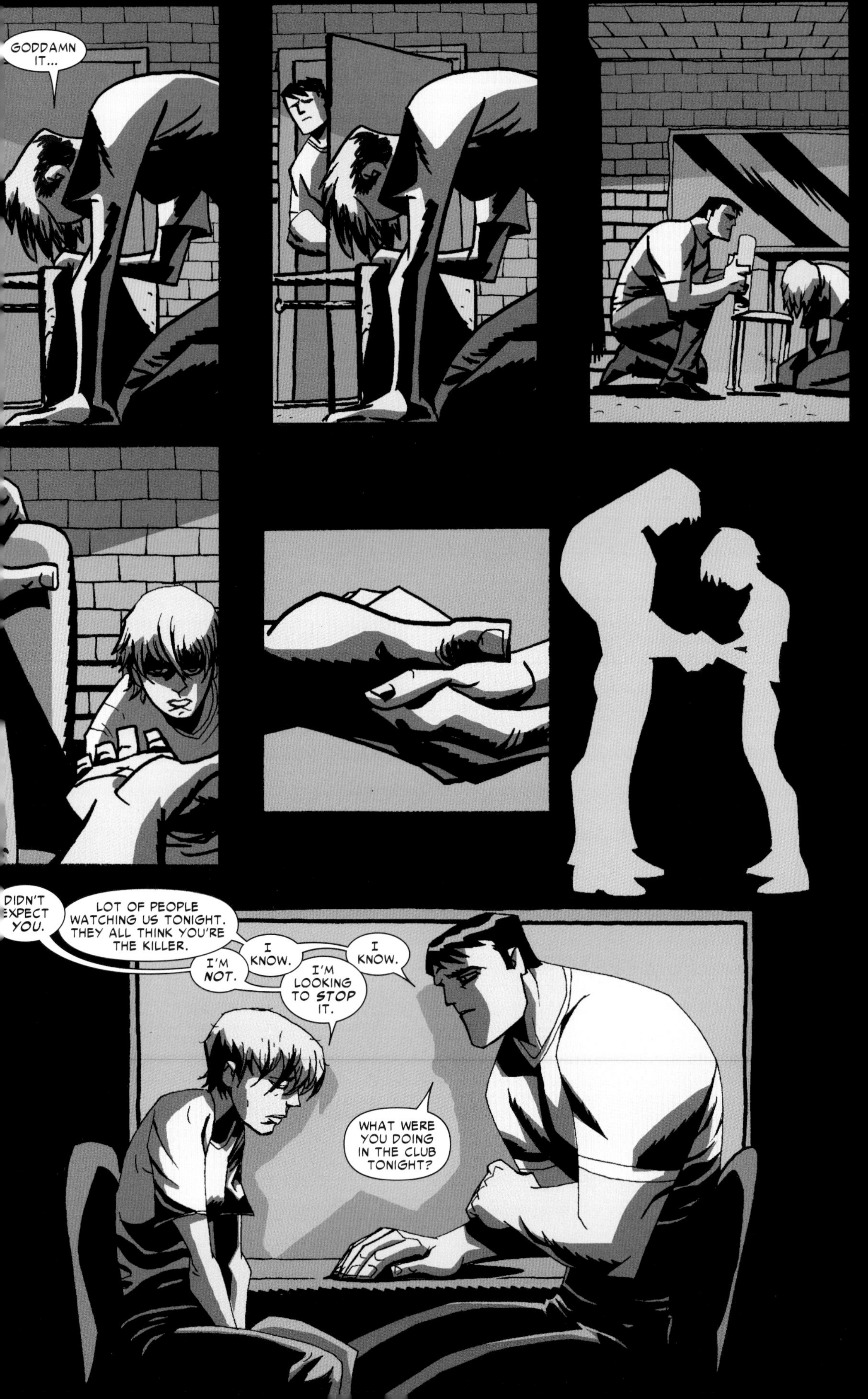
GODDAMN IT...
DIDN'T EXPECT YOU.
LOT OF PEOPLE WATCHING US TONIGHT. THEY ALL THINK YOU'RE THE KILLER.
I'M NOT.
I KNOW.
I KNOW.
I'M LOOKING TO STOP IT.
WHAT WERE YOU DOING IN THE CLUB TONIGHT?

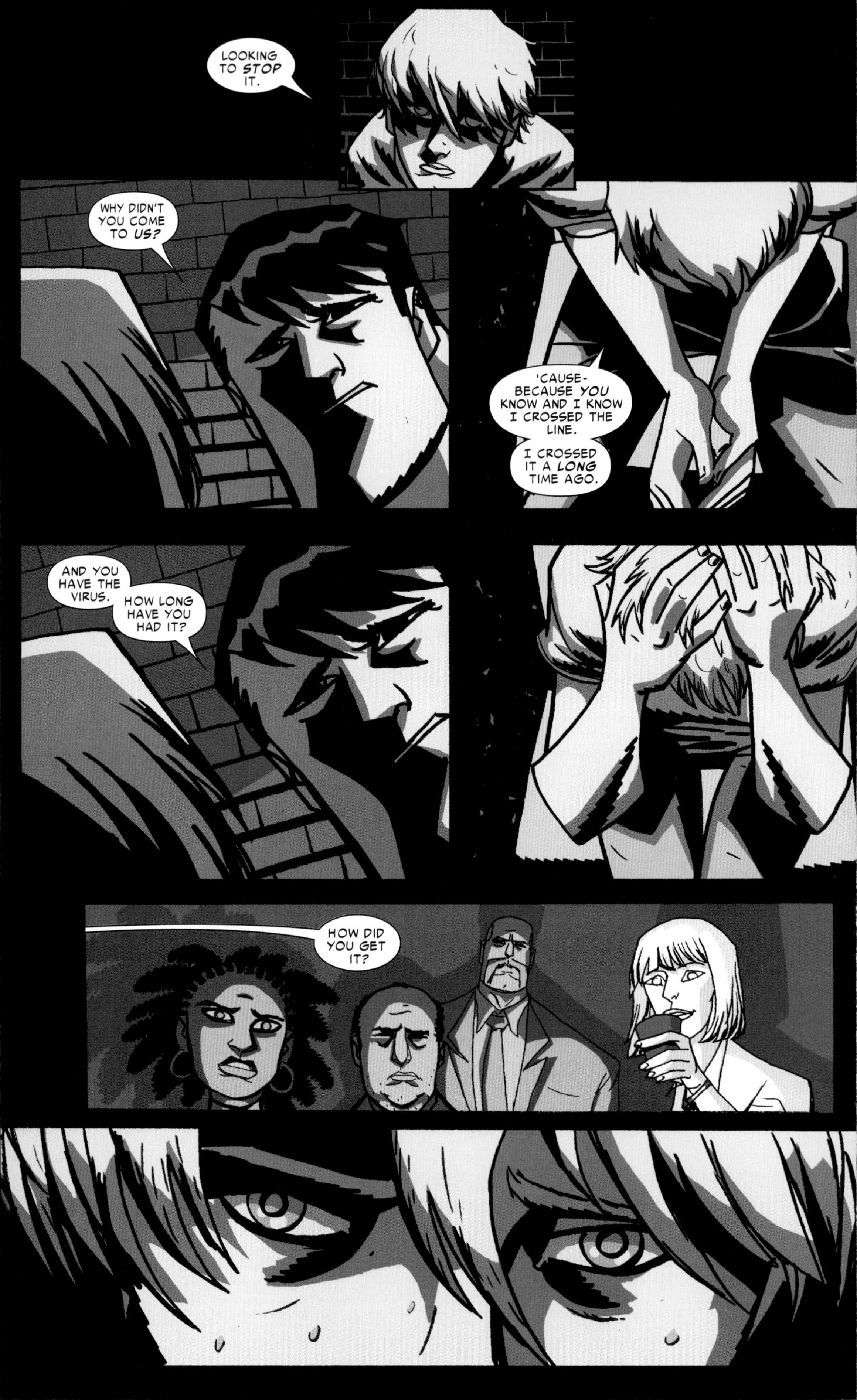
LOOKING TO STOP IT.
WHY DIDN'T YOU COME TO US?
'CAUSE- BECAUSE YOU KNOW AND I KNOW I CROSSED THE LINE.
I CROSSED IT A LONG TIME AGO.
AND YOU HAVE THE VIRUS.
HOW LONG HAVE YOU HAD IT?
HOW DID YOU GET IT?

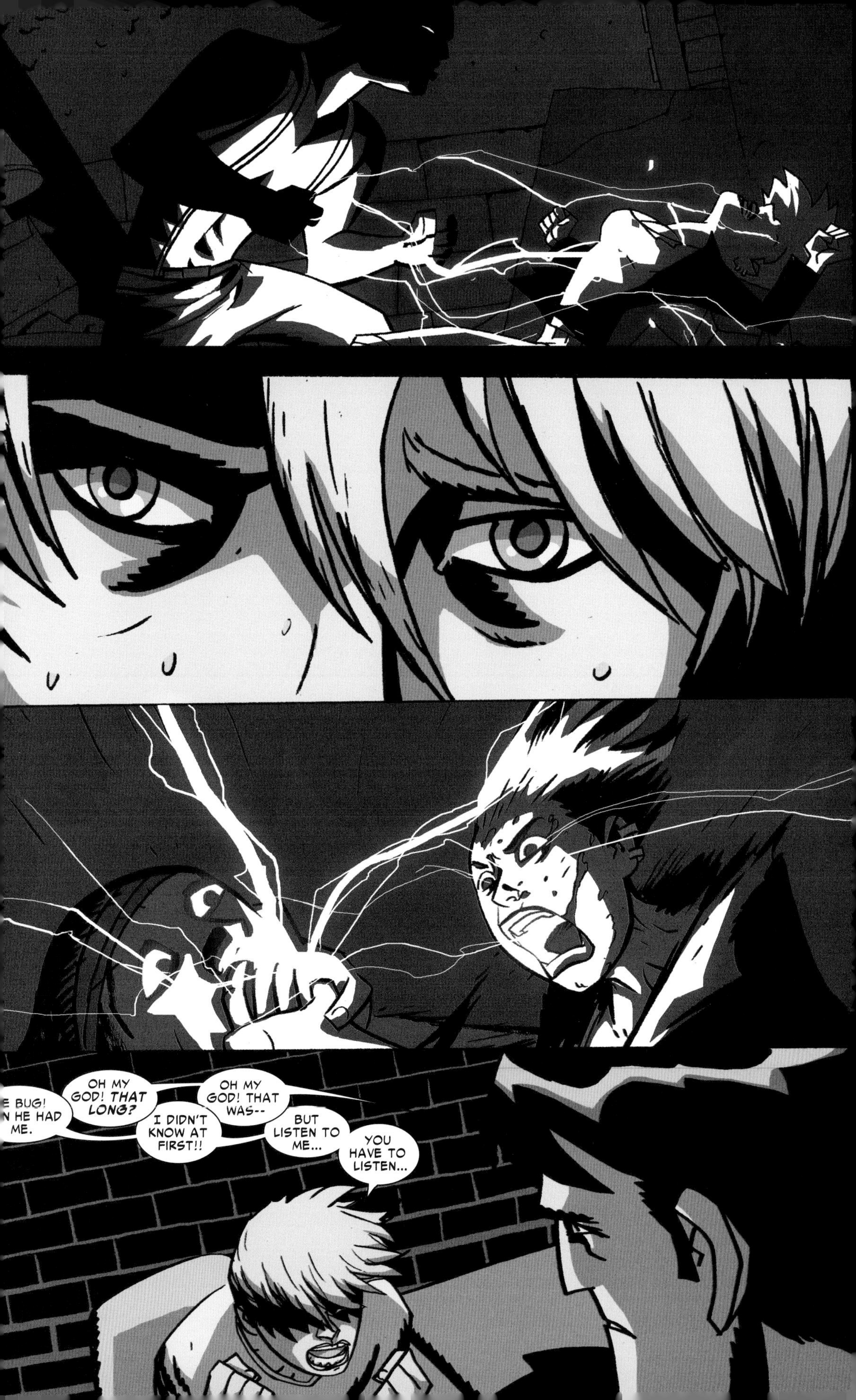
E BUG! N HE HAD ME.
OH MY GOD! *THAT LONG?*
I DIDN'T KNOW AT FIRST!!
OH MY GOD! THAT WAS--
BUT LISTEN TO ME...
YOU HAVE TO LISTEN...

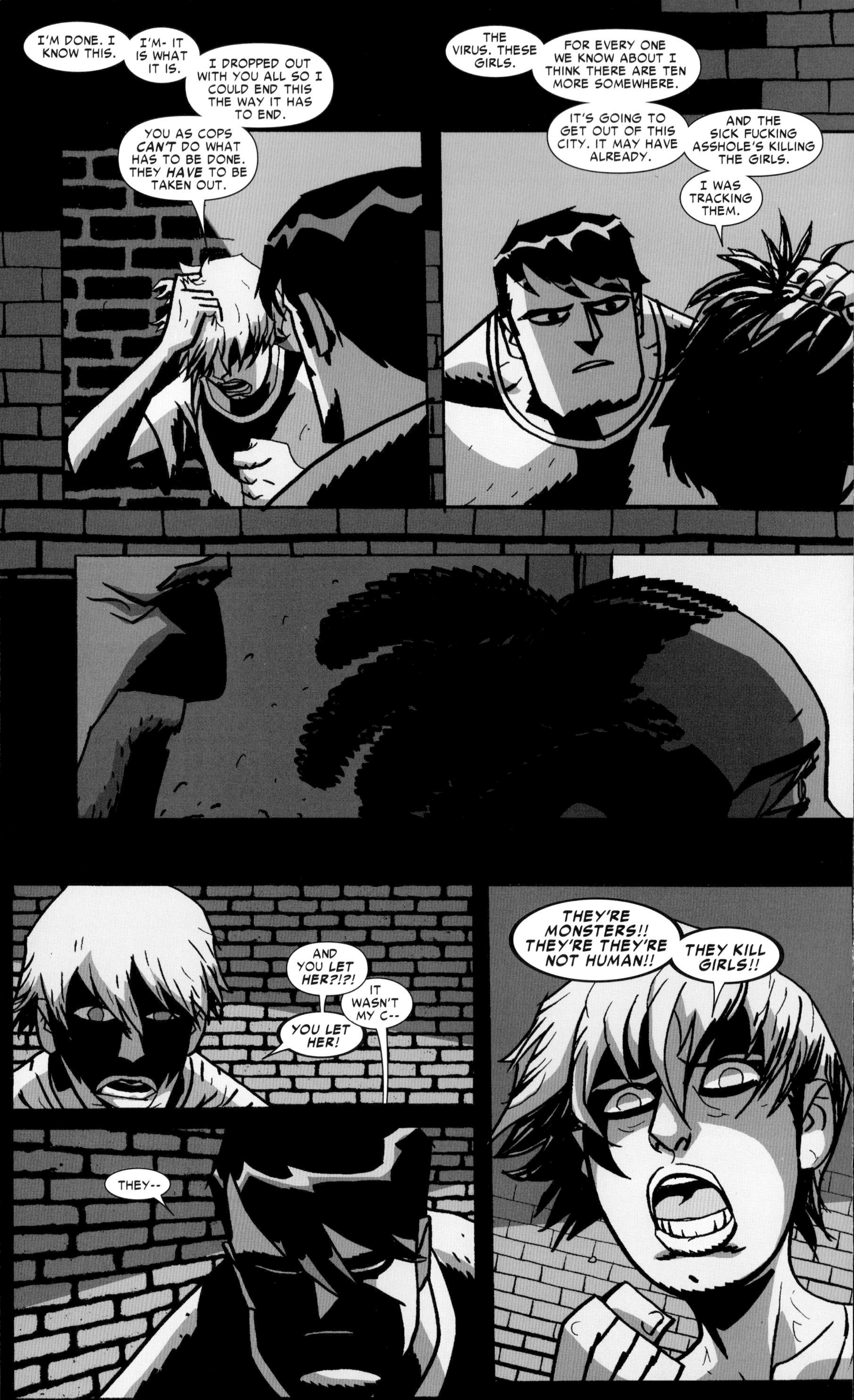
I'M DONE. I KNOW THIS.
I'M- IT IS WHAT IT IS.
I DROPPED OUT WITH YOU ALL SO I COULD END THIS THE WAY IT HAS TO END.
YOU AS COPS CAN'T DO WHAT HAS TO BE DONE. THEY HAVE TO BE TAKEN OUT.
THE VIRUS. THESE GIRLS.
FOR EVERY ONE WE KNOW ABOUT I THINK THERE ARE TEN MORE SOMEWHERE.
IT'S GOING TO GET OUT OF THIS CITY. IT MAY HAVE ALREADY.
AND THE SICK FUCKING ASSHOLE'S KILLING THE GIRLS.
I WAS TRACKING THEM.
AND YOU LET HER?!?!
IT WASN'T MY C--
YOU LET HER!
THEY--
THEY'RE MONSTERS!! THEY'RE THEY'RE NOT HUMAN!!
THEY KILL GIRLS!!

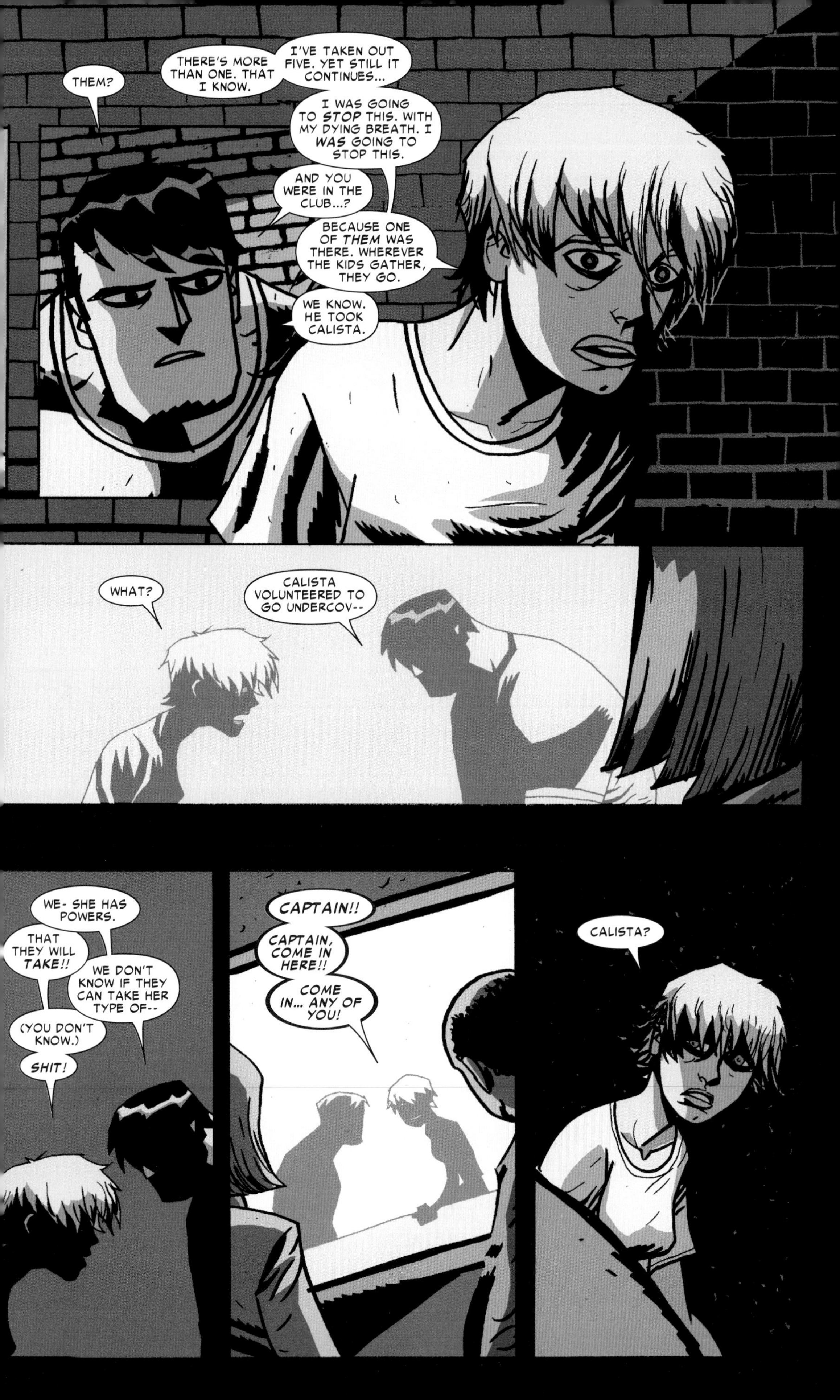
THEM?
THERE'S MORE THAN ONE. THAT I KNOW.
I'VE TAKEN OUT FIVE. YET STILL IT CONTINUES...
I WAS GOING TO STOP THIS. WITH MY DYING BREATH. I WAS GOING TO STOP THIS.
AND YOU WERE IN THE CLUB...?
BECAUSE ONE OF THEM WAS THERE. WHEREVER THE KIDS GATHER, THEY GO.
WE KNOW. HE TOOK CALISTA.
WHAT?
CALISTA VOLUNTEERED TO GO UNDERCOV--
WE- SHE HAS POWERS.
THAT THEY WILL TAKE!!
WE DON'T KNOW IF THEY CAN TAKE HER TYPE OF--
(YOU DON'T KNOW.)
SHIT!
CAPTAIN!!
CAPTAIN, COME IN HERE!!
COME IN... ANY OF YOU!
CALISTA?

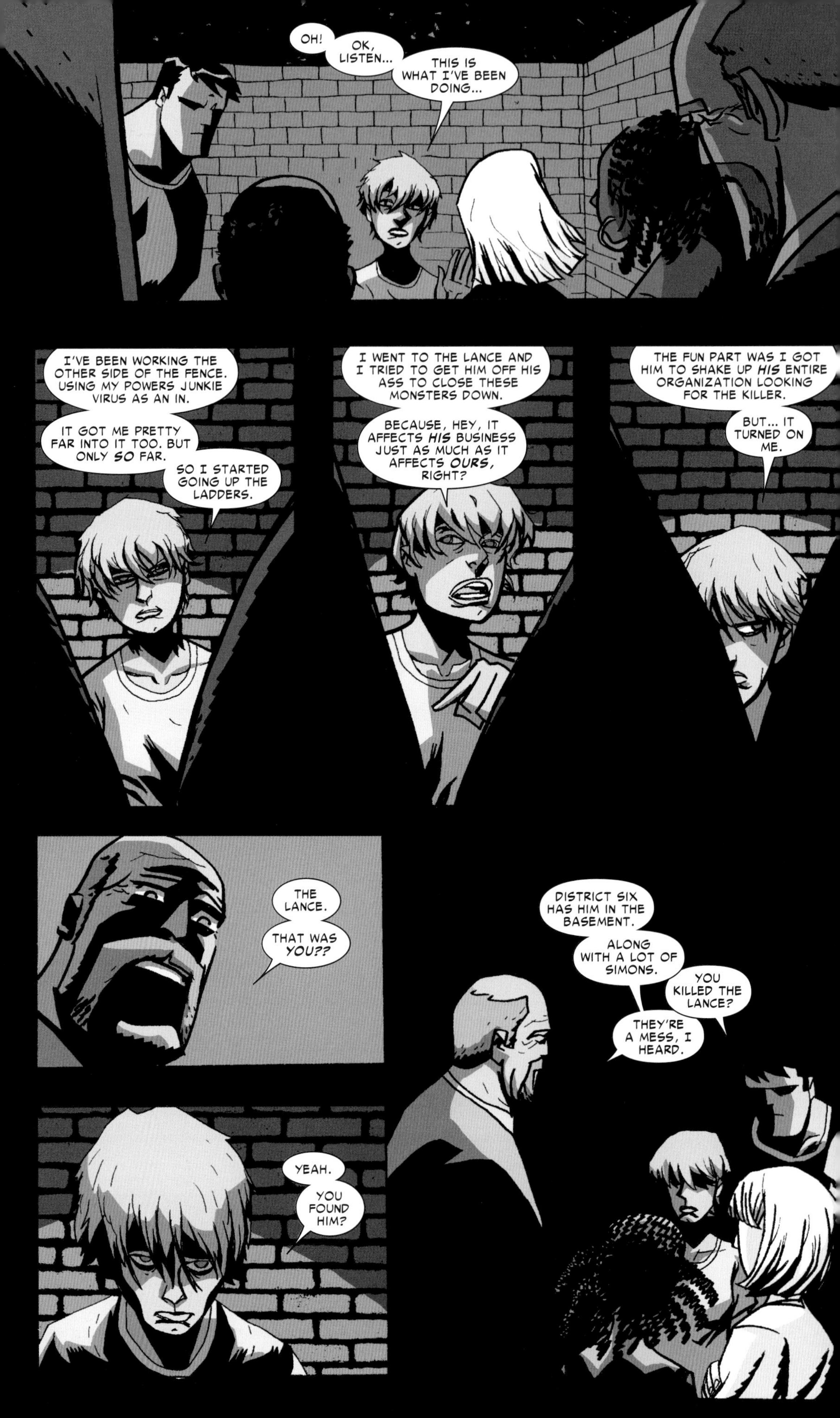
OH!
OK, LISTEN...
THIS IS WHAT I'VE BEEN DOING...
I'VE BEEN WORKING THE OTHER SIDE OF THE FENCE. USING MY POWERS JUNKIE VIRUS AS AN IN.
IT GOT ME PRETTY FAR INTO IT TOO. BUT ONLY SO FAR.
SO I STARTED GOING UP THE LADDERS.
I WENT TO THE LANCE AND I TRIED TO GET HIM OFF HIS ASS TO CLOSE THESE MONSTERS DOWN.
BECAUSE, HEY, IT AFFECTS HIS BUSINESS JUST AS MUCH AS IT AFFECTS OURS, RIGHT?
THE FUN PART WAS I GOT HIM TO SHAKE UP HIS ENTIRE ORGANIZATION LOOKING FOR THE KILLER.
BUT... IT TURNED ON ME.
THE LANCE.
THAT WAS YOU??
YEAH.
YOU FOUND HIM?
DISTRICT SIX HAS HIM IN THE BASEMENT.
ALONG WITH A LOT OF SIMONS.
YOU KILLED THE LANCE?
THEY'RE A MESS, I HEARD.

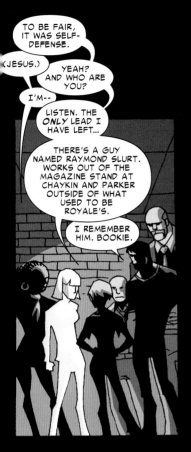

TO BE FAIR, IT WAS SELF-DEFENSE.

(JESUS.)

YEAH? AND WHO ARE YOU?

I'M--

LISTEN. THE *ONLY* LEAD I HAVE LEFT...

THERE'S A GUY NAMED RAYMOND SLURT. WORKS OUT OF THE MAGAZINE STAND AT CHAYKIN AND PARKER OUTSIDE OF WHAT USED TO BE ROYALE'S.

I REMEMBER HIM. BOOKIE.

GUY'S IN THE SAME SITUATION AS ME. HE'S GOT THE VIRUS TOO.

BUT HE AIN'T HAPPY WITH IT AND HE'S JUST TRYING TO LIVE.

HE'S BEEN FEEDING ME INTEL. DRIPS AND DRABS. RUMORS. SOME PAN, SOME DON'T.

GUY SENT ME TO THE CLUB TONIGHT.

HE *KNOWS* STUFF. HE KNEW THE GUY WAS GOING TO BE THERE. YOU *GO* TO HIM AND YOU GET HIM TO TAKE--

SHIT.

HE WON'T TALK TO YOU. YOU'RE FUCKING COPS.

WHY WOULD HE TALK TO YOU?

'CAUSE HE *LIKES* ME.

AND I THINK...

HE'S NOT A *BRIGHT* GUY, BUT HE KNOWS THIS IS OFF THE RAILS. I THINK HE WANTS ME TO END THIS.

SO YOU WANT *US* TO LET *YOU* OUT?

AND *YOU* GO TALK TO HIM?

YOU CAN FOLLOW.

NO.

CAPTAIN?

AND THEN WHAT?

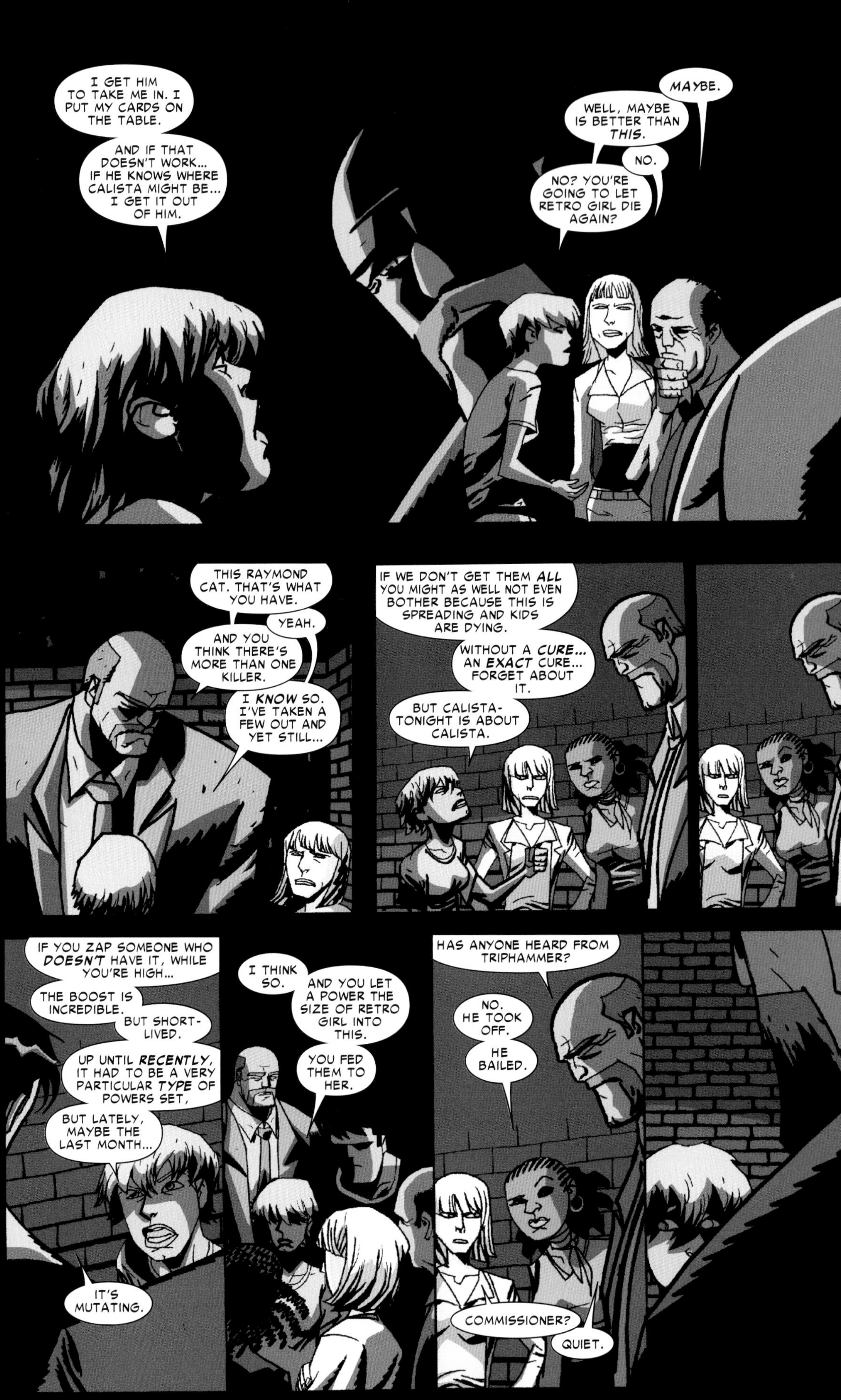
I GET HIM TO TAKE ME IN. I PUT MY CARDS ON THE TABLE.
AND IF THAT DOESN'T WORK... IF HE KNOWS WHERE CALISTA MIGHT BE... I GET IT OUT OF HIM.
MAYBE.
WELL, MAYBE IS BETTER THAN THIS.
NO.
NO? YOU'RE GOING TO LET RETRO GIRL DIE AGAIN?
THIS RAYMOND CAT. THAT'S WHAT YOU HAVE.
YEAH.
AND YOU THINK THERE'S MORE THAN ONE KILLER.
I KNOW SO. I'VE TAKEN A FEW OUT AND YET STILL...
IF WE DON'T GET THEM ALL YOU MIGHT AS WELL NOT EVEN BOTHER BECAUSE THIS IS SPREADING AND KIDS ARE DYING.
WITHOUT A CURE... AN EXACT CURE... FORGET ABOUT IT.
BUT CALISTA-TONIGHT IS ABOUT CALISTA.
IF YOU ZAP SOMEONE WHO DOESN'T HAVE IT, WHILE YOU'RE HIGH...
THE BOOST IS INCREDIBLE.
BUT SHORT-LIVED.
UP UNTIL RECENTLY, IT HAD TO BE A VERY PARTICULAR TYPE OF POWERS SET,
BUT LATELY, MAYBE THE LAST MONTH...
IT'S MUTATING.
I THINK SO.
AND YOU LET A POWER THE SIZE OF RETRO GIRL INTO THIS.
YOU FED THEM TO HER.
HAS ANYONE HEARD FROM TRIPHAMMER?
NO. HE TOOK OFF.
HE BAILED.
COMMISSIONER?
QUIET.

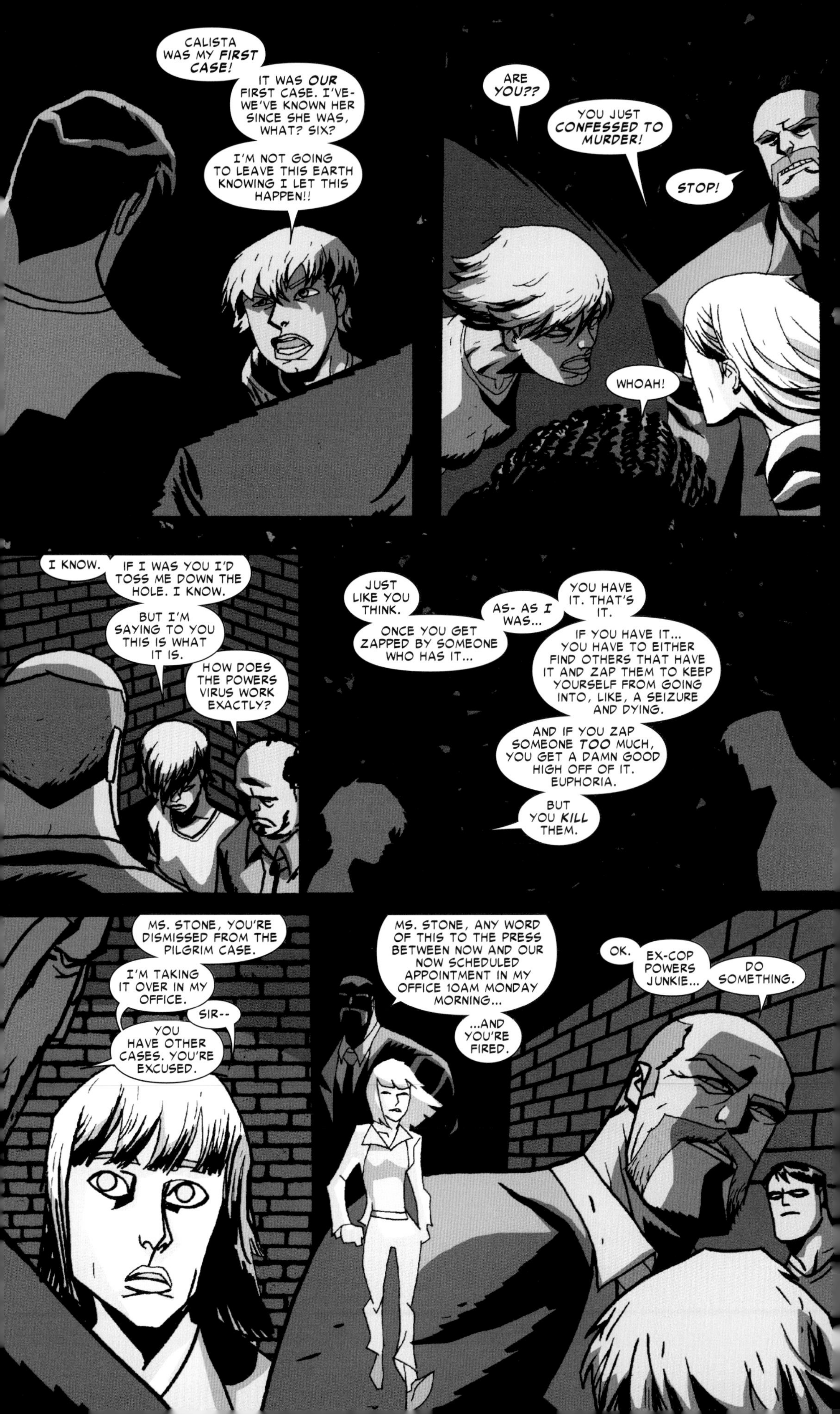
CALISTA WAS MY *FIRST CASE!*
IT WAS *OUR* FIRST CASE. I'VE-WE'VE KNOWN HER SINCE SHE WAS, WHAT? SIX?
I'M NOT GOING TO LEAVE THIS EARTH KNOWING I LET THIS HAPPEN!!
ARE *YOU??*
YOU JUST *CONFESSED TO MURDER!*
STOP!
WHOAH!
I KNOW.
IF I WAS YOU I'D TOSS ME DOWN THE HOLE. I KNOW.
BUT I'M SAYING TO YOU THIS IS WHAT IT IS.
HOW DOES THE POWERS VIRUS WORK EXACTLY?
JUST LIKE YOU THINK.
ONCE YOU GET ZAPPED BY SOMEONE WHO HAS IT...
AS- AS *I* WAS...
YOU HAVE IT. THAT'S IT.
IF YOU HAVE IT... YOU HAVE TO EITHER FIND OTHERS THAT HAVE IT AND ZAP THEM TO KEEP YOURSELF FROM GOING INTO, LIKE, A SEIZURE AND DYING.
AND IF YOU ZAP SOMEONE *TOO* MUCH, YOU GET A DAMN GOOD HIGH OFF OF IT. EUPHORIA.
BUT YOU *KILL* THEM.
MS. STONE, YOU'RE DISMISSED FROM THE PILGRIM CASE.
I'M TAKING IT OVER IN MY OFFICE.
SIR--
YOU HAVE OTHER CASES. YOU'RE EXCUSED.
MS. STONE, ANY WORD OF THIS TO THE PRESS BETWEEN NOW AND OUR NOW SCHEDULED APPOINTMENT IN MY OFFICE 10AM MONDAY MORNING...
...AND YOU'RE FIRED.
OK.
EX-COP POWERS JUNKIE...
DO SOMETHING.

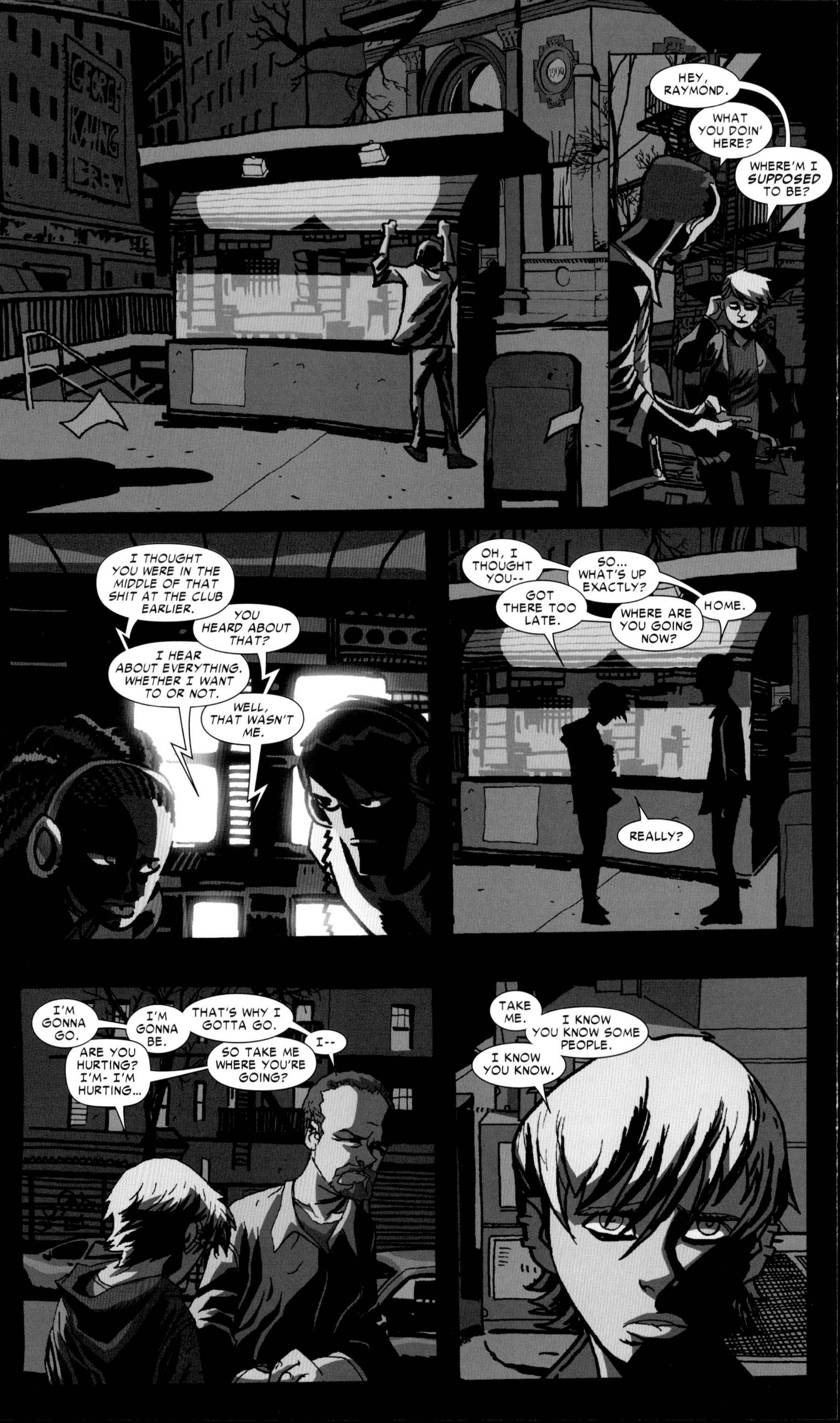
HEY, RAYMOND.
WHAT YOU DOIN' HERE?
WHERE'M I SUPPOSED TO BE?
I THOUGHT YOU WERE IN THE MIDDLE OF THAT SHIT AT THE CLUB EARLIER.
YOU HEARD ABOUT THAT?
I HEAR ABOUT EVERYTHING. WHETHER I WANT TO OR NOT.
WELL, THAT WASN'T ME.
OH, I THOUGHT YOU--
GOT THERE TOO LATE.
SO... WHAT'S UP EXACTLY?
WHERE ARE YOU GOING NOW?
HOME.
REALLY?
I'M GONNA GO.
I'M GONNA BE.
THAT'S WHY I GOTTA GO.
I--
ARE YOU HURTING? I'M- I'M HURTING...
SO TAKE ME WHERE YOU'RE GOING?
TAKE ME.
I KNOW YOU KNOW SOME PEOPLE.
I KNOW YOU KNOW.

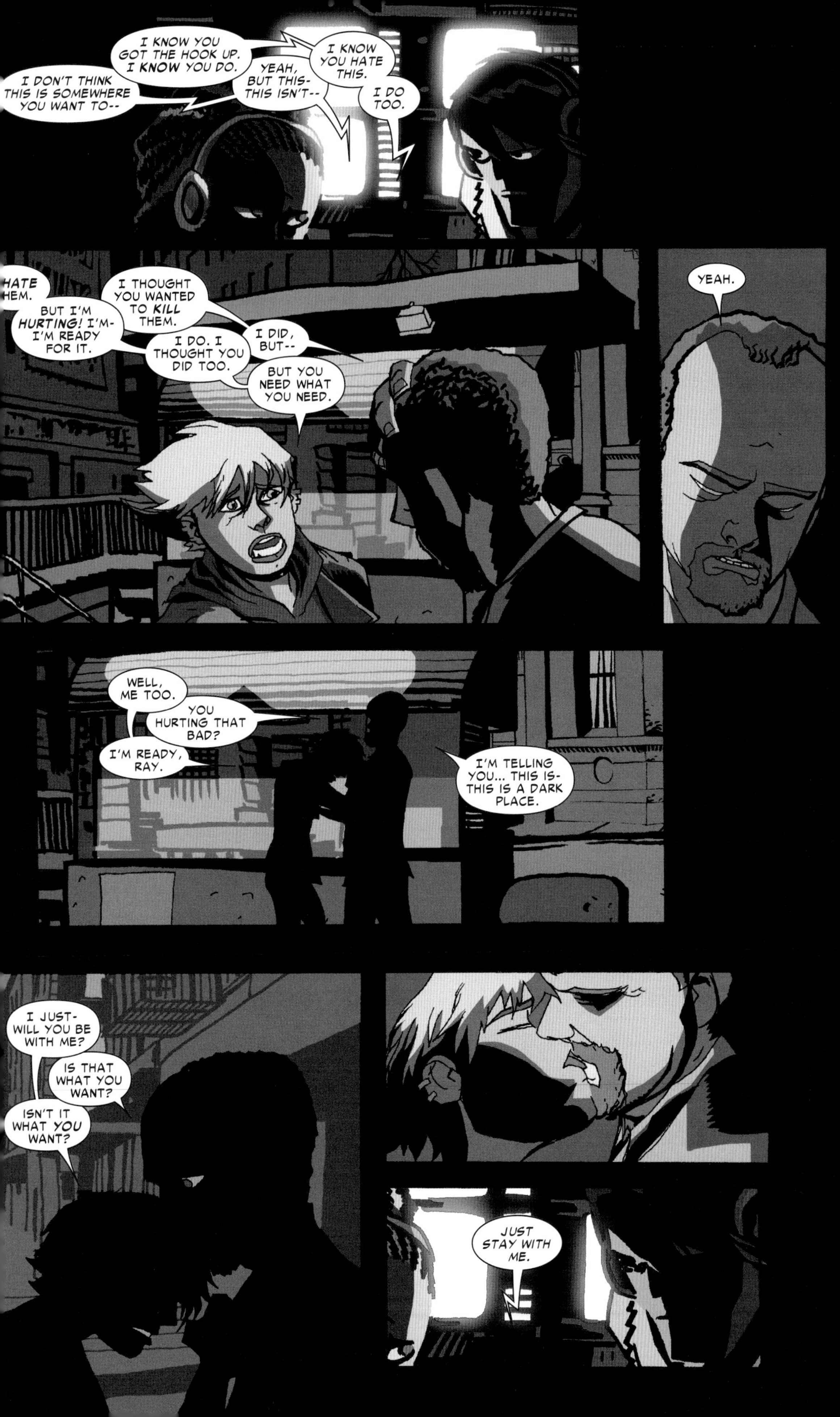
I DON'T THINK THIS IS SOMEWHERE YOU WANT TO--
I KNOW YOU GOT THE HOOK UP. I KNOW YOU DO.
YEAH, BUT THIS-THIS ISN'T--
I KNOW YOU HATE THIS.
I DO TOO.
HATE
HEM.
BUT I'M HURTING! I'M-I'M READY FOR IT.
I THOUGHT YOU WANTED TO KILL THEM.
I DID, BUT--
I DO. I THOUGHT YOU DID TOO.
BUT YOU NEED WHAT YOU NEED.
YEAH.
WELL, ME TOO.
YOU HURTING THAT BAD?
I'M READY, RAY.
I'M TELLING YOU... THIS IS-THIS IS A DARK PLACE.
I JUST-WILL YOU BE WITH ME?
IS THAT WHAT YOU WANT?
ISN'T IT WHAT YOU WANT?
JUST STAY WITH ME.

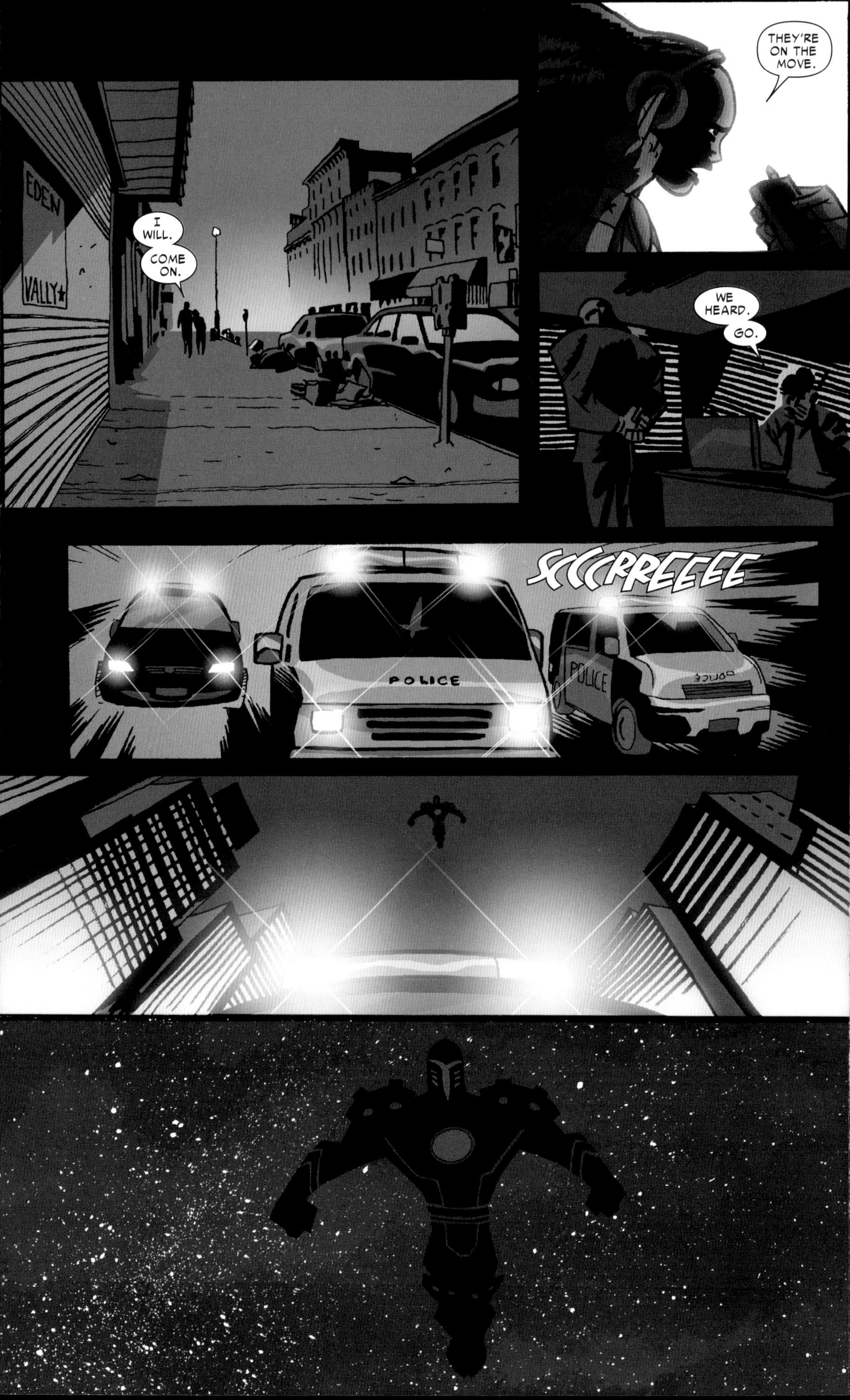
THEY'RE ON THE MOVE.
I WILL.
COME ON.
EDEN
VALLY
WE HEARD.
GO.
SCCCRREEEEE
POLICE
POLICE

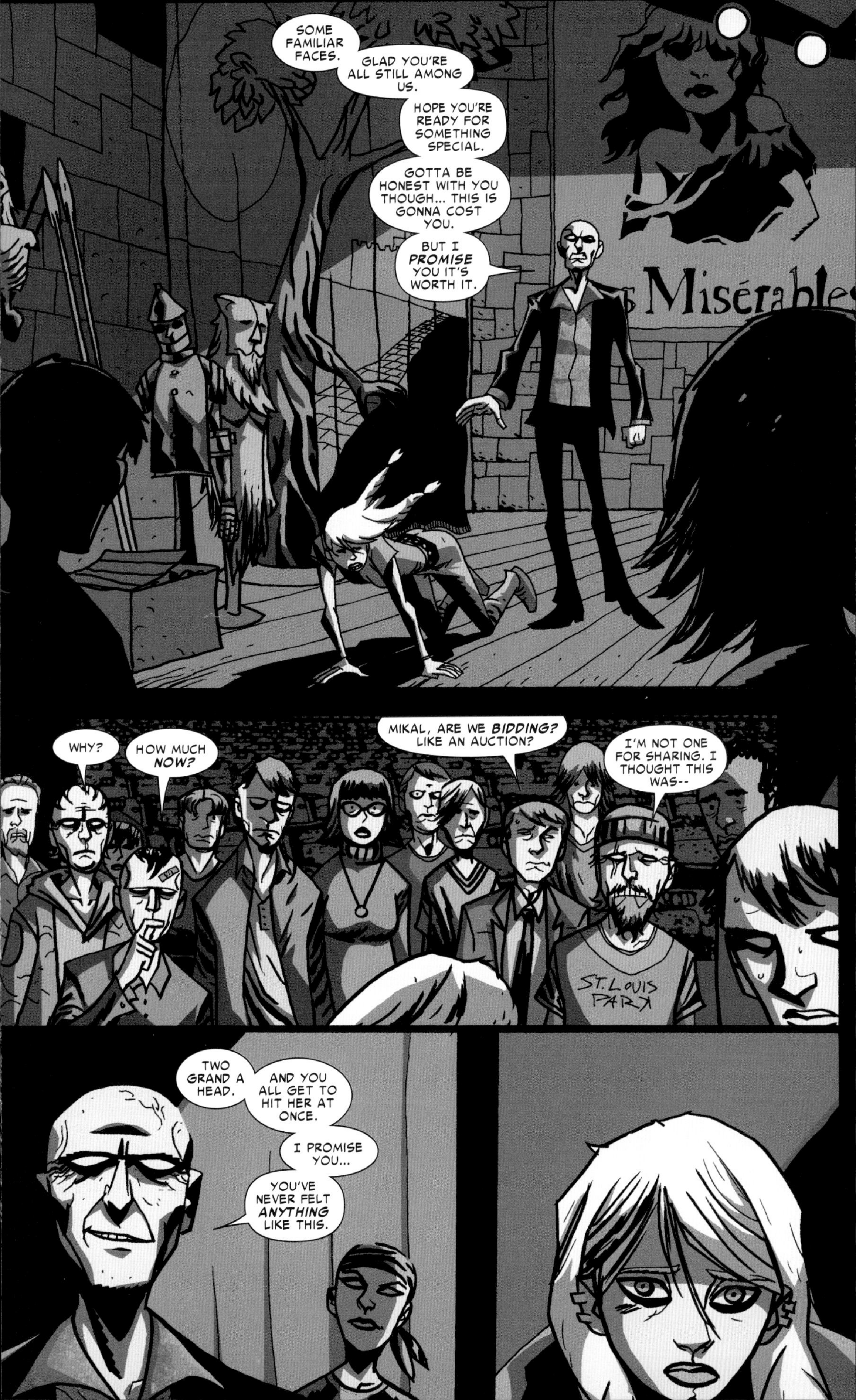
SOME FAMILIAR FACES.
GLAD YOU'RE ALL STILL AMONG US.
HOPE YOU'RE READY FOR SOMETHING SPECIAL.
GOTTA BE HONEST WITH YOU THOUGH... THIS IS GONNA COST YOU.
BUT I *PROMISE* YOU IT'S WORTH IT.
Misérables
WHY?
HOW MUCH *NOW?*
MIKAL, ARE WE *BIDDING?* LIKE AN AUCTION?
I'M NOT ONE FOR SHARING. I THOUGHT THIS WAS--
ST. LOUIS PARK
TWO GRAND A HEAD.
AND YOU ALL GET TO HIT HER AT ONCE.
I PROMISE YOU...
YOU'VE NEVER FELT *ANYTHING* LIKE THIS.

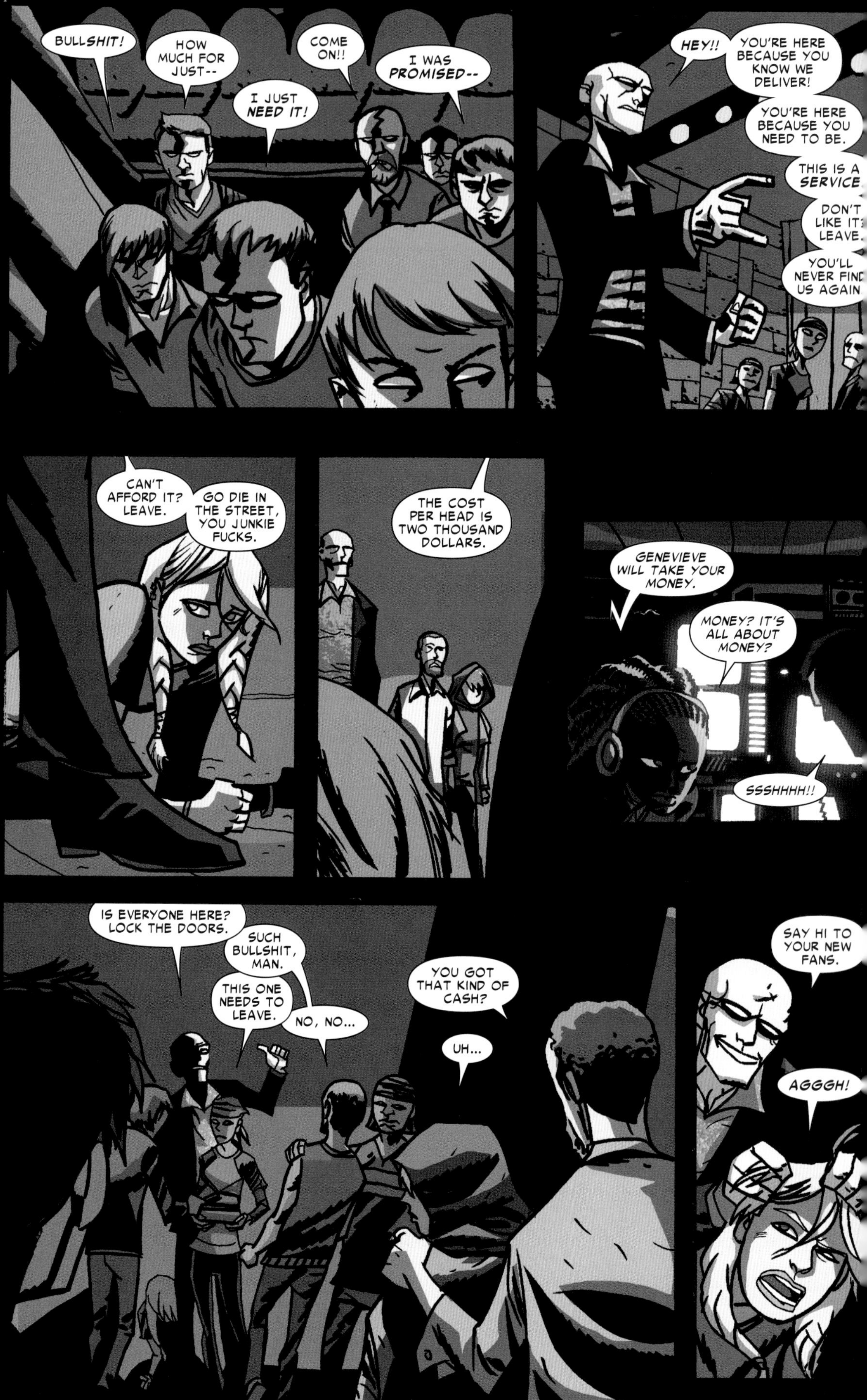
BULLSHIT!
HOW MUCH FOR JUST--
I JUST NEED IT!
COME ON!!
I WAS PROMISED--
HEY!!
YOU'RE HERE BECAUSE YOU KNOW WE DELIVER!
YOU'RE HERE BECAUSE YOU NEED TO BE.
THIS IS A SERVICE
DON'T LIKE IT: LEAVE.
YOU'LL NEVER FIND US AGAIN
CAN'T AFFORD IT? LEAVE.
GO DIE IN THE STREET, YOU JUNKIE FUCKS.
THE COST PER HEAD IS TWO THOUSAND DOLLARS.
GENEVIEVE WILL TAKE YOUR MONEY.
MONEY? IT'S ALL ABOUT MONEY?
SSSHHHH!!
IS EVERYONE HERE? LOCK THE DOORS.
SUCH BULLSHIT, MAN.
THIS ONE NEEDS TO LEAVE.
NO, NO...
YOU GOT THAT KIND OF CASH?
UH...
SAY HI TO YOUR NEW FANS.
AGGGH!

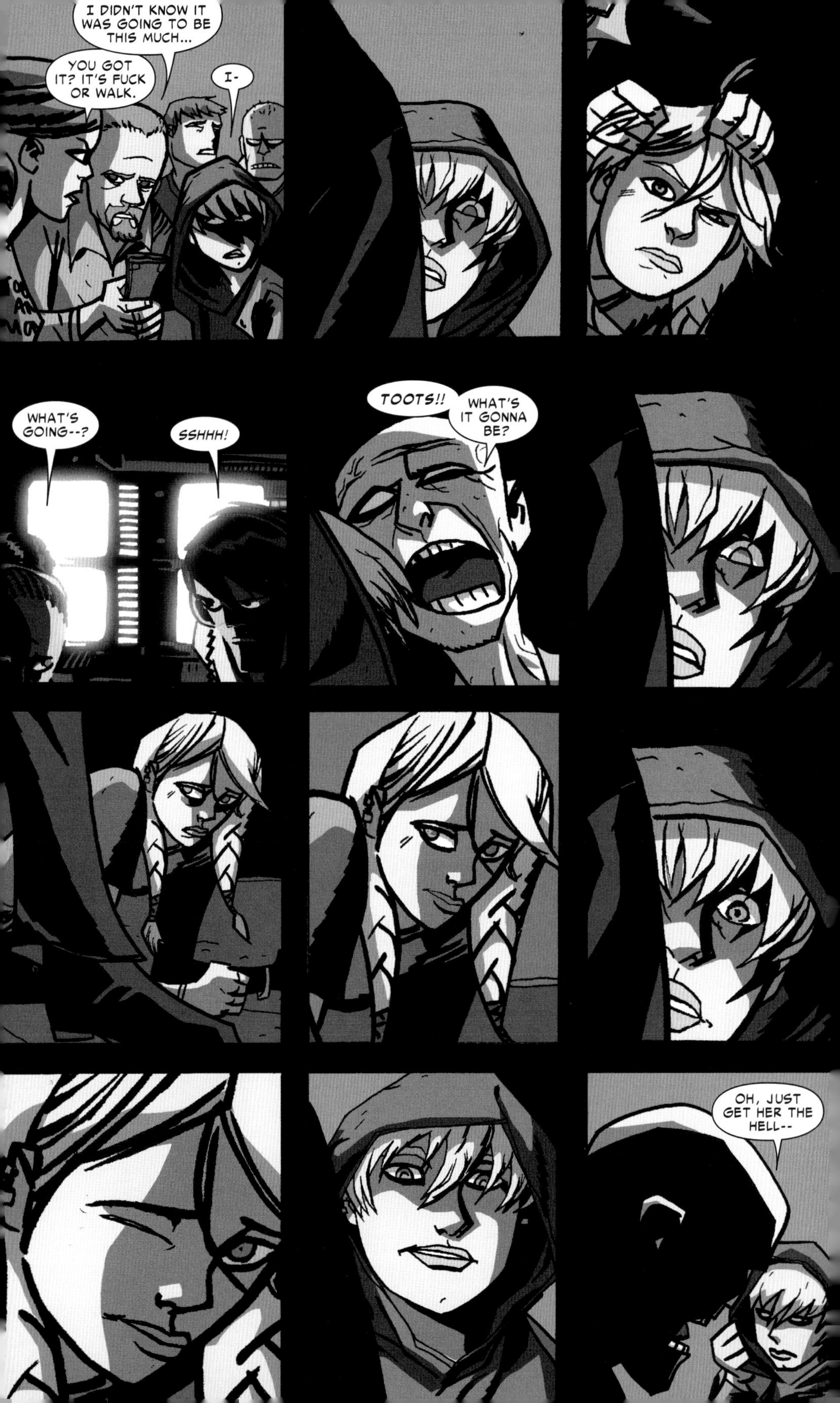
I DIDN'T KNOW IT WAS GOING TO BE THIS MUCH...
YOU GOT IT? IT'S FUCK OR WALK.
I-
WHAT'S GOING--?
SSHHH!
TOOTS!!
WHAT'S IT GONNA BE?
OH, JUST GET HER THE HELL--

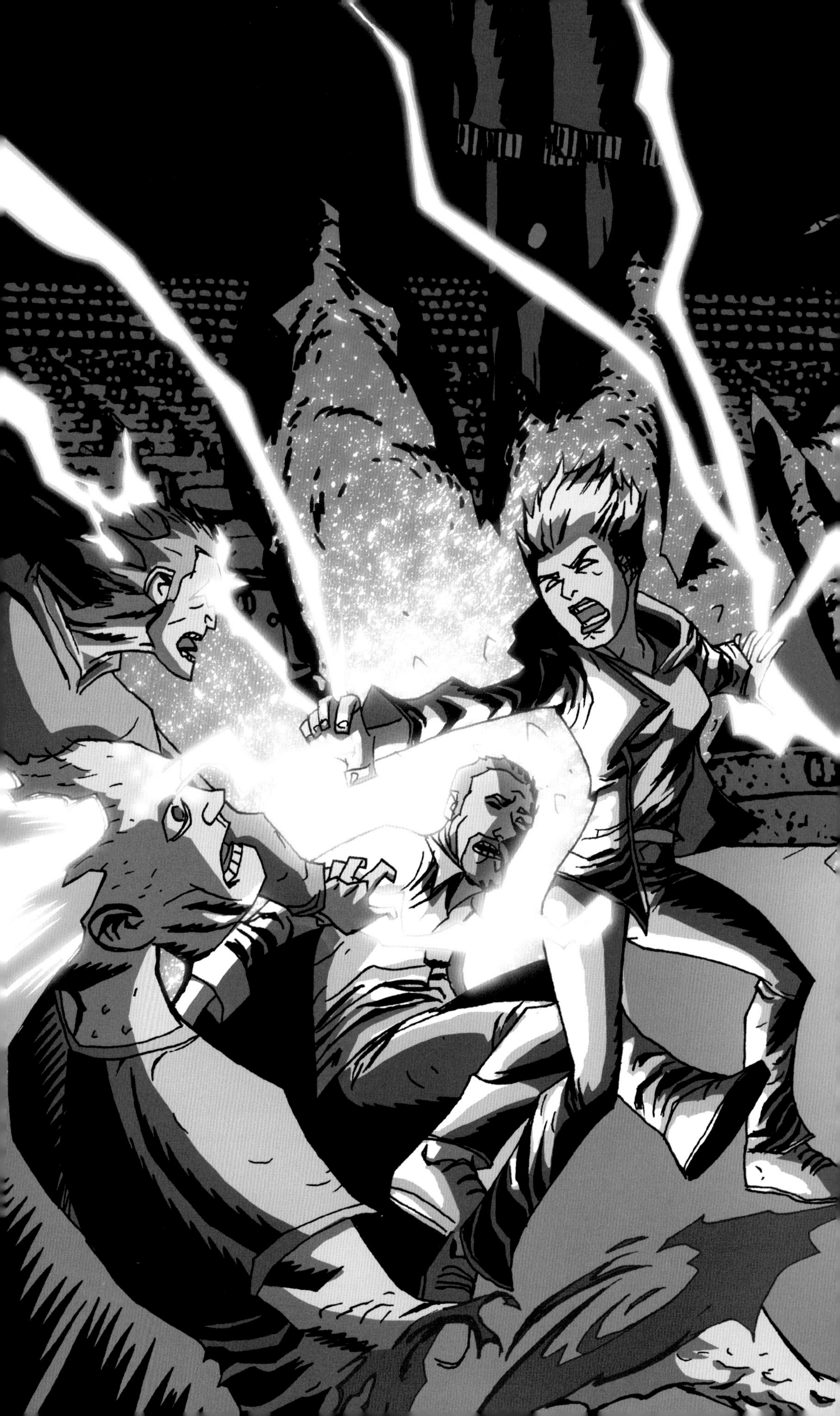

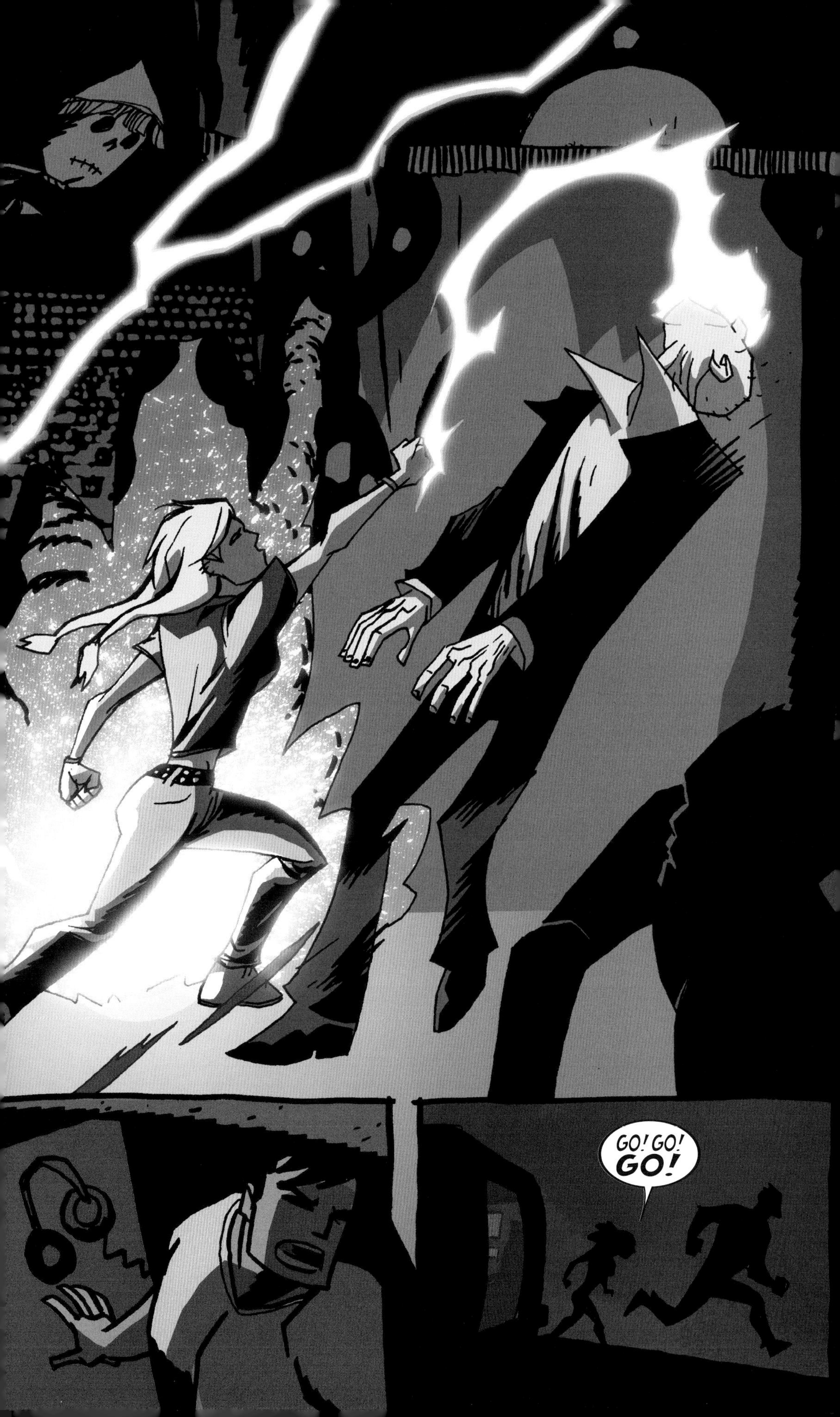
GO! GO! GO!

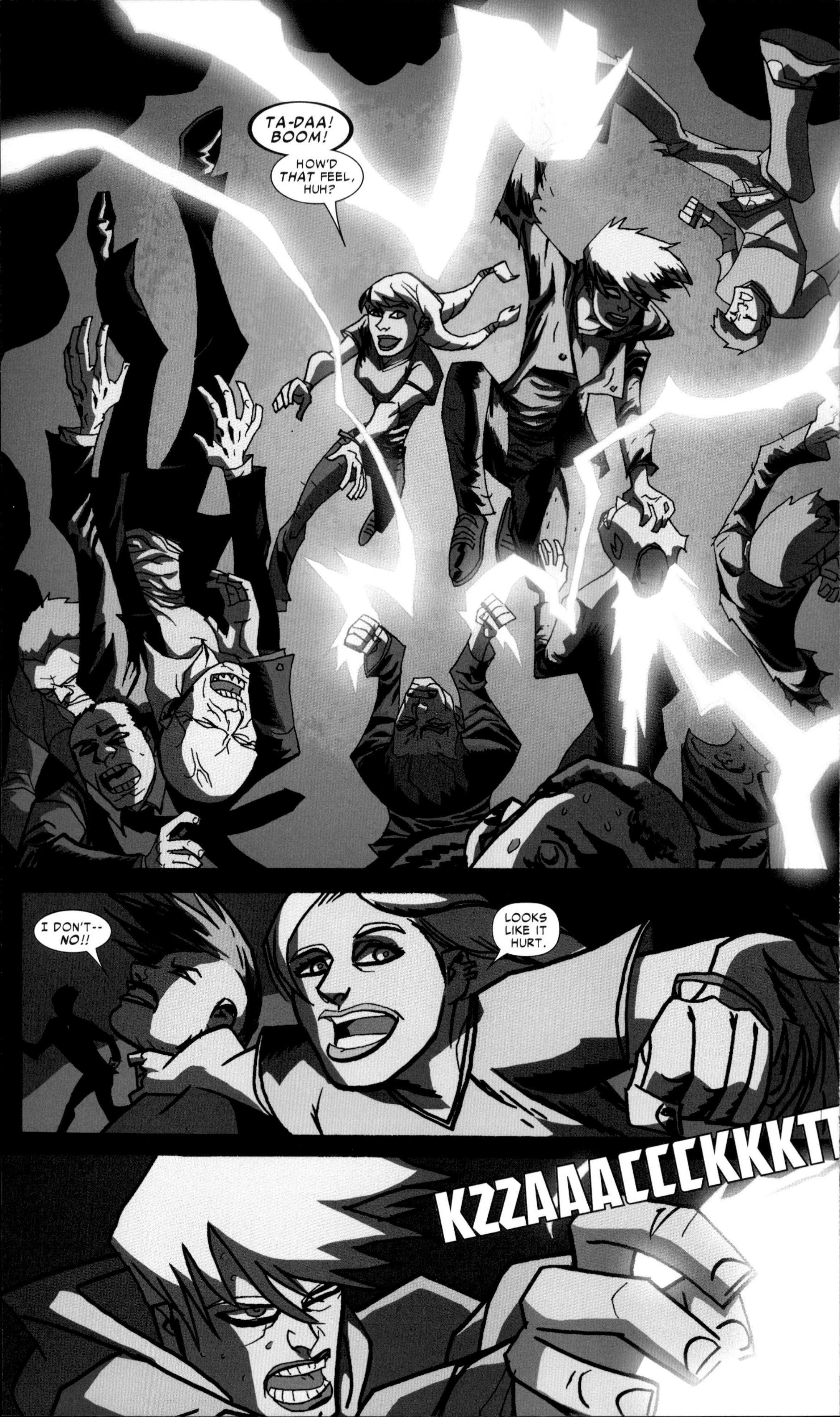
TA-DAA! BOOM!
HOW'D THAT FEEL, HUH?
I DON'T-- NO!!
LOOKS LIKE IT HURT.
KZZAAACCCKKKT

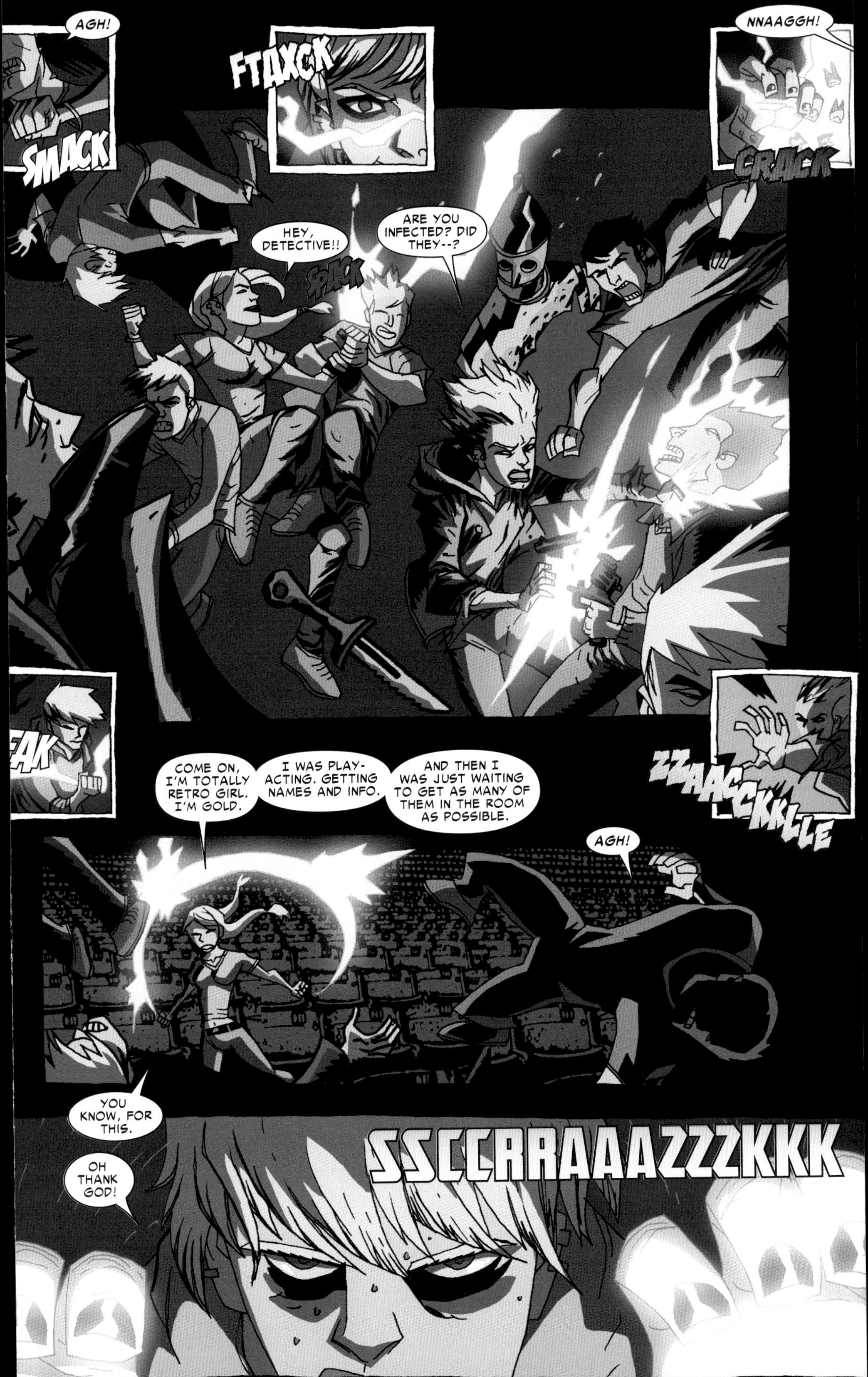
AGH!
SMACK
FTAXCK
NNAAGGH!
CRACK
HEY, DETECTIVE!!
SPACK
ARE YOU INFECTED? DID THEY--?
EAK
COME ON, I'M TOTALLY RETRO GIRL. I'M GOLD.
I WAS PLAY-ACTING. GETTING NAMES AND INFO.
AND THEN I WAS JUST WAITING TO GET AS MANY OF THEM IN THE ROOM AS POSSIBLE.
ZZAACCKKLLE
AGH!
YOU KNOW, FOR THIS.
OH THANK GOD!
SSCCRRAAAZZZKKK

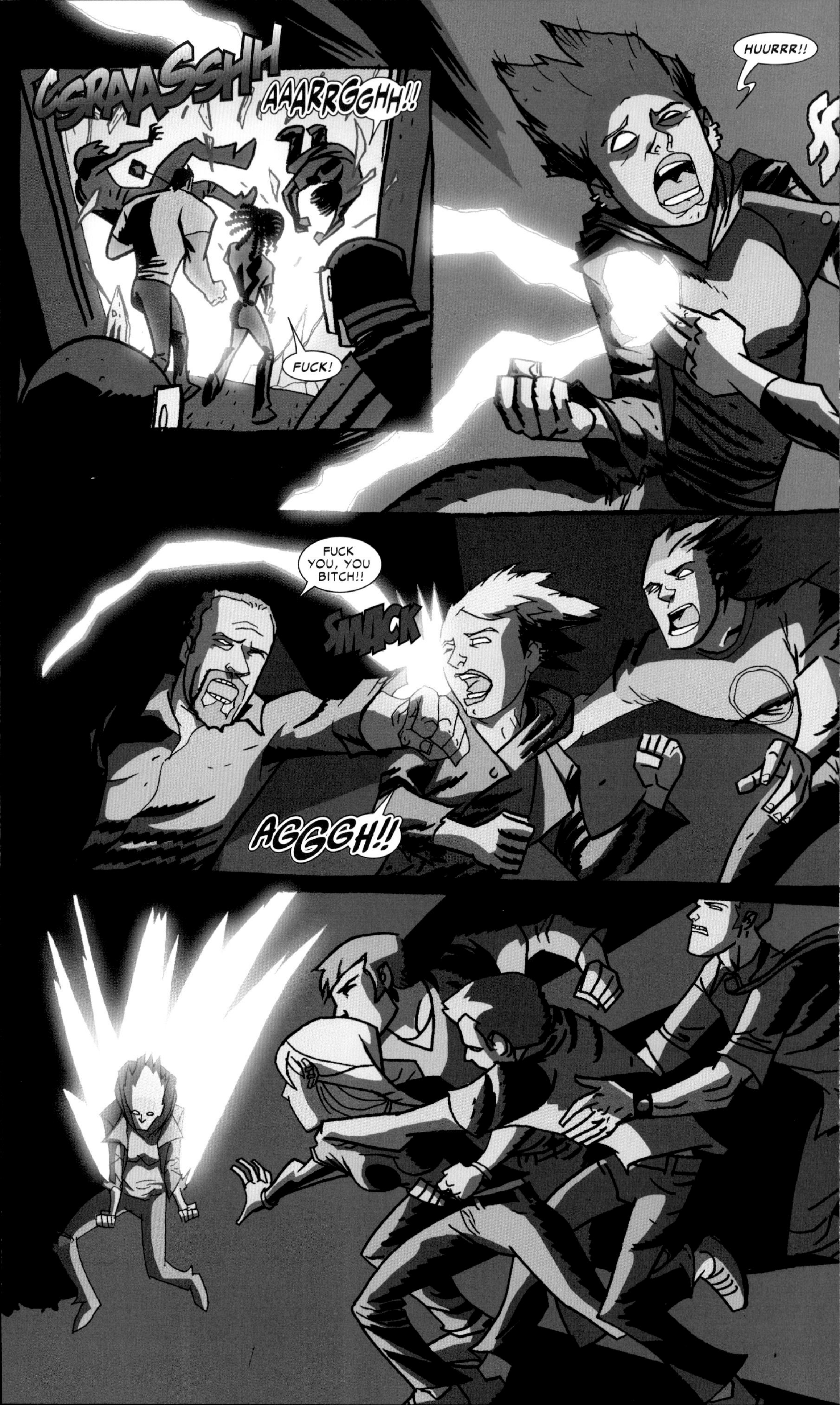

GRAASSHH
AAARRGGHH!!
FUCK!
HUURRR!!
FUCK YOU, YOU BITCH!!
SMACK
AGGGH!!

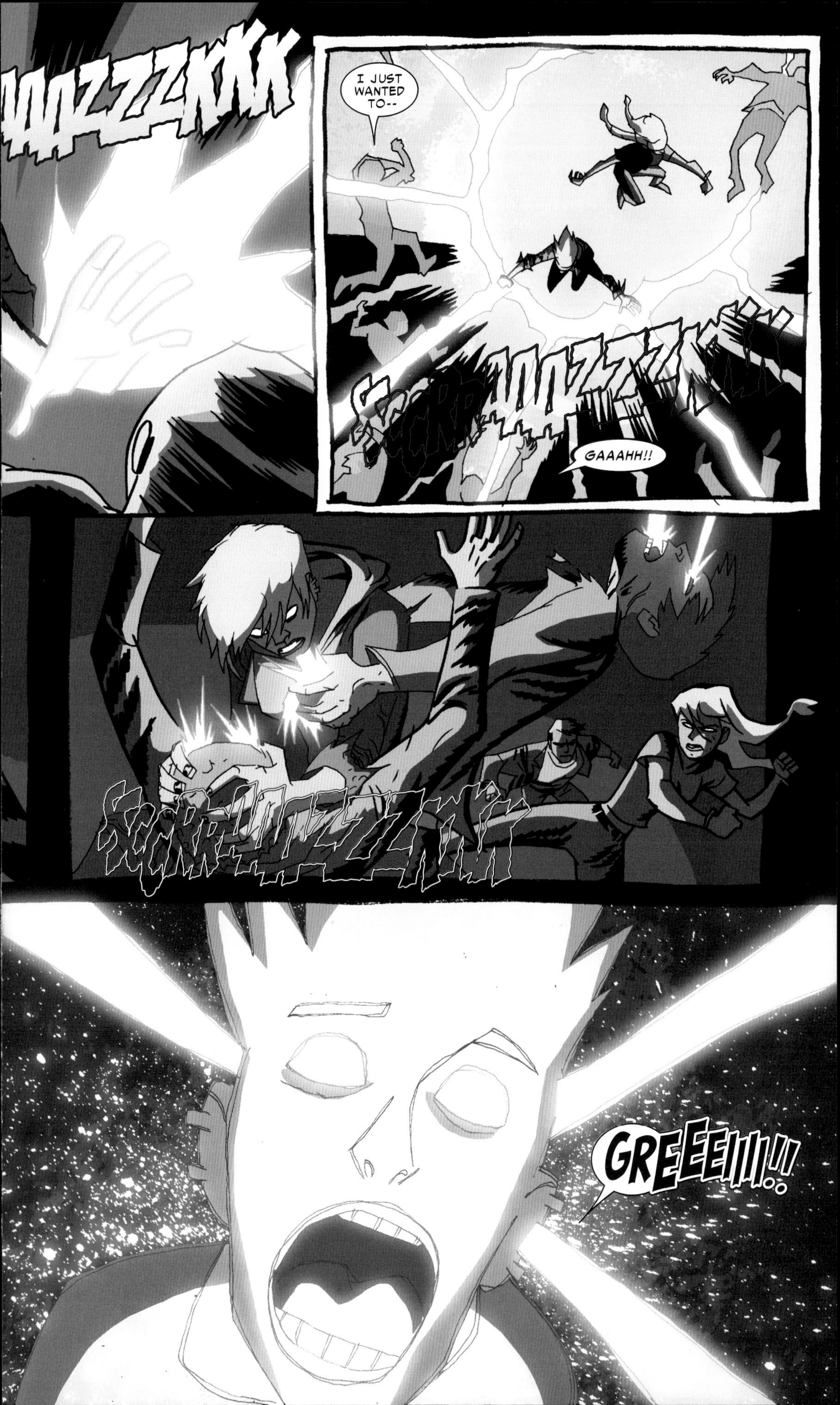

ZZZKKK
I JUST WANTED TO--
SSCRRAAZZZKKK
GAAAHH!!
SSCRRAAZZZKKK
GREEEIIII!!

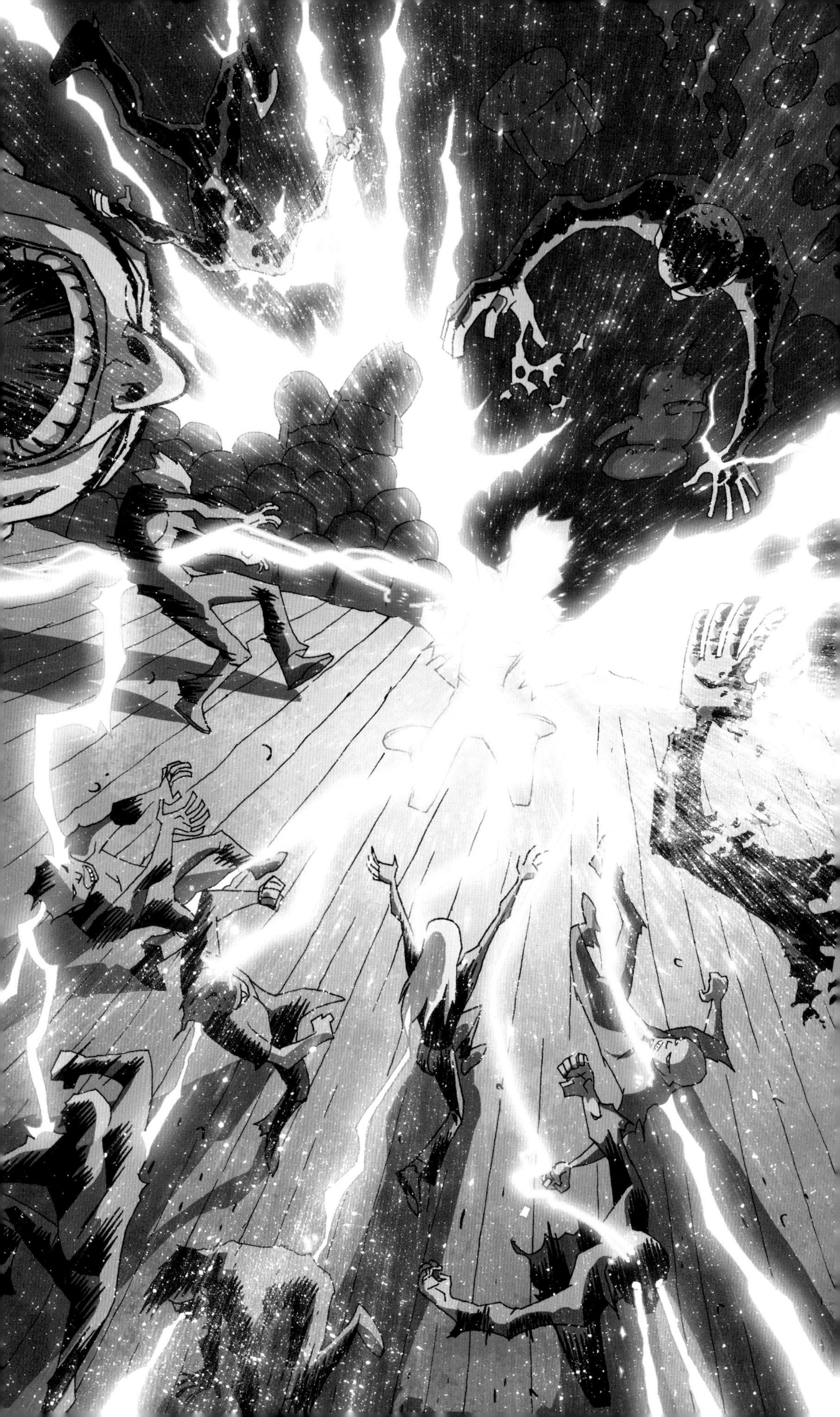

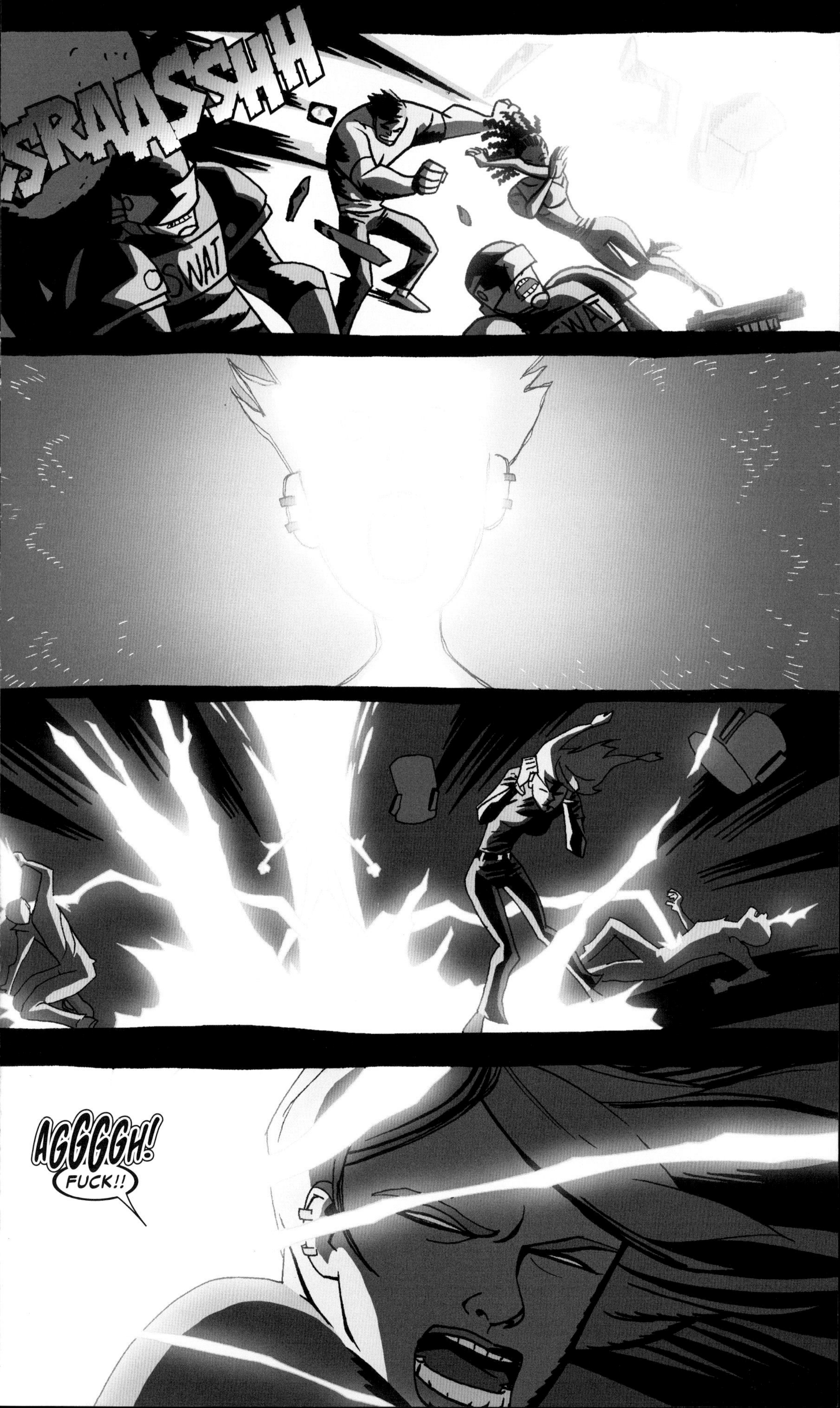
SRAASSHH
SWAT
SWAT
AGGGGH!
FUCK!!

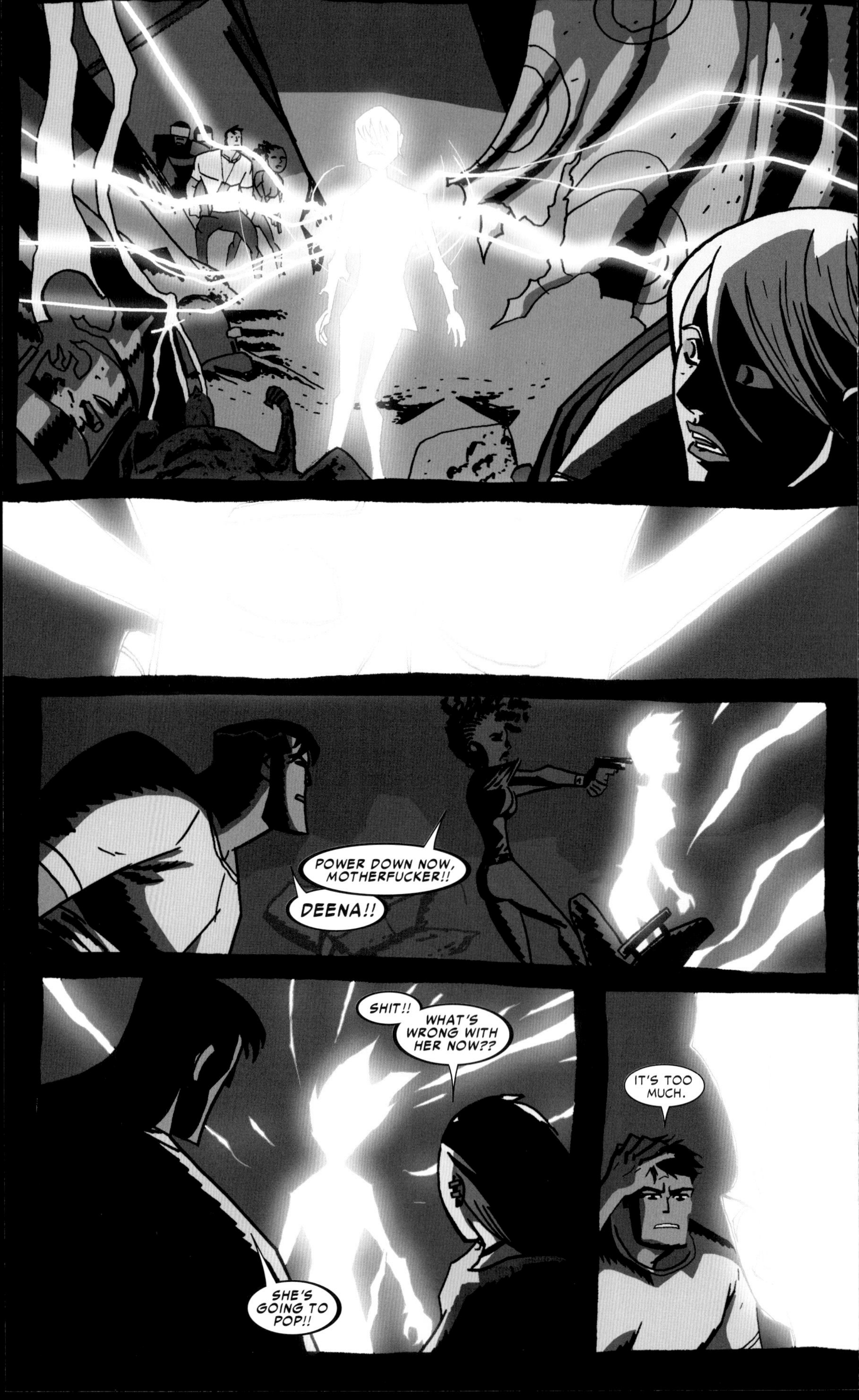
POWER DOWN NOW, MOTHERFUCKER!!
DEENA!!
SHIT!!
WHAT'S WRONG WITH HER NOW??
SHE'S GOING TO POP!!
IT'S TOO MUCH.

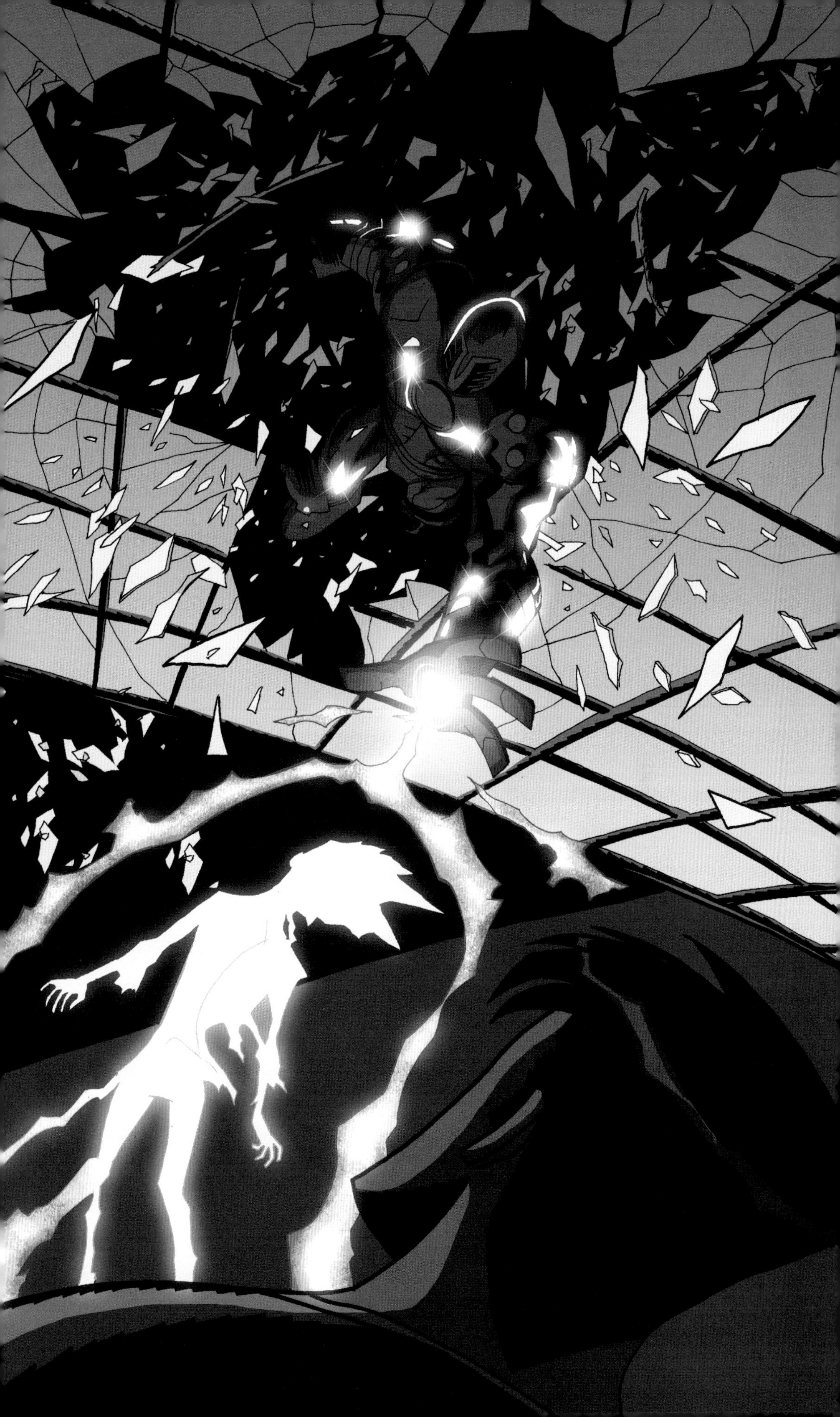

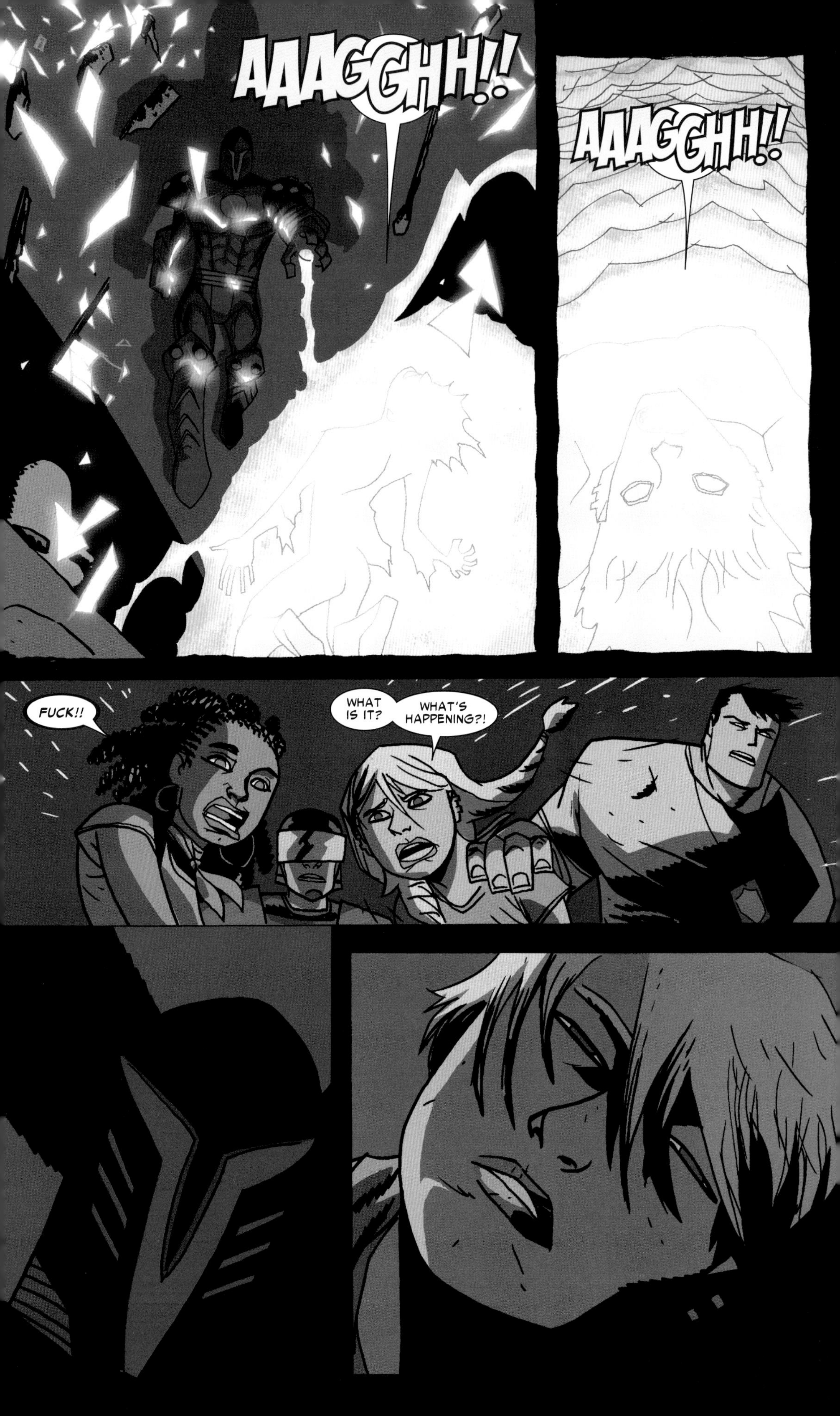
AAAGGHH!!
AAAGGHH!!
FUCK!!
WHAT IS IT?
WHAT'S HAPPENING?!

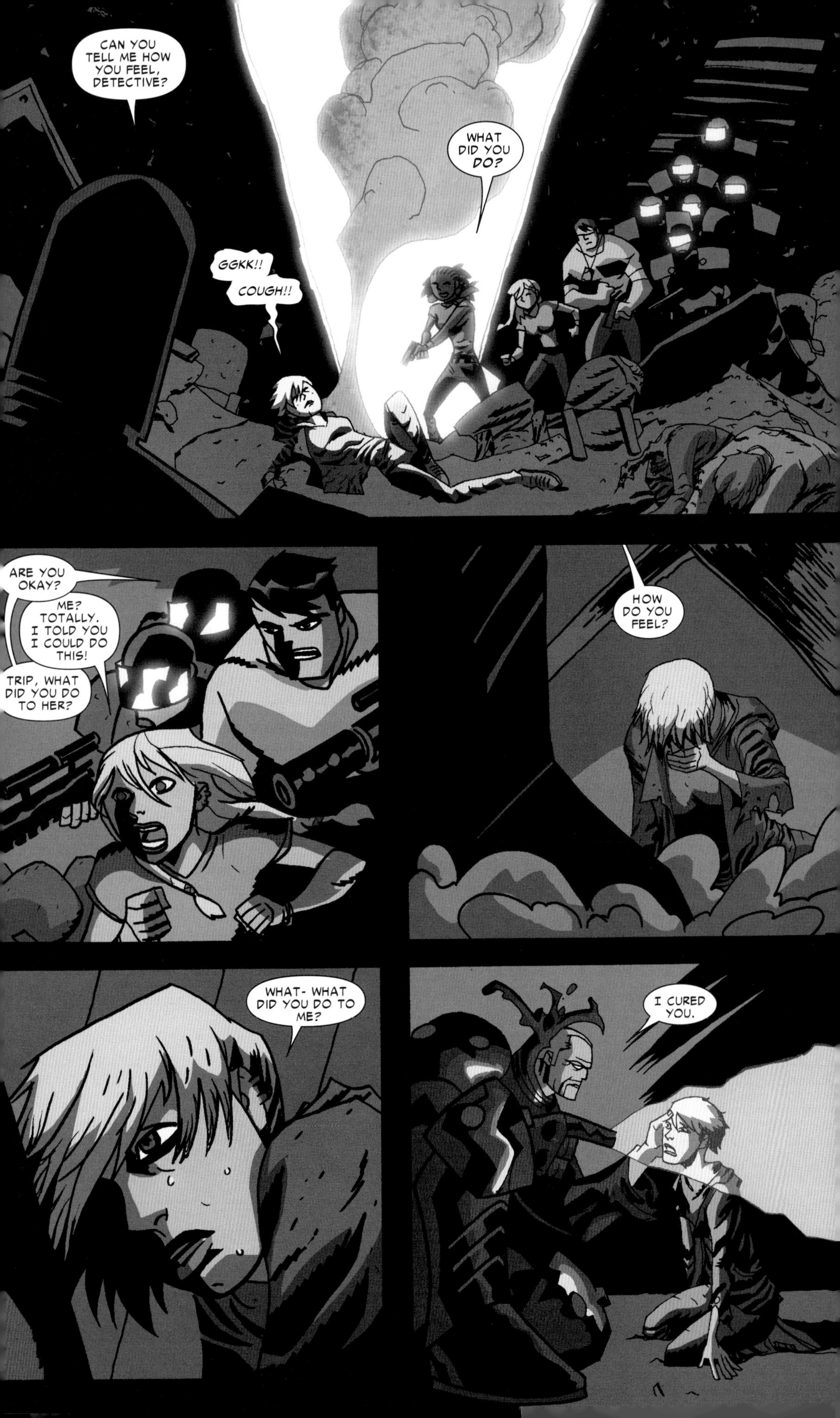
CAN YOU TELL ME HOW YOU FEEL, DETECTIVE?
WHAT DID YOU DO?
GGKK!!
COUGH!!
ARE YOU OKAY?
ME? TOTALLY. I TOLD YOU I COULD DO THIS!
TRIP, WHAT DID YOU DO TO HER?
HOW DO YOU FEEL?
WHAT- WHAT DID YOU DO TO ME?
I CURED YOU.

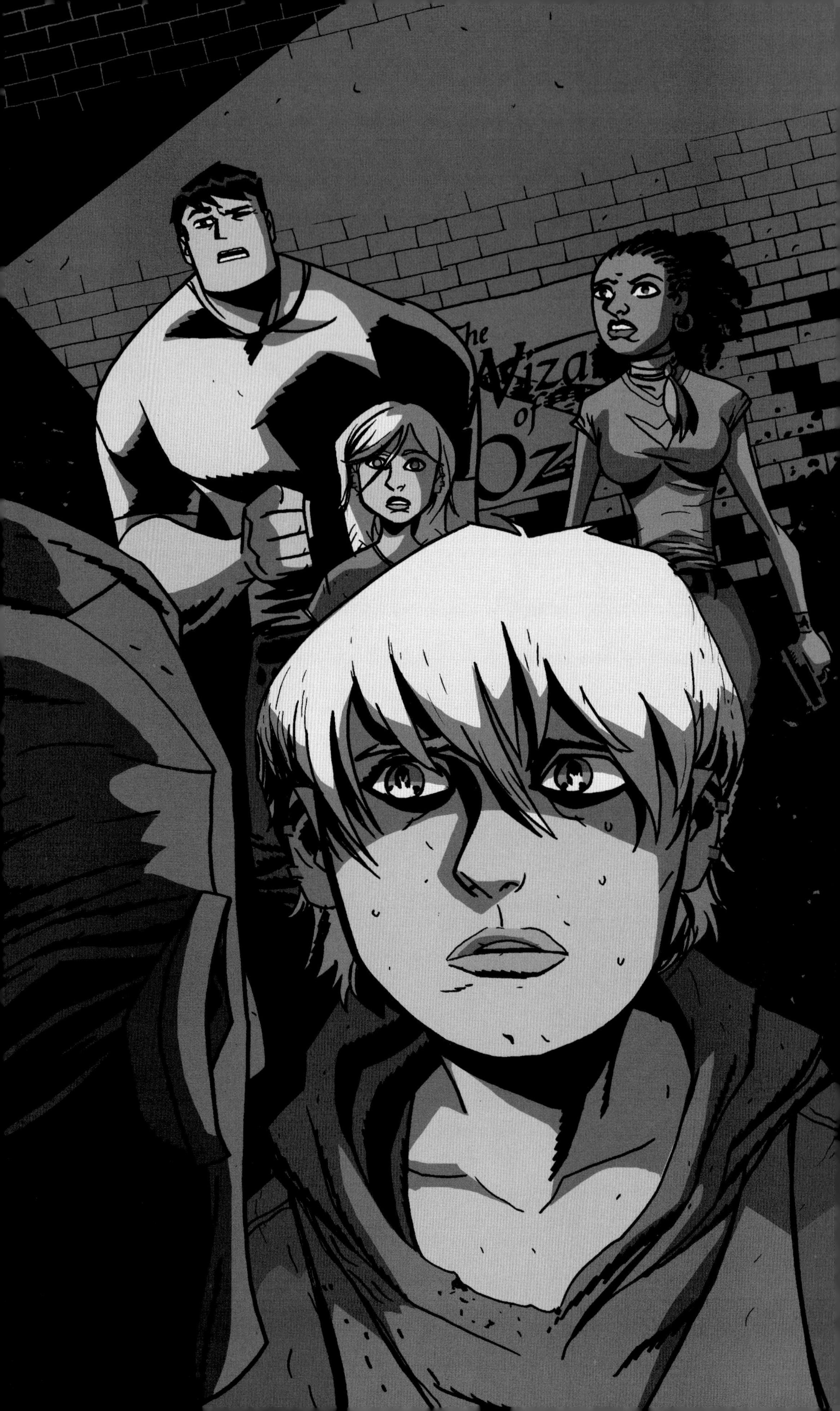

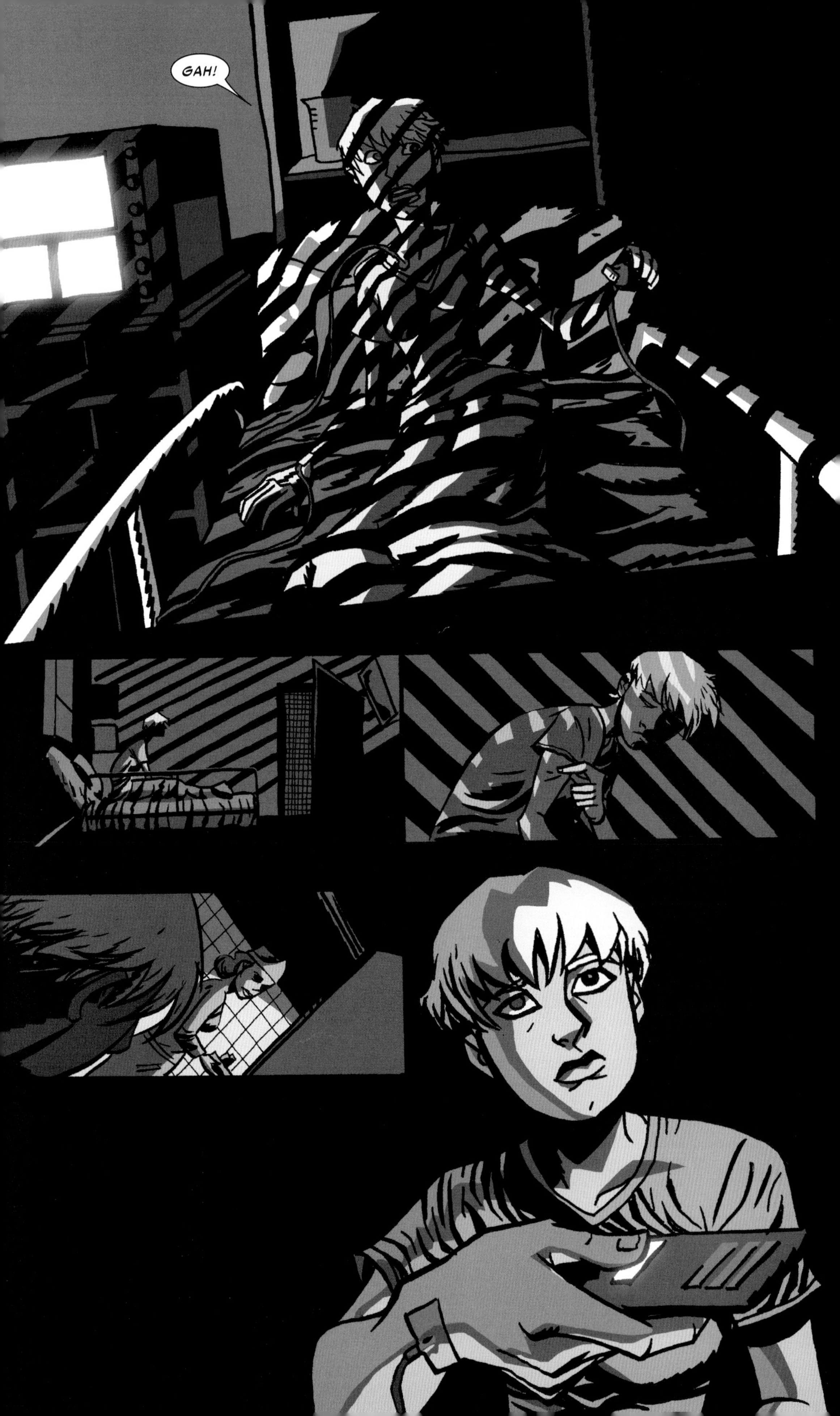
GAH!

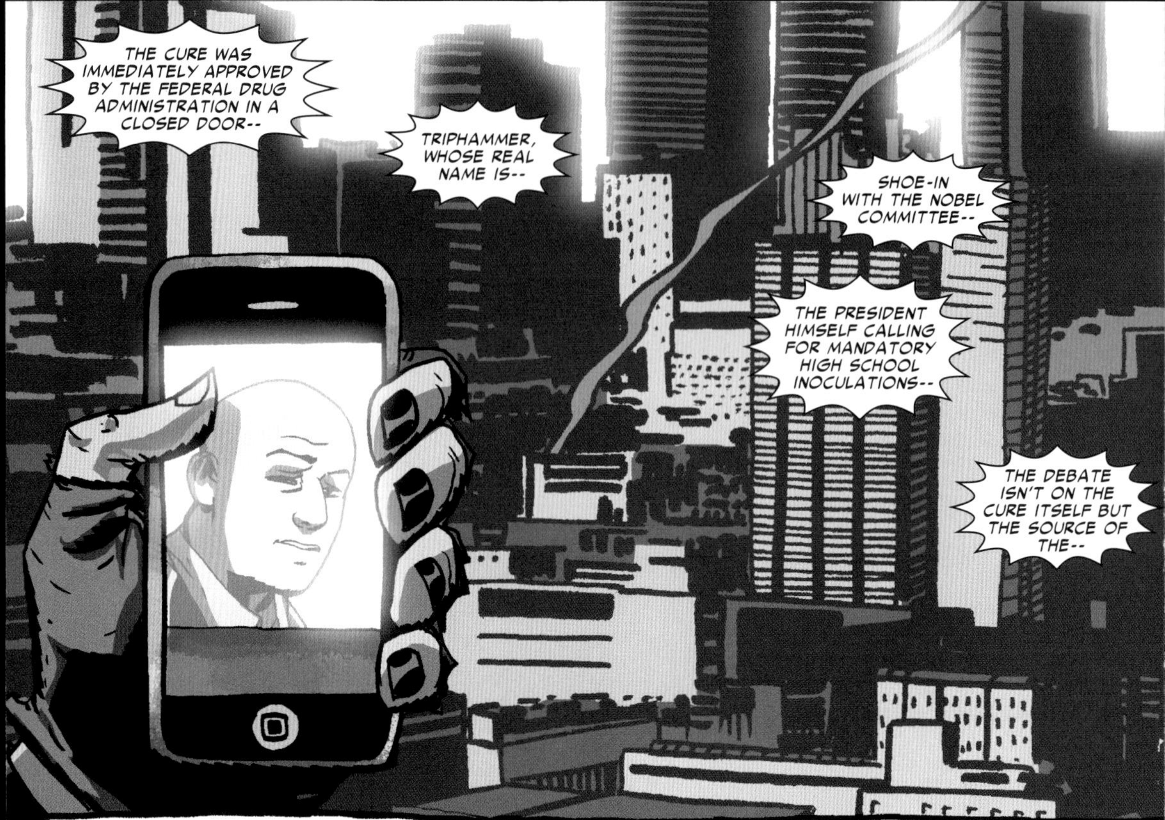
THE CURE WAS IMMEDIATELY APPROVED BY THE FEDERAL DRUG ADMINISTRATION IN A CLOSED DOOR--
TRIPHAMMER, WHOSE REAL NAME IS--
SHOE-IN WITH THE NOBEL COMMITTEE--
THE PRESIDENT HIMSELF CALLING FOR MANDATORY HIGH SCHOOL INOCULATIONS--
THE DEBATE ISN'T ON THE CURE ITSELF BUT THE SOURCE OF THE--

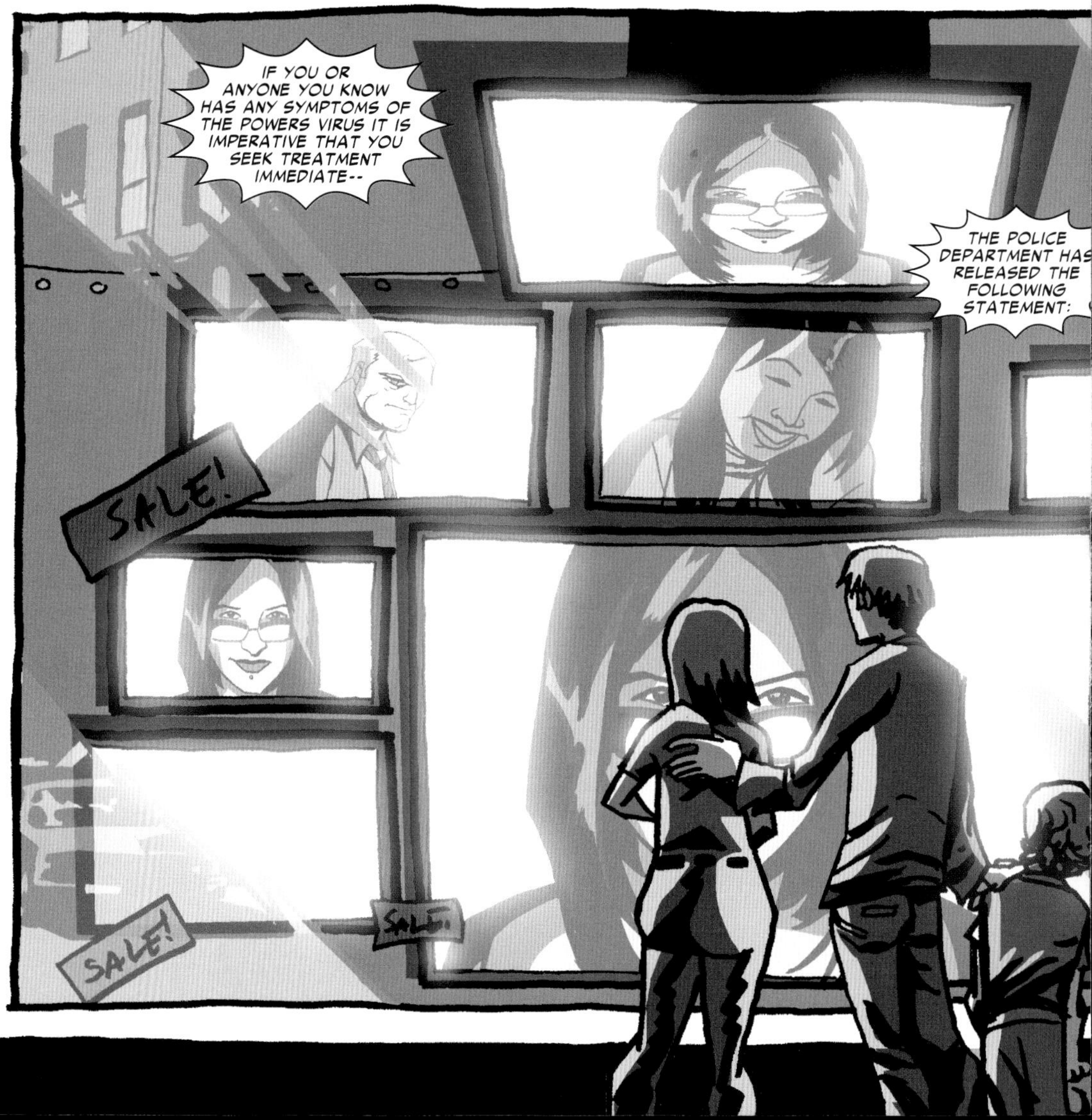
IF YOU OR ANYONE YOU KNOW HAS ANY SYMPTOMS OF THE POWERS VIRUS IT IS IMPERATIVE THAT YOU SEEK TREATMENT IMMEDIATE--
THE POLICE DEPARTMENT HAS RELEASED THE FOLLOWING STATEMENT:
SALE!
SALE!
SALE!

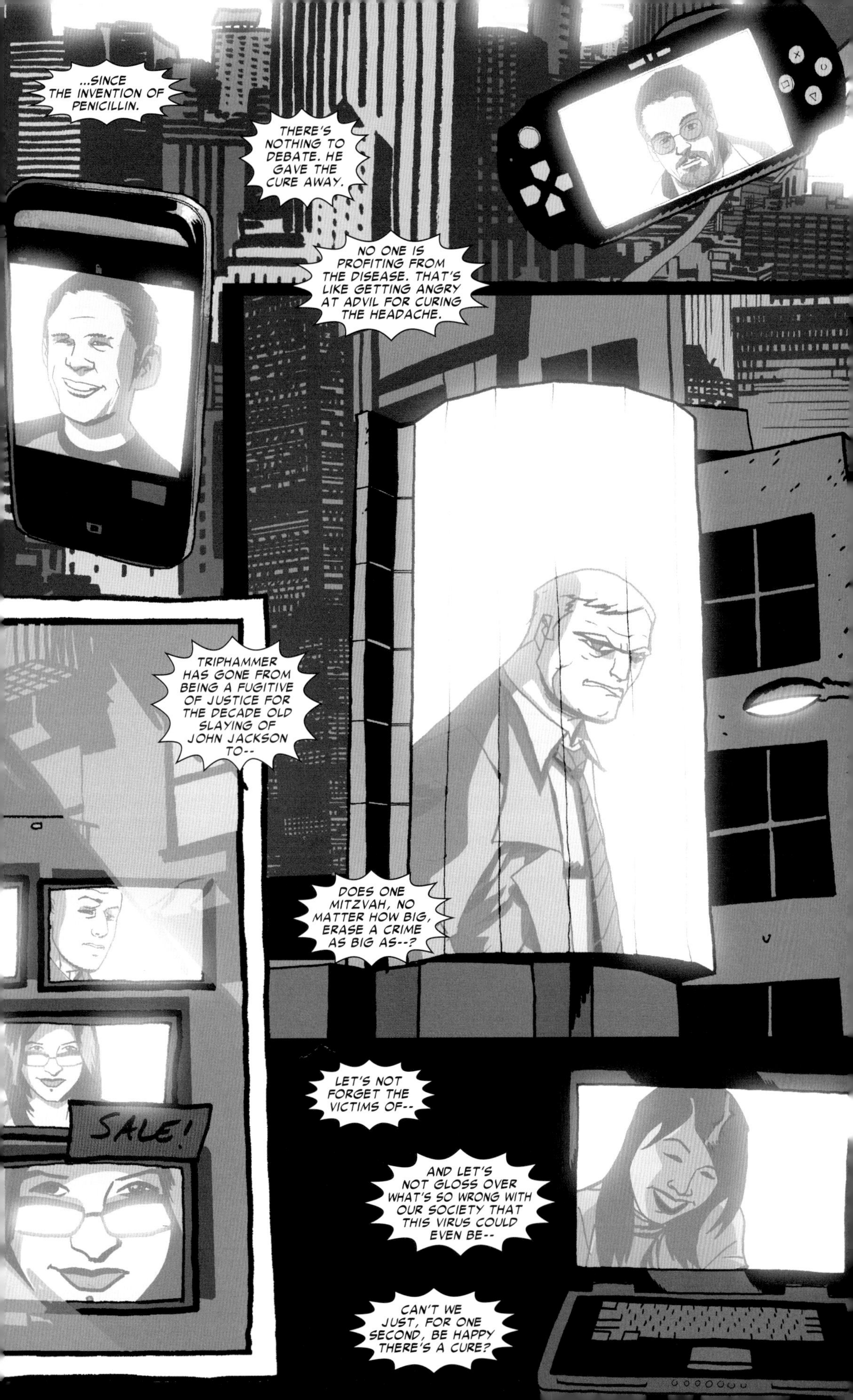
...SINCE THE INVENTION OF PENICILLIN.
THERE'S NOTHING TO DEBATE. HE GAVE THE CURE AWAY.
NO ONE IS PROFITING FROM THE DISEASE. THAT'S LIKE GETTING ANGRY AT ADVIL FOR CURING THE HEADACHE.
TRIPHAMMER HAS GONE FROM BEING A FUGITIVE OF JUSTICE FOR THE DECADE OLD SLAYING OF JOHN JACKSON TO--
DOES ONE MITZVAH, NO MATTER HOW BIG, ERASE A CRIME AS BIG AS--?
SALE!
LET'S NOT FORGET THE VICTIMS OF--
AND LET'S NOT GLOSS OVER WHAT'S SO WRONG WITH OUR SOCIETY THAT THIS VIRUS COULD EVEN BE--
CAN'T WE JUST, FOR ONE SECOND, BE HAPPY THERE'S A CURE?

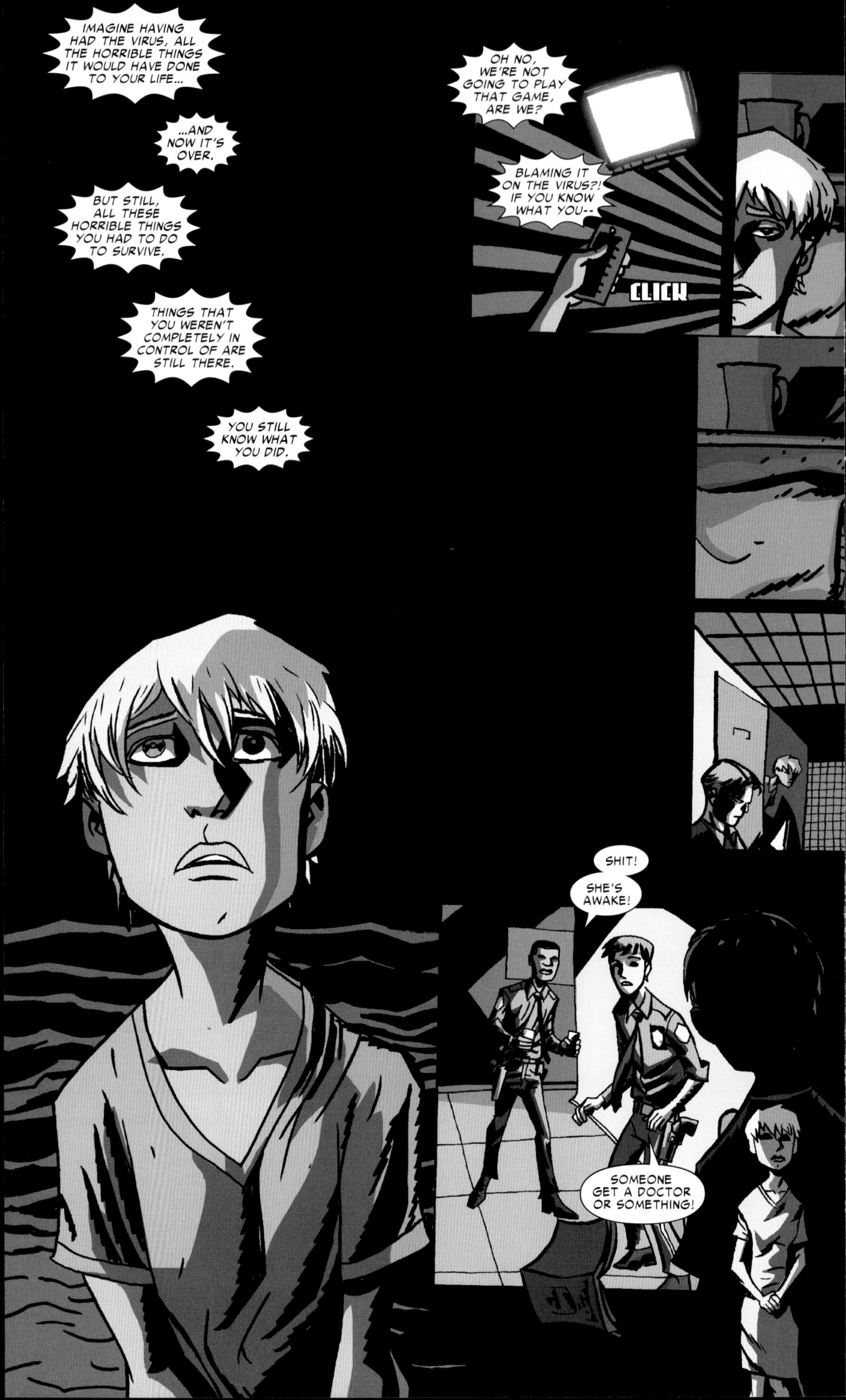
IMAGINE HAVING HAD THE VIRUS, ALL THE HORRIBLE THINGS IT WOULD HAVE DONE TO YOUR LIFE...
...AND NOW IT'S OVER.
BUT STILL, ALL THESE HORRIBLE THINGS YOU HAD TO DO TO SURVIVE.
THINGS THAT YOU WEREN'T COMPLETELY IN CONTROL OF ARE STILL THERE.
YOU STILL KNOW WHAT YOU DID.
OH NO, WE'RE NOT GOING TO PLAY THAT GAME, ARE WE?
BLAMING IT ON THE VIRUS?! IF YOU KNOW WHAT YOU--
CLICK
SHIT!
SHE'S AWAKE!
SOMEONE GET A DOCTOR OR SOMETHING!

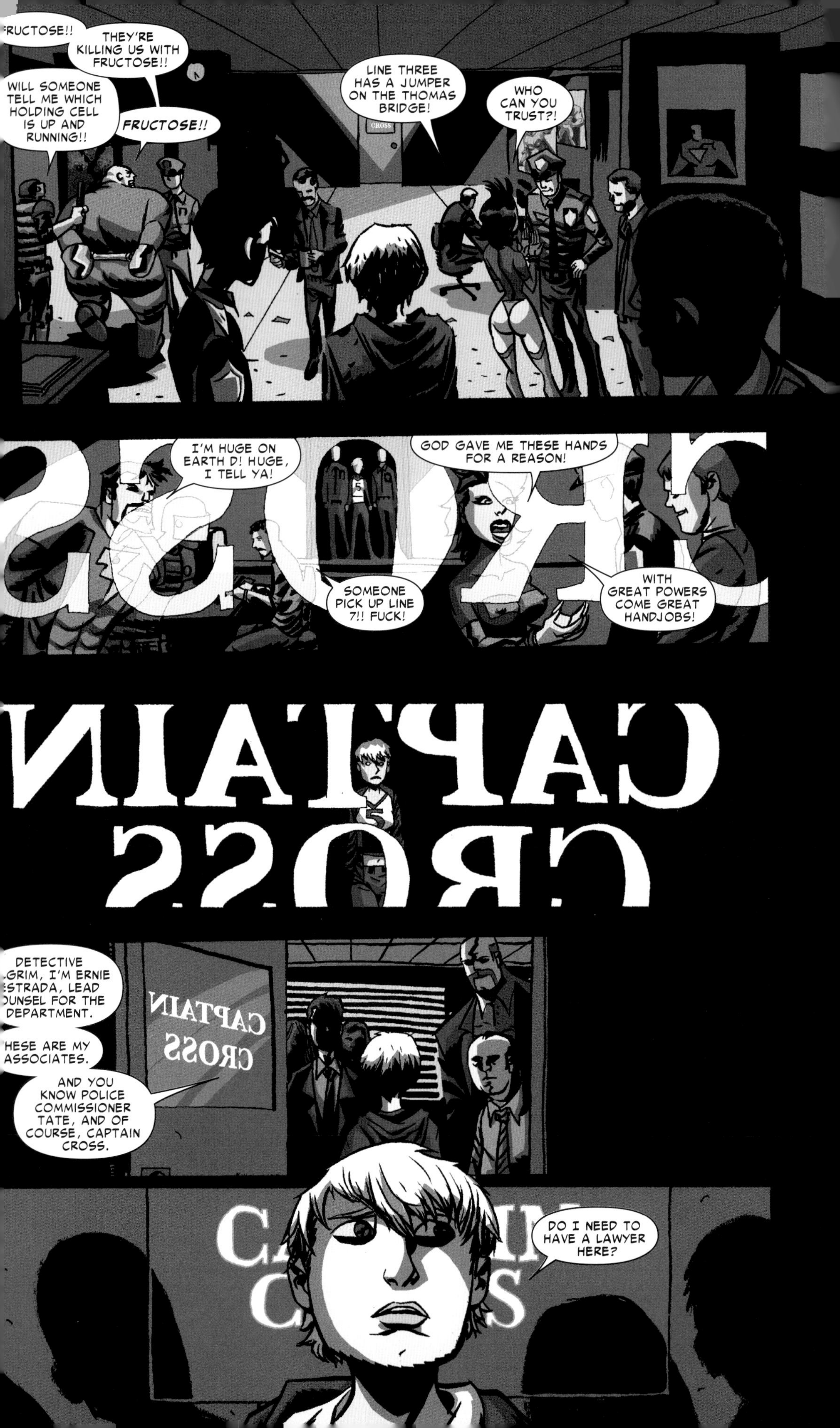

FRUCTOSE!!
THEY'RE KILLING US WITH FRUCTOSE!!
WILL SOMEONE TELL ME WHICH HOLDING CELL IS UP AND RUNNING!!
FRUCTOSE!!
LINE THREE HAS A JUMPER ON THE THOMAS BRIDGE!
WHO CAN YOU TRUST?!
I'M HUGE ON EARTH D! HUGE, I TELL YA!
GOD GAVE ME THESE HANDS FOR A REASON!
SOMEONE PICK UP LINE 7!! FUCK!
WITH GREAT POWERS COME GREAT HANDJOBS!
CAPTAIN CROSS
DETECTIVE GRIM, I'M ERNIE ESTRADA, LEAD COUNSEL FOR THE DEPARTMENT.
THESE ARE MY ASSOCIATES.
AND YOU KNOW POLICE COMMISSIONER TATE, AND OF COURSE, CAPTAIN CROSS.
CAPTAIN CROSS
DO I NEED TO HAVE A LAWYER HERE?

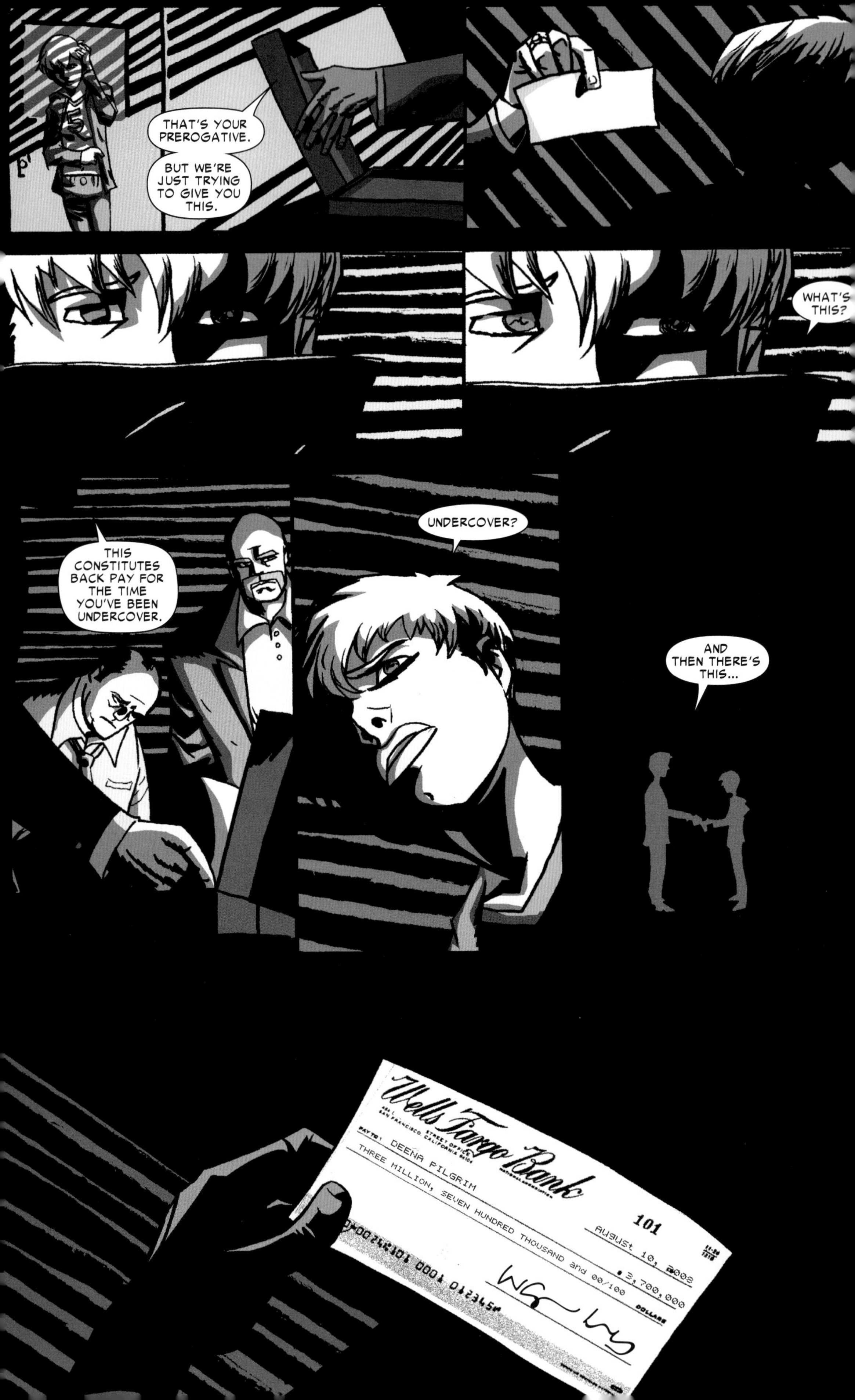
THAT'S YOUR PREROGATIVE.
BUT WE'RE JUST TRYING TO GIVE YOU THIS.
WHAT'S THIS?
THIS CONSTITUTES BACK PAY FOR THE TIME YOU'VE BEEN UNDERCOVER.
UNDERCOVER?
AND THEN THERE'S THIS...
Wells Fargo Bank
PAY TO: DEENA PILGRIM
THREE MILLION, SEVEN HUNDRED THOUSAND and 00/100
101
AUGUST 10, 2008
$3,700,000
DOLLARS

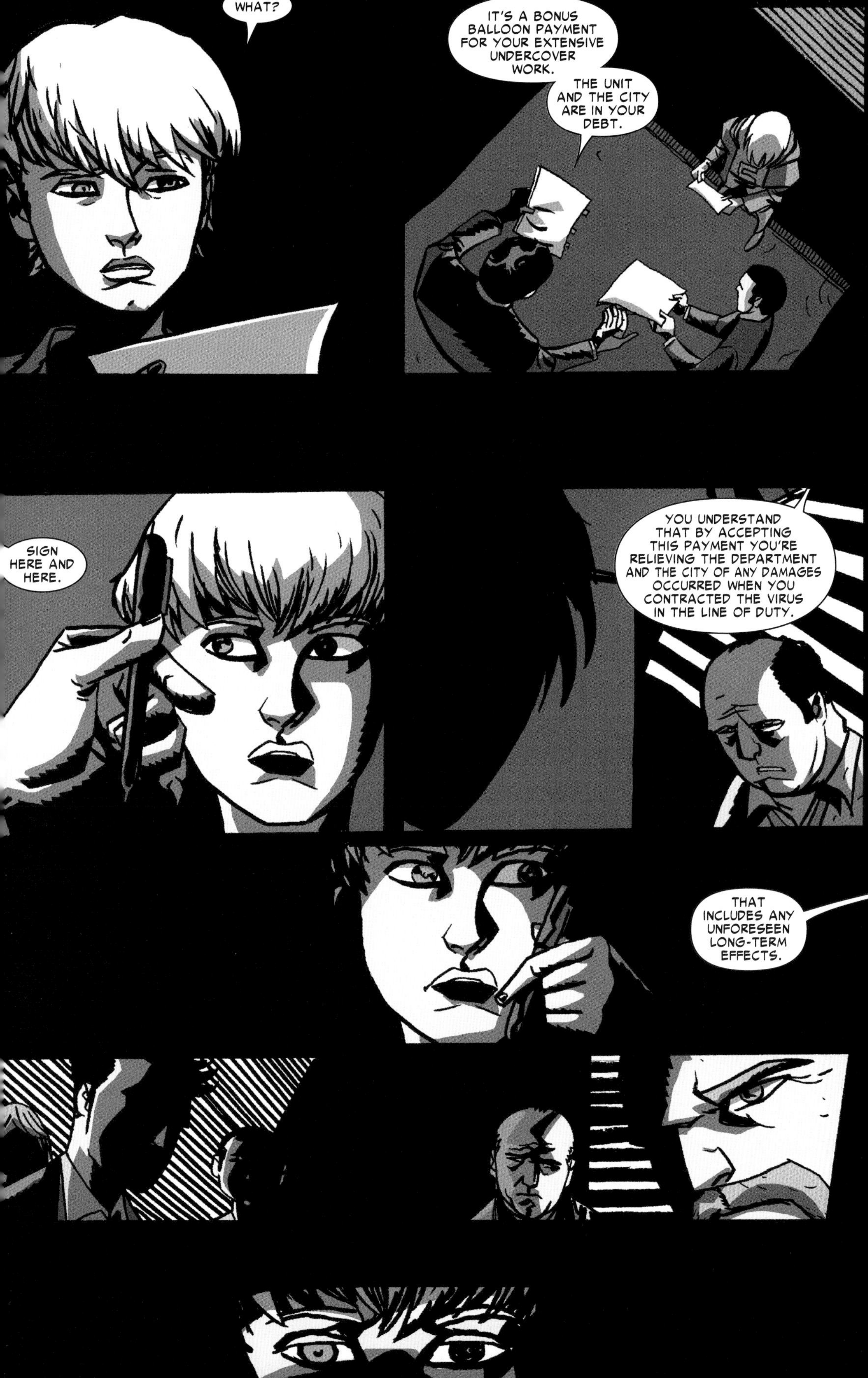
WHAT?
IT'S A BONUS BALLOON PAYMENT FOR YOUR EXTENSIVE UNDERCOVER WORK.
THE UNIT AND THE CITY ARE IN YOUR DEBT.
SIGN HERE AND HERE.
YOU UNDERSTAND THAT BY ACCEPTING THIS PAYMENT YOU'RE RELIEVING THE DEPARTMENT AND THE CITY OF ANY DAMAGES OCCURRED WHEN YOU CONTRACTED THE VIRUS IN THE LINE OF DUTY.
THAT INCLUDES ANY UNFORESEEN LONG-TERM EFFECTS.

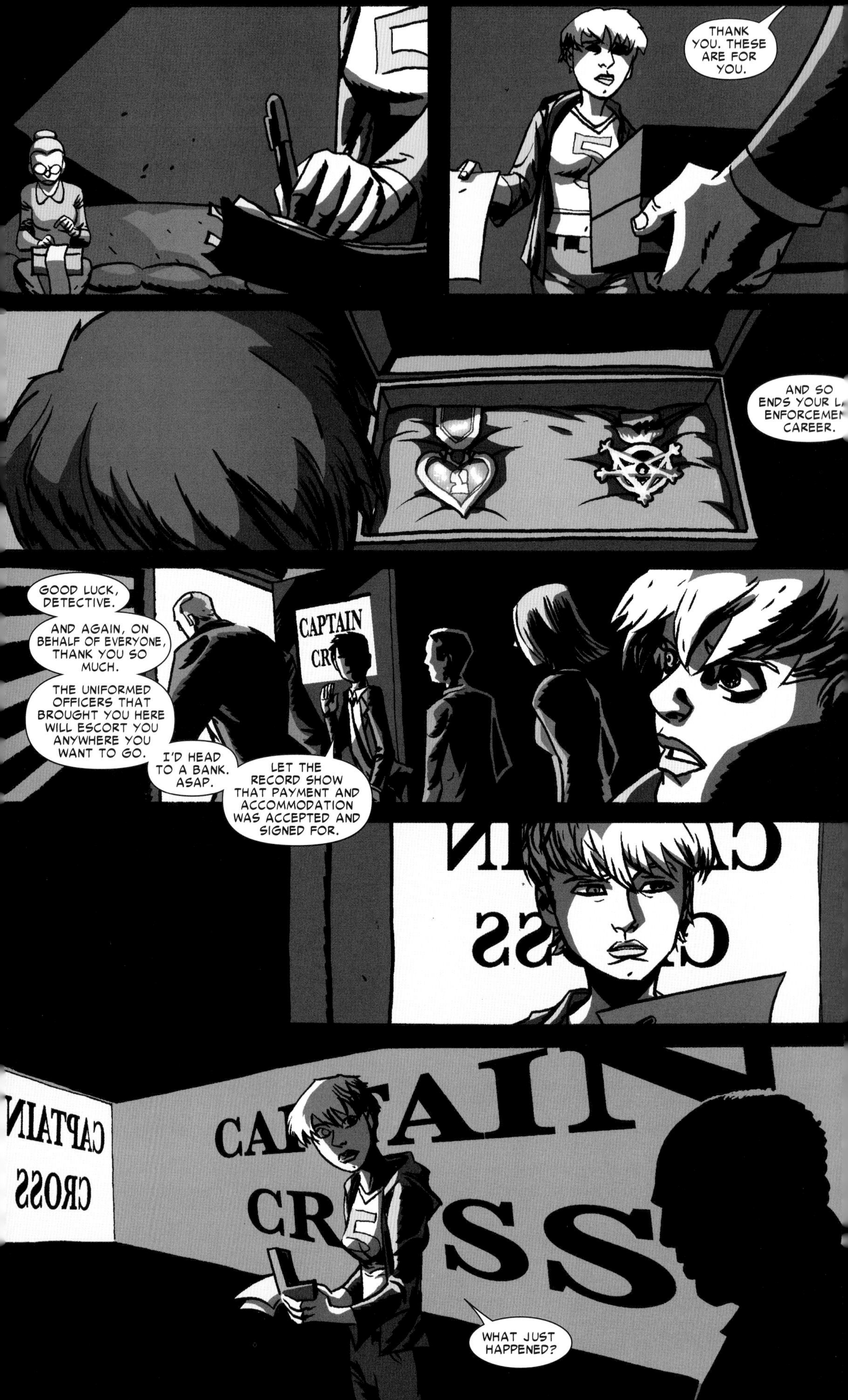
THANK YOU. THESE ARE FOR YOU.
AND SO ENDS YOUR L/ ENFORCEMEN CAREER.
GOOD LUCK, DETECTIVE.
AND AGAIN, ON BEHALF OF EVERYONE, THANK YOU SO MUCH.
THE UNIFORMED OFFICERS THAT BROUGHT YOU HERE WILL ESCORT YOU ANYWHERE YOU WANT TO GO.
I'D HEAD TO A BANK. ASAP.
LET THE RECORD SHOW THAT PAYMENT AND ACCOMMODATION WAS ACCEPTED AND SIGNED FOR.
CAPTAIN CR
CAPTAIN CROSS
CAPTAIN CROSS
WHAT JUST HAPPENED?

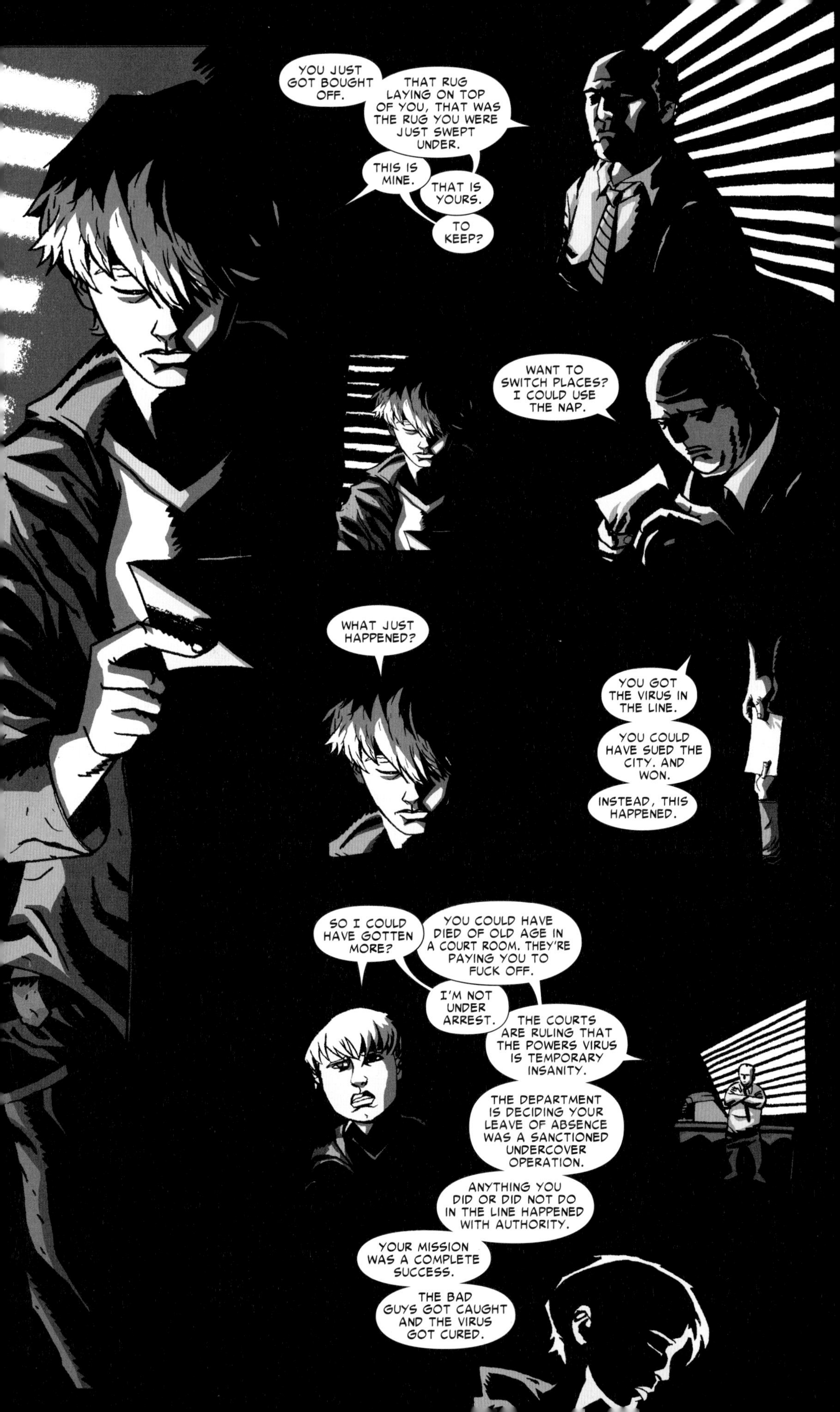
YOU JUST GOT BOUGHT OFF.
THAT RUG LAYING ON TOP OF YOU, THAT WAS THE RUG YOU WERE JUST SWEPT UNDER.
THIS IS MINE.
THAT IS YOURS.
TO KEEP?
WANT TO SWITCH PLACES? I COULD USE THE NAP.
WHAT JUST HAPPENED?
YOU GOT THE VIRUS IN THE LINE.
YOU COULD HAVE SUED THE CITY. AND WON.
INSTEAD, THIS HAPPENED.
SO I COULD HAVE GOTTEN MORE?
YOU COULD HAVE DIED OF OLD AGE IN A COURT ROOM. THEY'RE PAYING YOU TO FUCK OFF.
I'M NOT UNDER ARREST.
THE COURTS ARE RULING THAT THE POWERS VIRUS IS TEMPORARY INSANITY.
THE DEPARTMENT IS DECIDING YOUR LEAVE OF ABSENCE WAS A SANCTIONED UNDERCOVER OPERATION.
ANYTHING YOU DID OR DID NOT DO IN THE LINE HAPPENED WITH AUTHORITY.
YOUR MISSION WAS A COMPLETE SUCCESS.
THE BAD GUYS GOT CAUGHT AND THE VIRUS GOT CURED.

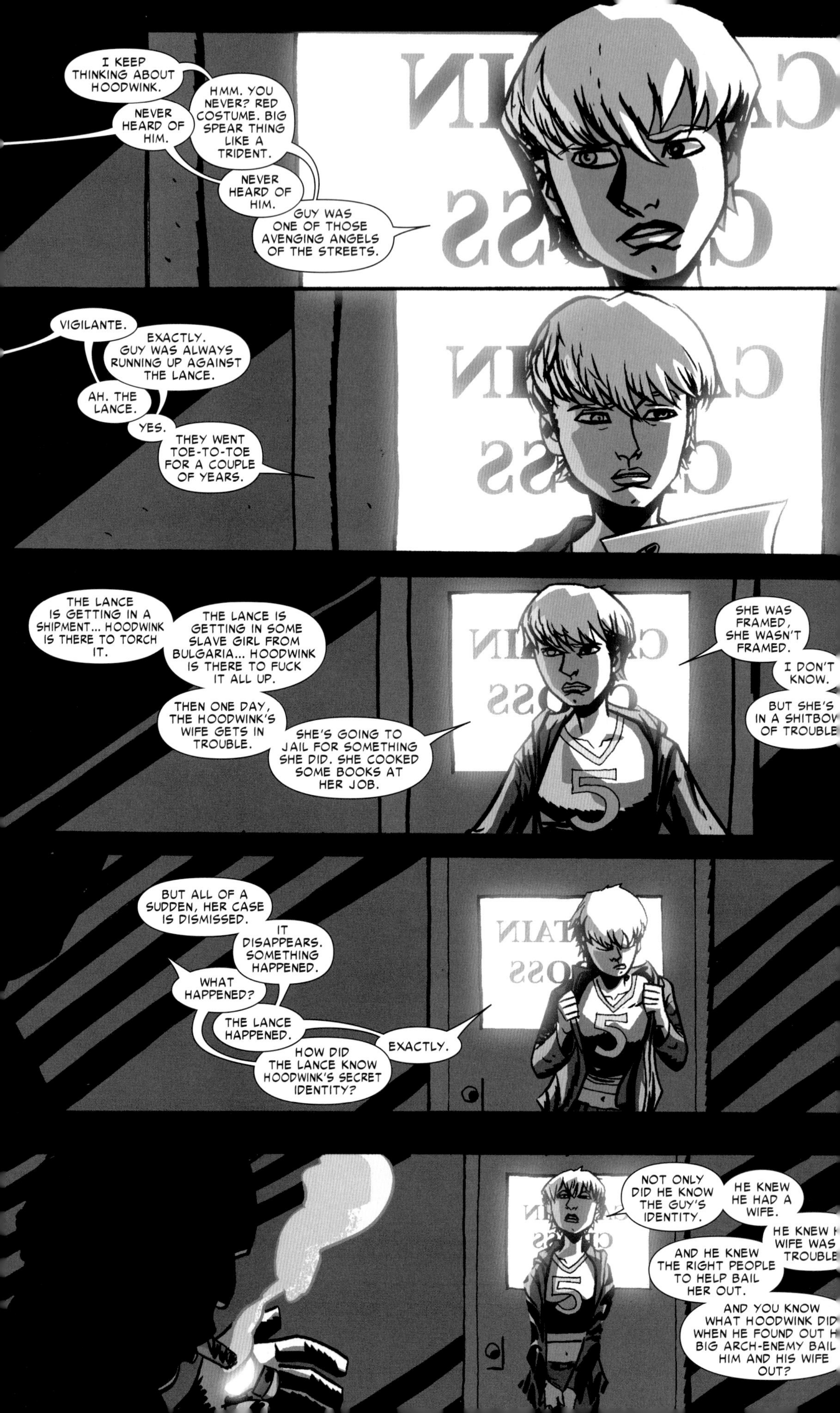
I KEEP THINKING ABOUT HOODWINK.
HMM. YOU NEVER? RED COSTUME. BIG SPEAR THING LIKE A TRIDENT.
NEVER HEARD OF HIM.
NEVER HEARD OF HIM.
GUY WAS ONE OF THOSE AVENGING ANGELS OF THE STREETS.
VIGILANTE.
EXACTLY. GUY WAS ALWAYS RUNNING UP AGAINST THE LANCE.
AH. THE LANCE.
YES.
THEY WENT TOE-TO-TOE FOR A COUPLE OF YEARS.
THE LANCE IS GETTING IN A SHIPMENT... HOODWINK IS THERE TO TORCH IT.
THE LANCE IS GETTING IN SOME SLAVE GIRL FROM BULGARIA... HOODWINK IS THERE TO FUCK IT ALL UP.
THEN ONE DAY, THE HOODWINK'S WIFE GETS IN TROUBLE.
SHE'S GOING TO JAIL FOR SOMETHING SHE DID. SHE COOKED SOME BOOKS AT HER JOB.
SHE WAS FRAMED, SHE WASN'T FRAMED.
I DON'T KNOW.
BUT SHE'S IN A SHITBOW OF TROUBLE
BUT ALL OF A SUDDEN, HER CASE IS DISMISSED.
IT DISAPPEARS. SOMETHING HAPPENED.
WHAT HAPPENED?
THE LANCE HAPPENED.
EXACTLY.
HOW DID THE LANCE KNOW HOODWINK'S SECRET IDENTITY?
NOT ONLY DID HE KNOW THE GUY'S IDENTITY.
HE KNEW HE HAD A WIFE.
HE KNEW WIFE WAS TROUBLE
AND HE KNEW THE RIGHT PEOPLE TO HELP BAIL HER OUT.
AND YOU KNOW WHAT HOODWINK DID WHEN HE FOUND OUT H BIG ARCH-ENEMY BAIL HIM AND HIS WIFE OUT?

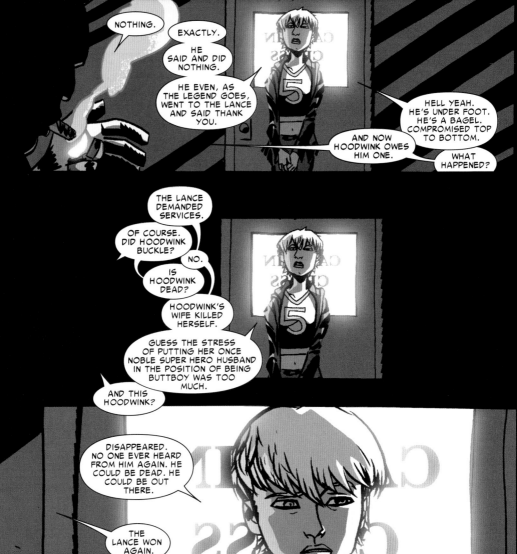

NOTHING.

EXACTLY. HE SAID AND DID NOTHING.

HE EVEN, AS THE LEGEND GOES, WENT TO THE LANCE AND SAID THANK YOU.

HELL YEAH. HE'S UNDER FOOT. HE'S A BAGEL. COMPROMISED TOP TO BOTTOM.

AND NOW HOODWINK OWES HIM ONE.

WHAT HAPPENED?

THE LANCE DEMANDED SERVICES.

OF COURSE. DID HOODWINK BUCKLE?

NO.

IS HOODWINK DEAD?

HOODWINK'S WIFE KILLED HERSELF.

GUESS THE STRESS OF PUTTING HER ONCE NOBLE SUPER HERO HUSBAND IN THE POSITION OF BEING BUTTBOY WAS TOO MUCH.

AND THIS HOODWINK?

DISAPPEARED. NO ONE EVER HEARD FROM HIM AGAIN. HE COULD BE DEAD. HE COULD BE OUT THERE.

THE LANCE WON AGAIN.

HOODWINK WAS MY BROTHER.

AND WITH THE SHACKLES OF MY DUTY AS A COP FINALLY OFF MY SHOULDERS AND THAT POWER IN MY VEINS...

WHAT DO I DO?

TORTURE AND KILL THE LANCE.

I KILLED HIM WITH MY BARE HANDS.

I WENT AFTER HIM AND I FUCKED HIM OVER AND THEN I KILLED HIM.

SO TELL ME HOW TEMPORARILY INSANE I WAS.

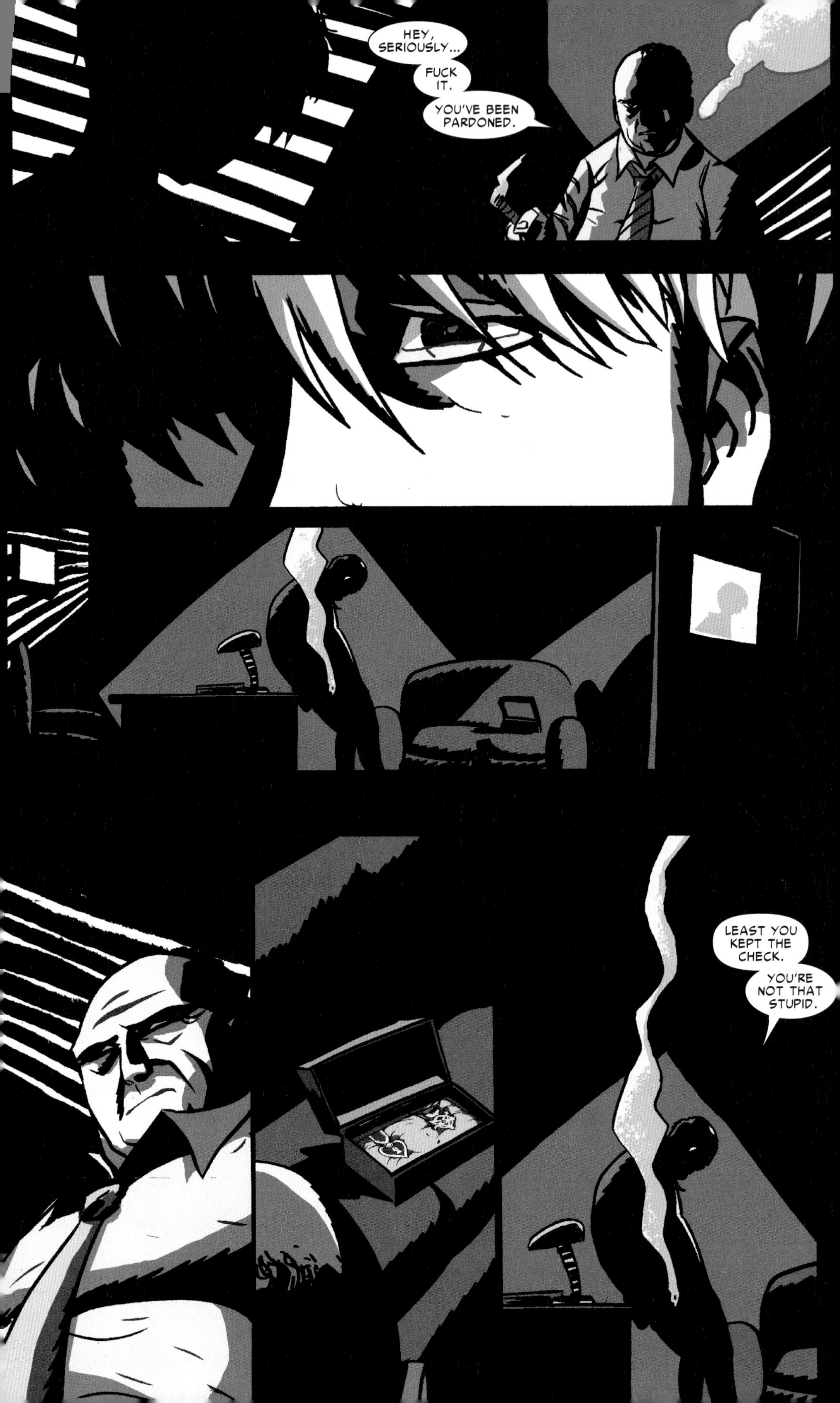
HEY, SERIOUSLY...
FUCK IT.
YOU'VE BEEN PARDONED.
LEAST YOU KEPT THE CHECK.
YOU'RE NOT THAT STUPID.

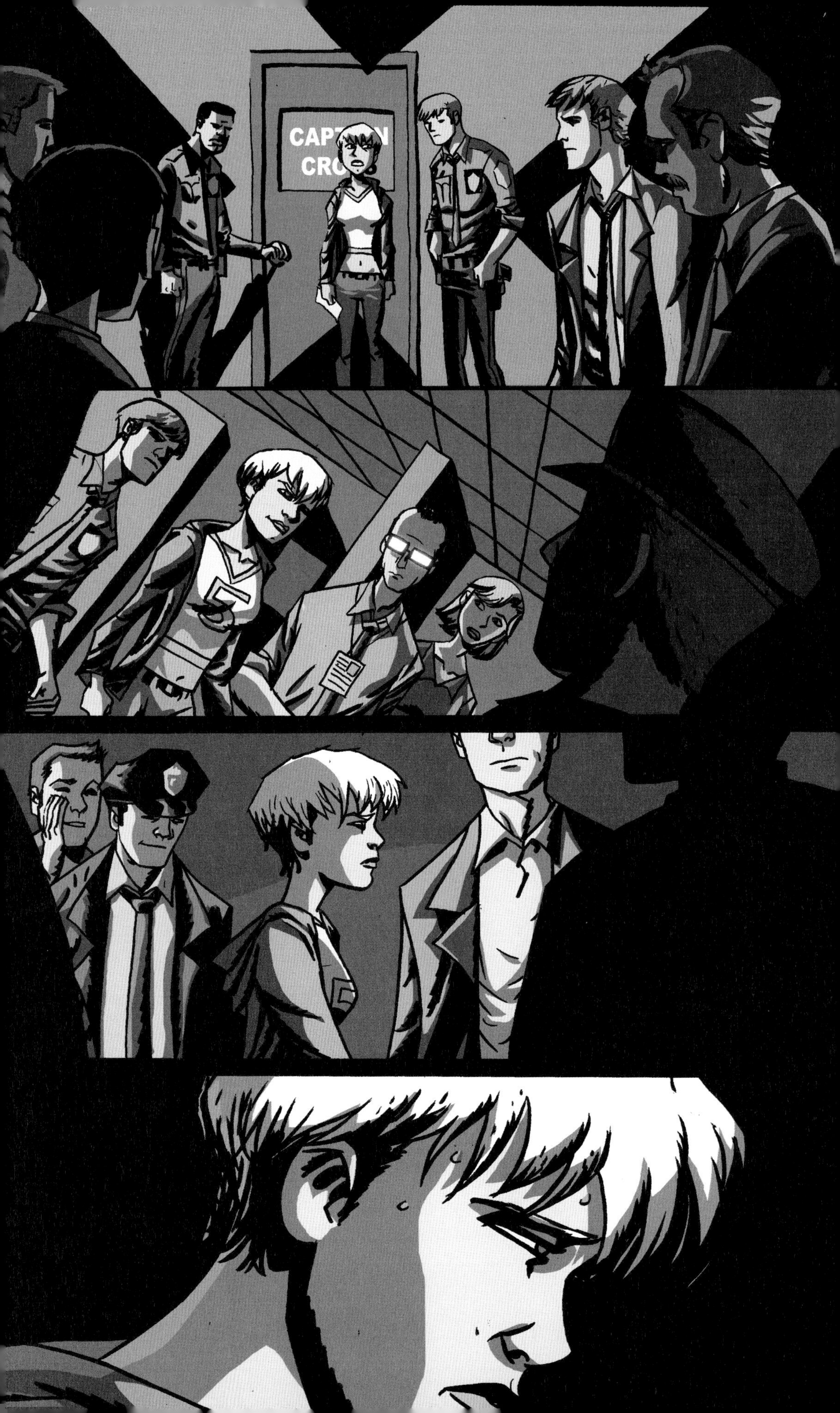

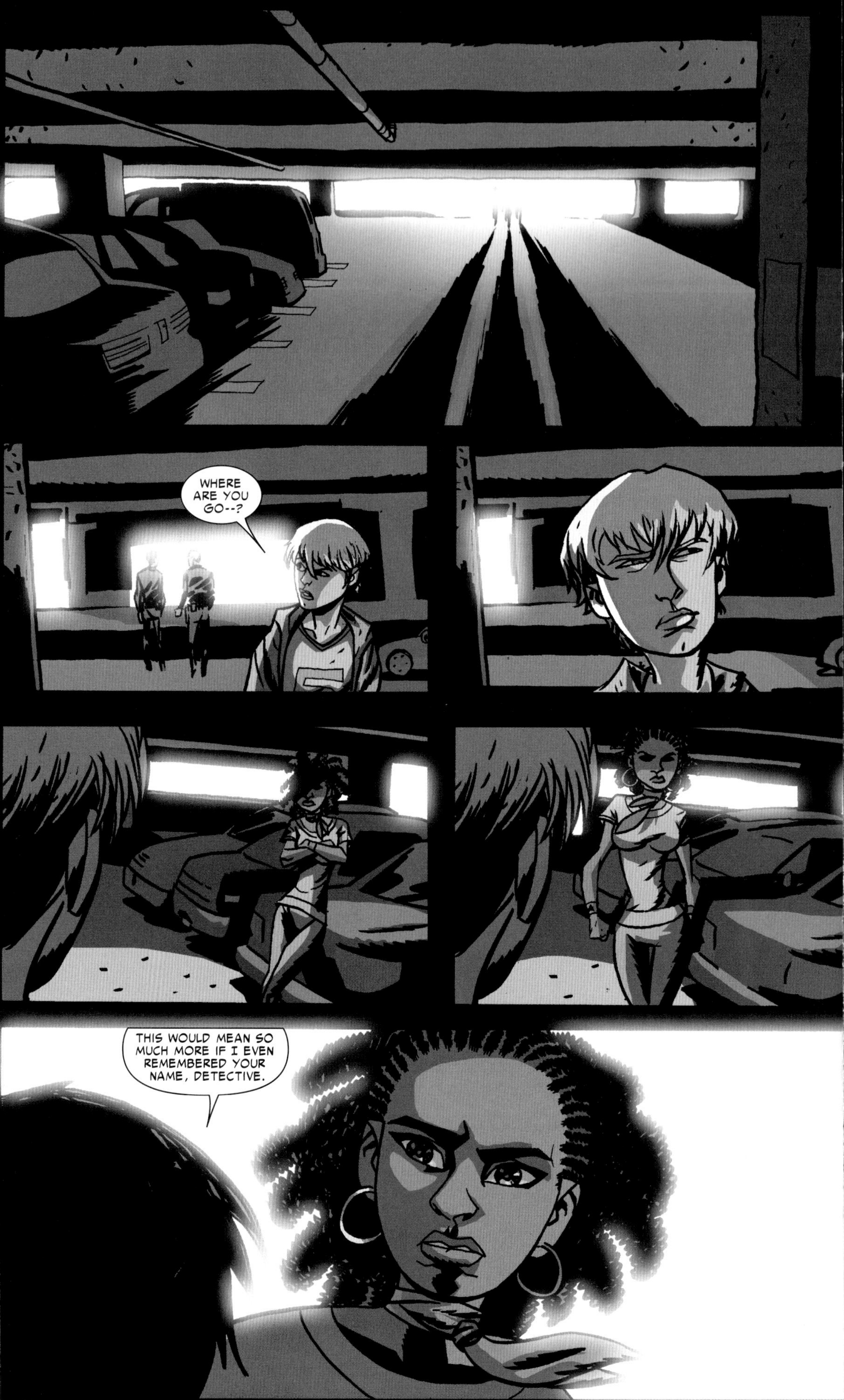
WHERE ARE YOU GO--?
THIS WOULD MEAN SO MUCH MORE IF I EVEN REMEMBERED YOUR NAME, DETECTIVE.

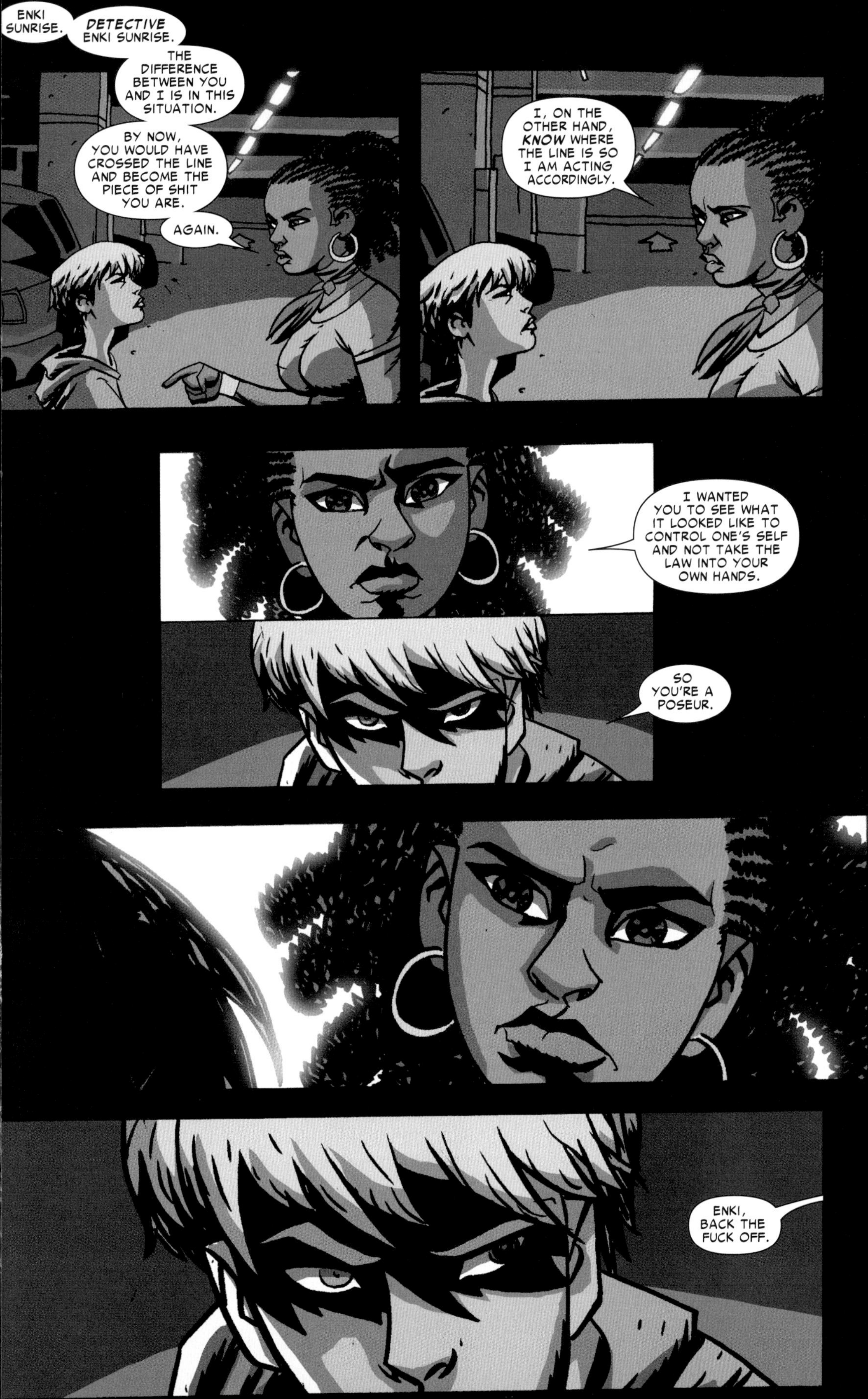
ENKI SUNRISE.
DETECTIVE ENKI SUNRISE.
THE DIFFERENCE BETWEEN YOU AND I IS IN THIS SITUATION.
BY NOW, YOU WOULD HAVE CROSSED THE LINE AND BECOME THE PIECE OF SHIT YOU ARE.
AGAIN.
I, ON THE OTHER HAND, KNOW WHERE THE LINE IS SO I AM ACTING ACCORDINGLY.
I WANTED YOU TO SEE WHAT IT LOOKED LIKE TO CONTROL ONE'S SELF AND NOT TAKE THE LAW INTO YOUR OWN HANDS.
SO YOU'RE A POSEUR.
ENKI, BACK THE FUCK OFF.

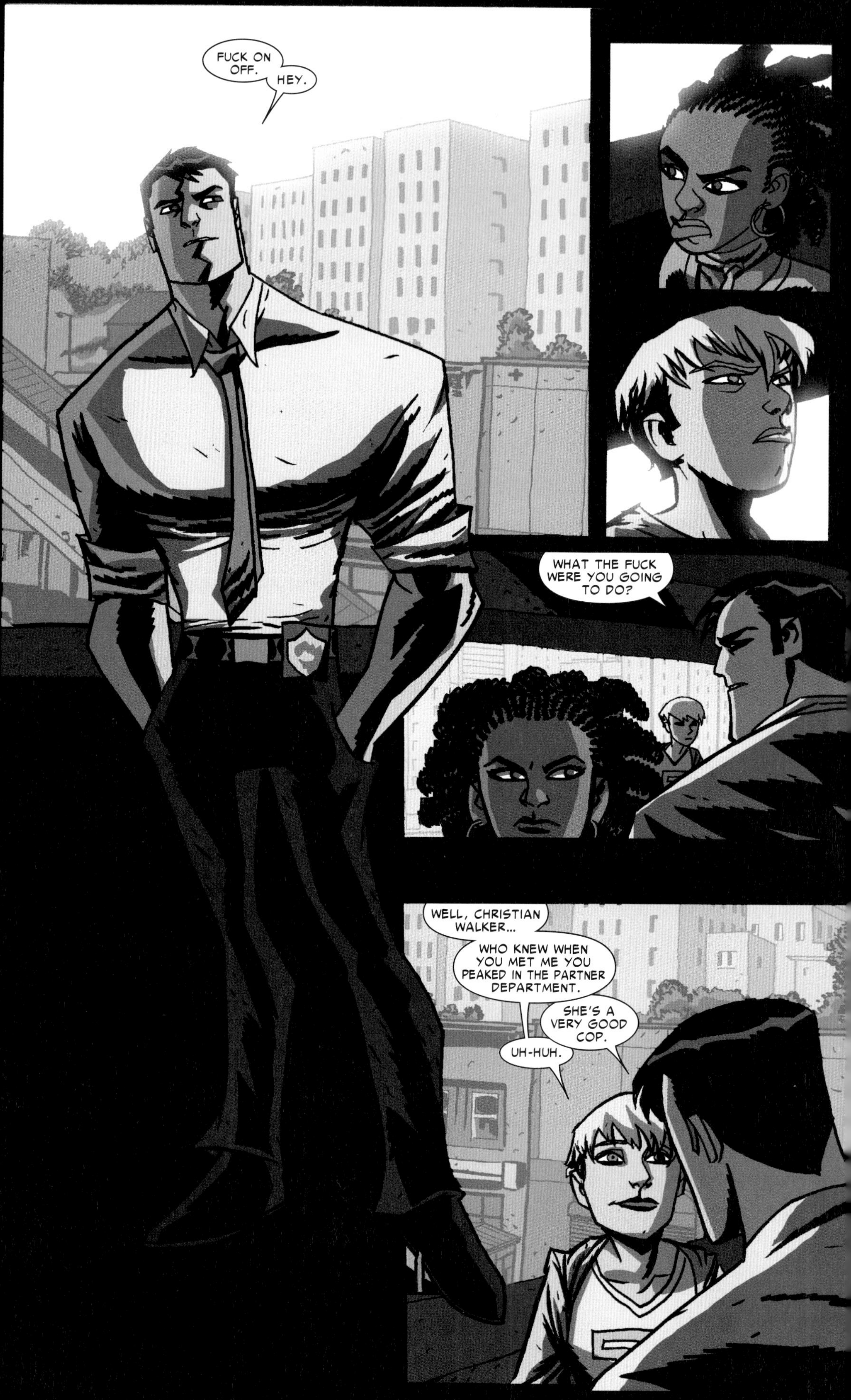
FUCK ON OFF.
HEY.
WHAT THE FUCK WERE YOU GOING TO DO?
WELL, CHRISTIAN WALKER...
WHO KNEW WHEN YOU MET ME YOU PEAKED IN THE PARTNER DEPARTMENT.
SHE'S A VERY GOOD COP.
UH-HUH.

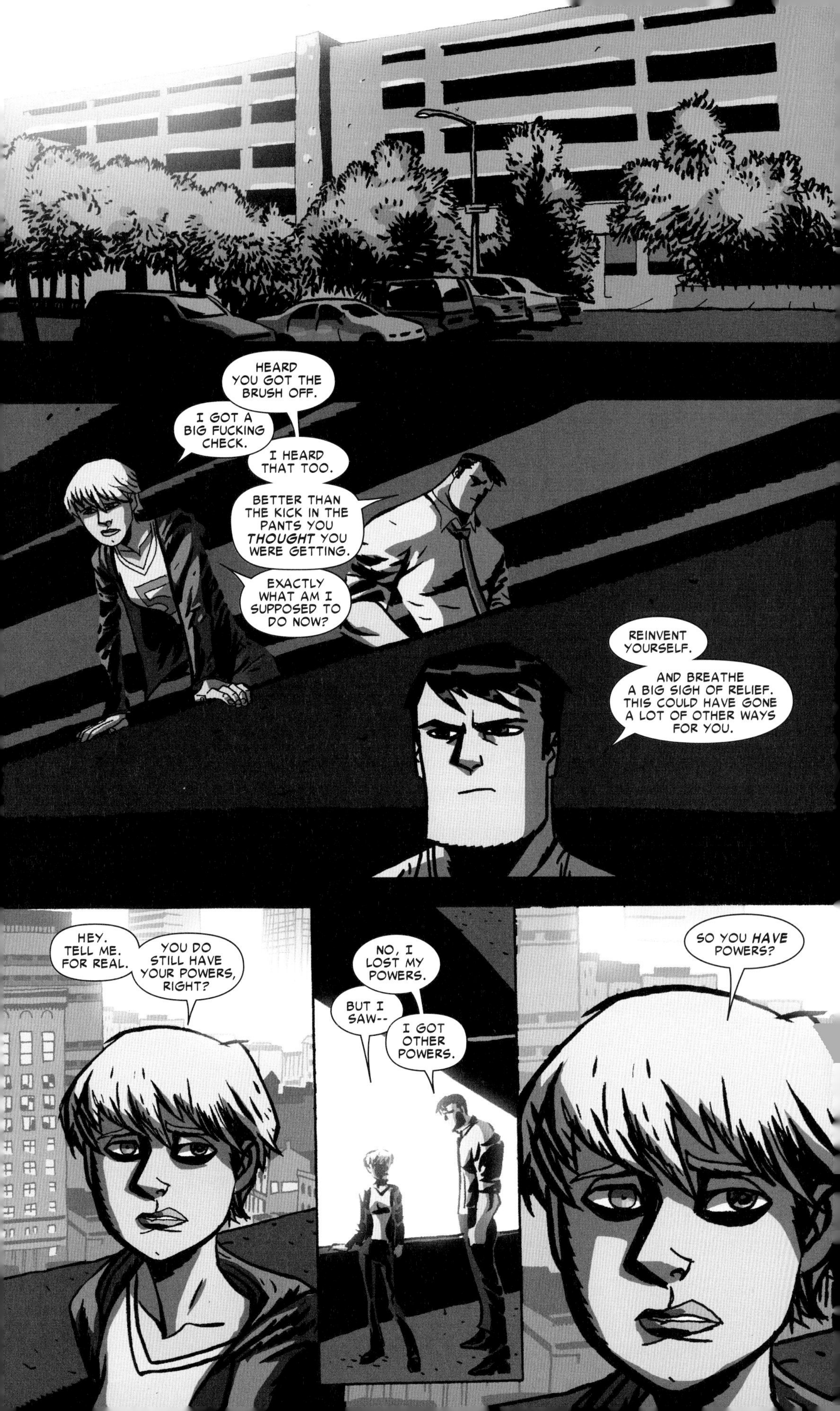
HEARD YOU GOT THE BRUSH OFF.
I GOT A BIG FUCKING CHECK.
I HEARD THAT TOO.
BETTER THAN THE KICK IN THE PANTS YOU *THOUGHT* YOU WERE GETTING.
EXACTLY WHAT AM I SUPPOSED TO DO NOW?
REINVENT YOURSELF.
AND BREATHE A BIG SIGH OF RELIEF. THIS COULD HAVE GONE A LOT OF OTHER WAYS FOR YOU.
HEY. TELL ME. FOR REAL.
YOU DO STILL HAVE YOUR POWERS, RIGHT?
NO, I LOST MY POWERS.
BUT I SAW--
I GOT OTHER POWERS.
SO YOU *HAVE* POWERS?

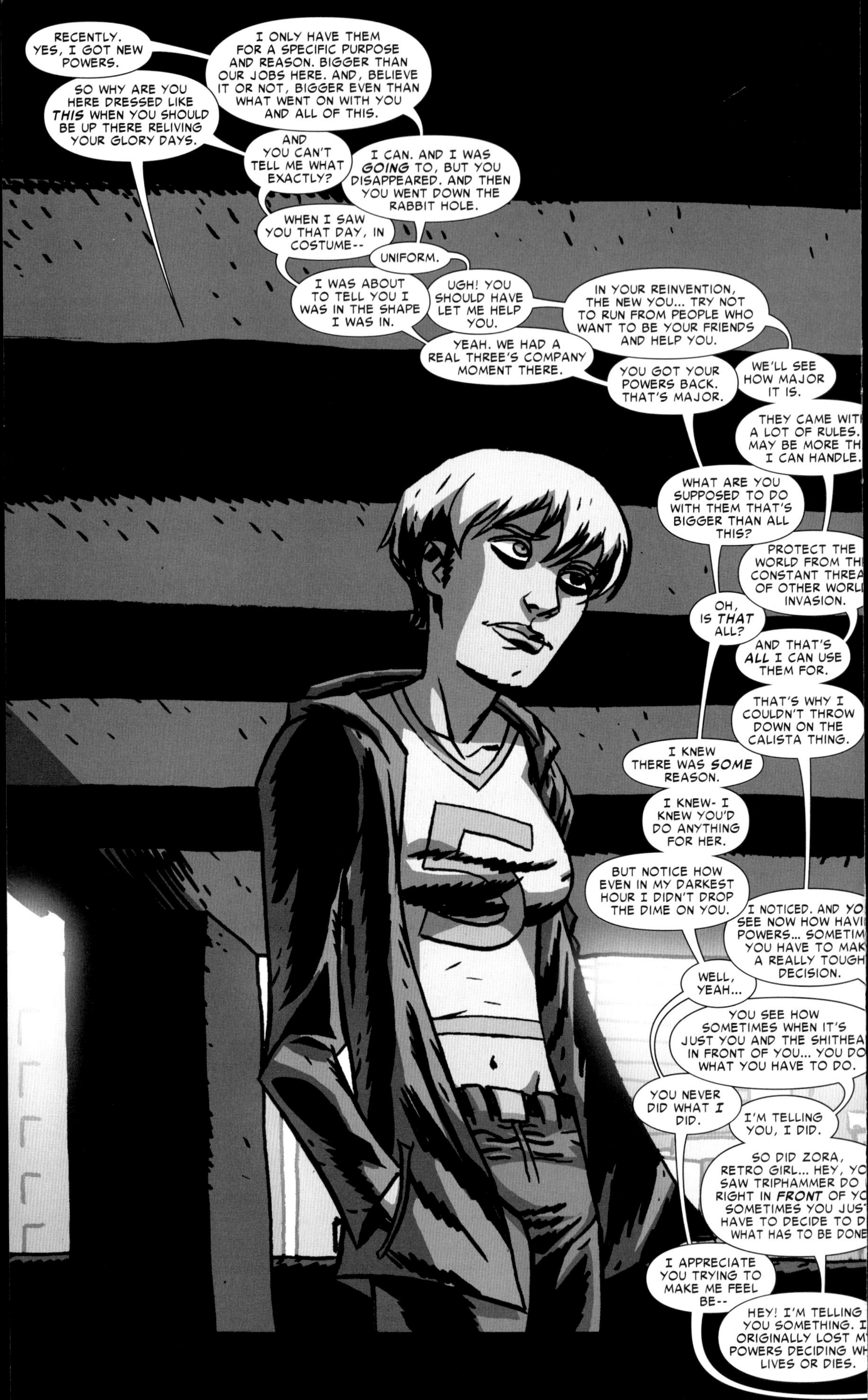
RECENTLY. YES, I GOT NEW POWERS.
I ONLY HAVE THEM FOR A SPECIFIC PURPOSE AND REASON. BIGGER THAN OUR JOBS HERE. AND, BELIEVE IT OR NOT, BIGGER EVEN THAN WHAT WENT ON WITH YOU AND ALL OF THIS.
SO WHY ARE YOU HERE DRESSED LIKE THIS WHEN YOU SHOULD BE UP THERE RELIVING YOUR GLORY DAYS.
AND YOU CAN'T TELL ME WHAT EXACTLY?
I CAN. AND I WAS GOING TO, BUT YOU DISAPPEARED. AND THEN YOU WENT DOWN THE RABBIT HOLE.
WHEN I SAW YOU THAT DAY, IN COSTUME--
UNIFORM.
I WAS ABOUT TO TELL YOU I WAS IN THE SHAPE I WAS IN.
UGH! YOU SHOULD HAVE LET ME HELP YOU.
IN YOUR REINVENTION, THE NEW YOU... TRY NOT TO RUN FROM PEOPLE WHO WANT TO BE YOUR FRIENDS AND HELP YOU.
YEAH. WE HAD A REAL THREE'S COMPANY MOMENT THERE.
YOU GOT YOUR POWERS BACK. THAT'S MAJOR.
WE'LL SEE HOW MAJOR IT IS.
THEY CAME WITH A LOT OF RULES. MAY BE MORE TH I CAN HANDLE.
WHAT ARE YOU SUPPOSED TO DO WITH THEM THAT'S BIGGER THAN ALL THIS?
PROTECT THE WORLD FROM TH CONSTANT THREA OF OTHER WORL INVASION.
OH, IS THAT ALL?
AND THAT'S ALL I CAN USE THEM FOR.
THAT'S WHY I COULDN'T THROW DOWN ON THE CALISTA THING.
I KNEW THERE WAS SOME REASON.
I KNEW- I KNEW YOU'D DO ANYTHING FOR HER.
BUT NOTICE HOW EVEN IN MY DARKEST HOUR I DIDN'T DROP THE DIME ON YOU.
I NOTICED. AND YO SEE NOW HOW HAVI POWERS... SOMETIM YOU HAVE TO MAK A REALLY TOUGH DECISION.
WELL, YEAH...
YOU SEE HOW SOMETIMES WHEN IT'S JUST YOU AND THE SHITHEA IN FRONT OF YOU... YOU DO WHAT YOU HAVE TO DO.
YOU NEVER DID WHAT I DID.
I'M TELLING YOU, I DID.
SO DID ZORA, RETRO GIRL... HEY, YO SAW TRIPHAMMER DO RIGHT IN FRONT OF YO SOMETIMES YOU JUST HAVE TO DECIDE TO D WHAT HAS TO BE DONE
I APPRECIATE YOU TRYING TO MAKE ME FEEL BE--
HEY! I'M TELLING YOU SOMETHING. I ORIGINALLY LOST MY POWERS DECIDING WH LIVES OR DIES.

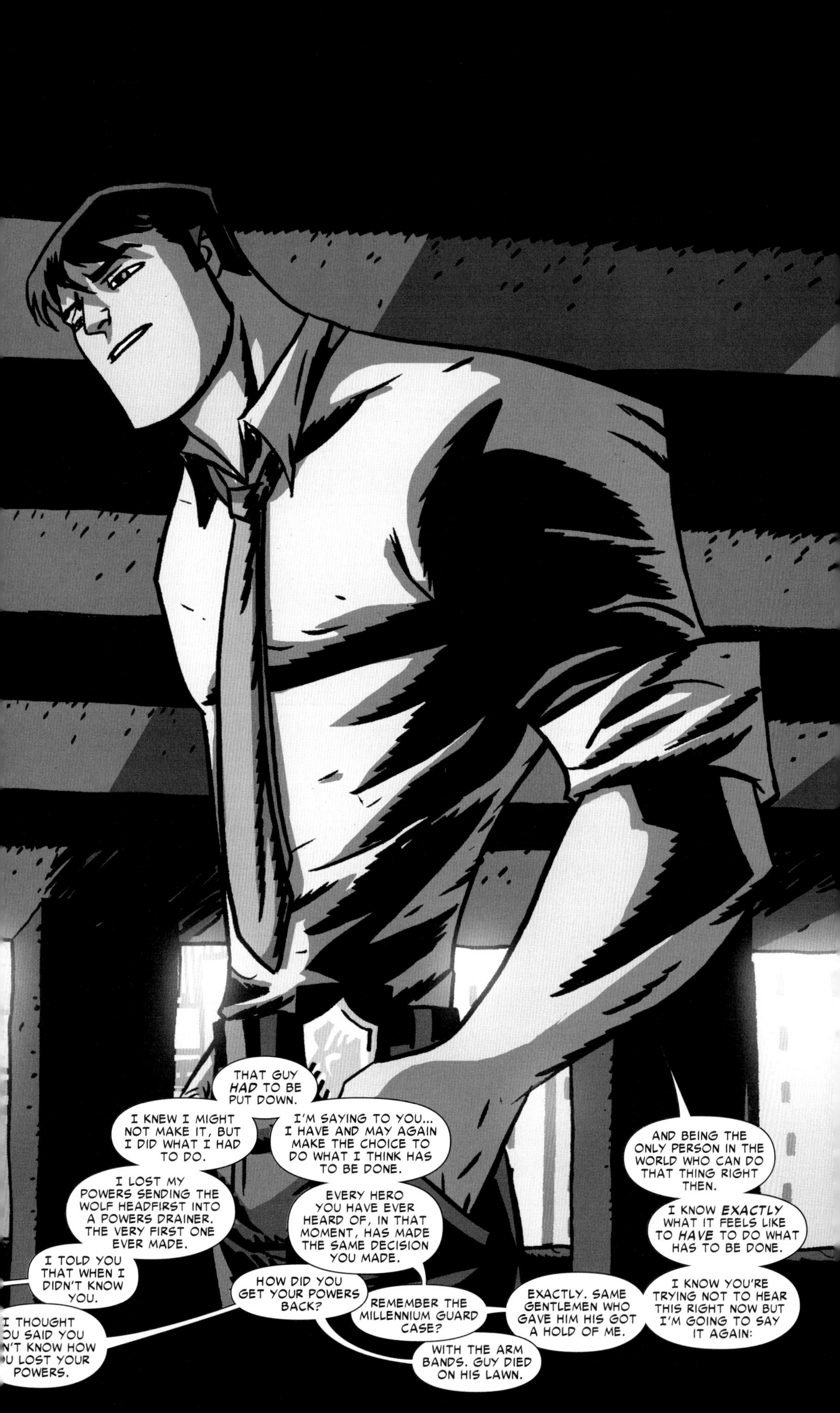

I THOUGHT
OU SAID YOU
N'T KNOW HOW
U LOST YOUR
POWERS.
I TOLD YOU THAT WHEN I DIDN'T KNOW YOU.
I LOST MY POWERS SENDING THE WOLF HEADFIRST INTO A POWERS DRAINER. THE VERY FIRST ONE EVER MADE.
I KNEW I MIGHT NOT MAKE IT, BUT I DID WHAT I HAD TO DO.
THAT GUY *HAD* TO BE PUT DOWN.
I'M SAYING TO YOU... I HAVE AND MAY AGAIN MAKE THE CHOICE TO DO WHAT I THINK HAS TO BE DONE.
EVERY HERO YOU HAVE EVER HEARD OF, IN THAT MOMENT, HAS MADE THE SAME DECISION YOU MADE.
HOW DID YOU GET YOUR POWERS BACK?
REMEMBER THE MILLENNIUM GUARD CASE?
WITH THE ARM BANDS. GUY DIED ON HIS LAWN.
EXACTLY. SAME GENTLEMEN WHO GAVE HIM HIS GOT A HOLD OF ME.
I KNOW YOU'RE TRYING NOT TO HEAR THIS RIGHT NOW BUT I'M GOING TO SAY IT AGAIN:
I KNOW *EXACTLY* WHAT IT FEELS LIKE TO *HAVE* TO DO WHAT HAS TO BE DONE.
AND BEING THE ONLY PERSON IN THE WORLD WHO CAN DO THAT THING RIGHT THEN.

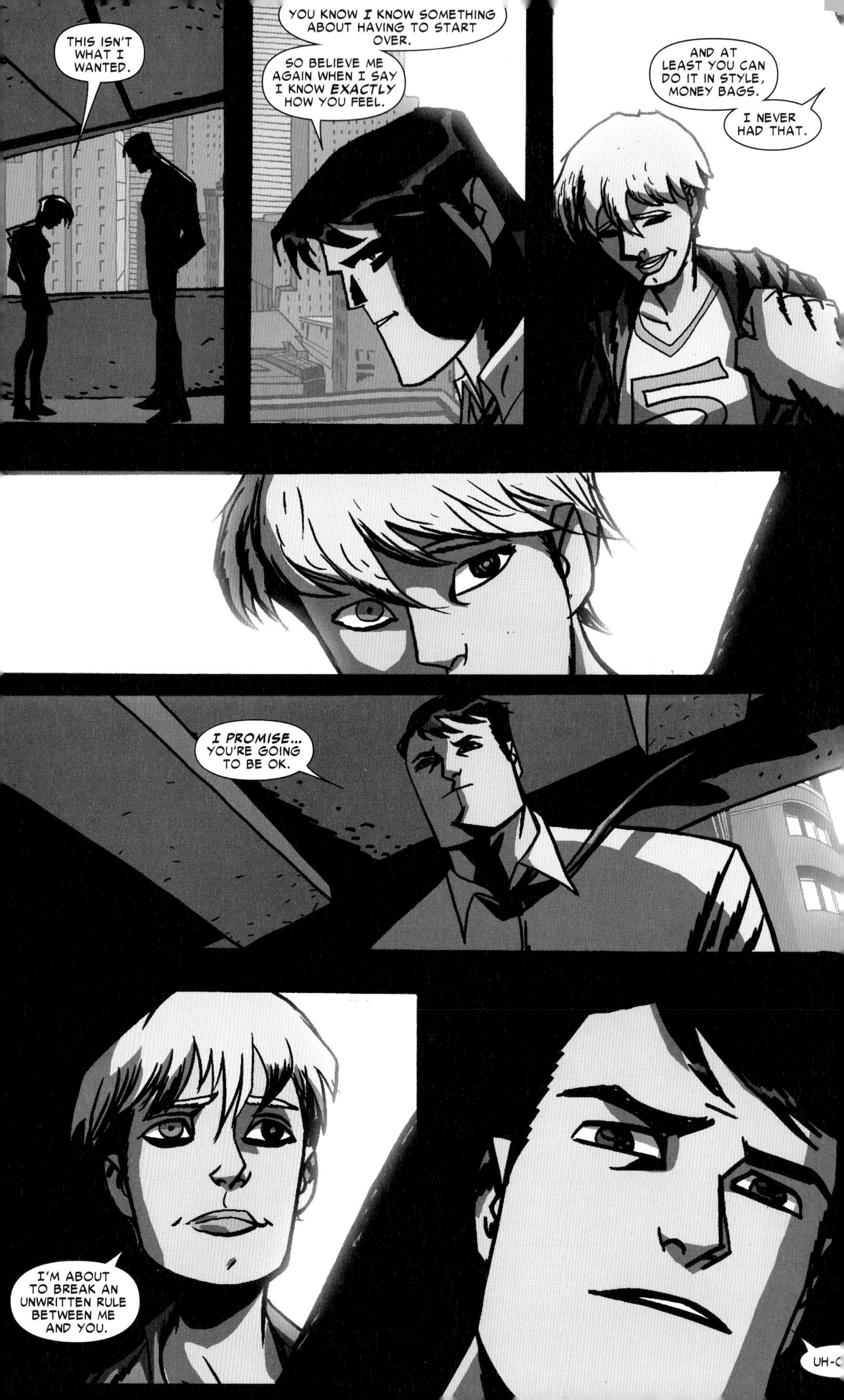
THIS ISN'T WHAT I WANTED.
YOU KNOW I KNOW SOMETHING ABOUT HAVING TO START OVER.
SO BELIEVE ME AGAIN WHEN I SAY I KNOW EXACTLY HOW YOU FEEL.
AND AT LEAST YOU CAN DO IT IN STYLE, MONEY BAGS.
I NEVER HAD THAT.
I PROMISE... YOU'RE GOING TO BE OK.
I'M ABOUT TO BREAK AN UNWRITTEN RULE BETWEEN ME AND YOU.
UH-

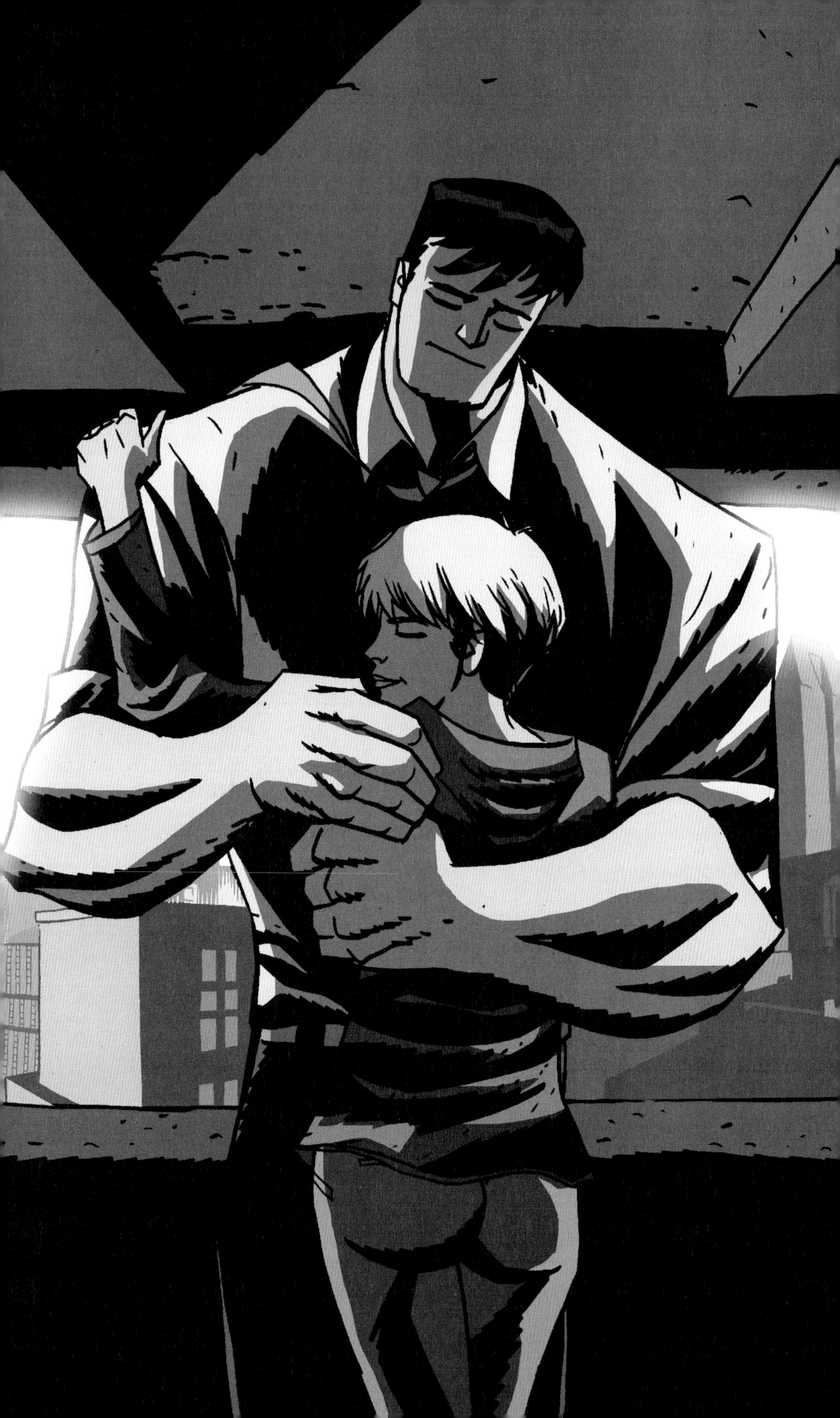

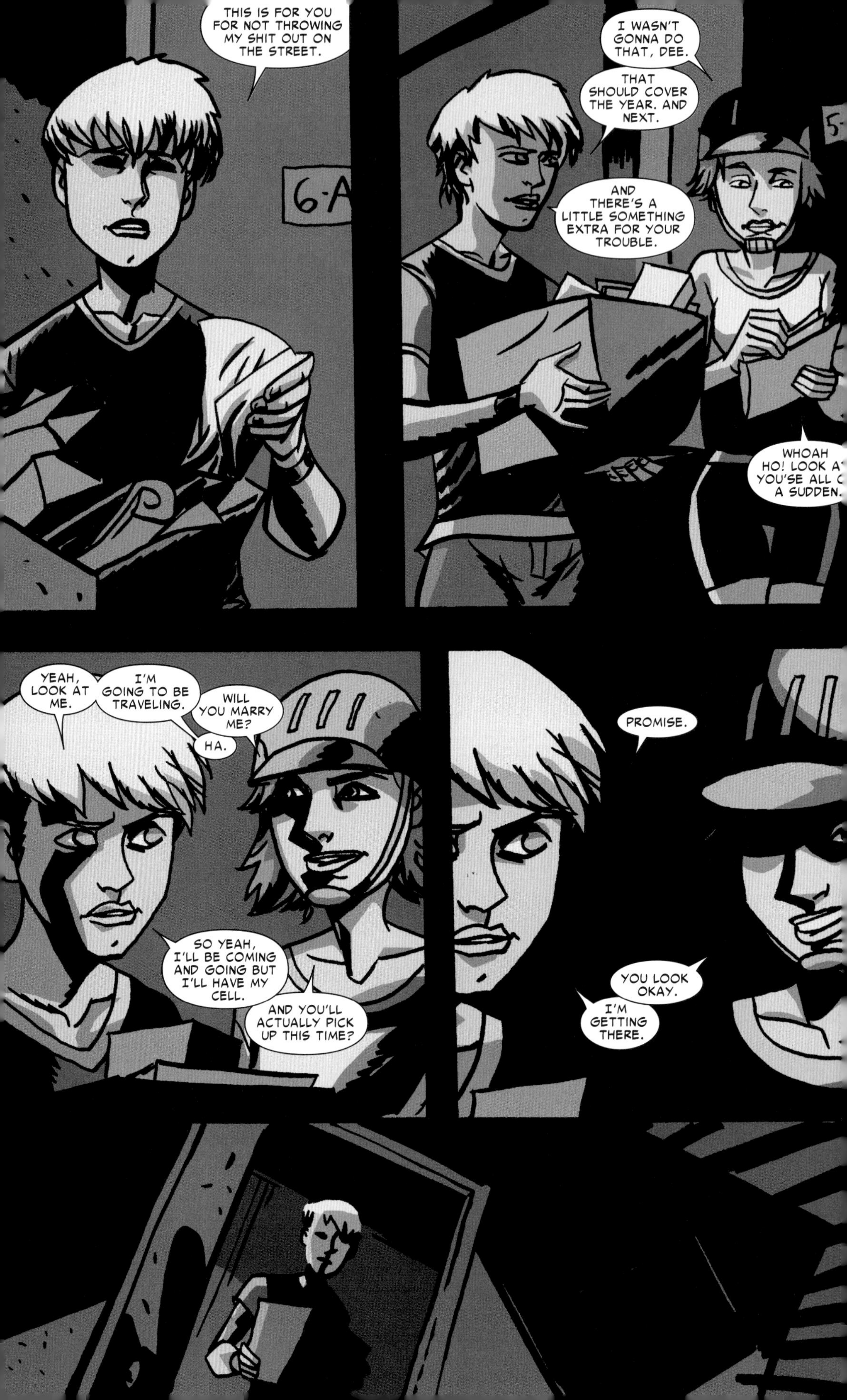
THIS IS FOR YOU FOR NOT THROWING MY SHIT OUT ON THE STREET.
I WASN'T GONNA DO THAT, DEE.
THAT SHOULD COVER THE YEAR. AND NEXT.
AND THERE'S A LITTLE SOMETHING EXTRA FOR YOUR TROUBLE.
WHOAH HO! LOOK AT YOU'SE ALL OF A SUDDEN.
YEAH, LOOK AT ME.
I'M GOING TO BE TRAVELING.
WILL YOU MARRY ME?
HA.
SO YEAH, I'LL BE COMING AND GOING BUT I'LL HAVE MY CELL.
AND YOU'LL ACTUALLY PICK UP THIS TIME?
PROMISE.
YOU LOOK OKAY.
I'M GETTING THERE.

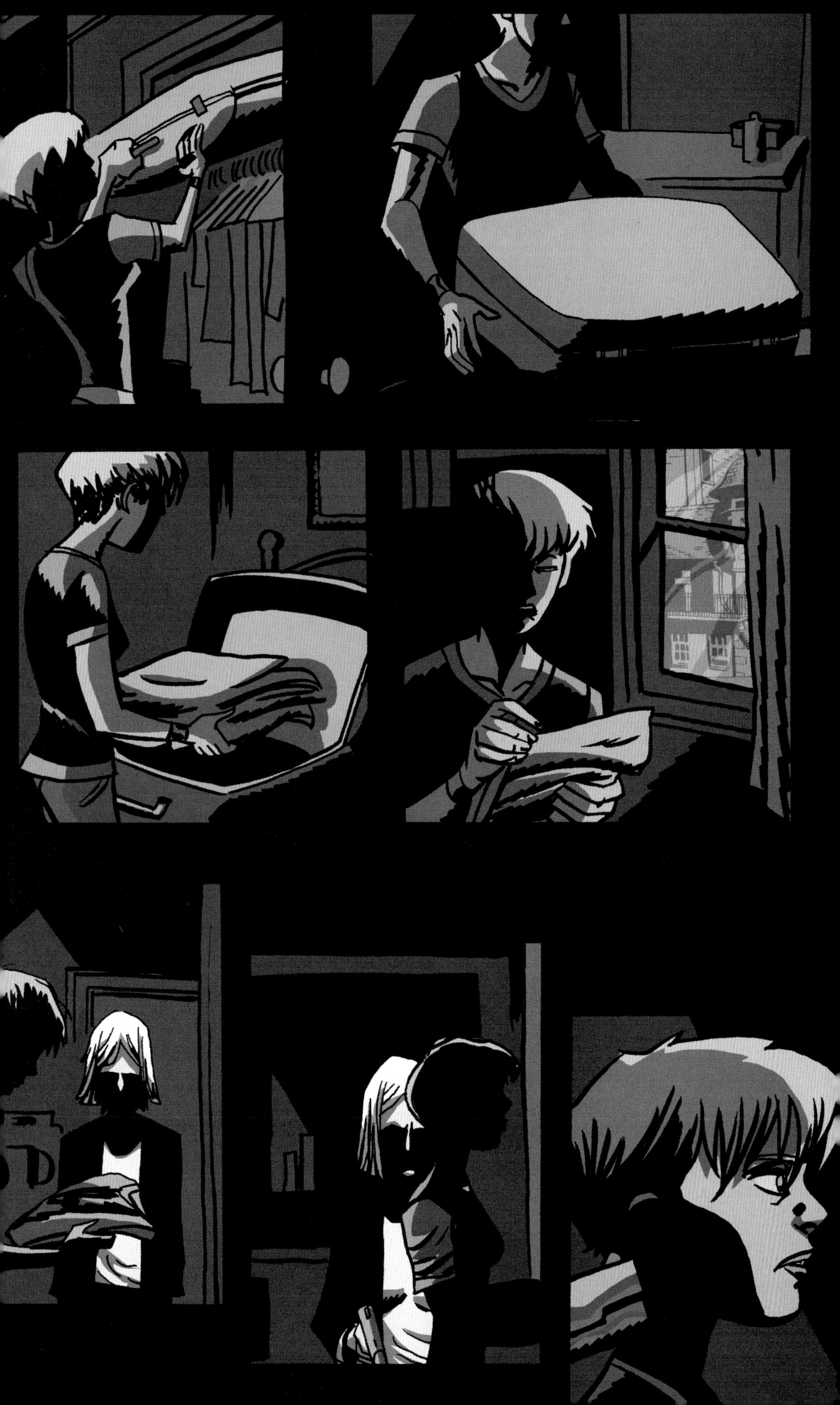

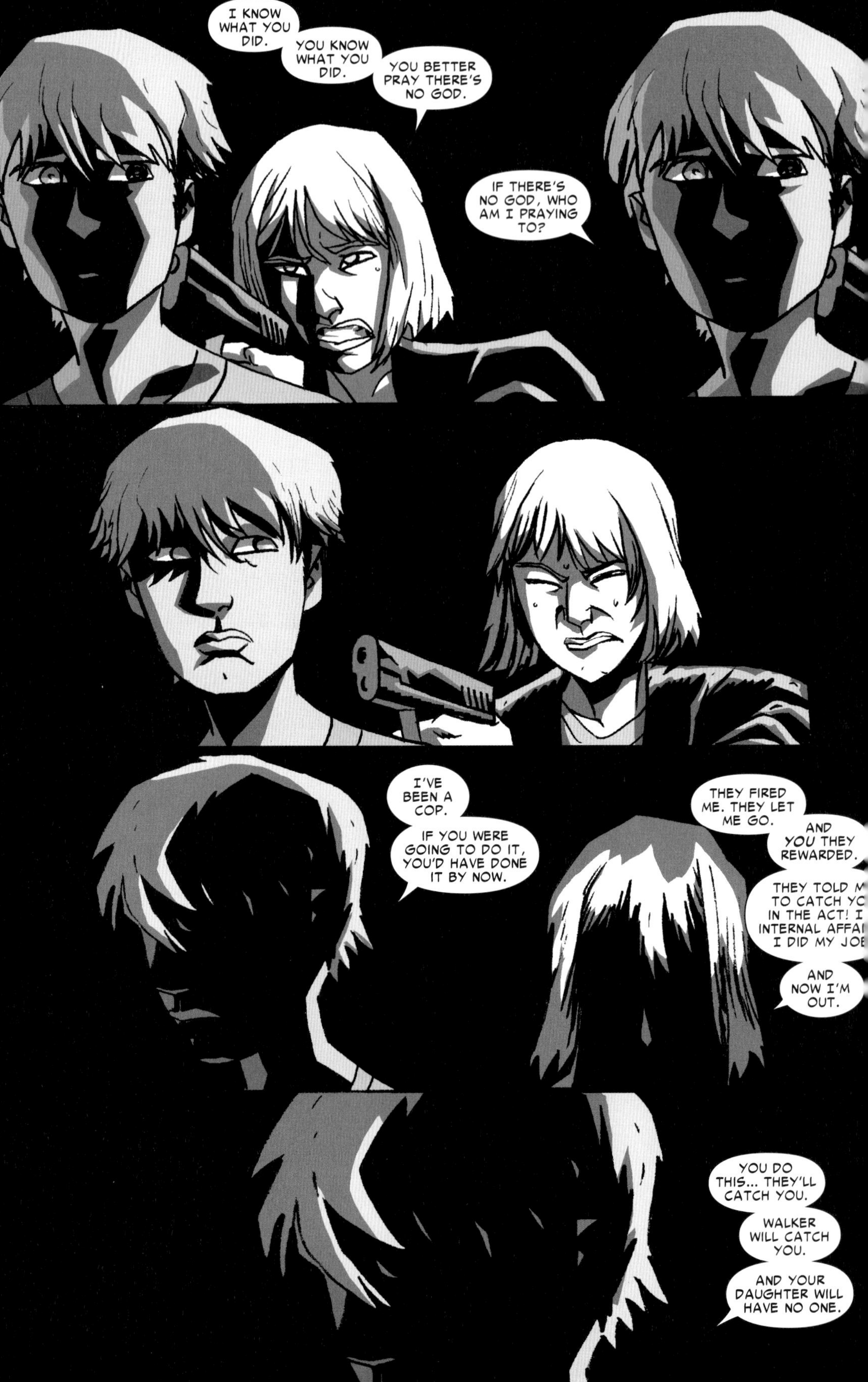
I KNOW WHAT YOU DID.
YOU KNOW WHAT YOU DID.
YOU BETTER PRAY THERE'S NO GOD.
IF THERE'S NO GOD, WHO AM I PRAYING TO?
I'VE BEEN A COP.
IF YOU WERE GOING TO DO IT, YOU'D HAVE DONE IT BY NOW.
THEY FIRED ME. THEY LET ME GO.
AND *YOU* THEY REWARDED.
AND NOW I'M OUT.
YOU DO THIS... THEY'LL CATCH YOU.
WALKER WILL CATCH YOU.
AND YOUR DAUGHTER WILL HAVE NO ONE.

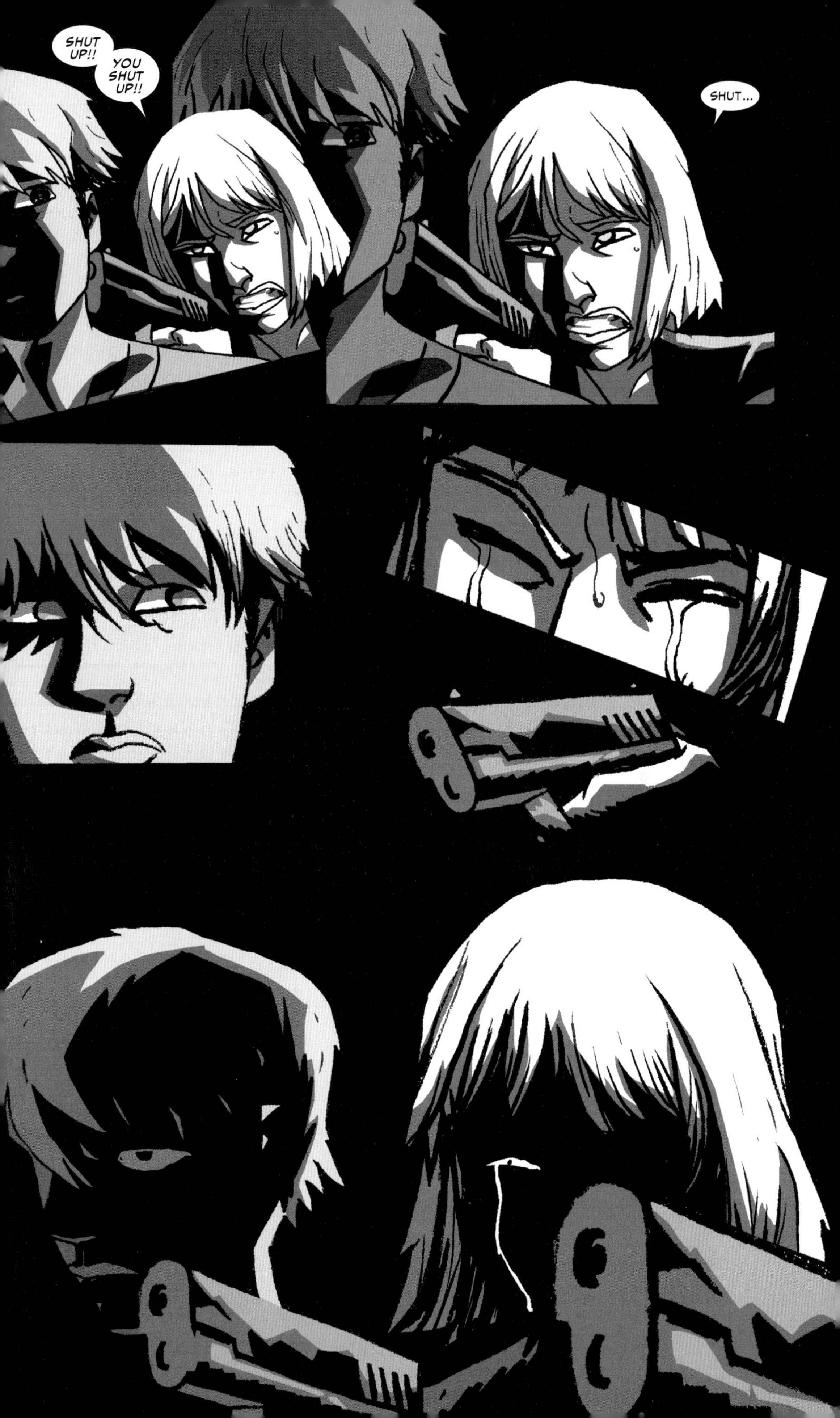
SHUT UP!!
YOU SHUT UP!!
SHUT...

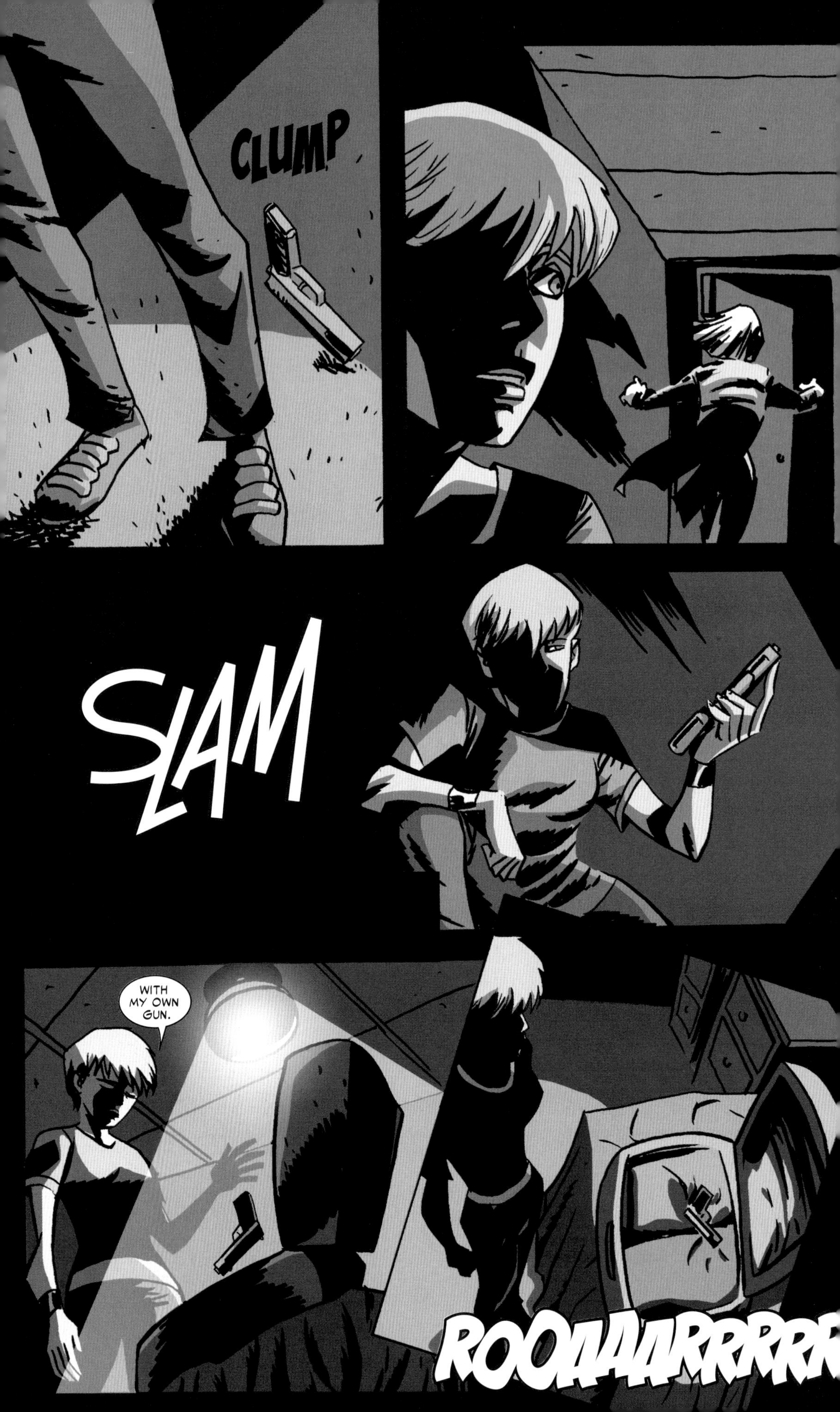
CLUMP
SLAM
WITH MY OWN GUN.
ROOOAAARRRRR

CRRAASSSHHH

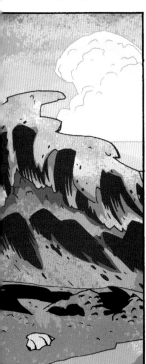

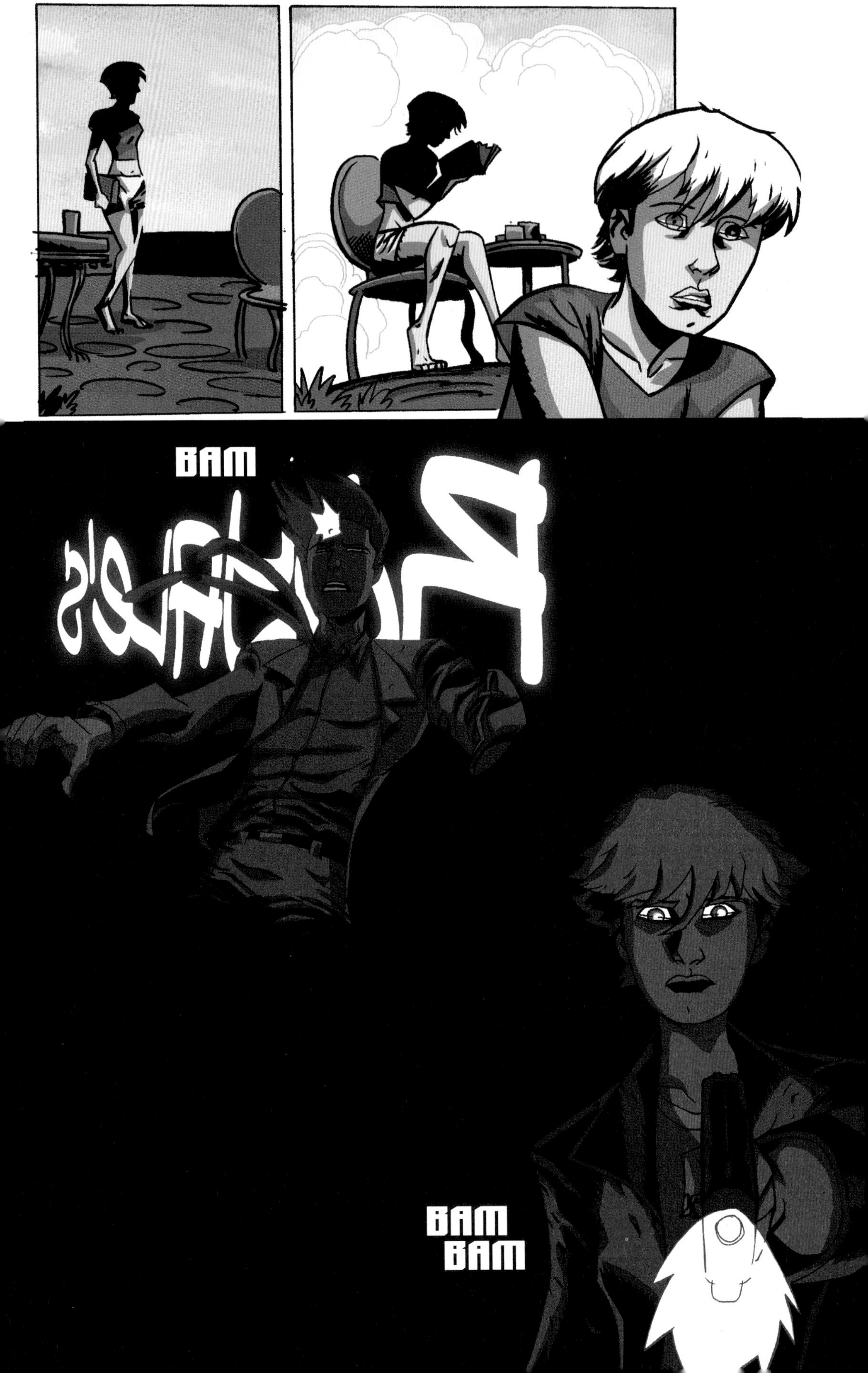
BAM
BAM
BAM

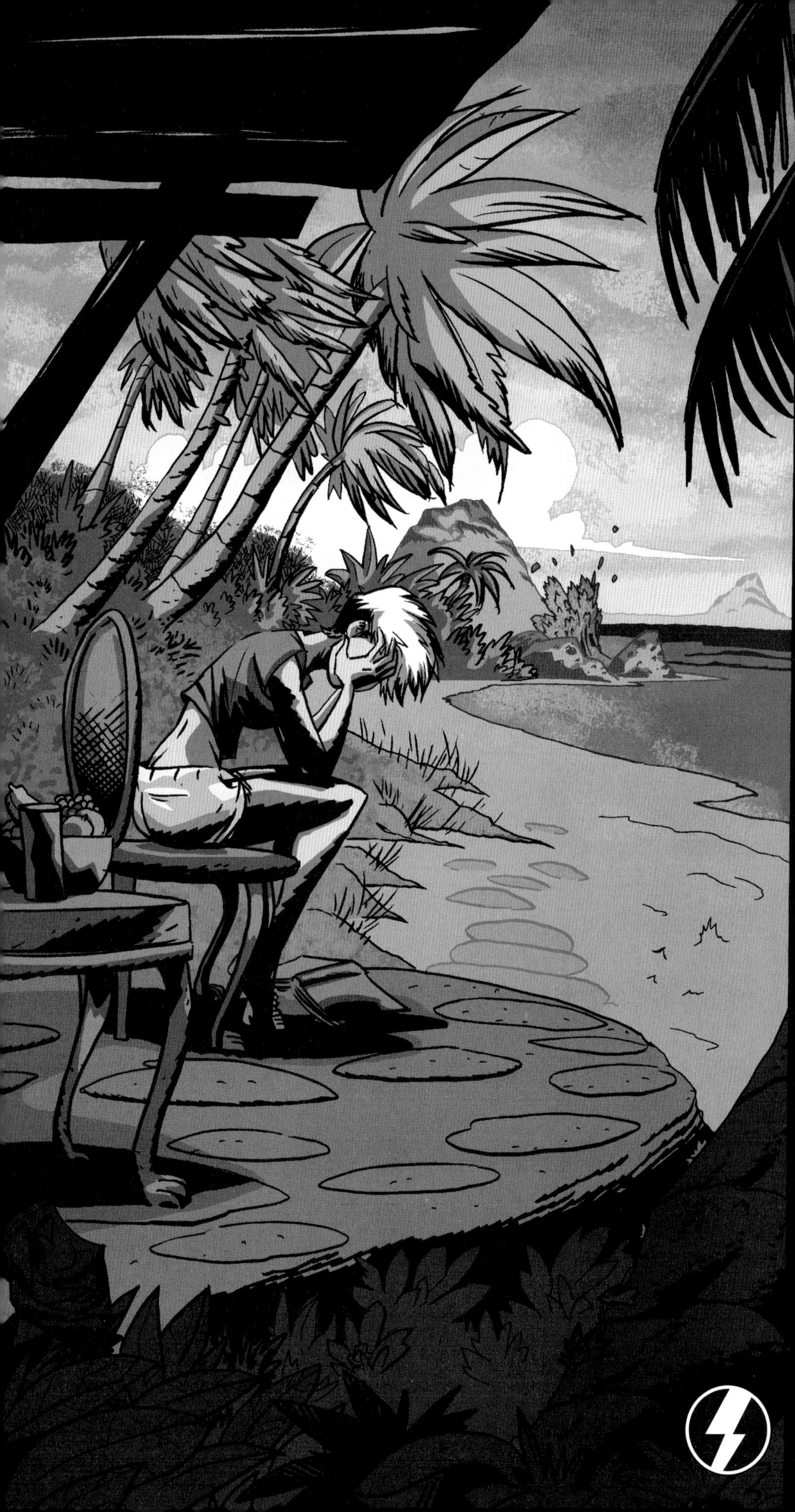

#25

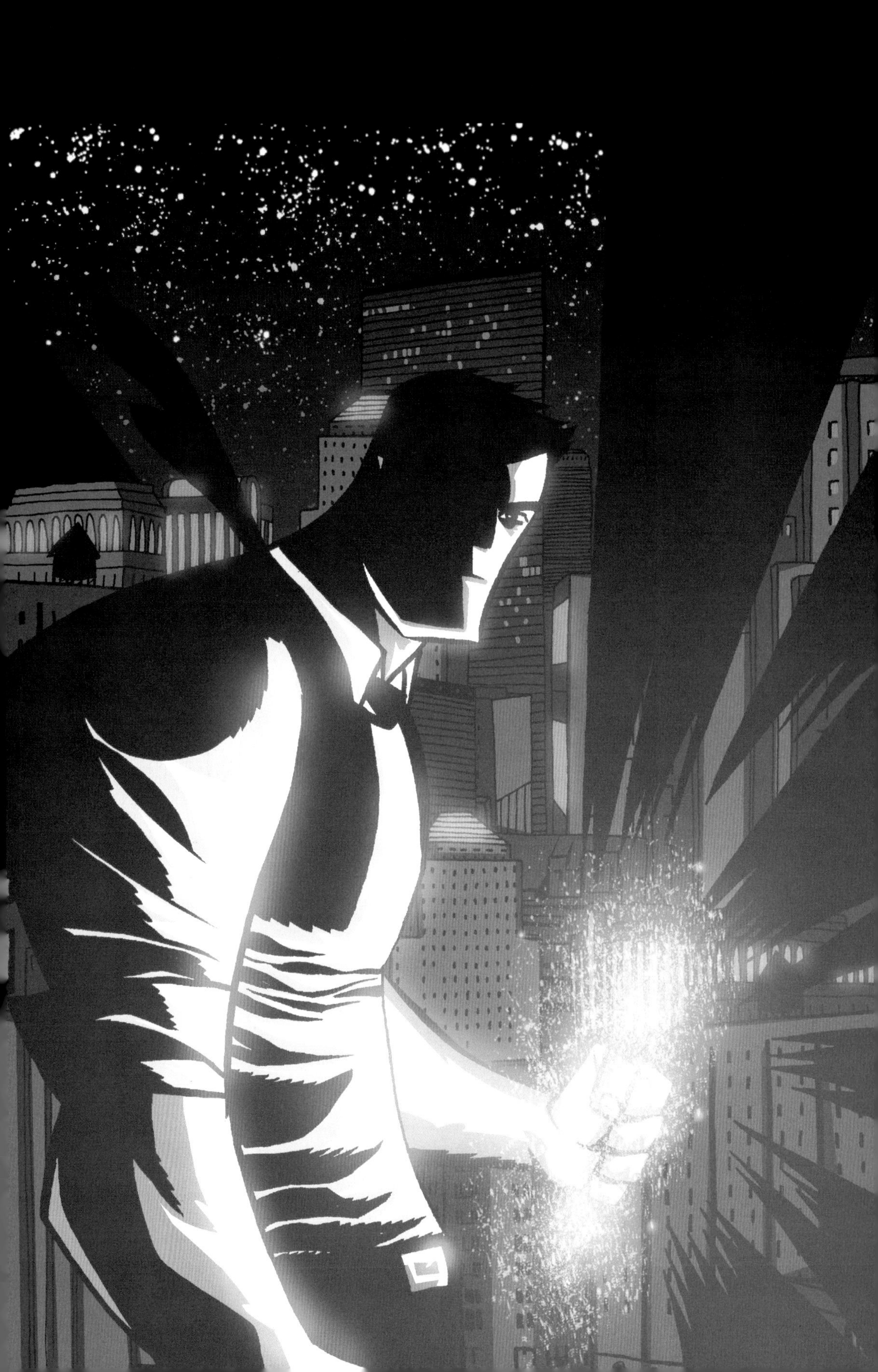

#25 VARIANT COVER
By Brian Michael Bendis

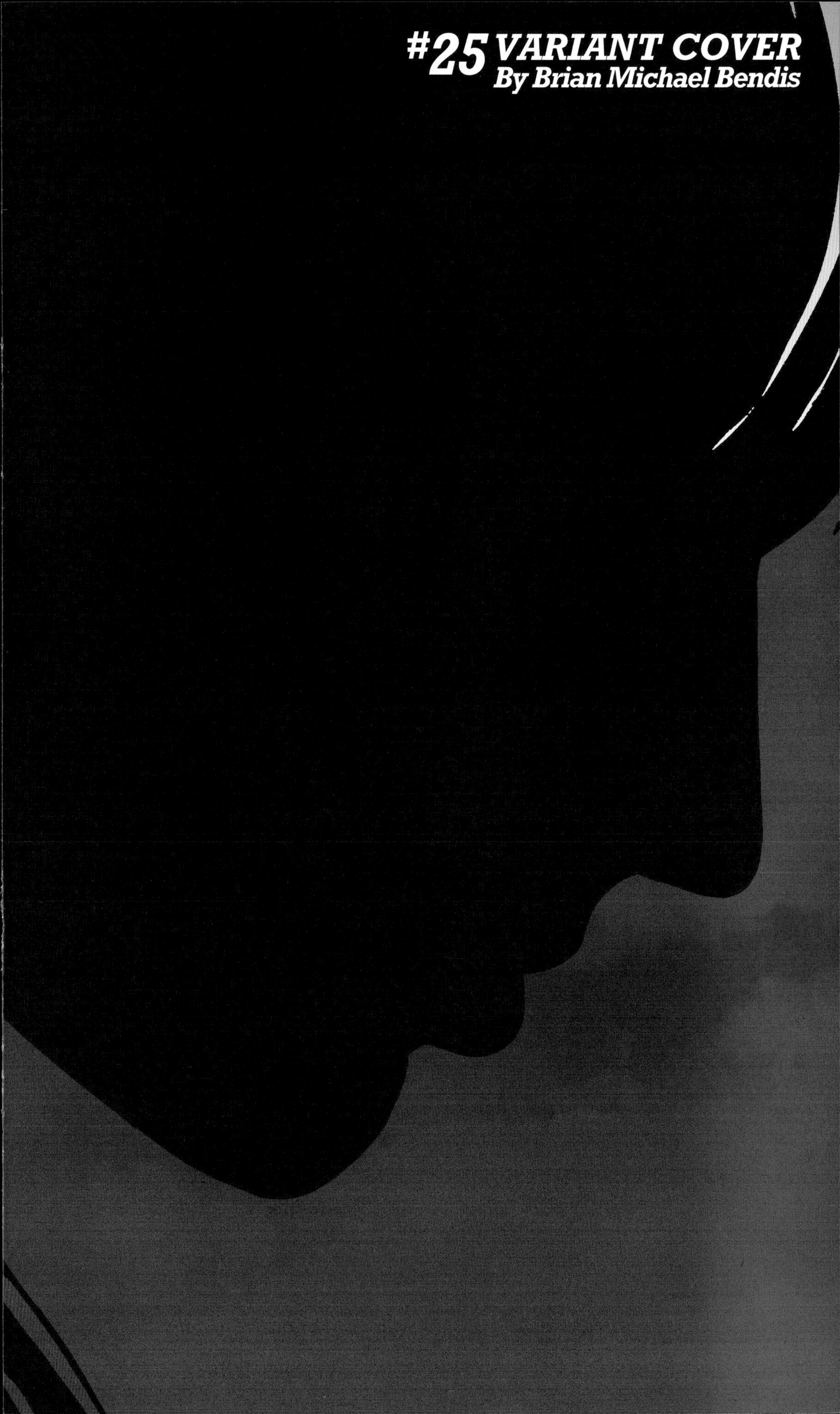

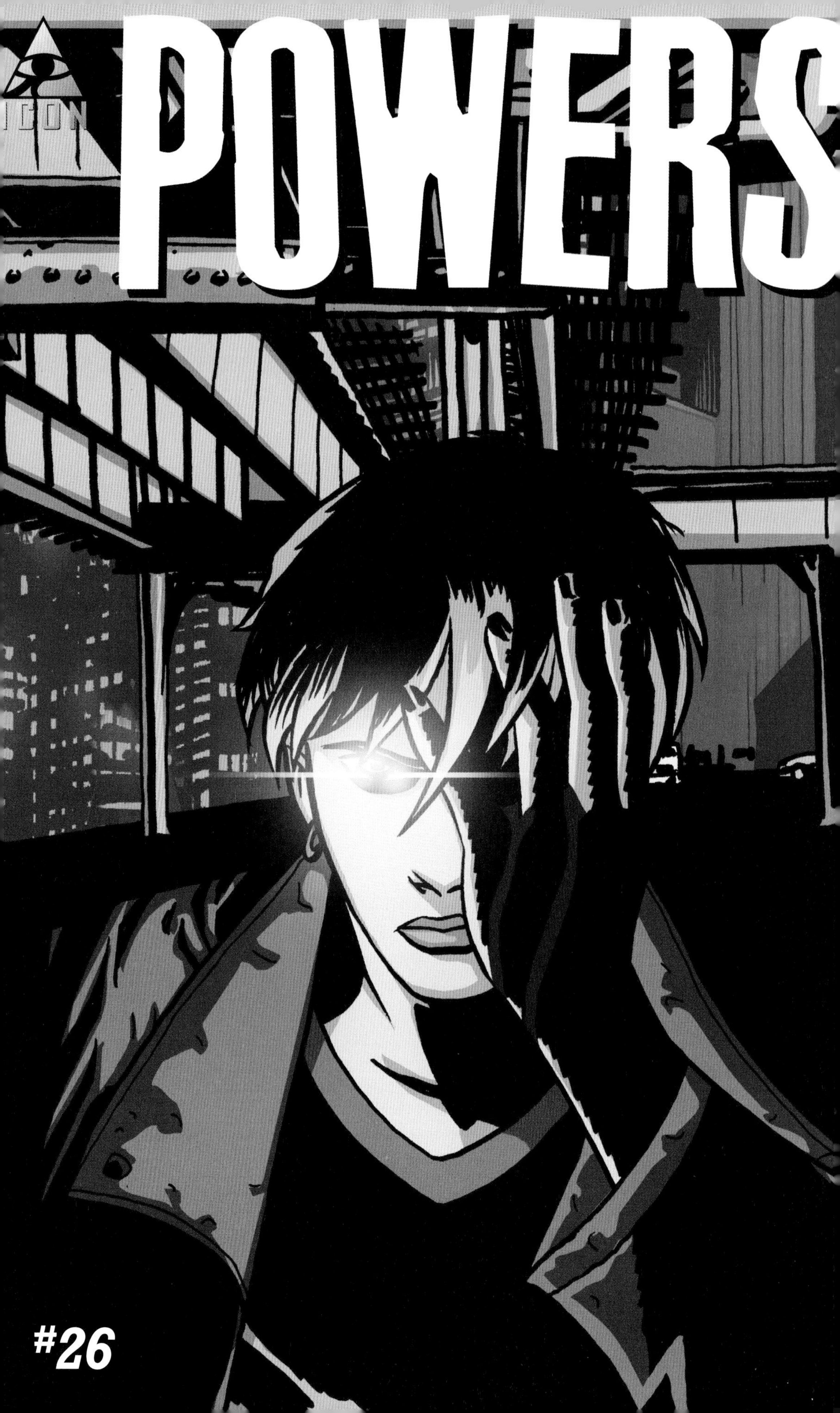
ICON
POWERS
#26

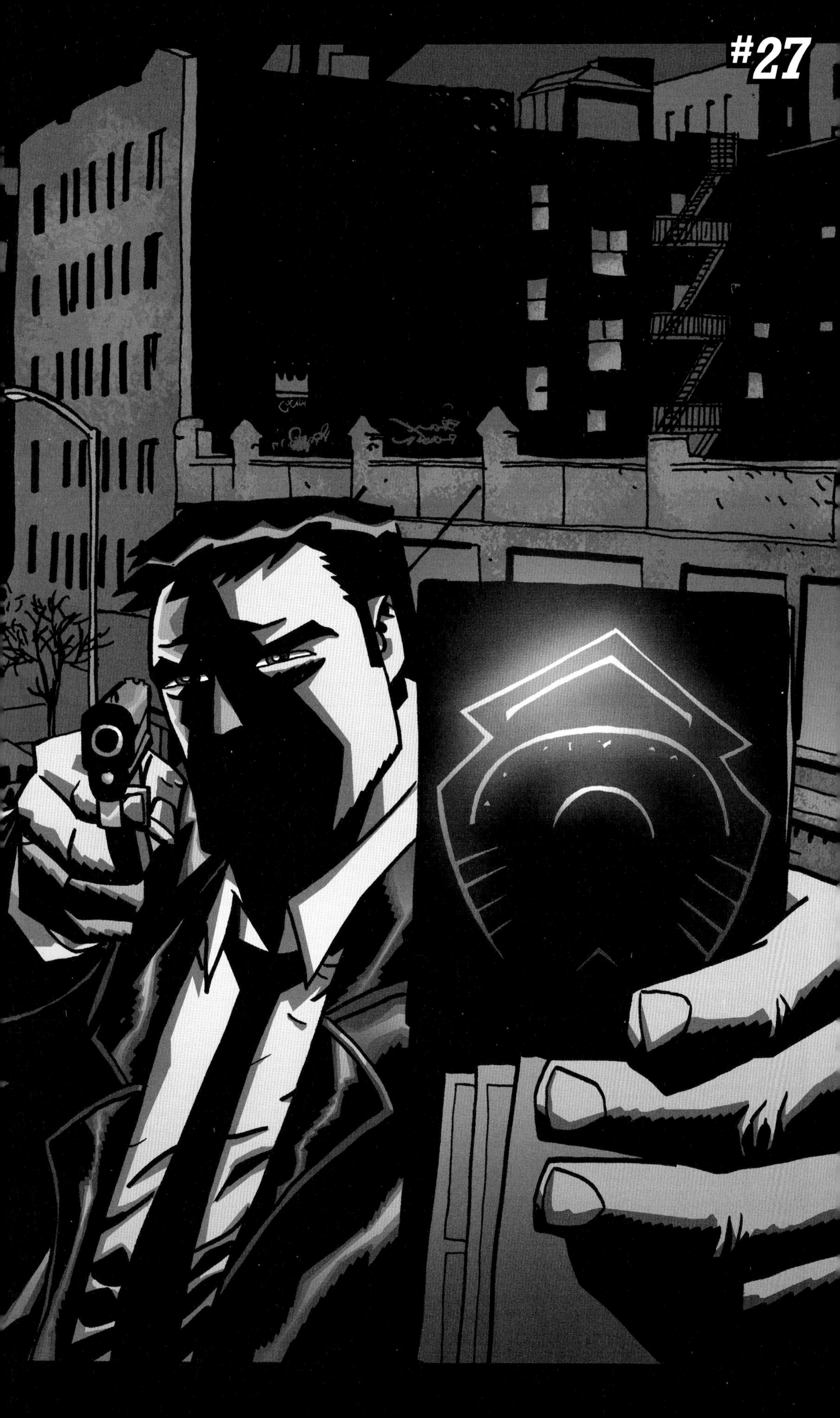
#27

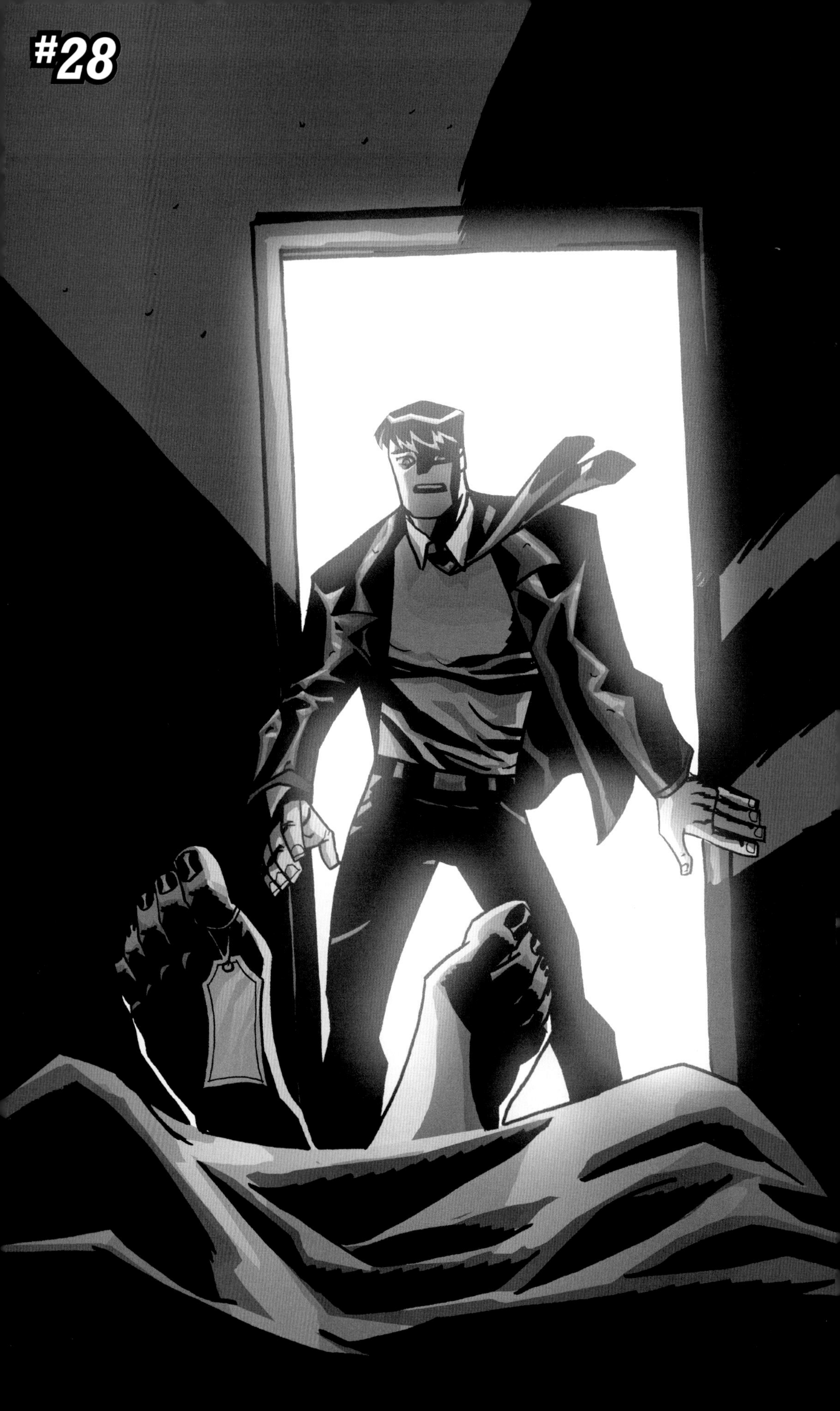
#28

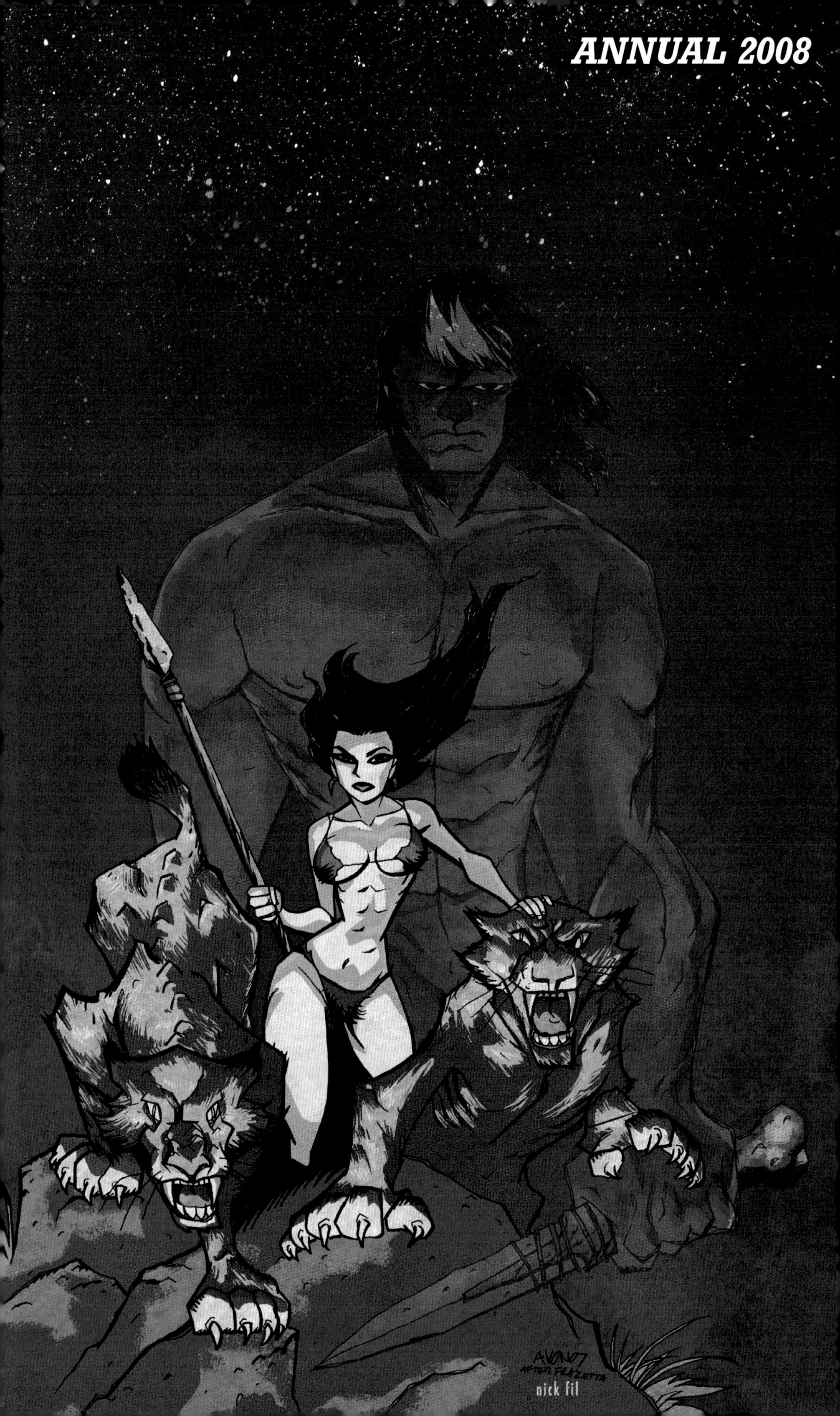
ANNUAL 2008
AVON 07
AFTER FRAZETTA
nick fil

#29

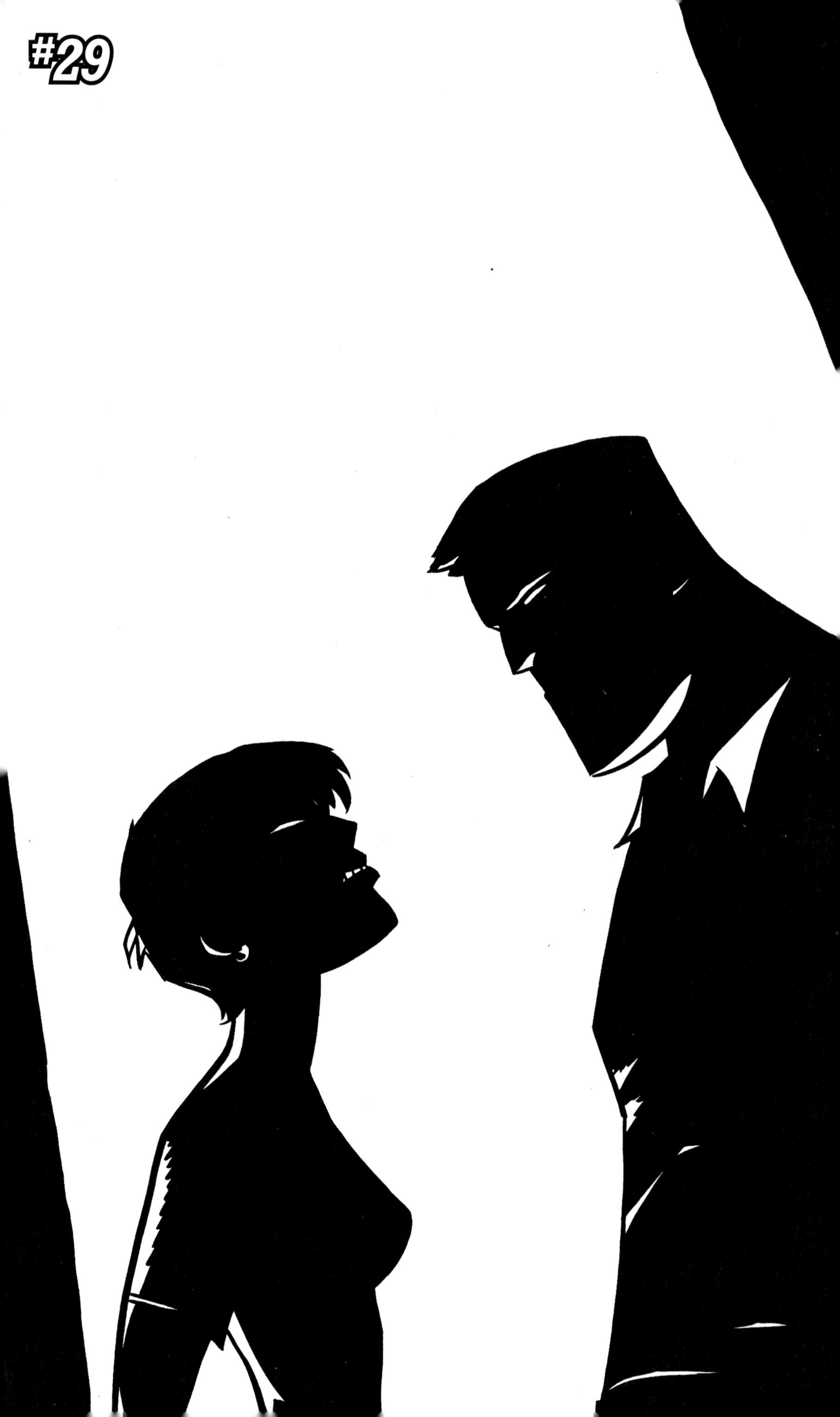

#30

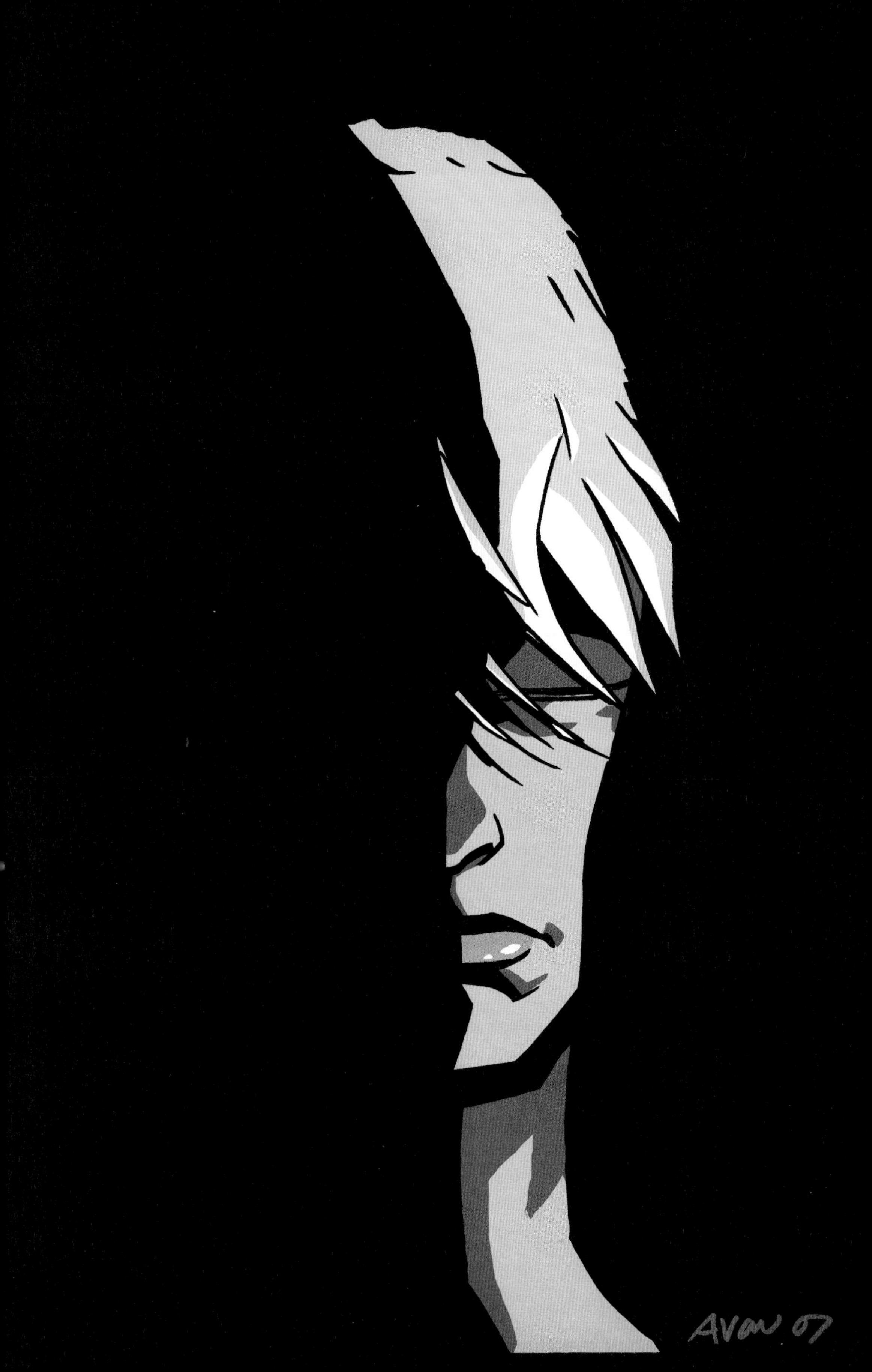
Avon 07

SKETCH GALLERY

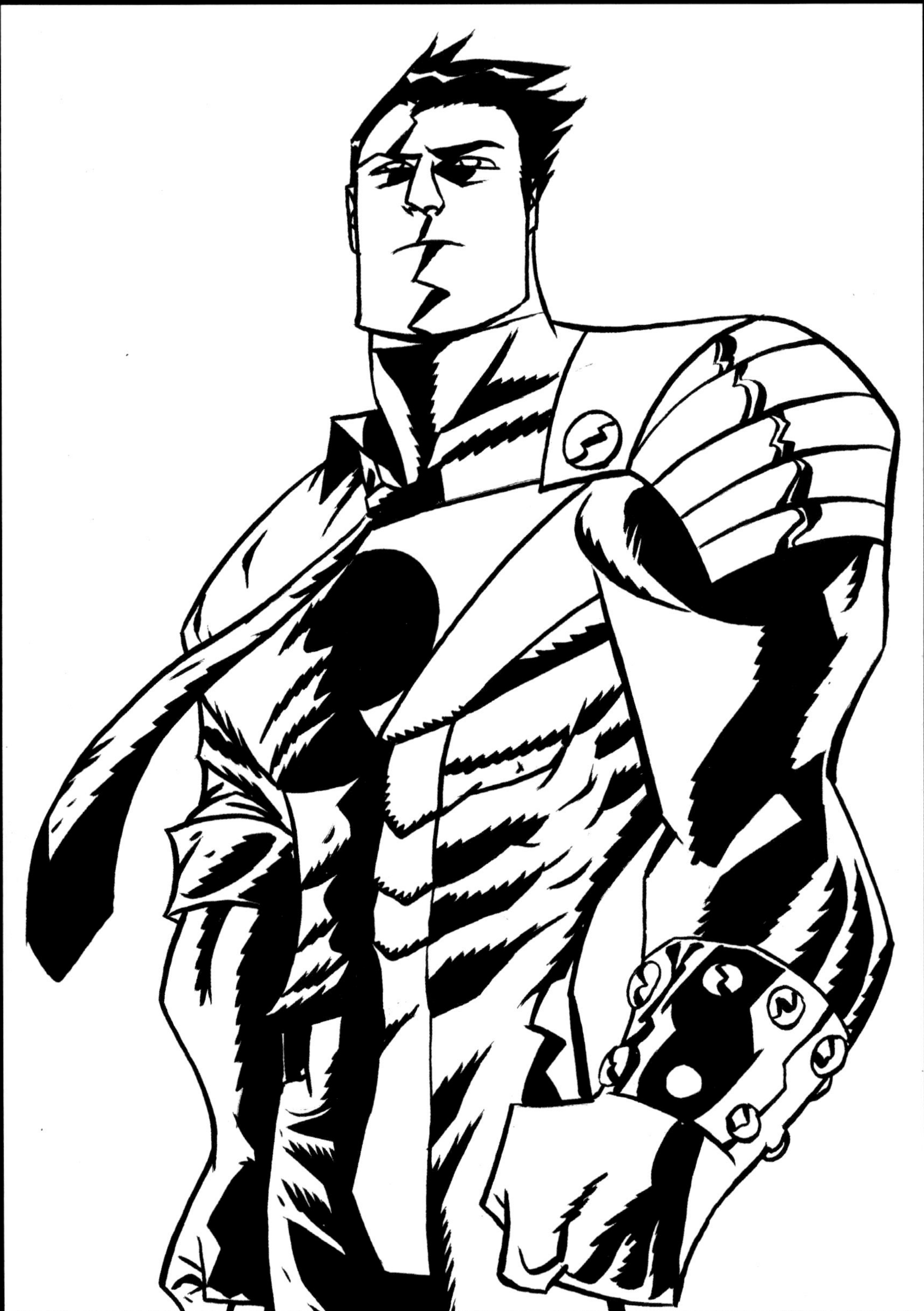

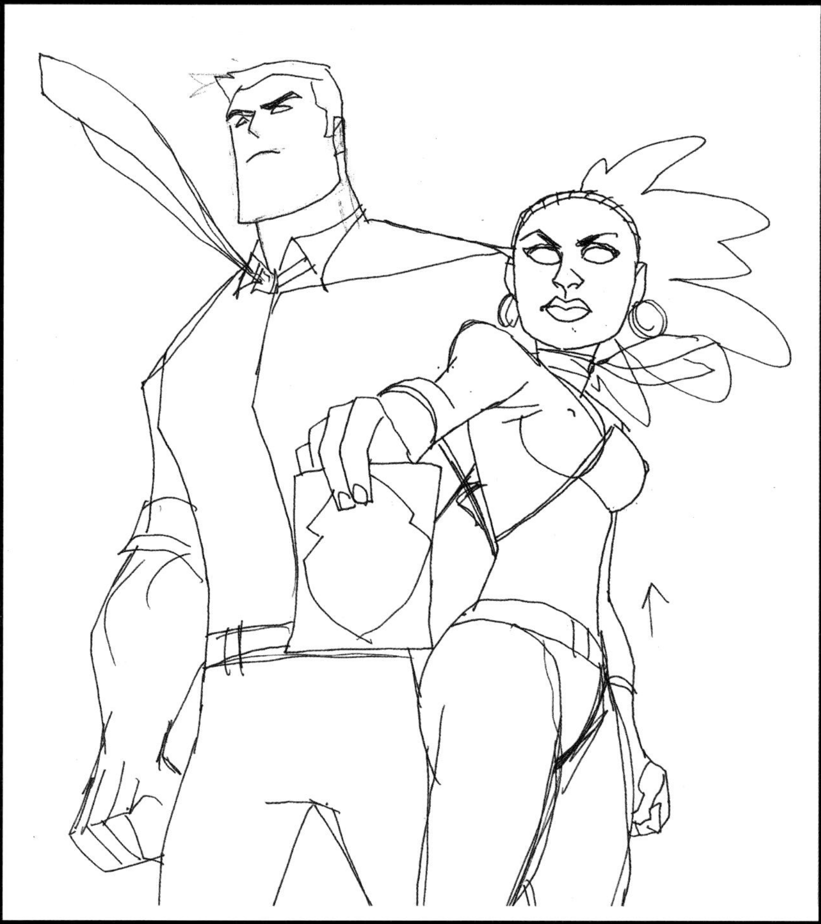

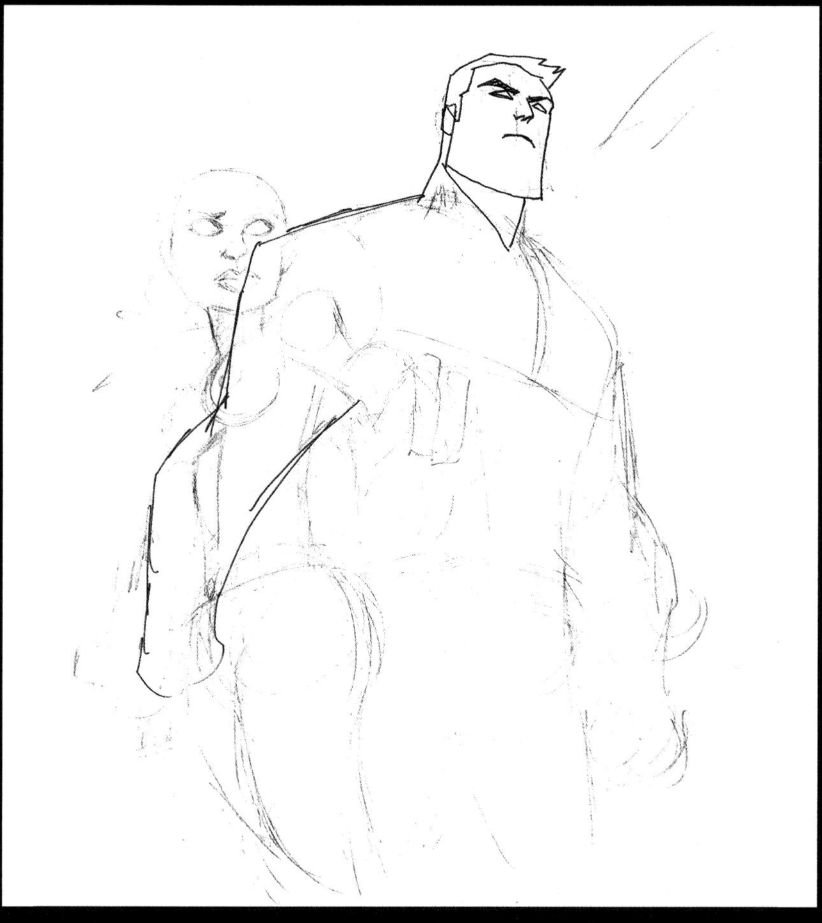

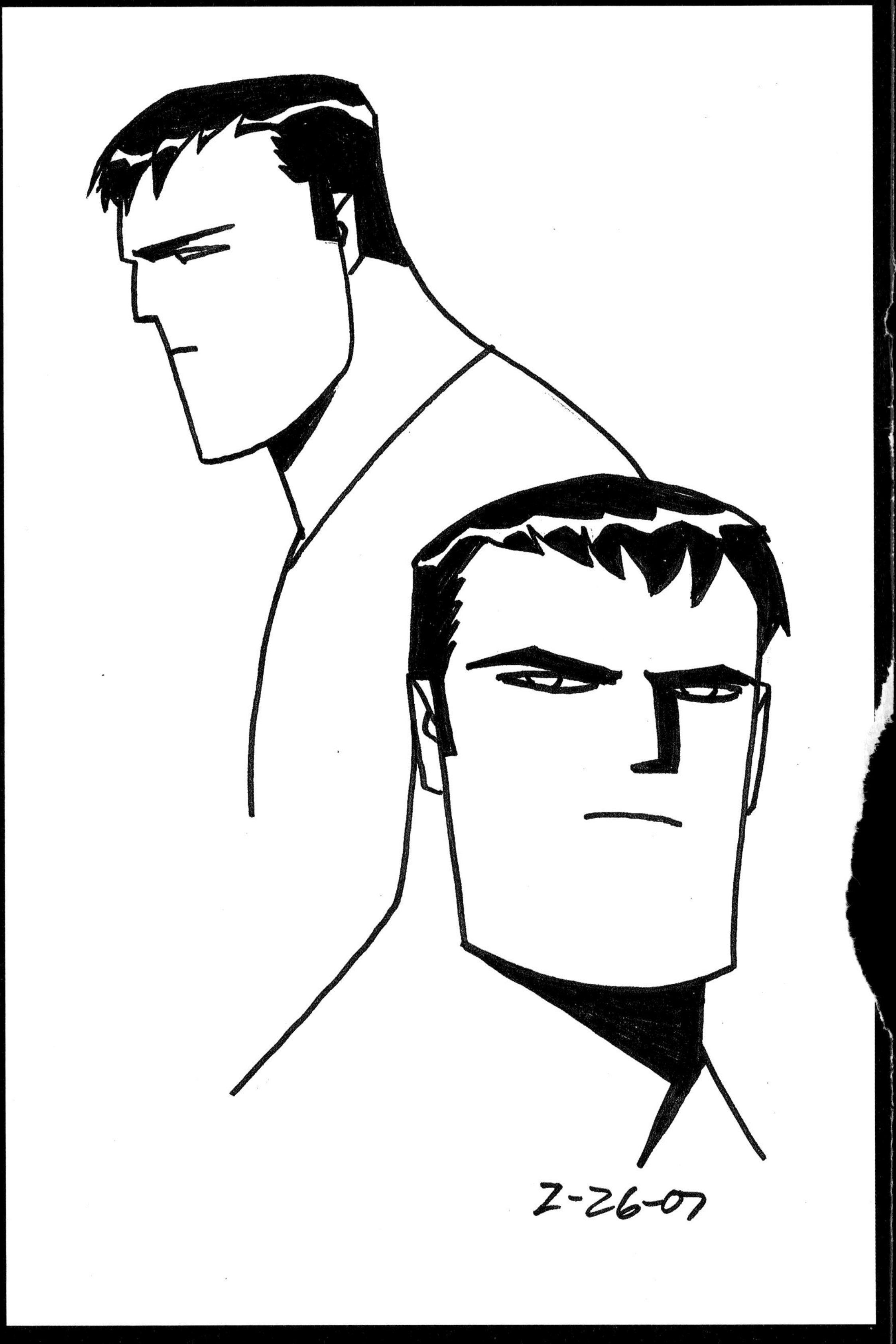
2-26-07